SOCIAL MEDIA

AND MOBILE

MARKETING

STRATEGY

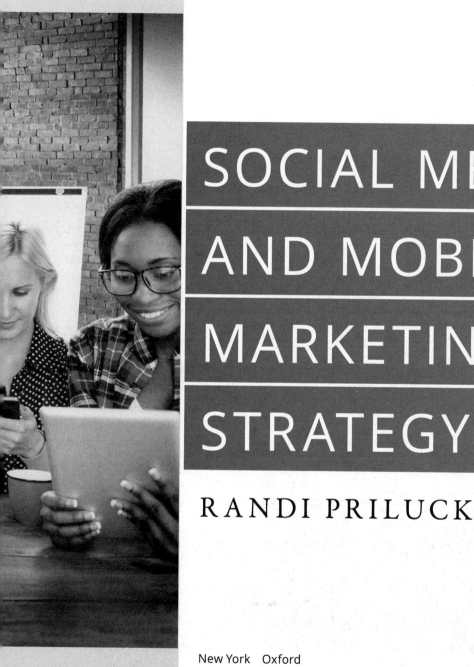

SOCIAL MEDIA AND MOBILE MARKETING STRATEGY

RANDI PRILUCK

New York   Oxford
OXFORD UNIVERSITY PRESS

Library of Congress Cataloging-in-Publication Data

Names: Priluck, Randi, author.
Title: Social media and mobile marketing strategy / Randi Priluck.
Description: Oxford ; New York : Oxford University Press, [2017] | Includes
   bibliographical references and index.
Identifiers: LCCN 2016014658 (print) | LCCN 2016023707 (ebook) | ISBN
   9780190215071 (pbk.) | ISBN 9780190215088 ()
Subjects: LCSH: Internet marketing. | Mobile commerce. | Social media. |
   Marketing—Management.
Classification: LCC HF5415.1265 .P74 2017 (print) | LCC HF5415.1265 (ebook) |
   DDC 658.8/72—dc23
LC record available at https://lccn.loc.gov/2016014658

Printing number: 9 8 7 6 5 4 3 2 1

Printed by R.R. Donnelley in the United States of America

THIS BOOK IS DEDICATED TO MY FATHER, HOWARD PRILUCK;
HIS NEVER-ENDING LOVE AND SUPPORT WILL ALWAYS BE WITH ME.

ABOUT THE AUTHOR

Randi Priluck is a Professor of Marketing at Pace University and Academic Director of the joint Lubin School of Business and Media Storm Master's program in Social Media and Mobile Marketing. She received a PhD in business with a specialization in marketing from Drexel University and an MBA from New York University. Her research in the area of consumer learning has appeared in *The Journal of Advertising, Journal of Current Issues and Research in Advertising, Psychology & Marketing, Journal of Marketing Education, Journal of Consumer Marketing, Journal of the Academy of Marketing Science,* and *The Journal of Brand Management.* Her blog on social media research may be read at www.socialmediaandmobileresearch.com.

CONTENTS IN BRIEF

CONTENTS

PREFACE

The practice of marketing has changed drastically in the past ten years and represents both challenges and opportunities for those who study the field. We are now firmly in the digital marketing era in which firms conduct business online and communicate with customers through a variety of digital and traditional media.

As a student of marketing, you should know that though the tools of the trade have changed, the basic theories and underlying principles remain consistent. This book takes our current knowledge of the field and applies the best ideas to the world of social media and mobile marketing. Effective marketing strategies begin by segmenting and targeting markets, researching the environment, and understanding consumer behavior, and that is why this book focuses heavily on planning the strategy prior to execution. Since you are probably familiar with the four P's of the marketing mix, the chapters build on this perspective by covering product development, distribution, pricing, and promotion.

A social media and mobile communications strategy also requires that one establish a strong digital presence on the Web and through online marketing prior to executing any campaign. Therefore, this book emphasizes planning and executing communications strategies, while keeping a clear focus on measuring the outcomes using clearly established goals and metrics. Finally, because there are legal issues involved in many executions, the final chapter reviews the law as it relates to digital marketing.

The examples throughout the text and the exhibits present content that should be familiar to you; they will also engage you in discussing the issues with your friends and professors. The case studies feature products and services you use every day, such as the backpacks made by Hershel Supply Co., Spotify, Axe Body Wash, Coke, and Snapchat. There are also some brands that you may admire, such as Porsche or Apple Pay. As you read, you will be challenged to "Consider This . . .": to draw your attention to interesting examples, specific problems that companies have faced, or related research on social media or mobile technology.

Some highlights of *Social Media and Mobile Marketing Strategy* include:

- A clear preview and detailed outline for each chapter
- Exhibits with data on social media and mobile marketing usage and strategies
- Summary review questions based on the content of each chapter
- Application questions that ask you to delve more deeply into specific issues, requiring research and careful consideration

- Compact case studies with questions for discussion and opportunities for analysis
- A companion website (www.oup.com/us/priluck) where you'll find links to videos relevant to each chapter, copies of all the images in the text, and other links and resources.
- For instructors, also available at www.oup.com/us/priluck, all the materials needed to teach a robust social media and mobile marketing course: an instructor's guide with additional assignments, video links, test questions, and PowerPoint lecture slides.

You know that the digital world is fast-paced and you move between social media sites, mobile apps, and other digital services quickly and throughout the day. Now it's time to stop and think how to use these technologies to enhance marketing strategy. After you have read this book, you will be ready to identify and research potential customers, set measurable goals, develop and curate content, create social media and mobile strategies, and evaluate the impact of your efforts.

ACKNOWLEDGMENTS

I would like to thank Oxford University Press and my wonderful editor Ann West for her guidance and advice. Emily Mathis and Claudia Dukeshire were instrumental in securing the images and formatting the document, and I greatly appreciate their help.

My two assistants, Elizaveta Ross and Elena Svintsova, were extremely helpful in researching social media strategies and completing the glossary. Thanks to you both.

Two friends and a colleague who have published books offered specific and sound advice on how to achieve the ultimate goal. Specifically, Joe Wisenblit, author of *Consumer Behavior,* advised on content, exhibits, and images. Julia Rothenberg, author of *Sociology Looks at the Arts,* provided guidance on the publishing industry and Ibraiz Tarique, author of *International Human Resource Management*, offered help at a crucial moment in the process.

In addition, I'd like to thank the reviewers who read and commented on chapters at various stages of the book's development. Their feedback and suggestions were extremely helpful:

Elena Bernard, University of Portland
Colin Campbell, Kent State
Melissa Clark, Coastal Carolina University
Diana-Joy Colarusso, Daytona State College
Terry Stringer Damron, Austin Peay State University
Naveen Donthu, Georgia State University
Rosario (Bud) Drago, Villanova University
Curtis Haugtvedt, The Ohio State University
Kathleen Houlihan, Wilkes University
Ira Kaufman, Lynchburg College
Pat Marzofka, Loras College
Joseph P. Mazer, Clemson University
Susan Mudambi, Temple University
Evan Neufeld, Baruch College, The City University of New York
Lou E. Pelton, University of North Texas
David F. Smith, Bemidji State University
Andrew Stephen, University of Pittsburgh
Wendy Wells-O'Rear, Central Georgia Technical College
Matthew Wilson, University of Northern Iowa

My colleagues in the Marketing Department at Pace University's Lubin School of Business and especially its Chairs, Martin Topol and Mary Long, supported my efforts to develop the MS in the Social Media and Mobile Marketing program and continue to offer the right courses and opportunities for its growth. Dean Neil Braun provided faculty development opportunities to support my interest in teaching digital marketing, which, in part, led to my decision to write this book.

My friends and family have been wonderfully supportive. Tom Goodrich helped with early drafts and offered writing advice. Alexandra Levinsohn provided endless support and positive energy. My mother Judi Priluck provided inspiration for the project and support throughout, as did my sister Jill and brother Gary.

And, of course, special thanks are owed to my son Harper Gold, who loves marketing and advertising, and my partner Ira Gold, who could do without it. Both put up with my writing this book at all hours and locations around the world, while they went swimming and hiked to waterfalls.

Randi Priluck
August, 2016

SOCIAL MEDIA AND MOBILE MARKETING STRATEGY

© Shutterstock/yukipon

CHAPTER ONE

THE NEW DIGITAL LANDSCAPE

Chapter One serves as our jumping-off point for exploring social media and mobile marketing strategy. We start with a discussion of the current marketing environment in which new media operate, including how firms are changing to address new consumption behaviors. The chapter defines social media and mobile marketing, introduces the seven C's framework to guide you through the new digital landscape, and describes the methods marketing managers use to interact with and engage customers. Social and mobile communications must be part of an integrated communications strategy, but marketers often jump into social media or mobile advertising without considering the underlying marketing principles. The chapter will also review the key marketing principles and describe how new media have changed the overall marketing mix.

LEARNING OBJECTIVES

After reading this chapter, you will be able to:

- EXPLAIN THE TRAJECTORY OF GROWTH IN SOCIAL MEDIA AND MOBILE TECHNOLOGY USE.

- DEFINE BASIC TERMS WITHIN THE FIELDS OF SOCIAL MEDIA AND MOBILE MARKETING.

- DESCRIBE THE NEW DIGITAL LANDSCAPE AND ITS INFLUENCE ON MARKETERS.

- EXPLAIN THE WAYS IN WHICH SOCIAL MEDIA AND MOBILE MARKETING CAN BE INTEGRATED INTO THE MARKETING MIX FOR A PARTICULAR PRODUCT OR SERVICE.

- IDENTIFY SUCCESSFUL SOCIAL MEDIA AND MOBILE MARKETING STRATEGIES.

- OUTLINE THE TRENDS ASSOCIATED WITH DIGITAL MEDIA AND ONLINE MARKETING.

Have you used Yik Yak? It's the social media site that allows you to remain anonymous while sharing whatever comes to mind with users within a 1.5-mile radius. Yik Yak got in some pretty hot water when a professor complained that students were harassing her on the social site and high school kids started posting nasty racist comments and bullying classmates [1]. These situations prompted the Yak to post the following message when certain negative keywords appeared:

> Pump the brakes, this yak may contain threatening language. Now it's probably nothing and you're probably an awesome person but just know that Yik Yak and law enforcement take threats seriously. So you tell us, is this yak cool to post?

Yik Yak was founded by Tyler Droll and Stephen "Brooks" Buffington when they were students at Furman University in South Carolina. Launched in the app store in November 2013, adoption quickly grew and by 2016 the app had spread to over 2,000 college campuses and had millions of monthly users [2]. The rapid-fire adoption of Yik Yak shows how quickly new social networks can grow and the challenge for marketers who want to keep up with trends.[3]

You may have noticed that marketing is a lot different than it was only a few years ago. From the consumer's perspective, there are many new ways to find products and services, learn about their pros and cons, shop 24/7 from almost anywhere in the world, and share satisfaction and dissatisfaction with a potentially global audience. Consumers have embraced social media for connecting with friends and family, but they also meet strangers online who can influence their purchase behavior. Marketers have been profoundly affected by the rapid technological change in the marketplace. Brands are having trouble maintaining their dominance as consumers gain more information from one another and rely less on brand name as the primary indicator of quality. New companies that once might have found it difficult to enter the market in the face of strong brand competition are finding quick success using new techniques to gain and hold consumer attention.

In the past, branding led to customer trust because brands delivered consistent and certain outcomes. Now, lesser known brands can make a mark for themselves by building trust through online buzz. Today, fewer than 25% of Americans say that brands affect their shopping behavior; loyalty among car buyers is dropping; and price premiums—higher prices consumers pay for brand names—have declined. A brand name alone no longer guarantees a higher price. On the flip side, unknown brands now have a chance to get noticed and compete with the big market players.[4]

Social media and mobile technology also have the potential to give back to brands some of the cache formerly associated with strong names. Social media can offer brands an outlet for connecting and engaging with customers. When customers choose to interact with brands, they can drive awareness and even reduce costs for a firm by providing information or service to other customers. For example, Microsoft's Xbox division monitors Twitter to determine product failures and addresses them early. Xbox is able to sift through the excessively colorful language that teens sometimes tweet and uncover any product problems that need to be fixed.[5]

Brands investing in mobile technology can offer consumers desirable mobile services, drive repeat purchase with mobile loyalty programs, and engage with customers as they interact with a company's offerings. Mobile marketing may be the key for marketers who wish to maintain their customer base and deliver value to market segments that return profits to the firm. For example, Pampers' Hello Baby Pregnancy Calendar mobile app allows prospective parents to view a developing baby. The app builds brand recognition and potential loyalty that can last long after the baby is born.

As social media connect customers, mobile technologies offer the one-to-one customization that people have come to expect from brands. In this chapter, we'll explore the strategies that can help build brand value to achieve business objectives.

WHAT ARE SOCIAL MEDIA AND MOBILE TECHNOLOGIES?

This book will expose you to a variety of new terms that represent the backbone of digital media marketing. Many of the terms are familiar to you and you often use them, but do you really know what they mean?

In this book, we define **social media** as a set of platforms that allow individuals to connect with a specified group of friends and family with whom they choose to share **content** such as stories, pictures, or video online. These platforms typically have a format that is created by the company and that users must follow—and a set of rules for behavior and sharing on the site. **Mobile technologies** refer to the hardware and cellular and wireless services for accessing and storing data on a mobile device. Because people use their mobile devices to access social media, any effective brand strategies take into account both types of social interaction.

Whereas mobile strategies have only been relevant since the first iPhones and mobile devices became available, social media have actually been around for at least twenty years. The earliest social media sites were text-based bulletin boards where people shared news and events. Early Internet providers like AOL offered

EXHIBIT 1.1

Top Global Sites on the Web

SITE	MAJOR FUNCTION(S)
Google	Search engine
Facebook	Social network
YouTube	Social network
Yahoo	Portal
Baidu	Search engine
Wikipedia	Social network
QQ	Portal and social network
Twitter	Social network

chat rooms where people gathered to meet and greet. The first actual social networking sites were Geocities, Sixdegrees.com, Blackboard's college management system, and Friendster. MySpace did not come onto the scene until 2003 and Facebook followed in 2004.[6]

Social media platforms are some of the most widely used websites online, reflecting their popularity with individuals around the world. The top sites include social networks on which people post profiles and connect with friends and relatives, video-sharing platforms, and content sites like Reddit or Wikipedia. Though the top sites reach billions of people, new social networks pop up all the time and often steal users from one of the established networks. The trend is likely to continue as different networks specialize to serve niche groups of consumers with specific needs and desires (see Exhibit 1.1).

SOCIAL MEDIA AND MOBILE MARKETING FOR BRANDS

Should brands engage in social media and mobile marketing activities? While social media and mobile marketing strategies often work hand in hand, marketers need to make separate decisions about the value of each of these strategies for their particular situation.

BENEFITS OF SOCIAL MEDIA MARKETING

A person unfamiliar with brand strategy might think that a company should execute a social media strategy simply because the platforms are free to use and reach a lot of potential customers. However, students of social media should know that social media are NOT free. Though Facebook, Pinterest, Instagram, Tumblr, LinkedIn, and Twitter do not charge fees to open basic accounts, brands must go to significant time, effort, and expense to execute strategies on these platforms. The major expense is hiring people to develop content, monitor the platforms, respond to consumers, and evaluate the strategy. In addition, whereas an individual can use a social media platform to communicate with friends, brands are often not allowed to freely interact with their followers and have to pay for ads to reach them. Snapchat originally charged firms $750,000 a day to run ads that disappeared.[7]

Even so, there are numerous advantages to social media strategies for brands, which might explain why companies have widely adopted social media marketing. Some of the key advantages include:

1. Brands can engage their current customers on platforms and communicate with them at times when people are receptive to messages.
2. Social media strategy can help increase a firm's **organic rankings** when people share content online. Organic rankings are the lists of nonpaid results that a **search engine**, like Google or Bing, returns when users type in words or phrases into the search box on the site.
3. Social media can help a brand build a strong image with positive buzz among influencers on various platforms.
4. Social media can be used for customer service purposes and can lead to cost savings over other methods.
5. Firms have successfully leveraged social media for product development, ideation, and strategy formulation to enhance their businesses.
6. Social media may help reduce media expenses if customers are using social media to engage with brands and firms can spend less in the mass media.
7. Sometimes social media can be more efficient than traditional media in reaching and motivating customers or social media can enhance a strategy to add value. For example, in the entertainment sphere, television shows such as the *Walking Dead* have strong Twitter audiences who communicate with one another while watching the program, thus enhancing the value of the show to those individuals.

consider this . . .

ARE SOCIAL MEDIA WORTH IT?

According to a study measuring the amount of online buzz about brands and their financial performance the answer is . . . yes. Researchers found that social media strategy has a positive impact on financial performance.[8]

Another study found that the more people participate in a company's social media platforms, the more likely those people are to do business with that firm. Individuals with the highest levels of activity in a brand's social media are more likely to buy premium products, are less deal-conscious, and contribute more profitability to the firm.[9]

BENEFITS OF MOBILE MARKETING

Though a brand may have a strong social media presence, it doesn't necessarily follow that the brand will also want to execute other mobile marketing strategies. As with any strategy, the brand must first determine the mobile marketing goal before devoting time, energy, and/or funds to such efforts. Mobile strategy consists of a variety of potential communications including setting up a mobile website, using text messaging to communicate with customers, building an email strategy (because many people access their email via mobile), mobile advertising, or mobile applications. For a brand to spend money in mobile, its customers must have mobile access and use mobile in situations that will directly or eventually result in a sale or the equivalent for a brand. As with social media, mobile technology strategies are not free and can require a significant start-up cost that must be recouped in order to make them worthwhile investments. Though it might be fun for a brand to make a new gaming application, the strategy has to deliver a measureable return. For example, only 20% of Walmart's shoppers are aware the store has a mobile app.[10] If most customers do not use the app, the company should decide whether it makes sense to continue to offer the service.

Some marketers have argued that **return on investment (ROI)** isn't a consideration in social or mobile because the brand is building an image. However, return on investment is the best way to measure the effectiveness of any strategy and compare it to other strategies that a firm might undertake. Return on investment refers to the amount of revenue (in a currency) a strategy delivers after accounting for expenses. Brands can generate a lot of buzz and not make any money. For example, WhatsApp was purchased by Facebook for $19 billion, but at that time the texting business was fragmented with many different texting applications popular in different locations. For example, WeChat was the popular texting app in China, Telegram in Germany, and Kaokao Talk in South Korea. Though WhatsApp may have had 450 million users signed up, it was by no means the dominant force in the industry despite the hype. One way to reduce risk in social media and mobile strategies is to use return on investment as a measure of effectiveness. In this case Facebook could examine WhatsApp's revenues relative to its expenses to determine the value of the investment.

LIFE IN A SOCIAL MEDIA AND MOBILE WORLD

There is no doubt that people around the world are altering the ways in which they interact with technology, media, marketers, and one another. Humans are evolving into multimedia multitaskers who are almost always wired—connected to devices and to others. Digital interaction in all forms of media is growing as more and more people log onto social media sites, interact via mobile devices, and live their day-to-day lives in a connected world.

Social media and mobile marketing have provided both opportunities and challenges for brands. Brands have new outlets for connecting with customers in more interactive ways than in the past, a deluge of information for understanding and reaching customers with messages, and richer, more varied platforms for developing brand experiences. In addition, marketers can use social media and mobile for other marketing functions such as product development, customer service, and distribution. These opportunities can reduce costs for firms and add to the bottom line.

On the flip side, social media and mobile technologies have complicated matters for marketers. There are new competitors who can enter the market and steal share by attracting customers online, many more places for consumers to focus their attention and avoid marketing communications, and new paths to purchase that marketers must understand so they can execute effective strategies.

SOCIAL MEDIA ARE CONSTANTLY EVOLVING

Once marketers figure out an effective branding strategy, the platforms, consumers, or competitors change. Brands must be constantly monitoring and altering strategy to properly reach and serve their customers.

Even small changes can cause problems. For the past few years, marketers have relied on Facebook to help them build engagement, but the platform is evolving. Originally, Facebook allowed brands to set up pages to connect with its customers for free. As Facebook has grown, the platform no longer allows brands to message its customers, deeply analyze the data associated with Facebook response, or even reach customers in its newsfeeds. Facebook has become an advertising platform and its popularity among certain demographic groups (such as teens) has declined. For most brands, only 1–2% of their postings go into the feeds of those individuals who "like" them. As a result, companies are starting to recognize that owning their own strategy and online content is important.

Millennials taking selfies to post on social media.

© Shutterstock/Lucky Business

ARE TEENS DONE WITH FACEBOOK?

Facebook use among younger teens has been dropping as they migrate to newer social media platforms. Teens prefer to communicate with their friends on messaging services, rather than broadcasting on social media platforms. Now that everyone's mom is on Facebook, kids no longer feel like it is their space or that it is cool to use. Teens view Snapchat as more private because messages go to individuals and disappear after a set time period as long as they are not quickly saved.[11]

Social Sites Used by Teens and Young Adults

SERVICE	PERCENTAGE WHO HAVE EVER USED	SERVICE	PERCENTAGE WHO HAVE EVER USED
Snapchat	72%	Vine	26%
Facebook	68%	Tumblr	24%
Instagram	66%	Google Plus	21%
Twitter	36%	WhatsApp	10%
Kik	29%	LinkedIn	9%
Pinterest	27%	Tinder	4%

United States; Edison Research; Triton Digital; January to February 2016; total survey n=2,002; 12 to 24 years http://www.statista .com.rlib.pace.edu/statistics/199242/social-media-and-networking-sites-used-by-us-teenagers/

SOCIAL MEDIA ARE DISRUPTIVE

Social media and mobile technologies are disruptive innovations because they transform business, lives, and the global economy. In order to be disruptive, a technology must have broad potential impact and significant economic value, and change how people live and work [12] (see Exhibit 1.2).

In spite of their disruptive nature, digital technologies have now become essential for brand communications strategy. Digital advertising spending has surpassed all other forms of media with the exception of television. Advertising agencies now view digital as the lead medium for executing communications strategy in many cases and brands have continued to allocate increasing shares of budget to search, display advertising, social media, and mobile marketing strategies. Each year the digital portion of the pie continues to grow, taking share from

EXHIBIT 1.2

Social Media and Mobile as Disruptive Technologies

DISRUPTIVE TECHNOLOGIES	SOCIAL MEDIA	MOBILE
1. Impact revenue and require increased investment by firms.	Lenovo attributes a 20% drop in service center calls to social media.	Global mobile ad spending will surpass $40 billion by 2020.
2. Are ubiquitous.	Facebook has billions of global users and is growing.	Wireless Internet access has exceeded wired access.
3. Shift the balance of power.	Brands now "listen" to social media for insights and are directly affected by buzz, both good and bad.	The Westpac Impulse Saver allows banking customers in New Zealand the chance to save a certain amount when they buy things.
4. Change lives and work.	Brands crowdsource new ideas and people share their intimate lives.	People wake up with their phones and spend over an hour a day using them without talking.

Sources: J. Sciarrino, "Leveraging the Virtuous Circle of Brand and the Extended Self," Journal of Marketing Theory and Practice, vol. 22, no. 2, pp. 147–148, Spring 2014; Total Media Ad Spending Growth Slows Worldwide Downward revision due to developments in North America, Latin America and Western Europe September 15, 2015 | Media Buying-See more at: http://www.emarketer.com/Article/Total-Media-Ad-Spending-Growth-Slows-Worldwide/1012981#sthash.4C8HU4XQ.dpufhttp://www.emarketer.com/Article/Total-Media-Ad-Spending-Growth-Slows-Worldwide/1012981

television, magazines, and newspaper advertising. The trend is likely to continue as the number of digital properties grows and as consumers spend even more time with digital devices. Marketers who execute successful digital strategies and can demonstrate measureable returns on their investments will have even more incentive to allocate funds to social media and mobile communications.

ENGAGEMENT AMONG AND BETWEEN CUSTOMERS AND BRANDS

One of the most important developments for marketers and consumers is the connectedness among individuals and between individuals and brands. Consumers can widely communicate brand preferences, reviews, attitudes, and actions related to the brands they respect, utilize, purchase, or shun. Marketers must be aware of consumer responses to their strategies and proactively seek out information to enhance brand experiences or risk letting the market control the message. The market has become **fragmented**, meaning that customers interact with brands and each other in a variety of ways, both online and offline. Fragmentation also means the extent to which viewers expose themselves to different communications such that marketers find it difficult to reach people using a limited set of media options; that no one medium, location, or strategy can reach broad groups of consumers to drive desired actions as in the past mass media environment.

Individuals now maintain digital selves, or **personas**, which interact with brands. A person's **digital self** is the person he or she shows online, which may differ from his or her true personality or physical self. Most people act differently online. For instance, take a moment to look at your Facebook newsfeed. Review the last ten posts from your friends and relatives. What percent of the posts are positive and negative? Have you noticed that everyone on Facebook is always happy, shares good news, or has attended a fascinating event? Reality may be somewhat different as sometimes people are sick, depressed, or even just not fantastic all the time.

Brands have the opportunity to connect and engage customers' personas by humanizing the interaction; dealing with people in authentic, transparent, and meaningful one-to-one relationships; offering value to them; and following up with people in the real world.[13] For example, part of Starbucks's emotional attachment strategy was to build strong ties between customers and individual baristas who would know their order. To solidify the strategy, Starbucks executed Mystarbucks idea.com, allowing people to further engage with the brand and signify their loyalty both online and through a mobile application. These strategies operate in tandem to encourage return visits to Starbucks and grow sales for the brand.

THE SEVEN C'S OF SOCIAL MEDIA AND MOBILE MARKETING

The **four P's of the marketing mix** (Product, Price, Place or Distribution, and Promotion) has been the dominant framework for developing marketing strategy for many years. These strategies are still important and continue to play a key role in the realm of social media and mobile marketing. The basic underlying marketing concepts have not changed, but the tools to execute strategy have evolved and social media and mobile influence each of the four P's significantly (see Exhibit 1.3).

Though the four P's of the mix are still critical to a strategy, marketers have many more challenges in the digital arena. The seven C's framework provides some of the background in thinking about social media and mobile strategies and shows how digital technology has evolved.

In the seven C's framework, social media and mobile marketing are:

EXHIBIT 1.3

The Impact of Social Media and Mobile on the Four P's

	IMPACT OF SOCIAL MEDIA	EXAMPLE(S)
Product	Marketers engaged in product development use crowdsourcing to pull together various aspects of the marketing mix for a brand. Mobile marketers have developed a number of new products aimed at smartphone users.	The company Quirky.com used social media to choose the best products to bring to market and then leveraged the knowledge of the crowd to develop the marketing strategy. Angry Birds, Snapchat, and Instagram are all products developed specifically for mobile devices.
Price	Prices of products are transparent online, deal sites influence consumers' perceptions of price and value, and consumers use mobile devices to seek out lower prices.	Groupon's original discounts of 50% appealed to highly deal-prone consumers who often failed to repeat purchase at the regular price. Best Buy created its own shelf tags for consumers to use with mobile devices to help limit the need to search for lower prices on their mobile phones.
Place or distribution	Marketers can now distribute products via social media, and social media sites drive traffic to marketer websites and brick and mortar retailers. People can also buy digital products on their phones or tablets any time when they are wirelessly connected.	Marketers can set up stores on Facebook. com, and traffic from Pinterest can be a strong sales generator for particular brands. Fandango's mobile app sells movie tickets via mobile. The service is useful when people are out and about, and decide to see a movie.
Promotion	Many aspects of promotion have been influenced by social media and mobile marketing. For example, brands can build awareness, encourage engagement, provide product information, and drive purchase behavior.	Consumers communicate about products and services on social media sites, and this type of word of mouth can strongly influence purchase as consumers continue to deny that traditional advertising influences them. McDonald's uses Snapchat to communicate with its young mobile customers.

- Convergent
- Community-oriented
- Comprehensive
- Chaotic
- Content-driven
- Commercial
- Calculable

Each of these factors is described below.

CONVERGENT

Convergent industries are those that merge in a synergistic manner to create new outcomes. A number of industries have converged to create new opportunities and challenges for brands. For instance, when the advertising and entertainment industries converged, Scott Donaton, an editor at *Advertising Age* magazine, wrote a book titled *Madison & Vine* (2004). The name of the book represents the intersection of the street known for the advertising industry in New York City (Madison Avenue) and the street in Hollywood known for the entertainment business (Vine). At that time, brands were experimenting with entertainment properties to sponsor them, incorporating product placement in movies and television shows, and using some of their content and talent in advertising brands. Brands continue to use concepts from the entertainment industry. For example, Nike created a short film honoring LeBron James, one of its celebrity endorsers, to highlight the brand and connect with sports fans.[14]

In the digital world, convergence refers to the media and technology industries in which information technology, communications networks, and content publishers share information across broadband and wireless networks. These entities have converged at a macro level to create a new environment for interaction, commerce, communities, and computing.

At the micro level, social media and mobile technology have converged and now mobile is the primary method for accessing social media platforms. The most downloaded and utilized apps are social media sites such as Facebook, Twitter, Instagram, and WeChat (see Exhibit 1.4). Mobile is also converging with the World Wide Web and mobile access accounts for close to 40% of website visits globally. [15] Even online commerce and publishing are converging as Jeff Bezos, the founder of Amazon.com, now owns the venerable *Washington Post*. You can see the convergence in social media and mobile technology by looking at YouTube, a social media site with content from a variety of marketers, which can be accessed 24/7 from computers, smartphones, tablets, Google glass, and even smartwatches.

Convergence benefits firms by allowing companies greater variety in their content and helps locate more potential customers who are interested in the content or its delivery. From the consumer's perspective, the offerings seem more diverse because they combine technology and media to create cool new products. You can get shows like *Orange Is the New Black* and *Game of Thrones*. But, convergence also leads to less competition and possibly higher prices because power becomes concentrated with a few players.

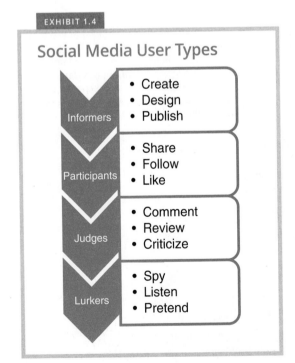

EXHIBIT 1.4

Social Media User Types

Informers
- Create
- Design
- Publish

Participants
- Share
- Follow
- Like

Judges
- Comment
- Review
- Criticize

Lurkers
- Spy
- Listen
- Pretend

COMMUNITY-ORIENTED

Community refers to a unified group of individuals with common interests linked by social, economic, professional, or political concerns.[16] People participating in communities typically have a feeling of belonging, need fulfillment, commitment to the group and relationships within the group. Since social media are built on human interaction and are by nature cooperative, social media platforms can be communities. On social networking sites, people share their stories, lives, feelings, and impressions of experiences. Other sites bring people together to complete projects, help others, raise money, complete tasks, or provide experience and advice. There are a significant number of people helping others often for no material gain. Many support groups have sprung up and these groups are, in essence, social communities. For example, Canceractive is a website devoted to the disease that connects people with others who suffer. Sometimes online connections lead to off-line meetings. There are venues for people who want to meet in the real world as well as through organized sites like Meetup.com or Match. com. Professionals use social media to network within their industries. LinkedIn is a popular online site for business connections. According to Alexa.com, LinkedIn is among the top ten global websites generating most of its traffic from the United States, India, United Kingdom, Canada, and Spain.[17] As you start your career, you should consider checking out LinkedIn because it has jobs and industry information.

Social networks help people fight diseases like cancer.

CancerActive, www. canceractive.com

Communities engage in political or social change through social media, and can activate large groups of protesters who communicate on platforms such as Twitter. People convene on social media sites because these companies are not controlled by governments, though governments can shut down platforms or heavily regulate their content. People view social media sites as a safe place to anonymously convey information to large groups of people. The result can be for the social good or for more nefarious activities. For example, Coca-Cola and Pepsi agreed to remove brominated vegetable oil from soft drinks after teenager Sarah Kavanagh posted two petitions on Change.org. The petition against PowerAde was signed by 59,000 people and another for Gatorade resulted in 200,000 online signatures.[18] On the more nefarious side, Mexican drug cartels post violent videos on YouTube as a warning to those who oppose them.[19]

Consumers cooperate via social media to share brand information and make recommendations. Review sites provide an avenue for strangers to interact regarding particular products and services. Gamers join forces on social media to meet while playing to enhance their shared enjoyment. Artists and fundraisers come together on sites to generate funds for projects and charities. Within social media, there are diverse sites for people with all types of interests, activities, and behaviors. There are sites for knitters, people who want to share their dreams, those who love mustaches, and even Bronies, adults who like *My Little Pony*.

Social networks can build communities for social change.

*Change.org, Inc.,
www.change.org*

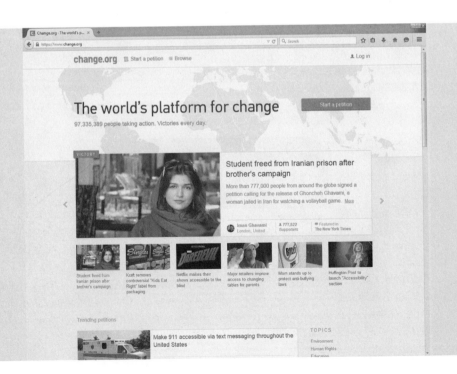

CHAPTER ONE The New Digital Landscape

Though social media sites rely on mobile to provide access to the platforms at all times, mobile by nature is less community-oriented than social media. The cell phone is a personal device that is tied to individuals and their preferred methods of interacting with the world. In the developed world, people do use their mobile devices to build community as when they access social media or use mobile to check into certain locations to meet friends. Mobile can facilitate community by providing methods by which people can share dinners and parties. For example, the mobile payment system Venmo allows groups of people to pay a bill, apportioning each person's share properly and access their banking systems to execute the transaction.

Mobile is even more important for communities in the developing world, serving as a lifeline by providing access to communications networks. For example, Medic Mobile connects patients and health workers using text messaging. When patients live in remote areas, Medic Mobile can provide advice between appointments and supply distant communities with medical supplies when outbreaks occur.[20]

consider this...

HOW MUCH DO YOU SHARE ONLINE?

A study by IPSOS found that people in certain countries were more likely than others to "share everything online." Can you guess where? The countries are: Saudi Arabia, India, Indonesia, Turkey, China, Poland, South Africa, Italy, Brazil, Argentina, Russia, Mexico. Worldwide, 24% of people, on average, say they "share everything online".[21]

COMPREHENSIVE

Social media and mobile technology are considered comprehensive in that broad members of the world community participate in them and the information available through these technologies is vast. On the social media side, 81% of the users of the top Internet properties reside outside of the United States.[21] In addition, Internet growth is driven by the developing world in countries such as China, India, Indonesia, Iran, Russia, Nigeria, Philippines, Mexico, and Brazil. There are now few places in the world where the population cannot connect. Presently about 2/3rds of the world's population use the Internet. The dominant mode of connection in the developing world is mobile, with an increased likelihood of accessing the Web via mobile than in the developed world, which has long relied on wired connections.[22]

On the content side, social media is comprehensive by connecting broad swaths of people who have access to vast amounts of data and who may assist in creating content. Wikipedia is a social media site at which global editors have created the world's largest online encyclopedia. Wikipedia reports over 30 million articles in 287 languages curated by 129,828 active editors globally.[23]

The comprehensiveness of social media allows individuals to connect and crowdsource information, often with greater accuracy than experts. **Crowdsourcing** refers to groups of strangers who come together to solve a problem by providing their expertise online to the group. There is some evidence to suggest that crowds of people make good estimates. A company called Estimize thinks so and uses the stock predictions of 25,000 people, half of whom are amateurs, to estimate company earnings for investment purposes. Deutsche Bank reported that the estimates were more accurate than those offered by professional analysts 66% of the time.[24]

Mobile is quickly becoming equally content-comprehensive as social media because smartphones can access similar amounts of data. As technology advances and connections get faster, people will be able to use mobile with the same expectation of information and response as a desktop connected computer. Google uses data from mobile in its rankings algorithm because mobile is a key method for connecting people.

CHAOTIC

Have you ever posted anything on a social network that you later wish you could take back? You are not alone and many companies have tweeted messages to the whole world that were supposed to be private. Both social media and mobile have been chaotic at the macro level, upsetting the nature of business and changing relationships among people. The chaos also refers to the fact that social media are open to anyone and shareable by all. Once an individual creates and posts content, it is difficult to rein in the consequences.

While social media are chaotic in that everyone can partake and add almost any kind of information, there are ways to organize the chaos. Firms such as Salesforce.com or Klout use technical methods to cull through the vast amounts of data in an attempt to make sense of the chaos. These types of services suggest:

1. There is a hierarchy of contributions that can be ranked and that some hold more influence than others.
2. The process is iterative when some content is shared and amplified by people who build on it.
3. The Web is organized and can be sorted for distinct purposes.
4. The significant growth in content and information makes it more difficult to be heard.

Companies are still acclimating to the realities of social media and the growing influence of mobile technology. The chaos can be problematic for brands who seek to maintain an image. Businesses must manage their social media and mobile strategies and determine who may speak on behalf of the company. In some firms, an individual or a small group is responsible for social media and mobile messages. In other firms, every employee may use social media to communicate and connect. The decision regarding who should be permitted to represent the business on social media platforms depends on the goals a firm wants to achieve and the level of risk a company accepts. Some firms use brand ambassadors, dedicated people who have express permission to represent the brand. For example, Google calls its spokespeople "evangelists."

Allowing all employees to represent the brand has some advantages. For example, LinkedIn found that employees are the key to boosting a company's social media presence. Using its Content Marketing Score, a measure of engagement the site determined that the more a firm's employees post, the higher that company's score.[25] The risks are also something to consider. An employee of HMV, the music chain, tweeted about the firing of 190 staff members on the brand's Twitter feed and then the marketing director tweeted, "How do I shut down Twitter?"[26] These kinds of embarrassments affect a brand's image.

CONTENT-DRIVEN

As a user of social networks, you have probably both consumed and created content. Content can be as simple as a post you write on Facebook, a picture you put on your Instagram account, or a review you write on Yelp. Marketers are interested in the content you create related to brands and develop content of their own that they hope people will share.

Content refers to creative communications developed by people, firms, and non-profits that are distributed online. There are many forms of digital content including:

blogs, "web logs" that are discussion-based or informative websites often presented in reverse chronological order

white papers, authoritative reports or guides helping readers understand an issue, solve a problem, or make a decision,

podcasts, episodic audio or video series that can be downloaded or streamed.

Brands can develop and then leverage content to build a reputation and subsequent business. Some of the early creators of content were business-to-business firms that distributed free white papers to clients, who provided email contact information. White papers show individual and company expertise in an industry and build loyalty among a set of customers or clients who could later be tapped for business.

These days, a variety of businesses create content to enhance their brand identities, share with current and potential customers, and collect email addresses for future communications. However, the content must be high quality and valued so that others share it online. Certain individuals are more likely to create brand content or share it online. Forrester Research categorized people into groups: creators, joiners, critics, and spectators, depending on their level of participation in online activities (see Exhibit 1.4). Some people create, while others simply spectate, but each group may be valuable to marketers who want to reach them.

Content development is an important component of a digital strategy, but content must be managed. To do so, brands should research target markets to determine the information that is important to them, rather than publishing general information that is not deeply important to customers. Firms benefit when they develop systems of content execution and treat content as a shared asset of an organization.

Content is important because information can be shared by people online, in social media and via mobile. When people share a brand's content embedded with keywords, search engines are more likely to highly rank the content when people search those keywords and the brand name. Content and sharing have become the currencies of the Web that produce desirable search engine rankings for brands.

COMMERCIAL

Social media and mobile technology are commercial directly, through actual buying and selling, and indirectly, in their influence over other buying and selling situations, whether or not the execution occurs on one of these platforms. For example, Sara can purchase a pair of sunglasses on her mobile phone or use her phone to get information about sunglasses she intends to purchase from comments made by friends or Pinterest pictures she saw posted. The commercial nature of social networks and mobile technology makes the platforms interesting and important to marketers who have new opportunities to influence sales and threats from potential competitors at the store level. In either case, marketers must plan for the new commercial environment to maximize profitability.

A number of common social websites are commercial in nature. In terms of direct commerce, eBay is a platform that generates quarterly e-commerce volume in excess of $50 billion,[27] with $11 billion in transactions from mobile. eBay was one of the earlier "social networks" because it paired together buyers and sellers to engage in trade. Though it did not have the features of Facebook, people were able to build relationships on the site by interacting online. Buyers and sellers continue to interact on eBay by connecting through sales, social media, and reviews. eBay also makes a concerted effort to encourage sellers to use social networks such as Facebook and Twitter to drive sales.

The largest online marketplace in the world is a site you may have never encountered. It's called Alibaba, and it is a popular e-commerce platform in the world's second largest economy, China. The founder of Alibaba, Jack Ma, appealed to Chinese consumers and vendors when starting his first site Taobao by not charging consumer and vendor fees, allowing bargaining, and adding an online chat function to make the site more social. In addition, Alibaba operates a virtual mall where brands such as Nike, Disney, Procter & Gamble, and Apple host their own stores; has its own payment system called Alipay; and makes a 45% profit margin. eBay's profit margin is under 18%. Not only that, but half of China's population is still not online, representing a huge potential area for Alibaba's growth.[28]

Social media networks can also be commercial. Social sites generate traffic to websites that sell merchandise, but they are also commercial themselves. **F-commerce** refers to stores that operate on Facebook, meaning they sell merchandise through Facebook's platform, though only 2% of Facebook users indicate they have purchased directly through the site.[29] Pinterest no longer takes a cut of business that originates from its platform, but the site is commercial when people showcase items that they love and wish to buy. Review sites are also commercial in that they directly influence the clientele of large groups of businesses.

Daily deals sites are commercial sites that promote businesses through their social platforms. Groupon and LivingSocial encourage businesses to offer deep discounts to their daily deal site members. Originally, in order to get a deal on a particular service, a person had to encourage friends to join the deal via social media.

Have you purchased anything using your cell phone in the last seven days? Chances are you have downloaded apps or music, but what about physical products? Mobile is becoming more transactionally commercial as more commerce is executed via cell phones and tablets. eBay reports that more than 10% of its transactions take place via mobile and sees mobile as an area of growth for the company going forward.[27] Exhibit 1.5 shows the most downloaded iPhone shopping apps in the U.S. over a one-week period in 2016.

Mobile sales will grow 16% annually through 2018 when a third of online sales are expected to occur through mobile devices, representing more than $600 billion in revenue.[30] Mobile also strongly influences how people shop both in the store and at home. Within stores people use their phones to obtain information on products, their prices, and their competitor's prices. Tablets are a

EXHIBIT 1.5

App Annie's Top Shopping Apps in the U.S.

FREE	PAID	TOP GROSSING
Amazon	Qseer Coupon Reader	Our Groceries Shopping List
OfferUp	Coupons for Amazon	Makr Logo Design
Wish	Shirtsy Design and Mail	QSeer Coupon Reader
Jet	Myibidder Auction Bid Snipper	Myibidder Auction Bid Snipper

Source:AppAnnie Top Shopping Apps IOS store 2016, Week of March 21, 2016. https://www.appannie.com/apps/ios/top-chart/united-states/shopping/?device=iphone

growing means of buying items at home because it is much more comfortable to sit on the couch and shop with your iPad than at a desktop computer when you want to relax. Tablets are expected to represent over 70% of mobile transactions over the next five years.[31]

CALCULABLE

One of the important benefits social media and mobile can offer a brand is the ability to measure performance. Brands can determine the impact of a social media or mobile strategy by setting clear goals and examining key performance indicators and return on investment. **Key performance indicators (KPIs)** are variables or metrics that measure a brand's success, and return on investment. (ROI), as previously defined, is the amount of revenue a brand makes as a result of a strategy after expenses. Strategies are only successful if they deliver measurable return with a direct impact on revenue. Some brands rely on metrics such as "tweets" or "likes," but these measures only show a part of the picture. Just because someone likes your posting doesn't mean they will buy the product or service or even recommend it to others. Though such measures may show whether a brand is on the right track toward a goal, the ultimate measure of success is often financial.

In the digital world, many brands want to drive traffic to websites. In the United States, the most effective way to determine the origin of a click is through the Google Analytics platform. Google's search engine represents over two-thirds of all U.S. search traffic[32] and is the number one website globally. The only places in the world where Google's competitors are stronger are in China (Baidu and 360 Search), Russia (Yandex), South Korea (Naver and Daum), and Japan

DORITOS'S DIP DESPERADO STRATEGY

Pepsi's Doritos brand demonstrates how social media strategies can resonate with marketing-resistant target markets. Doritos is a top-ten brand in the United Kingdom, but faces strong competition in a competitive, but growing market with a significant amount of advertising clutter. Clutter refers to the competitive advertising in a medium that potentially interferes with a brand's message.

In the Dip Desperado strategy, Pepsi targeted 16- to 24-year-old active millennials, encouraging them to buy both chips and dip to increase overall sales. The goal of the strategy was to drive brand engagement with millennials and increase positive attitudes among retailers who sold the brand. To achieve these two goals, Pepsi used traditional advertising to set the stage for a more engaging digital campaign. The television commercial told the story of Esteban Ortega who could accurately flick tortilla chips world-class distances into bowls of dip. At one point, Estaban is defeated in a chip-flicking competition and has to regain his title. At the end of

the ad, there is a call to action to enter a contest that will award prizes by going to a designated website and playing the Dip Desperado chip-flicking game. During the campaign, Doritos gave out £770,000 worth of prizes. The result was a 25% increase in dip sales and a 10% increase in single-serving sizes of Doritos.[33]

Doritos relies on customers to generate social media content.

© Shutterstock/Sean Locke Photography

(Yahoo! Japan). Google's analytics platform allows brands to track their online strategies.

INTEGRATED MARKETING COMMUNICATIONS, TRADITIONAL AND DIGITAL MEDIA

You are probably familiar with the expression **Integrated Marketing Communications (IMCs)** from your first marketing class. IMC refers to blending various forms of promotion that all work together to create a clear and distinctive message aimed at a particular target market. The concept suggests that brands develop strategies to ensure that communications are consistent across different forms of media. Brands use a combination of traditional media, such as television, radio, and outdoor, together with digital media, such as buying ads for keywords that people use to search online, and social media, and mobile. Marketers should integrate these channels to optimize their communications efforts. A person who views the brand messaging in a print advertisement should not be confused or unable to identify the brand advertising aimed at him or her on billboards, YouTube videos, or a mobile app. The main message should remain consistent across consumer touchpoints to create a clear set of associations in the mind of the consumer. When the campaign is strongly integrated, consumers should be able to clearly indicate the meaning of the brand and the brand personality.

The newest way to refer to branded communications strategies is to divide the efforts into paid media, social media, owned media, and earned media. Paid media are the methods firms use to advertise when the brand purchases advertising time in digital or traditional media. Social media are the platforms we discuss in this book that brands can use for communication. Owned media are the properties that the brand creates, such as its blog or website. Finally, earned media refer to the amplification of online communications when people share content across the Web. The brand "earns" free media time because people share the information, but the company doesn't pay for media space to run the message.

PREREQUISITES FOR SOCIAL AND MOBILE STRATEGIES

So, you think you may be ready to jump into a social media or mobile marketing solution? Not so fast. There is a lot of preliminary work that you must complete before embarking on such a venture. First of all, you may not even need a social or mobile strategy and a marketer should *never* begin by saying, "I want to set up a Pinterest site" or "Let's make a mobile application." These two statements suggest that the marketer has already decided on the plan before determining whether the strategies make sense for the brand or the target market. To reduce the risk inherent in executing any marketing strategy, good marketers do their research and set clear measureable goals so that after executing the strategy, the marketer can determine the degree of success. In digital marketing, the feedback from an execution is very important to inform the next level of the strategy. Since one can directly measure the reach of any message online, marketers can leverage the best strategies for the future.

To execute a strategy, the marketer must segment and target markets, conduct consumer behavioral research, set appropriate goals, develop creative messaging, consider various forms of media, test the strategy, determine the metrics and measures for evaluation, and establish legal boundaries. The remaining chapters of this book describe these steps toward building a strong social media or mobile marketing strategy.

SUMMARY AND REVIEW

CHAPTER SUMMARY

Social media and mobile marketing are part of a firm's digital marketing strategy. Both can be used to communicate with and engage target markets, but must be carefully planned and managed. The marketing environment has changed how marketers interact with consumers and has both opened up doors and posed significant challenges to brand strategies. Brands are still adjusting to the new reality and will continue to see new opportunities and threats as digital marketing progresses.

KEY TERMS

blog	four P's of the	Key Performance	return on investment
content	marketing mix	Indicators (KPIs)	(ROI)
crowdsourcing	fragmented	mobile technologies	search engine
digital self	Integrated Marketing	organic rankings	social media
F-Commerce	Communication	personas	white paper
	(IMC)	podcast	

SUMMARY REVIEW QUESTIONS

1. Describe three major changes that have influenced marketing since the advent of social media. How has mobile changed marketing for retailers?
2. Social media and mobile technologies are often described as "disruptive." What does the term disruptive mean and how can social media or mobile technology disrupt an industry?
3. In what forms of media do brands spend most of their advertising dollars? What do you expect to happen with regard to global ad spending going forward?
4. What are the most used mobile applications and explain why they are popular based on your knowledge and use of the apps.
5. What are the advantages of using social media for brands?

APPLICATION QUESTIONS

1. How hard would it be to edit a Wikipedia site? Now is your chance to find out. Choose a topic you know something about or one that you would like to know more about. Go to Wikipedia.com and locate the page on your topic. Read the article to see whether there may be points that need

clarification. Often Wikipedia will request that more information be added to a particular page. Before you actually edit anything on the site, try to use the Sandbox feature. This allows you to see how your post will look before it is seen by the whole world. Your assignment is to write at least one line of information for an actual Wikipage or, alternatively, show your work in the Sandbox.

2. Locate an online community that shares a common goal. What is the key driver of a person's participation in the community, and how can the community engage participants so they continue to remain part of the community?

3. Social media has been described as "chaotic." Go online and find an example of a company that ran into problems in executing a social media strategy. Describe the problem and how the company could have prevented the resulting chaos.

4. Choose a new mobile application (app) that was introduced in the past year. Describe the basic functionality of the app. How will the app make money? Consider one brand that could use the application to add value to a particular customer base. Explain.

5. What will digital life be like in 2025? Find the Pew Internet Research report on this subject and write a short summary. What are some of the theses that Pew has considered about the digital future?

case study Herschel Supply's Social Strategy

Herschel Supply Co. was a manufacturer of backpacks, bags, and travel accessories based in Vancouver, Canada. Founded in 2009 by Brothers Jamie and Lyndon Cormack, the company's goal was "to create a timeless product with fine regard for detail."[34]

Herschel designed its own products, produced them in China, and sold bags in over sixty countries. In North America, the brand had 5,000 retailers including Nordstrom and Urban Outfitters and also sold on the company website run on Shopify's platform.[35]

Backpacks represented a $13 billion global market, with projected stable growth of about 4% a year through 2018 due to the product's relatively reasonable price. Most of the expected growth was from China and the United States, which had large populations of travelers with the money to spend on accessories.

The market was fragmented with no single player dominating and the top brand, Jansport, commanded only about a 7% global share. The remaining top brands were Nike, The North Face, Adidas, Eastpak, Samsonite, Sestini, Xeryus, High Sierra, and Coach. Herschel was still too small to rank in the top twenty global competitors, but was gaining traction in a number of countries including France and Japan.[36]

By 2015 Herschel's sales "were in the tens of millions" according to one brother and the brand had grown 22,000% over the four prior years.[37] The major growth was achieved without a significant advertising budget. The brand relied on organic buzz and little paid advertising. The company instead used social media to introduce new products and designs and never prompted customers with aggressive calls to action. The brand leveraged storytelling to drive sales and all marketing was done in-house.

Herschel used social media as a way to reach its target customer base of 18- to 25-year-old adventurers who like to talk about travel and exploration. Using the hashtag #WellTravelled, Herschel built an audience on social media sites, harnessing Hootsuite to deliver the message across media formats. Hootsuite was a platform that brands used to distribute social media content to a variety of social sites and to track and manage the response.

A big component of the social strategy was Instagram, where the brand posted high-quality travel photos, 95% of which hit the Instagram popular page. The brand had also been suggested to users on the platform, which drew attention to the brand and led to growth. To further build its social presence, Herschel developed the Wander the World contest, giving away a trip to Peru. Partnering with Intrepid Traveler, the brand offered the travel prize for people in the United States and Canada who posted pictures on Instagram. The winner was chosen based on the "ability to deliver a unique perspective on the location being shot" and judged on the following criteria:

1. Ability to portray a story through images
2. Photographic ability
3. Sense of awe[34]

The brand followed up with additional contests such as the holiday Pinterest contest and the #CityLimitless Instagram contest. In the latter, the brand asked people to share imagery that embodied the urban existence. The #CityLimitless contest offered a grand prize of a $1,000 Herschel Supply e-gift card and a City Survival Essentials Pack. The brand supplied the required extensive contest rules, such as "no purchase necessary." However, in order to participate, people had to upload photos to their Instagram accounts, follow Herschel Supply, and tag their photos with the #CityLimitless and #HerschelSupply hashtags. Participants agreed to grant Herschel the exclusive rights to their photos for marketing purposes.

Travelers were an interesting demographic for a brand like Herschel because typical travelers were couples over 50 with high incomes. The average age of leisure travelers was 47.5. However, even if Herschel's target customer did not travel, the theme resonated with the young educated customer who could imagine traveling to exotic locations by engaging with Herschel's social media content.[38] In addition, millennials were expected to grow their spending as they aged and to increase their number of international trips 47% by 2020.[39]

Herschel also used social media for customer service. When Herschel was founded, the company had one customer service representative to handle complaints via email and telephone. Though the person usually responded quickly, the company wanted to be more present in the lives of its target customers. Herschel management decided instead to leverage social media to respond to its young demographic where they were most active.

By responding to and engaging customers on Facebook and Twitter, Herschel increased customer service satisfaction by 20% and brand sentiment by 60%, a direct result of the sharing that occurred through the social customer service outreach.[40]

In 2015 @HerschelSupply had 29.4k followers and 1,385 tweets. On its Twitter description, the brand provided the customer service handle @HSC_Support so that customers with complaints would be serviced elsewhere. This feed had only 268 followers who were often asked to contact the company via email, rather than use the Twitter feed for specific issues/complaints.[40] Some of the complaints involved the product ripping and people posted pictures of the damage. Others had tried alternative methods of reaching the company and were only able to do so via Twitter.

Herschel and its competitors were active in social media as shown in Exhibit 1.6. Though Herschel used less traditional media than competitors there were some targeted efforts to broaden the appeal. Specifically the brand launched a magazine called *The Journal*,

publishing 150,000 print copies and a digital version. The brand regularly exhibited its products at Agenda, a streetwear trade show held in Las Vegas, New York, and Long Beach, running bi-annual ads in the show's guide and magazine's back cover. Herschel's in-house agency also placed ads in magazines in Japan, Hong Kong, Italy, France, Australia, and even North America. Online, it ran ads in blogs and on Facebook.[41] Herschel maintained a budget of $770 per month to buy search engine keywords to direct potential customers to its website.[42]

Herschel Supply Company saw quick success with its well-made and fashionable bags. As the brand continued to grow, how would the company use social media and would traditional advertising add to the brand's value going forward?

QUESTIONS FOR DISCUSSION

1. What are three types of content that Herschel can create and share on social media? What has it shared, and has such a strategy been successful relative to its competitors?

EXHIBIT 1.6

Social Media Presence for Three Competitors

SOCIAL MEDIA PRESENCE (2015)	HERSCHEL	JANSPORT	EASTPAK
Facebook likes	271,000	1,618,343	1,710,715
Twitter followers	29,400	22,100	3,222
Instagram followers	497,000	51,000	19,400

Sources: Facebook, Twitter, and Instagram

2. The case indicates that Herschel has a limited ad budget, but does the company spend money on advertising? What are its expenses?
3. Who creates and who owns Herschel's social media content?
4. Why did Herschel add the #CityLimitless hashtag to its marketing effort? What could this achieve for the brand?
5. If you were working in Herschel's marketing department, how would you pick the winner of the #CityLimitless contest? Might the brand consider other qualities of the entrant aside from his or her talent?
6. Herschel also uses social media for customer service. What are the pros and cons of this strategy?
7. Does the brand run paid advertising? Are paid media necessary for a successful strategy? Explain.
8. Give an example of each of the 7 C's using ideas and concepts from the case.
9. Do you have a Twitter account? If not, go ahead and create one. Post three tweets about where you would like to travel and what you would take with you. Next, go to Hootsuite and authorize the platform to access your Twitter account. What are three things a marketer could do with Hootsuite to assist with social media marketing?

REFERENCES

[1] J. Mahler, "Who Spewed That Abuse? Anonymous Yik Yak App Isn't Telling," *The New York Times,* 8 March 2015.

[2] A. Shontell, "How 2 Georgia Fraternity Brothers Created Yik Yak, a Controversial App that Became a ~$400 Million Business in 365 Days," *Business Insider,* March 2015.

[3] http://digiday.com/publishers/how-bbc-is-using-yik-yak-to-talk-to-millennials-and-get-them-to-talk-back/

[4] J. Surowiecki, "Twilight of the Brands," *The New Yorker,* 17 and 24 February 2014.

[5] C. Hibbard, "How Microsoft Xbox Uses Twitter to Reduce Support Costs," *Social Media Examiner,* 27 July 2010.

[6] A. Curtis, "A Brief History of Social Media," 2013. [Online]. Available: http://www2.uncp.edu/home/ acurtis/NewMedia/SocialMedia/SocialMediaHistory.html.

[7] G. Sloan, "Snapchat Is Asking Brands for $750,000 to Advertise and Won't Budge," *AdWeek,* 14 Jan 2015.

[8] D. Schniederjans, E. S. Caob and M. Schniederjans, "Enhancing Financial Performance with Social Media: An Impression Management Perspective," *Decision Support Systems,* vol. 55, no. 4, pp. 911–918, November 2013.

[9] R. Rishika, A. Kumar, R. Janakiraman, and R. Bezawada, "The Effect of Customers' Social Media Participation on Customer Visit Frequency and Profitability: An Empirical Investigation," *Information Systems Research,* vol. 24, no. 1, pp. 108–127, March 2013.

[10] C. Heine, "Brand Apps Need to Provide a Utility to Stay Visible," *Adweek,* 3 February 2014.

[11] J. Stern, "Teens are Leaving Facebook and This is Where They are Going," *ABC News Blog,* October 2013.

[12] McKinsey, "Disruptive Technologies: Advances That Will Transform Life, Business, and the Global Economy.," 2013.

[13] J. Sciarrino, "Leveraging the Virtuous Circle of Brand and the Extended Self" *Journal of Marketing Theory and Practice,* vol. 22, no. 2, pp. 147–148, Spring 2014.

[14] Creativity, "Watch Nike's Short Film Celebrating LeBron James' Return to Cleveland," *Creativity,* 30 October 2014.

[15] Worldwide; StatCounter; 2009 to 2016 We Are Social 2016

[16] Merriam-Webster, 2014.

[17] Alexa, "Top 500 Sites on the Web," 8 May 2014. [Online]. Available: http://www.alexa.com/topsites. [Accessed 2014].

[18] Z. Schlanger, "Coke to Remove Flame-Retardant Chemical From All Its Drinks," *Newsweek,* 5 May 2014.

[19] Carnegie Mellon, "Science Daily," March 2014. [Online]. Available: http://www.sciencedaily.com/releases/2014/03/140304130027.htm.

[20] L. Fisher, "How Crowdsourcing is Tackling Poverty in the Developing World," *Forbes,* 21 March 2012.

[21] M. Meeker, "2013 Internet Trends," *Kleiner Perkins Insights,* 2013.

[22] E. Poushter, "Smartphone Ownership and Internet Usage Continues to Climb in Emerging Economies," Pew Research Center, February 22, 2016.

[23] Wikipedia, [Online]. Available: www.wikipedia.com. [Accessed 30 April 2014].

[24] E. Griffen, "Crowdsourced Stock Site Estimize Adds M&A Predictions (and $1.5 Million in Venture Funding)," *CNN Money,* 26 March 2014.

[25] G. Sloan, "Brand Sitting on Secret Army of Marketers," *Adweek,* 28 March 2014.

[26] S. Kleinberg, "Top Social Media Fails of 2013," *Chicago Tribune,* 31 January 2013.

[27] eBay, "eBay Inc. Reports First Quarter 2014 Results," 29 April 2014.

[28] V. Goel, M. J. D. L. Merced, and N. Gough, "Chinese Giant Alibaba Will Go Public, Listing in U.S.," *New York Times,* 6 May 2014.

[29] Rooke, "Is Facebook Commerce Already Dead?," *iMedia,* 9 October 2013.

[30] Goldman Sachs, "eCommerce Expected to Accelerate in 2014," 2014.

[31] eMarketer, "Smartphones, Tablets Drive Faster Growth in Ecommerce Sales - See more at: http://www.emarketer.com/Article/Smartphones-Tablets-Drive-Faster-Growth-Ecommerce-Sales/1009835#sthash.zCbKKvPU.dpuf," *eMarketer,* 24 April 2013.

[32] ComScore, "comScore Releases January 2014 US Search Engine Rankings," 18 February 2014.

[33] Austin Return on Now Internet Marketing , "2013 Search Engine Market Share By Country," 2013. [Online]. Available: http://returnonnow.com/internet-marketing-resources/2013-search-engine-market-share-by-country/.

[34] G. Rossolatos, "Doritos: The Dip Desperado Strategy," in *Encyclopedia of Major Marketing Strategies*, Gale, 2013, pp. 121–124.

[35] Herschel Supply, "About," 2015. [Online]. Available: http://www.herschelsupply.com/about/.

[36] P. Demery, "How Herschel Straightens its Product Data to Back its Growth," *Internet Retailer,* 8 March 2014.

[37] Euromonitor, "Euromonitor Luggage Report ABackpacks: Current and Future Drivers Datagraphic," *Euromonitor,* March 2014.

[38] J. Horn, "Brands of the Year: Herschel's Cool Factor Takes it Global," *Strategy,* 9 October 2014.

[39] US Travel Association, "Travel Facts and Statistics," *US Travel Association,* 2015.

[40] J. Sullivan, "Millenials: A New Breed of Travelers," *Euromonitor,* 25 February 2015.

[41] HootSuite, "Success Story Herschel Supply Co," Hootsuite, 2014.

[42] K. Gold, "Herschel Supply Has it in the Bag," *Marketing Magazine,* 25 October 2013.

[43] Spyfu, "Search Terms Herschel Supply," 2015.

© Shutterstock/Goodluz

CHAPTER TWO

IDENTIFYING CUSTOMERS

The best marketing strategies are aimed at specific groups of customers. In order to identify the most lucrative targets, marketing managers must clearly divide consumers into groups and then evaluate the segments. Strong marketing efforts outline and deeply describe segments beyond simple demographics, providing many alternative targets to evaluate for achieving specific objectives. In the current fragmented media market, segmentation can be the key to developing an efficient strategy and effective execution. Chapter Two describes segmentation and targeting for social media and mobile strategies and presents the concept of social positioning for brands.

LEARNING OBJECTIVES

After reading this chapter, you will be able to:

- SEGMENT A SPECIFIC MARKET FOR SOCIAL MEDIA AND MOBILE STRATEGIES.

- DETERMINE APPROPRIATE TARGETS FOR SELECTED MARKETING ACTIONS.

- TARGET DIGITAL CONSUMERS BASED ON THEIR ONLINE BEHAVIOR.

- EVALUATE COMPETITORS' STRATEGIES USING SHARE OF VOICE.

- UTILIZE SOCIAL MEDIA TO POSITION BRANDS RELATIVE TO COMPETITORS.

You may not realize this, but Chinese consumers love luxury products. The vast middle class in China now earns the equivalent of $836-$3,304 a month and 77% of these consumers say they purchase luxury goods in a given year [1]. Can you guess which brands are their favorites?

As China's luxury markets in China's largest cities such as Beijing, Shanghai, and Guangzhou mature, marketers have begun to notice upscale consumers in second- and third-tier cities as well—including Chongqing, Xi'an, and Hangzhou. The city of Chengdou has 7 million people whose incomes have increased as much as 20% over the past few years and the province claims an estimated 1,800 superwealthy residents with incomes over $16 million a year [2].

The British retailer Burberry leverages both social media and mobile marketing to expand aggressively in China's "emerging" cities. The Chinese store's employees use iPads, to allow customers to shop easily and showcase merchandise in a beautiful and engaging manner. To build buzz, a video of the Beijing Burberry store opening was featured on Sina Weibo, one of China's social media sites, and it had 3 million online opening-day viewers [3].

Other marketers are also looking to China for growth. Ford Motors wants to increase its global sales 50% by 2050, and introducing the Lincoln brand to Chinese luxury consumers is an important part of the strategy [4]. Ford is building social media relationships by making the Sina Weibo mobile application available in Ford cars, so drivers can get news, weather, information, and location services [5]. With the help of social media and mobile, Ford is poised to outsell its major Japanese rivals, Toyota and Honda in China [6].

Upscale Chinese shop globally.

© Shutterstock/MJTH

Chinese annual disposable income is expected to double by 2020 to $8,000, approaching the incomes of South Koreans. By then, approximately 6% (60 million) of Chinese consumers will be considered affluent, with household incomes over $34,000 annually. The wealthiest thirteen Chinese cities hold 27% of the total urban gross domestic product, an important geographic consideration for marketers [7].

China's population is aging. Whereas 55- to 65-year-olds spend 50% of their income on food, those 34–54 spend only 34% on groceries and allocate more toward apparel, suggesting a shift in purchasing patterns in the future. These behavioral differences also affect luxury consumption in the world's largest potential market, a country that is already outspending Japan in luxury consumption [6].

FAVORED CHINESE LUXURY ITEMS

So, what are the favorite brands among Chinese luxury consumers? Burberry is number one followed by Chanel, Gucci, Louis Vuitton, and Prada [8].

Burberry and Ford have penetrated the Chinese market in the hopes of riding the tide of growing affluence. To be successful, the brands had to examine the market, segment Chinese consumers geographically, and develop optimal strategies to reach their target markets and maximize revenues.

In general, marketers who segment customers, understand the various target markets, and engage customers in meaningful ways will be more successful implementing strategies. Though luxury consumers around the world share some similarities, local differences could make or break a brand. This chapter will help you plan and develop strategies for defining, locating, and reaching the best target markets to meet organizational objectives.

SEGMENTATION BASICS

Segmentation is the process of dividing the broad market into groups based on certain predefined characteristics that often relate to consumer behavior. Marketers are interested in determining which groups of consumers are likely to respond to marketing communications, engage in particular market behaviors such as a purchase, or communicate satisfaction or dissatisfaction with products or services.

Determining customer segments is an important prerequisite to any social media or mobile strategy for both the **business-to-consumer market (B2C)** and **business-to-business market (B2B)**. Businesses who market to final consumers use social media and mobile to communicate with and engage with their business so that they may share experiences online and ultimately purchase. B2B marketers are also interested in communicating and engaging their targets and can use social media to reach them. For example, many B2B firms who sell to marketing clients publish white papers that emphasize a business topic of interest to their customers. The reports emphasize the company's expertise and potential clients may be attracted to the firm because of their content and the company's reputation. Business-to-business firms rely on relationships to build their business and social media can facilitate these relationships. One popular site for business-to-business marketing is LinkedIn, which connects people in a variety of firms. Marketers can use LinkedIn to reach out to potential clients. Selling to other businesses is complicated because the process often involves multiple players with various goals. Therefore, when B2B marketers segment clients, they may consider the following criteria:

- Individual or company behavior
- Size and composition of the decision-making team
- Potential for profitability
- Firm lifetime customer value
- Desired benefits of the product/service
- Use or application of the product/service
- Final customers in the marketing channel
- Price/quality demands
- Competitors in the market

For example, the B2B marketer for SAP, the German software company, segmented the social media market in Latin America by language. The company now has multiple Facebook pages, Twitter feeds, and LinkedIn accounts in both Spanish and Portuguese [9].

In the B2C arena, marketers must consider a broad range of possible consumer groups in order to hone in on the people who are most receptive to the brand and who will deliver company profits. Consumers in the most successful target markets have the following characteristics:

- Ability and willingness to purchase
- Receptiveness to marketing messages and products
- Potential to deliver profitability (with revenues over expenses)

Nokia emphasized its Lumina 1020 smartphone's camera function and aimed ads at parents who take pictures of their kids. The target market of parents meets the criteria of adequate size and potential profitability.

UNDERSTANDING THE TARGET MARKET

Marketers do not always recognize the best target market when they first conceive of a strategy. Sometimes, marketers think of a likely target before they consider all the possible characteristics of consumers that influence their purchase likelihood, their shopping and buying habits, or their responsiveness to various communications. As a result, some marketers begin the process by jumping straight into locating targets without completing a full segmentation. This kind of snap decision approach could cause a marketer to overlook potentially viable and profitable targets.

When it comes to social media and mobile market segmentation, marketers must determine where consumers seek brand- and purchase-related information and how they engage with various services and devices. For example, if the target market does not use social media, it would be wasteful to try to reach them with tweets. Therefore, marketers must examine a series of behaviors that may differentiate groups of consumers as they interact with the brand online. These behaviors are factors that influence the segmentation and targeting process because consumers vary in their responses to brand communications. Exhibit 2.1 lists the factors to consider when segmenting markets for social or mobile strategies.

Factors Influencing B2C Segmentation in Social Media or Mobile Technology

Preferences for particular social networks
Online activities such as content developing, spectating, or criticizing
Media viewing and response habits
Social media influence and interactions
Use of particular devices
Level of online risk tolerance or aversion
Likelihood of engaging and sharing
Shopping and buying habits

LOOKING BEYOND DEMOGRAPHICS

Demographics are an important part of segmentation and targeting strategies. Demographics are the statistical data associated with a particular population and include variables such as age, income, marital status, and ancestry. Many marketers use the variables age and gender to choose consumer groups for marketing strategies, though other factors may be more indicative of people's purchase behavior. For example, Burton may target men or women, but is much more interested in whether they snowboard. Burton's social media contest asked people to "regram" (on Instagram) a photo of Mark McMorris to win a trip to snowboard with the star athlete.

In the past, the emphasis on age and gender made sense for many marketers in the B2C arena because of the heavy emphasis on commercial television to deliver messaging. Successful television shows had high ratings determined by A.C. Nielsen, and Nielsen's electronic monitoring system consisted of a set top box that recorded television viewing among a representative sample of households. Though the data had the potential to provide detailed family information, most advertisers focused on consumers' ages and genders.

With digital media, marketers are no longer limited to Nielsen data and have a host of new characteristics with which to segment the market beyond demographics. For example, Facebook allows advertisers to narrow down the universe of Facebook users by segmenting on demographics, hobbies and activities, life events, device ownership, and product categories purchased.

Exhibit 2.2 shows the four basic segmentation methods and some of the sub-segments that are offered to advertisers on Facebook. Marketers can target their ads to these narrow categories of Facebook's audience.

Facebook also recognizes that marketers may have different goals and encourages marketers to select from the following campaign objectives:

- Increasing page likes
- Generating website clicks and conversions
- Installing and engaging with applications
- Responding to events
- Claiming offers
- Gaining Video Views

Marketers who have set clear goals will be more successful in reaching the right target market and executing strategies that will attract and encourage purchase for better firm results. Some brands have been very successful in using Facebook's precise targeting. On Facebook's platform, Budweiser offered a free beer to those people who had just turned 22 and was able to target only those individuals. HSBC wanted to reach university students in Europe and Asia after a number of students protested new charges for overdrafts on Facebook. Groupon and Living Social use Facebook data to determine people's locations and preferences for services [11].

INFLUENCERS

Marketers are particularly interested in **influencers**—consumers who are highly engaged with their brands, communicate with their connections through social

consider this . . .

UNLEASHING THE JOY OF REDDI-WIP

ConAgra's Reddi-wip brand knew a lot about the people who bought whipped cream. Yes, they were women, but that wasn't the only factor that mattered. Most purchases were related to the holiday season and certain foods were more likely to be topped—such as gelatin, pies, and pudding. One food that often went naked was fruit, but it was the most eaten food that could take a squirt of whipped cream. Reddi-wip developed a campaign aimed at its target group, women, encouraging them to eat whipped cream on fruit, which added only 15 calories. The ads featured two women returning from their work-out and rewarding themselves with a low-calorie snack of fruit and Reddi-wip. The brand ran television and Web banners and grew its Facebook engagement with an offer of a free berry-keeper container for people who "liked" Reddi-wip. The results were impressive. Sales in each month following the campaign were 6–18% higher than in the prior year, when the brand only expected sales increases of 3% [10].

EXHIBIT 2.2

Segmentation and Sub-segmentation Options on Facebook

SEGMENTATION METHODS	FACEBOOK SUB-SEGMENTS
Geographic	City, country, local by postal code
Demographic	Age (13 and above): Advertisers can match to exact ages, such as 31. Gender (male or female) Languages spoken Education Workplace (advertise to people who work at a specific company) Relationship status
Psychographic	Precise interest such as console gamers, people who watch specific television shows, or read select magazines Broad categories of interest such as business and industry, family and relationships, fitness and wellness, food and drink, and hobbies and activities Interests in particular activities, music genres, movie categories, and sports Life events such as the birth of a child, new job, or upcoming birthday
Behavioral Social media–related Purchase-related Mobile usage	People's connections and their friends' connections People who buy beauty products, fashion, or luxury goods Owners of old computers Mobile feature phone vs. smartphone owners Mobile operating system and brand of phone Mobile devices such as iPad or iPhone

media or mobile properties and may affect the attitudes and behavior of others. Influencers can be regular people, opinion leaders who have a particular interest in a product or service and who choose to share information, or they may be professionals with specialized knowledge or elevated status, such as experts, bloggers, or celebrities.

TYPES OF INFLUENCERS

Opinion leaders are highly involved with a product or service and enjoy sharing information on the category with friends and family. These advice-givers have close personal relationships with the people they advise, but know a little more about a particular product or service. An opinion leader usually recommends in one or two product categories where he or she has the most knowledge. How do you hear about new television shows to watch? If you listen to your friends' advice about what to watch, your friends are your opinion leaders. In the past, opinion leaders were limited to sharing with their close companions, but online connectedness allows opinion leaders to share attitudes with anyone online.

Endorsers are professionals who may share product category information online and include experts and celebrities. **Experts** are those with professional knowledge regarding products or services, such as doctors or bloggers who focus on a particular area. The influence of experts can be strong when they are viewed as credible and knowledgeable by others. Celebrities may also endorse products, but their influence lies in their trustworthiness and attractiveness to their followers. Ads with celebrities may also be funny so that people share them. Kevin Bacon does ads for eggs, because what goes better with eggs than Bacon? As egg consumption grew, the industry decided to boost its visibility with Kevin Bacon as a celebrity endorser for eggs with the tagline "Wake up with the strength to endure a lifetime of bacon jokes." In the online video ad, Kevin Bacon suddenly appears lying on the counter in a woman's kitchen offering healthy tips on eggs, but takes offense to bacon references [12].

Research has found that influence is strongest when the persuader is credible and knowledgeable and does not intend to persuade. Attractive persuaders are more successful in changing people's attitudes than unattractive ones, as are those with special expertise and status. Of course, the message itself and the person hearing the communication also determine the likelihood that he or she will be persuaded, so social media is a small component of overall influence.

Marketers can measure social media influence through a number of online services. For example, Klout uses data from a variety of social media sites to determine an individual's Klout score. Those with higher scores are more influential than those with lower scores. Klout divides influencers into sixteen types, depending on how much original content the person creates and his or her reach, and the number of people with whom he or she interacts. There are curators, broadcasters, socializers, dabblers, observers, thought leaders, and specialists to name a few [13]. Celebrities have strong reach and may tweet about a product or brand and can boost a strategy because of people's desire to emulate them. Of course, sometimes celebrities tweet about products and it may not benefit the company. Martha Stewart dropped her iPad and sent out a tweet announcing that the product had broken and made clear that Apple customer service was not as good as she expected. "I just dropped my iPad on the ground and shattered two glass corners. What to do? Does one call Apple to come and pick it up or do I take it?" [14].

FINDING AND ENGAGING INFLUENCERS

Marketers can identify influencers and encourage them to share brand messages. Since influencers are already engaged with the product category, marketers should be able to locate them within their customer base. Opinion leaders are likely to have had contact with the brand and may be on its email list or subscribe to its newsletter. Very often, small incentives and recognition can be effective in building loyalty among opinion leaders. Bloggers, experts, and celebrities are easy to identify as well, but more effort may be required to encourage them to share. Blogger strategy is an important component of some social media campaigns, and techniques for Blogger outreach are covered in Chapter Nine. Reaching out to celebrities requires getting in touch with agents and publishers and may involve fees for endorsements, but some brands get lucky and are mentioned by celebrities because they are customers.

Mobile applications can be used to engage influencers and keep them connected to a brand. SocialLadder is a mobile app that rewards young adults when they engage in a set of brand challenges that they then share through social media. As people complete brand-related actions such as posting product use pictures, they earn points toward one-of-a-kind brand experiences. For example, a certain level of points can lead to backstage passes at concerts, sporting events, or fashion shows that ordinary people can't attend. Young people are likely to opt in to this platform to earn the points for the unique redemptions.

Building influence in social media can provide brands with benefits that have measurable results. First, when consumers are engaged, they communicate with the brand, expressing their thoughts, feelings, or ideas, and may help other consumers solve problems through online networks. Second, when a brand's content is shared throughout the online space, in social media and via mobile, the brand benefits from higher search engine rankings on the major search engines.

Going forward, marketers will attempt to identify and reward those who are strong influencers for their brand, and build strategies to encourage them to share and keep them interested. Honda used Pinterest to promote its campaign "get out and live life" by locating the five most influential pinners on Pinterest and encouraging them to take a 24-hour break from the site to participate in real activities. Honda gave each influential pinner $500 to allow the brand to take over his or her site with a "Pintermission" billboard as the pinners were off in the real world. The campaign earned over 16 million online impressions [15].

SocialLadder harnesses the power of the influential.

SocialLadder, http://socialladder.rkiapps.com/

consider this...

CELEBRITY Q SCORES

How do companies decide which celebrities should represent their brands? A variety of factors including trustworthiness, attractiveness, and fit with the product play a role. But brands have another tool at their disposal, Q scores. **Q scores** measure the likability of celebrities, icons, and known individuals and people's emotional connections to them. One of the highest-scoring celebrities is George Clooney, who has a Q score of 22, much higher than the average score of 16 for celebrities. The chart here shows the awareness levels and Q scores for celebrity endorsers for some popular brands and the company's ranking on *Fortune's* World's Most Admired Company list.

Brands with strong recognition prefer to work with celebrities who have strong Q scores [16].

BRAND	FORTUNE'S MOST ADMIRED COMPANY RANKING	CELEBRITY ENDORSER	CELEBRITY AWARENESS LEVEL	CELEBRITY Q-SCORE
Coke	6	Taylor Swift	82%	20
Procter & Gamble	15	Queen Latifah	76%	16
Pepsi	42	Beyonce Knowles	84%	20
Berkshire Hathaway	4	Warren Buffett The Geico Gecko	43% 93%	15 35
Samsung	21	David Beckham	66%	11

SEGMENTATION FOR MARKETING STRATEGIES

Segmentation allows marketers to determine where the customers are located, who they are, how they live their lives, what their media habits are, and how they use products and services. The process of segmenting for social media and mobile strategies is similar to traditional segmentation in that marketers consider some of the same variables. The first step is to determine the method to use to divide the market into groups. Typically, marketers divide the broad base of consumers by demographics, geographics, psychographics, behaviors, and combinations of these categories. Effective segmentation includes evaluating all of the sub-segments within the four categories and delving deeply into many potential consumer characteristics. Each of the categories is described in the next section with examples from social media and mobile marketing.

DEMOGRAPHIC SEGMENTATION

Demographic segmentation divides the market into groups based on the population characteristics of the market. Governments around the world collect a lot of information on the composition of their populations to provide proper services to citizens. Though not all governments complete a census of the population, some countries or organizations provide significant amounts of free data, such as the United States, European Commission, India, and Australia.

The demographic population characteristics include age, gender, marital status, family composition, presence of children, country of origin, religion, and occupation. If you delve deeply into the United States' Census website at census. gov, you may be surprised to find information on various industries, e-commerce, wealth, and social mobility. For example, the Census webpage offers reports on holiday shopping, candle purchases, retail sales, Christmas trees, toys, and even the annual Super Bowl [17].

Demographics of Social Media and Mobile Consumers

Social media and mobile usage differ by certain demographic characteristics. Specifically, women are more active on social media both in the United States and Europe, logging on and posting more often on Facebook, Twitter, and Pinterest than men. Women indicate that they engage in social networking to connect with family and friends and stay up-to-date with them. Men view social media as information sources and are more likely to be contributors of factual content on sites like Wikipedia, LinkedIn, and Google+ [18].

Social media usage differs by age, with younger people more actively engaged with more friends on social media sites and connecting more frequently with brands than older people. For example, those ages 18–29 are far more likely to be on Twitter than those 30–65+ [19]. Higher levels of education are also associated with more social media usage and Hispanics are slightly more likely to engage in social media than other ethnic groups.

Marital status is an indicator of social media usage, but it depends on whether you are talking about husbands or wives. Married women flock to social media, while married men shy away [20].

Mobile smartphone ownership skews slightly higher for women, and people with high incomes and more education are more likely to own both smartphones and tablet devices. Age also plays a role, with those 18–29 more likely to own smartphones than those 50–65+ and even a bit more than 30–49 year olds. More than half of smartphone owners in the United States have Android systems [21].

Global Mobile Demographics

Smartphone penetration is not as high in developing countries as in the developed world and mobile phone ownership differs by gender and other factors. For example, whereas most people in South Korea (88%) have a smartphone, only 58% of Chinese, 45% of Russians, 41% of Brazilians, and 17% of Indians have smartphones. In all these countries, men are somewhat more likely to own smartphones than women. Interestingly, British men are more likely to have smartphones than British women, but American women own more smartphones than American men [22]. Exhibit 2.3 shows smartphone penetration in the BRIC countries: Brazil, Russia, India, and China.

EXHIBIT 2.3

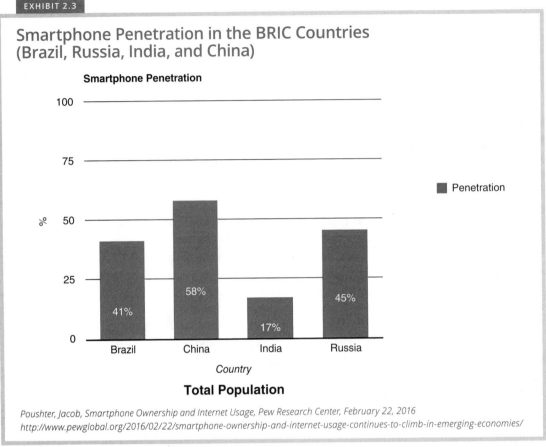

Smartphone Penetration in the BRIC Countries (Brazil, Russia, India, and China)

Smartphone Penetration

Poushter, Jacob, *Smartphone Ownership and Internet Usage, Pew Research Center, February 22, 2016*
http://www.pewglobal.org/2016/02/22/smartphone-ownership-and-internet-usage-continues-to-climb-in-emerging-economies/

GEOGRAPHIC SEGMENTATION

Geographic segmentation allows marketers to divide consumers based on their location—by country, city, metropolitan area, census tract, or neighborhood. Many social media sites can target individuals based on location. For instance, Pandora, the online Internet radio service, offers marketers the opportunity to target consumers in their homes, at their offices, and even in their cars with a personalized musical backdrop. Local businesses can use Pandora to reach only people in a retailer's immediate location.

Geographic breakdowns are important for mobile strategies because marketers can pinpoint mobile users and target them when their customers are seeking products or services. Smartphone users tend to engage in local search behavior to find locations of stores and restaurants on their phones. A study of 6,000 mobile searches by Nielsen and Google found that over half of these searches led to further engagement on the part of the customer through a phone call, store visit, or purchase [23].

Country-by-Country Segmentation

Geographic segmentation is also useful in identifying methods to reach global consumers because people in some countries are more active in social media than in other countries. Though the United States is the country with the largest percentage of Twitter users, Japan, India, the United Kingdom, Spain, and Russia also have large populations of people on Twitter [24]. The largest social media sites including Facebook and Twitter are available in many countries, but not all countries allow free social media access. In some countries the global social media sites are dominated by local versions that serve particular countries. In China, the dominant **microblogging** site is Sina Weibo, and in Russia, the dominant social media site is VKontakte or VK.

consider this . . .

COUNTRIES WITH HIGH SMARTPHONE PENETRATION

Mobile phone ownership differs by country. Can you name any countries with populations who have more smartphones per capita than in the United States? According to Google, smartphone penetration is higher in all these countries [22] compared to the United States:

United Arab Emirates
Saudi Arabia

South Korea
Singapore
Norway
Australia
Hong Kong
Israel
United Kingdom
Denmark
Ireland

Local Targeting with Review Sites

Marketers who segment geographically can also reach local customers through social media sites and track the success of these online efforts through Google Analytics to determine the location of customers. Google Analytics is a free tool that Google offers businesses to evaluate their website performance and to track the location of website visitors. Local social media sites are important for retail businesses such as shops and restaurants because people may be looking for locations when they are out and about. Local review sites can drive more customers to stores when the prospects examine reviews on their smartphones.

Yelp is a popular local review site operating in twenty-three countries that displays reviews of restaurants and retail locations for businesses in a particular area. When potential customers search Yelp on their mobile phones, tablets, and computers, they are usually looking for information they are likely to act upon right away. For instance, someone looking for a seafood retailer on their mobile phone is likely to purchase fish for their dinner that night. The searches yield purchase-specific information based on geographic location.

consider this . . .

TOP YELP CATEGORIES IN SELECTED CITIES ON ONE DAY

You are probably not surprised that restaurants are among the top Yelp categories, but other services are also demanded by online consumers in San Francisco, London, Dublin, and Singapore. [25]

The top Yelp categories in San Francisco:

1. Restaurants San Francisco
2. Dinner San Francisco
3. Lunch San Francisxo
4. Sushi San Francisco
5. Restaurant San Francisco

The top Yelp categories in London, England:

1. Cheap clothing stores London
2. Restaurants London
3. Call girls London
4. Salon names London
5. Brothels London

The top Yelp categories in Dublin, Ireland:

1. Restaurants in Dublin
2. Apple Store Dublin
3. Best Irish breakfast Dublin
4. Currency exchange Dublin
5. Birthday party venues Dublin

The top Yelp categories in Singapore:

1. Japanese buffet Singapore
2. Halal restaurant Singapore
3. Massage parlour Singapore
4. Best Korean restaurant Singapore
5. Swingers clubs Singapore

PSYCHOGRAPHIC SEGMENTATION

Psychographic segmentation divides the market into groups based on people's activities, interests, and opinions. When people connect on social media, the conversations often relate to their interests. Consider the last five tweets, Facebook posts, or status updates that you saw posted. What were they about? The top topics on both Facebook and Twitter tend to be related to news, celebrities, and sports [29]. According to Technorati, the blog-monitoring site, the most popular blogs are news-related ones, such as the Huffington Post, Mashable, and TechCrunch.

Many social media sites mine customer data to provide opportunities to segment the market by a variety of factors. Marketers who wish to communicate with customers may find that people's hobbies and interests coincide or at least correlate with their product or service. Nordstrom advertises on the Purse Blog to reach fashion shoppers. Additionally, the brand might consider other top fashion blogs, such as Fashionista, POPSUGAR, or Haute Magazine.

IS "THE SOCIAL HABIT" STRESSFUL?

The tendency to use social media several times a day is called **The Social Habit**. According to Social Media Examiner, about one-fifth of the U.S. population is part of this growing target market. These people use social media to stay connected with friends and family, for entertainment, and to learn about new products and services [30].

There is good news for heavy social media users: A Reuters study found no increased stress as a result of the social habit. People who were heavy users of social media did not have higher levels of stress than those who did not use social media. Women scored 10.8 on the Perceived Stress Scale and men scored 9.8 regardless of their social media usage. Some women even reported lower stress as a result of increased Twitter usage—perhaps due to perceived social support from the activity [31].

BEHAVIORAL SEGMENTATION

Behavioral segmentation divides up the market based on how people use or respond to a product category as shown in Exhibit 2.4. Behavioral segmentation starts with understanding patterns of product usage to group people based on factors such as the benefits they enjoy by using the product, when or how often they use the product, or whether they are regular purchasers in the category.

The retailer Macy's focuses on behavioral segmentation in its direct mail promotions to build store traffic. The company tracks its customers online and in-store using Acxiom Data Management, a firm that uses credit card data to examine purchase behavior. The company then targets

EXHIBIT 2.4

Four Behavioral Segments

Benefit: Which attributes are important to a consumer's value analysis of the product or service?

Usage: When, where, and how do customers use the product or service?

Usage rate: How often do people use and buy the product or service?

Loyalty: Are consumers loyal to a brand or prone to switching?

customers based on their most recent seven to ten purchases, the departments in which they bought something, and the specific designers. The direct mail division then creates and tests emails aimed at customers based on their past shopping behavior. In addition, Macy's segments by usage rate, dividing customers into three groups:

Consumers who have shopped in Macy's over the past year

Lapsed shoppers who have not shopped Macy's in the past year

Non-Macy's customers [32]

Segmenting on Product or Service Benefits

Social media and mobile marketing can enhance customer perceptions of benefits. Connecting with others regarding a product can add value to the offering, and some customer segments may use connectivity as a basis for determining their satisfaction. People who are very engaged with video games join communities to discuss the games and their strategies. Call of Duty has over 1 million Facebook "likes" and an engaged group of players.

Marketers can track consumer usage of a product or service and reach individuals at a moment when they are ready to buy again. For example, mobile reminders to take medications can also prompt reorder. The MedsLog mobile app will remind a person to take medication and warn when it is about to run out. MedsLog costs about $4.00, but this is exactly the type of app that a prescription drug seller might offer for free with the opportunity to reorder [33].

Usage Rate Segments

Usage rate segmentation refers to dividing the market of consumers into groups based on how much of the product or service they buy or consume. Some people buy a lot of a particular product category, while others buy very little. Segmenting the market by heavy, medium, and light users can help marketers determine how to serve special customers who spend more money than average customers. The segment of heavy users is important because of the amount they purchase and because they are likely more favorable toward the brand. Marketers may be able to turn these heavy users into brand advocates who might share content and positive reviews of brands. The website TripAdvisor runs on voluntary reviews written by travelers who book hotel rooms, fly on commercial airlines, and eat in destination restaurants. TripAdvisor does not pay people to review hotels and restaurants when they travel. Instead, the company offers badges to those who post reviews and special reviewer status. There is no tangible benefit to writing a review, only the psychic benefit of increased status on TripAdvisor.

HEAVY USERS ARE SOMETIMES TOO HEAVY

Some marketers seem to purposefully offend their heavy users. Though this sounds counterintuitive, marketers of cell phone services may actually hamper consumers because of the high cost of servicing them. A cell service provider could slow down its network data connection for some users who have unlimited data plans on their mobile devices and use a lot of bandwidth to stream movies. These consumers may object to reductions in their speed. Generally, when marketers have heavy users as customers and serve them well, these potential brand advocates deliver benefits back to the firm [34].

Locating and Rewarding Loyalty

Increasingly, mobile technology can help marketers build loyalty because a person's phone is with them at all times and the phone can store loyalty information. In the past, loyalty cards took up valuable wallet space and only a person's most used cards traveled with them. Now, a smartphone can store information on numerous brands, reducing the customer's initial commitment to participate in a loyalty program. Marketers can offer incentives to customers and track results easily with mobile technology.

Social media can also offer rewards for certain behaviors. Marketers can now target those individuals with many Twitter followers or people who have written numerous reviews to advocate for their brands. Of course, individuals who receive payment or free gifts must disclose their relationship with the firm by law.

CAN YOU BELIEVE ONLINE REVIEWS?

Have you ever written a review of a restaurant? Who is writing all these reviews anyway? Review sites attempt to judge which reviews are real and which reviews are fakes. Yelp reports that it removes about 20% of reviews from its site because the site suspects they are frauds. The company admits that it likely eliminates some real reviews, but prefers to err on the conservative side.

It may be easy to spot a fake review written by a computer program, but marketers can pay human beings to write reviews. Even so, there may be ways to ferret out a phony. A study by Cornell University using an algorithm to evaluate reviews found that fake reviews tended to be more likely when the reviews:

Were sole reviews written on a particular user's account
Came from many accounts on one computer
Differed from most other reviews of the business
Contained many gushing adjectives
Used vague terms rather than specifics [26], [27]

Scientists have also tried statistical techniques to determine which reviews are fakes.

The method examines statistical anomalies in graphed data. According to the researchers, ratings should resemble a J-shaped curve, with a high number of 1 star ratings followed by lower levels of 2, 3, and 4 star ratings and then a high number of 5 star ratings. The distribution represents the notion that people buy what they like, and since most purchases meet expectations, the majority of people are satisfied. However, only those with extremely positive or negative feelings would be motivated to write a review. Since fake reviews distort the curve, businesses with more 2, 3, and 4 star reviews may also have more fakes [28].

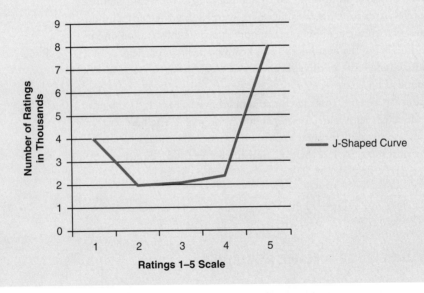

DIGITAL TARGETING WITH BIG DATA

Marketers now have access to a consumer's entire click stream multiplied across all potential prospects. The amount of data is staggering. Data analysts use statistical techniques to aggregate and organize the information to make sense of it all for marketing strategies. The data can be used to target consumers who fit certain profiles. Big data may provide the most powerful tool for marketing in the marketer's toolbox, but managing big data is a challenge.

Data analytics, the practice of mining information on consumer behavior and analyzing the data to provide insights, can help marketers determine optimal targets for a brand with incredible precision. Tracking the customer's behavior and delivering ads are actually a form of targeting because rather than divide the market into groups, the process hones in on specific targets and serves those people ads. For example, mobile payments are popular among an unexpected segment of consumers in Southeast Asia. Segmenting the consumer market by income, mobile payment companies have found that those with low incomes are using mobile phones to pay for groceries, medical bills, and tuition in Bangladesh, India, and Pakistan [35].

The vast amount of data marketers collect can be used to deliver targeted advertising to consumers who browse the Internet, read blogs and news sites, engage with friends on social media, or use apps on their mobile phones. Marketers may decide to deliver certain types of ads based on people's current or past online market behavior. Therefore, a number of digital targeting methods divide consumers based on their click streams to serve ads at the appropriate time and place when consumers may be ready, willing, and able to buy. The five methods of digital targeting are:

Behavioral

Contextual

Geographic

Day part

Affinity

Marketers use these five types of digital targeting to reach customers online through various websites, mobile sites, and social media sites. Each method pairs ads with either the content of the site or the actions the customer has taken in the past.

BEHAVIORAL TARGETING

In **behavioral targeting,** marketers determine the consumer's online actions, and when the person visits a website online or on a mobile device, an ad server delivers an advertisement that is targeted to that individual's behavior, regardless of the type of website the person is viewing. For example, Starwood Hotels identified a segment of consumers they called "globetrotters" by mining click stream data. Using this information, Starwood then targeted these consumers on websites regardless of whether the sites were travel-related. The result was a higher return on investment than if the company had sponsored a major market newspaper's travel site [36].

Behavioral targeting continues to increase in usage and complexity and is delivered from a number of potential sources such as ad servers, ad networks, publishers or through a system of real-time bidding (RTB). In RTB, ad networks sell ads on websites aimed at targets of consumers who have just completed a certain online action, such as viewed a particular product. The advertisers wish to reach these customers with targeted messages. For example, Jane might be searching for "summer sandals" on a search engine or she may be looking at pictures of sandals on Pinterest. An ad server can sell an advertisement aimed at Jane and other women looking at sandals to Zappos, which could then show her an ad for the perfect pair of shoes.

CONTEXTUAL TARGETING

Contextual targeting occurs when marketers reach consumers with ads on websites, mobile sites, or social media because the site is directly related to the product or service category. Marketers assume that if consumers are viewing a particular site, they are in the target markets for the products and services associated with it. Land Rover used Google's Display Network to attract people who were searching for a new car. The goals were to "reach consumers at all points of the purchase journey, create memorable interactions with the Land Rover brand and convert shoppers into sales." Google's Display Network can serve ads on car-related websites such as Road and Track and TopSpeed as well as in articles that discuss car buying. Land Rover ran ads that reached people on all their devices and were seen 100 million times. The car company reports that 15% of its leads are generated through online channels [37].

GEOGRAPHIC TARGETING

With geographic targeting, marketers use people's Internet Protocol (IP) addresses to pinpoint their locations and serve them ads. Serving ads in specific locations can reduce media costs for marketers who only seek consumers in a specific area. Marketers no longer have to rely on zip codes for targeting and can serve advertisements to individual consumers on their phones. Retailers are particularly interested in local advertising and location-based information to drive consumers to their stores. The McDonald's store locator app helps customers find Big Macs all over the world. These location-based strategies can be very effective. A study of mobile response found that when local information was paired with behavioral targeting, click-through rates increased from less than 1% to 8%, suggesting that the more criteria marketers use in targeting, the more successful the strategy [38].

DAY PART TARGETING

Day part targeting assumes that consumers act a certain way at a particular time of the day, and marketers can reach those consumers when they consider a purchase. In traditional media, day parts represent times during the day when an audience is tuned into a communication, such as AM drive time in radio or prime time in television. Each day part is associated with a certain level of viewership and an accompanying cost to reach those consumers. In digital segmentation, day parts are moments in the day when consumers may be receptive to marketers' messages.

Gourmet Ads is an Australia-based network that will serve ads to grocery shoppers in the United States, Canada, United Kingdom, Australia, and New Zealand. The network partners with a set of websites that grocery consumers read as part of their decision-making process. The network includes publishers of food, cooking, and recipe sites. Through the network, advertisers can choose specific times during each day of the week to run advertisements on the network. Aside from day part targeting, Gourmet Ads also serves ads to behavioral, contextual, and geographic targets for brands such as Campbell's and Nestlé.

AFFINITY TARGETING

Marketers use **affinity targeting** when they want to reach fans of particular television shows, movies, celebrities, or sports teams. Sometimes, fans who have strong emotional connections to a phenomenon purchase products or services

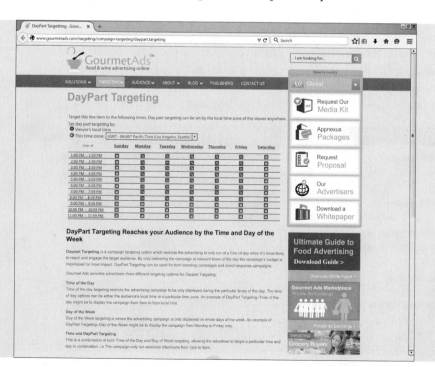

Gourmet Ads offers day part targeting to their advertisers.

GourmetAds, www.gourmetads.com

associated with their fandom. Marketers may wish to take advantage of that heightened emotion to sell a product.

The MTV show *Ridiculousness* wanted to reach a potential audience for the show. After using Google Key Words, the show's marketers noted that key targets were not noticing ads served to them. To enhance its strategy, the show chose affinity-inspired keywords that honed in on other shows the desired audience watched. Originally, *Ridiculousness* chose words such as the names of the host, guest, reality TV shows, and other MTV shows. When using affinity targeting, *Ridiculousness* added other shows and new search terms: *The Tonight Show Starring Jimmy Fallon,* Asher Roth, Shaun White, *30 for 30,* Mike Tyson, and ESPN. The strategy increased the click-through rate from .06% to .11% and reduced the cost of running the campaign [39].

Another type of affinity targeting assumes that individuals who visit the same user-generated social media content have a relationship and may buy similar types of products and services. Researchers determined that connected individuals have closer brand proximities and are better potential targets for a product than those who are not connected. In addition, when individuals are seeded with ads, members in the network are more likely to take action for product categories such as hotels and cell phones [40].

consider this . . .

CUSTOMER PROFILE DATA MINING ON TWITTER

Companies can harness the data in Twitter to learn more about target markets and their attitudes and behavior. Demographics Pro mines Twitter to determine the likely characteristics of individuals who may be targets for a brand.

Specifically, Demographics Pro matches likely characteristics of the population based on Twitter data and amplifies the results to provide a target profile of a brand's customers. For example, consider @lonelyplanet's profile shown here [41].

FOLLOWERS OF @LONELYPLANET	
Gender	58.2% Female
Average age Average income	28.1 $36.6k/year
Twitter activity	Tweet 1.7 times per week Number of followers: 78
Location	International: 7.8% London 3.8% New York 2.7% Jakarta 2.7% Seoul

FOLLOWERS OF @LONELYPLANET	
Occupations	11.9% Sales/marketing 10.2% Students 8.7% Senior managers 8.4% Journalists
Brands	43% Starbucks 25% McDonald's 21.3% Ikea 16.6% Whole Foods 8.3% Patagonia
Following	87.8% Lonely Planet 31.0% Barack Obama 25.1% *New York Times* 21.3 CNN News

SOCIAL POSITIONING

Positioning refers to a marketer's attempt to create an image for a brand in the minds of consumers relative to the competition. To position a brand, the marketer must first determine the types of associations that they would like or expect consumers to consider when people are presented with the brand and research competitive strategies to determine how consumers perceive the competition. For example, think about some of the social media sites you use. Which ones do you perceive as cool? Is Snapchat cooler than Facebook? That may be due to its positioning as the hip entrant in social media. Is there a site that is cooler than Snapchat? There probably is one because the definition of "cool" changes constantly. The diagram in Exhibit 2.5 is a perceptual map, which shows how a person or group of people may perceive brands on two sets of factors. In this case, the map shows perceptions of coolness (cool vs. boring) and purpose use (business vs. leisure) for a few social media sites.

How can a brand influence consumers' perceptions of it? Typically, marketers use messages in various forms of media to describe the brand and what it stands for. Brands can use social media to focus the brand conversation, provide relevant images, show the meaning of the brand, and hope that consumers build on it and share the message. One method for engaging consumers in social media is to ask them to develop their own brand content. Marketers sometimes run contests to encourage people to participate in message creation. The type of content that people create is called *user-generated content* and is often associated with a contest,

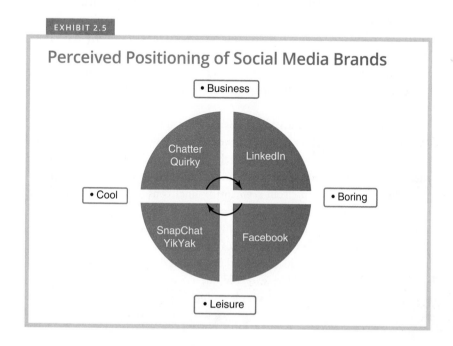

EXHIBIT 2.5

Perceived Positioning of Social Media Brands

as we learned in the previous chapter's case study on Herschel Supply, which asked people to post photos representing the #WellTravelled theme.

PULLING IT ALL TOGETHER

The key to developing an appropriate social media strategy is to know the social networks your consumers use most and find ways to engage them within that space. The difficult part of this process is that consumer tastes and usage patterns in social media change regularly. Consider the evolution within social media. One early social media site was Friendster, which began in 2002 and was adopted by 3 million users by 2004 [42]. Though it was at one time the top social media site, it was overtaken by Myspace in 2004. The rest of the story is well known as now Facebook dominates the social media scene. Facebook's dominance may not last as many new social media entrants are operating to attract niche markets of individuals who want a more specialized experience. For instance, Tinder competes with the big dating sites by offering a different experience in selecting people to meet. Of course, users should be careful. At the South by Southwest music and tech event in Austin, Texas, guys on Tinder encountered a beautiful girl named Ava who asked interesting questions of them, such as "What makes you human?" and "Have you ever been in love?" It turned out that Ava was Alicia Vikander, a Swedish actress starring in *Ex Machina,* a film that was premiering in Austin at that time [43].

Marketers need data to segment markets. In the B2C arena, *Simmons OneView* provides information on many consumer demographic, psychographic, media usage, and behavioral variables cross-referenced against product and service category data. A variety of online services provide customer data by mining search, social media, and mobile usage. With the data, the markets can lay out customer segments and then target appropriate groups for marketing strategies that reach specific goals.

It helps to begin with the goals the marketer would like to achieve so that the segmentation drives an appropriate business response with the right people. For example, if a marketer wants to build relationships with influencers, he or she might segment the blogosphere to determine which bloggers to target. Segmenting influencers is different from segmenting final consumers for a product or brand. B2B marketers will also use a different set of criteria for determining appropriate segments to identify targets using industry-related data.

Once marketers have established clear goals, the next step is to consider all possible segmentations by which the market could be divided. At this point in the process, segmentation should be "target-blind," meaning that when the segmentation process is under way, the people doing the segmentation refrain from considering the possible target markets. Often, when marketers attempt to segment markets, they really just jump ahead and go right to the targeting. The disadvantage of targeting without first carefully segmenting is that the marketer might miss potentially lucrative segments of the market or fail to consider secondary or tertiary markets for strategies. For example, who is the target for Coca Cola's classic drink? You might assume that kids and teens drink lots of cola; therefore, they are the target. And, you would be correct because younger people do drink more sugary sodas than older adults, who tend to choose diet drinks. The problem is that by jumping to the target of kids and teens, you would neglect a very important target market, the people who actually often buy the soda in the grocery store or give children money to purchase drinks. Those people are moms, who are the key decision-makers/gatekeepers in the cola market and who may respond differently to marketing strategies than children.

Another problem with jumping in and choosing targets before segmenting is that marketers tend to choose the same targets that may not drive consumer actions. A very popular target is women 18–49. While it is true that this group tends to do most of the household purchasing, there are many categories for which age and gender do not drive purchase. For example, many B2B decisions have nothing to do with a person's age or gender, but there are also consumer products that would benefit from a more nuanced segmentation. Consider bottled water, a product category with $13 billion in revenues within the United States [44]. What drives a customer to purchase bottled water? Perhaps they are thirsty at a particular point and need a drink, or they don't believe the water from their tap is pure. Neither one of these reasons has anything much to do with age or gender, though there may be some correlation. Instead, Poland Spring targets a psychographic group of runners with "Runner's Resource," a guide on its Facebook page providing training tips.

Once the marketer identifies a strong list of segments, he or she should determine a set of actions that would clearly pinpoint individuals who are in the target market. Some actions that consumers may undertake as a result of their segments are:

- Conduct a Google search for information on a brand.
- Consider appropriate retail locations for collecting brand information.
- Search in a store for brand information.
- Read reviews of brands on social media sites.
- Visit the websites of competing brands for information.
- Determine the important attributes for a brand decision.
- Compare several competing brands on attributes.
- Select a preferred set of brands to consider further.

- Focus on one brand to purchase.
- Set expectations for the performance of a brand.
- Evaluate the quality of a brand's performance based on expectations.
- Make a brand purchase.

For each of the actions that a consumer may take regarding a brand, the marketer must identify the key relevant segments of the market that can be identified.

For example, let's take the first consumer action: "Conducts a Google search for information on a brand." The marketer should then consider the relevant segmentation variables that will affect the desired outcome for the brand. In the case of a Google search, the search terms will be important and certain segmentation variables will come into play. For example, Exhibit 2.6 identifies keywords that a consumer might input in a search related to flat screen televisions. Some of the words have clear commercial intent, while others do not. This behavioral segmentation yields different groups based on their intent toward a brand.

The keywords that show an individual has commercial intent can be used to target customers who search these terms. Again, the search behavior is a much better predictor of the likelihood of purchase than a person's gender or age.

Once marketers determine the goal to reach and segments within the market, the targets to choose become clear because the customers show themselves as ready, willing, and able to purchase. The marketer can then develop the marketing strategy to reach those targets. The strategy is planned specifically for a target so that the prospects respond in the desired manner.

EXHIBIT 2.6

Keywords in Three Behavioral Segments

COMMERCIAL INTENT	NON-COMMERCIAL INTENT	AMBIGUOUS INTENT
Buy a flat screen television	How flat screen TVs work	Televisions
Samsung flat screen demo	Watch HBO on flat screen	LCD vs. plasma
Best Buy television brands	Cleaning flat screen	*Consumer Reports* TV ratings

SUMMARY AND REVIEW

CHAPTER SUMMARY

Segmenting markets is an important component of any digital strategy, so marketers can identify the right consumers to reach with their marketing efforts. As people influence one another through social networks, marketers can take advantage of these connections by encouraging sharing and engaging with customers. Brands should also determine consumer perceptions and those of competitors to properly position in the marketplace. Chapter Two makes clear that before reaching out to consumers with social media or mobile strategies, the marketer must first identify them.

KEY TERMS

affinity targeting
behavioral segmentation
behavioral targeting
business-to-business
    market (B2B)
business-to-consumer
    market (B2C)

contextual targeting
data analytics
day part targeting
demographic
    segmentation
endorsers
experts

geographic
    segmentation
geographic targeting
influencers
microblogging
millennials
opinion leaders

positioning
psychographic
    segmentation
Q scores
segmentation
The Social Habit
usage rate segmentation

SUMMARY REVIEW QUESTIONS

1. How does segmentation for B2C brands differ from that for B2B brands?
2. What is the problem with targeting before segmenting the market?
3. Describe behavioral segmentation and give an example.
4. What is the difference between behavioral and contextual digital targeting?
5. Give an example of a search term with commercial intent.
6. Describe heavy social media and mobile users.

APPLICATION QUESTIONS

1. Go to followerwonk.com and click on the tab that reads "Analyze Followers." Choose a Twitter handle and write a one-paragraph report on the people who follow that handle.
2. Use Google to explain the term "open API." Which platforms have open APIs?
3. Go to www.Alexa.com and browse the top websites. Choose one and scroll down to the bottom of the page. Indicate the countries that most use the site and the basic demographic profile of the users of the site.
4. Go to www.census .gov. Search for and locate the most recent e-commerce report. How much wholesale and retail business occurs via e-commerce according to the report?
5. Consider the mobile application Snapchat. What segmentation factors are important for this brand?
6. Let's say you are a marketer for a new brand of toothpaste and you want to segment by age. What are all the possible age segments? Be sure that each category is mutually exclusive (no overlaps) and the total list is exhaustive (contains all possible segments).

case study Spotify and the Digital Music Consumer

Spotify, the music streaming service, was first introduced in Finland, France, Norway, Sweden, Spain, and the United Kingdom in 2008. Soon thereafter, the company had expanded to offer music services in over fifty countries globally. Spotify wanted users to consider the service as a personal music collection or library with access to music anytime. The social media strategy was to encourage people to share music with friends, posting on Facebook, with whom Spotify had an integrated platform, and other social networks. By 2015 Spotify had over 60 million active users, 25% paying for premium services [45]. Music lovers were adopting music streaming services and moving away from music downloading.

THE MUSIC INDUSTRY

The music industry had undergone significant changes with new music delivery options for increasingly digital and mobile customers. The recording industry represented over 15 billion in global sales [46], with 39% of revenue generated by digital channels. However, by 2014 digital track sales began to weaken, falling 5.7% [47]. Exhibit 2.8 shows share of the music business by country and Exhibit 2.9 provides sales by music genre in North America.

Social media and mobile technology penetration contributed to the global surge in demand for music. Consumers adopted new digital platforms for listening and the digital music industry expanded worldwide from 23 countries in 2012 to 119 countries by 2014, mostly due to market penetration by iTunes. Though iTunes remained the global giant, its standard pricing strategy for single-track digital downloads left it vulnerable to competitors who offered unlimited music on a monthly basis, an attractive alternative for heavy music consumers.

DIGITAL MUSIC SUBSCRIPTION SERVICES

Subscriptions revenues represented 29% of total digital revenues and were expected to rise to over 50% by 2020 [48]. Penetration was higher in countries that had early exposure to the streaming services, such as in Sweden, where subscriptions represented 85% of digital revenues.

DIGITAL MUSIC COMPETITORS

The digital music streaming business was competitive, with many entrants vying for the same group of music customers who would be willing to pay for services. Due to low barriers to entry, most services including Spotify, Rhapsody, and Rdio operated in multiple countries. Spotify was seeing new competitors in key markets. Specifically, in the U.S. market, a number of streaming services already operated, including Rhapsody, Pandora, and Google Play. Apple bought Beats music and launched its new and upgraded service in 2015.

THE MUSIC TARGET MARKET

Globally, teens were the traditional music target market, listening to more music than other age groups [49]. Though the industry was concerned that teens pirated more music than other demographic groups, teens still represented the demographic most engaged with and interested in music. Additionally, teens were technologically capable of downloading or streaming music.

The global teen market represented over $100 billion in purchasing power. With significant discretionary incomes and few household responsibilities, middle- and upper-income young adults spent most of their money on cosmetics, hygiene, fast food, and music. Marketers found that teenagers did not respond to hard-sell approaches and preferred more subtle marketing efforts. As long-time consumers of advertising, teens were wary when messages were aimed at them and reacted positively when brands met their needs. Teens valued "cool," but did not want to be told what was cool by marketers or other adults. Advertising still represented "the establishment" to teens who tended toward "anti-establishment" [50].

While the populations in much of the West were aging, the youth market represented larger percentages of the population in developing countries (see Exhibit 2.7). By 2015 these children would become teenagers and a prime target for digital music as incomes grew in the developing world.

With the advent of the Internet, teens in the developed world became multitaskers connected to multiple devices and deeply involved with social networks. They expected and often found free music and videos on demand [51] through YouTube and other content sites. Streaming music was often free from services such as Pandora, but one important feature for teens was the ability to listen without an Internet connection, any place and any time.

EXHIBIT 2.7

Youth by Country

COUNTRY	PERCENTAGE AGED 14 OR YOUNGER IN 2002
China	23%
Argentina	28%
Brazil	29%
India	34%
Iran	31%
Malaysia	33%
Philippines	38%

World Bank, 2002, Population, ages 0–14 (% of total) Population between the ages 0 to 14 as a percentage of the total population. Population is based on the de facto definition of population.
http://data.worldbank.org/indicator/SP.POP.0014.TO.ZS?page=2

TARGET MARKET BEHAVIOR

Young adults across cultures were transitioning from childhood to adulthood and sought ways to develop identities of their own. Teens continued to struggle with the decisions of rebellion versus conformity, idealism versus pragmatism, and narcissism versus intimacy [52]. Attachment theory also provided some insights into teen consumption behavior. Teens with weak attachments to parents in childhood were more susceptible to influence from others, believed that peers had more purchase knowledge than they did, and spent more money when with peers than teens with strong parental attachments [53]. Teen shopping had also been characterized as hedonic versus utilitarian, suggesting that decision-making among some teens was based more on practical considerations than for others who valued social connections and entertainment when shopping [54].

In the United States, teens born between the late 1970s and early 1990s were sometimes referred to as Generation Y or **millennials.** This group was characterized as media savvy, with high expectations of choice and strongly image-conscious [55]. Teens continued to distinguish themselves by adopting behaviors in opposition to those of prior generations. Generation X had eschewed materialism by choosing grunge. To distinguish themselves from Generation X, millennials used consumption as a means of identifying themselves and adopted a "cult of celebrity" [55].

Teens around the world had access to global media and images of teen culture had traveled cross-culturally and outside of geographic boundaries to then be localized within each country [55]. Music was viewed as a central component of teen culture and an important expression of cool. Through music, teens exhibited identities, enhanced their moods, and maintained status within a group. Boys were particularly tied to music, using the language of music in conversation and to judge their compatibility with others. Girls were more likely to rely on fashion for expression of group conformity [56].

Teens living in step- or single-parent families were more likely to use music to escape. Young adults raised in nuclear families depended less on music as a coping mechanism and listened to wider varieties of genres. These more confident teens were clear about their preferences, were judgmental about music, more willing to

publicly share music, but less accepting of others' tastes. Teens also viewed music as a way to bond with family members [56].

Tweens were a group of young teens aged 9–12 years who controlled $1.5 billion in buying power. The group of youths was believed to be very brand-conscious in categories such as beauty, clothing, electronics, music, and entertainment and was strongly influenced by peers and through social media [57]. Tweens expected to be entertained, and were more likely than adults to click on ads that interested them [57]. Some of the research suggested that tweens in individualistic countries were more similar to each other than those in collectivist countries in their use of media, but this may have been dependent on access to media properties [57]. Celebrities were popular with teens around the world, but those celebrities differed by country.

One study of teens in France and Turkey segmented them into four groups based on apparel consumption patterns: fashion brand–conscious, indifferent consumers, recreation seekers, and quality seekers [58]. Another study of Indian teens divided them into these groups [59]:

1. **Get going adopters (27%):** Fashion-conscious; variety-seeking; interested and easily excited to try new products; with strong values and religious beliefs; politically aware; and sports-loving.
2. **Disinterested introverts (9%):** Not aware of fashion, sports, or political trends; few values; lacking confidence; and uninterested in activities.
3. **Confused followers (38%):** Having many interests, although not sports- or fashion-related; health-conscious; and somewhat value-oriented.

4. **Independent life lovers (26%):** Seeking variety and challenges; open to new things and sharing; encouraging of others; self-confident; sports lovers; religious; very price-conscious. Often leaders in the fashion industry.

Countries also differed in their cultural dimensions. Individuals in developing countries (BRICS and Mexico) were less individualistic than people in developed or industrial countries (the United States, Canada, Europe, and Oceania) [60]. Teens to some extent adopted their own culture's norms and attitudes as they struggled with identity issues. Exhibits 2.8–2.10 show data on the global music industry, digital sales in the US and population and GDP by country.

THE PROBLEM OF DIGITAL MUSIC PIRACY

Piracy remained a problem for the music industry, though a few countries introduced piracy

EXHIBIT 2.8

Share of Global Music and Value of Purchases per Person by Country

	SHARE OF GLOBAL MUSIC BUSINESS (U.S. $ MILLIONS)	VALUE OF PURCHASES PER PERSON (U.S. $ MILLIONS)
Japan	$25.4	$32.3
United States	22.5	11.7
Germany	10.6	20.8
United Kingdom	8.6	22.3
France	6.2	15.4
Australia	2.5	19.0
Canada	2.1	10.2
Italy	1.7	4.7
Netherlands	1.7	16.1
Brazil	1.6	1.3
Other	17.1	

(Recording Industry Association of Japan, 2012)

EXHIBIT 2.9

Digital Album Sales North America

DIGITAL ALBUM SALES BY GENRE	SALES IN MILLIONS (NORTH AMERICA)
Rock	43.1
Alternative	26.7
R&B	16.3
Rap	10.7
Metal	11.2
Country	11.2
Soundtrack	6
Electronic	4.9
Christian/gospel	5.3
Classical	2.6

The Nielsen Company & Billboard's 2012 Music Industry Report, http://www.businesswire.com/news/home/20130104005149/en/Nielsen-Company-Billboard%E2%80%99s-2012-Music-Industry-Report

EXHIBIT 2.10

Population by Country, GDP, and Median Age

RANK	COUNTRY OR AREA	POPULATION	GDP	MEDIAN AGE
1	China	1,330,141,295	$7.298 trillion	34.5
2	India	1,173,108,018	1.848 trillion	25.1
3	United States	310,232,863	15.09 trillion	36.9
4	Indonesia	242,968,342	847 billion	27.8
5	Brazil	201,103,330	2.477 trillion	29.1
6	Pakistan	184,404,791	211.1 billion	21.7
7	Bangladesh	156,118,464	110.6 billion	24.2
8	Nigeria	152,217,341	235.9 billion	18.5
9	Russia	139,390,205	1.86 trillion	37.9
10	Japan	126,804,433	5.87 trillion	44.7
11	Mexico	112,468,855	1.16 trillion	26.6
12	Philippines	99,900,177	224.7 billion	22.2
13	Vietnam	89,571,130	1.24 billion	28.2
14	Ethiopia	88,013,491	31.71 billion	18.7
15	Germany	81,644,454	3.57 trillion	44.3
16	Egypt	80,471,869	229.5 billion	24.4
17	Turkey	77,804,122	773.1 billion	28.3
18	Iran	76,923,300	331.0 billion	27.1
19	Congo (Kinshasa)	69,851,289	14.75b billion	19.6
20	Thailand	66,336,258	345.65 billion	34.2

U.S. Census (2010), *http://data.worldbank.org/country (2011)*
http://esa.un.org/unpd/wpp/Sorting-Tables/tab-sorting_ageing.htm

laws, including France (the HADOPI Law), South Korea, and New Zealand. The regulations educated and warned downloaders, encouraging them to move to legitimate sources. India, Malaysia, Belgium, Denmark, Italy, Spain, Austria, and Finland attacked piracy by blocking certain sites on the Internet [61].

CONCLUSION

Spotify became a global player in the highly competitive digital music streaming business, and by 2015 digital music revenues had overtaken the sales of physical formats [62]. New entrants threatened Spotify's position in the global music industry. For example, a group of musicians including Jay Z and Beyonce purchased the Tidal music streaming service and offered exclusive content. But, the real problem was Apple's streaming service that would provide monthly subscriptions for $7.99 and had over 800 million iTunes users as potential customers [63].

QUESTIONS FOR DISCUSSION

1. Does the global teen market represent a single unified group? What elements are similar and which are different?

2. Segment the teen market for music using demographic, geographic, psychographic, and behavioral criteria. Determine each and every possible segment within those categories. For instance, a marketer might segment demographically by age and the segments would be as follows: under 18, 18–34, 35–54, 55+. Note that each segment should be mutually exclusive and exhaustive.

3. Consider one of the advertisers on Spotify (Reebok, Coca-Cola, AT&T, Intel, or McDonald's). Explain the brand's use of behavioral targeting on Spotify. Are there other types of online advertising that these brands could consider using on Spotify?

4. Spotify was in over 50 countries. Should the brand continue to expand globally? Which countries should Spotify consider for new market entry and why? Use Exhibit 2.10 to help answer this question.

5. Are there additional questions you would like to have answered in any decision to enter a particular market? If so, what are those questions?

6. What are some strategies Spotify should consider given the threat of competition in 2015?

7. Choose one country that you think would be a good choice for Spotify's international expansion. Do some outside research and examine the demographic, cultural, political-legal, and technological information for that country to determine the likelihood of a successful market entry for Spotify in the country you chose.

REFERENCES

[1] L. Flora, "China's Middle-Class Luxury Consumers Loved Buying Abroad and Burberry in 2013," Jing Daily: The Business of Luxury and Culture in China, 6 January 2014.

[2] J. Lin-Liu, "China's Smaller Cities Thirst for the Luxe Life," *The New York Times,* 20 November 2013.

[3] J. Clode, "Burberry Builds Success with China's Luxury Consumers," Advertising Age Global, 10 May 2012.

[4] H. Greimel, "Ford Plans Launch of Luxury Lincoln Brand in China in 2014," Advertising Age Global, 28 August 2012.

[5] R. Martin, "Ford Makes Play for Chinese Drivers with In-Car Weibo App," 9 January 2013, http://www.techinasia.com/ford-sina-weibo-support/.

[6] N. Shirouzu, "ford Comes from Behind in China to Stun Japanese Rivals," Reuters, 2013.

[7] Y. Atsmon and M. Magni, "Meet the Chinese Consumer of 2020," McKinsey & Company, March 2012.

[8] L. Flora, "China's Middle Class Luxury Consumers Loved Buying Abroad and Burberry in 2013," Jing Daily, 6 January 2014.

[9] eConsultancy, "B2B Social: Five Case Studies from Brands Achieving Great Results," 2013.

[10] David Ogilvy Awards Advertising Research Foundation, "Unleasing the Joy of Redi-wip and Fruit," 2014.

[11] J. Edwards, "Meet the Thirty Biggest Advertisers on Facebook," Business Insider, 24 September 2012.

[12] T. Nudd, "Kevin Bacon Does Ads for Eggs, Because What Goes Better with Eggs Than Bacon?," *AdWeek,* 12 March 2015.

[13] R. Morin, "Five Types of Socia Media Influencers," Social Media Today, 18 February 2012.

[14] C. Moss and M. Kosoff, "Twenty–Eight Times Brands and Celebrities Completely Failed on Twitter," Business Insider, 9 January 2015.

[15] K. Piombino, "Honda's Shoestring Pinterest Campaign Attracts Millions," PR Daily, 21 February 2013.

[16] S. Mehta, "Most Admired Celebrity Endorsements," *Fortune,* 28 February 2014.

[17] United States Census, "Facts for Features: The 2013 Holiday Season," 2 December 2013, http://www.census.gov/newsroom/releases/archives/facts_for_features_special_editions/cb13-ff28.html.

[18] C. Taylor, "Women Win Facebook, Twitter, Zynga; Men Get Linkedin, Reddit," Mashable, 4 July 2012.

[19] Pew Research Center, "Tracking Study," Internet & American Life Project, Winter 2012.

[20] A. Hoffman, "The Social Media Gender Gap," *Business Week,* 2008.

[21] Smith, Aaron, "Chapter One a Portrait of Smartphone Ownership, Pew Research Center, April 1, 2015. http://www.pewinternet.org/2015/04/01/chapter-one-a-portrait-of-smartphone-ownership/

[22] J. Poushter, "Smartphone Ownership and Internet Usage Continues to Climb in Emerging Economies," Pew Research Center, February 22nd, 2016, http://www.pewglobal.org/2016/02/22/smartphone-ownership-and-internet-usage-continues-to-climb-in-emerging-economies/.

[23] Google and Nielsen, "Mobile Search Moments: Understanding How Mobile Drives Conversions," 2013.

[24] Alexa, 1 April 2013, http://www.alexa.com.

[25] Yelp, 31 March 2013, https://www.yelp.com.

[26] M. Learmonth, "As Fake Reviews Rise, Yelp, Others Crack Down on Fraudsters," *Advertising Age*, 30 October 2012.

[27] New York Times Blog, "Yelp Fights Fake Reviews with Shaming," *The New York Times,* 18 October 2012.

[28] N. Savage, "Statistics Unmask Phony Online Reviews," *MIT Technology Review*, 18 June 2012.

[29] CBS DFW, "Trending 2014 Topics on Facebook," CBS News, 9 December 2015.

[30] P. Redsicker, "9 Consumer Social Media Trends That Could Impact Marketers," Social Media Examiner, 6 February 2013.

[31] Reuters, "No Increased Stress from Heavier Social Media Use: Survey," 15 January 2015.

[32] Pace University IDM Lab, Retail Merchandising and Interactive Marketing, New York, 2013.

[33] B. Tedeschi, "Personal Tech," *The New York TImes,* 30 September 2010.

[34] N. Bolton, "Stuck with a Carrier for the Long Haul," *The New York Times,* 18 March 2013.

[35] R. Shaffer, "Mobile Payments Gain Traction Among India's Poor," *The New York Times*, 4 December 2013.

[36] K. Newcombe, "Study Shows Behavioral Targeting's Strengths, Weaknesses," ClickZ, 5 April 2005.

[37] Google, "Cross-Channel Marketing Drives Land Rover's Digital Sales," Think with Google, September 2014.

[38] C. Tode, "More Precise Mobile Location Targeting Use by Advertisers Is Skyrocketing: Report," Mobile Marketer, 11 March 2013.

[39] Affinity Answers, "Ridiculousness Effective Contextual Buys on Google," 2013.

[40] F. Provost, B. Delassandro, R. Hook, X. Zhang, and A. Murray, "Audience Selection for Online Brand Advertising: Privacy-Friendly Social Network Targeting," ACM NYU Stern School of Business, 2009.

[41] Demographics Pro, "Lonely Planet Profile," 2014.

[42] B. Schiffman, "In Praise of Friendster," *Wired*, 27 October 2008.

[43] T. Nudd, "Tinder Users at SXSW Are Falling for This Woman, but She's Not What She Appears," AdWeek, 15 March 2015.

[44] I. B. W. Association, "Bottled Water Sales and Consumption Projected to Increase in 2014, Expected to Be the Number One Packaged Drink by 2016," 4 December 2014. Press release.

[45] Spotify, What Is Spotify?," 27 May 2015, http://press.spotify.com/us/information.

[46] ifpi, 22 May 2014, http://www.ifpi.org/global statistics.php.

[47] E. Christman, "Billboard," 3 January 2014, www.billboard.com/biz/articles/news.digital-and-mobile/5855162.digital-music-sales.

[48] Generator Research, "Digital Music Subscription Services 2015," 2015.

[49] G. Peoples, "Business Matters: iTunes Global Revenue Was $6 Billion in 2011," Billboard.biz, 25 January 2012.

[50] S. Goodson, "Marketing to Youth Globally—It's Child's Play," *Forbes*, 1 July 2011.

[51] A. Goodstein, "What Would Madison Avenue Do? Marketing to Teens," *School Library Journal*, 1 May 2008.

[52] J. B. Kim, "For Savvy Teens: Real Life, Real Solutions," Advertising Age, 23 August 1993.

[53] Y. Huang, L. Wang, and J. Shi, "How Attachment Affects the Strength of Peer Influence on Adolescent Consumer Behavior," *Psychology & Marketing*, vol. 29, no. 8, pp. 558–567, August 2012.

[54] P. R. Cardoso and S. C. Pinto, "Hedonic and Utilitarian Shopping Motivations Among Young Portuguese Consumers," *International Journal of Retail and Distribution Management*, vol. 38, no. 7, pp. 538–558, 2009.

[55] S. Ferguson, "A Global Culture of Cool? Generation Y and Their Perceptions of Coolness," *Young Consumers*, vol. 12, no. 3, pp. 265–275, 2011.

[56] P. Nuttall, "Thank You for the Music? The Role and Significance of Music for Adolescents," *Young Consumers*, vol. 9, no. 2, pp. 104–111, 2008.

[57] D. Prince and N. Martin, "The Tween Consumer Marketing Model Significant Variables and Recommended Research Hypotheses," *Academy of Marketing Studies Journal*, vol. 16, no. 2, pp. 31–45, July 2012.

[58] A. Ulun, N. Tezcan, and A. Vignolles, "Segmenting Young Adults through Their Consumption Styles: A Cross-Cultural Study," *Young Consumers*, vol. 12, no. 4, pp. 348–360, 2011.

[59] R. Narang, "Psychographic Segmentation of Youth in the Evolving Indian Retail Market," *International Review of Retain, Distribution and Consumer Research*, vol. 20, no. 5, pp. 535–544, 2010.

[60] C. Jobs and D. M. Gilfoil, "Less Is More for Online Marcom in Emerging Markets: Linking Hofstede's Cultural and Higher Relative Preferences for Microblogging in Developing Nations," *Academy of Marketing Studies Journal*, vol. 16, no. 2, pp. 79–96, 2012.

[61] F. Moore, "Digital Music Report 2012," International Federation of the Phonographic Industry, 2012.

[62] J. Vincent, "Digital Music Revenues Overtake CD Sales First Time Globally," The Verge, 15 April 2015.

[63] D. Ethrington and J. Constine, "Apple's Streaming Music Service Will Debut in June," TechCrunch, 5 March 2015.

© Shutterstock/Crystal Home

CHAPTER THREE

DISCOVERING INSIGHTS

To discover insights, a marketer must plan a research strategy. Marketers should be aware of the environment in which they operate, the industry composition, competitors and their strategies, consumer tastes, preferences and attitudes, and effective and ineffective executions. Consumers who use social media and mobile devices generate reams of information that marketers can use to develop and track strategies. This chapter emphasizes the secondary sources of information applicable to social media and mobile marketing strategies and some methods for conducting primary research in digital.

LEARNING OBJECTIVES

After reading this chapter, you will be able to:

- DETERMINE INSIGHTS FROM INFORMATION OBTAINED THROUGH RESEARCH.

- CONDUCT A SITUATION ANALYSIS FOR A BRAND.

- LISTEN TO SOCIAL MEDIA TO EVALUATE SENTIMENT, MONITOR COMPETITORS, AND TRACK TRENDS.

- IDENTIFY AND EVALUATE BLOGGERS FOR POTENTIAL COMMUNICATIONS EXECUTIONS.

- REVIEW SITE ANALYTICS TO IMPROVE STRATEGIES.

- EXECUTE MOBILE RESEARCH STRATEGIES.

Dell Computer has had a lot of ups and downs with social media. Back in 2005, a customer named Jeff Jarvis posted an article titled "Dell Sucks" on his blog BuzzMachine after repeated frustrations over his broken computer and a lack of response from Dell (see the image, below, for the original blog post). It took about a year for Dell to figure out that social media could enhance the customer experience. In 2006 the company started Direct2Dell, a blog that was intended to deliver company news, but instead was forced to handle irate customers whose batteries had overheated [1]. These days, Dell is deep into social media. Dell's social media listening command center is a dedicated computer room that features customer conversations in real time and a team of representatives to respond.

Dell also runs IdeaStorm to solicit customer suggestions for the company. In its first five years, the site received 15,000 suggestions and made over 500 company changes based on that information [2]. Jeff Jarvis was an active member of the site and in 2010 criticized Dell for just listening and not participating in the Dell community. As a result, the company added Storm Sessions, with representatives scheduling time in a chat room to discuss particular issues with the community. Members could earn points toward Dell Rock Star status, the cream of the crop of Dell influencers [2] who earn recognition; invites to special conferences and merchandise [3]. Jarvis still blogs at BuzzMachine and still complains about poor service from tech companies.

Jeff Jarvis's famous blog post.

BuzzMachine,
http://buzzmachine.com/

Dell's social media strategy has become a standard for other companies. The brand generates over 25,000 worldwide conversations each day. Employees are trained on social media practices as well as listening platforms to pass insights throughout the organization [4]. A visit to Dell's social media page allows users to interact with a variety of social media platforms beyond the usual suspects. People can connect through Facebook, YouTube, LinkedIn, and Twitter, but Dell also provides icons for connecting through Slideshare, Storify, Xing, Renren, Sina Weibo and posts links to over fifty country-specific Facebook pages.

RESEARCH FOR STRATEGY DEVELOPMENT

You may have taken a course in market research because it is an important component of a marketing strategy and a key requirement of social media and mobile marketing campaigns. Research helps marketers reduce their risk in decision-making, but also plan their communications to efficiently reach audiences.

Marketers should develop a clear research plan before attempting to collect data. The purpose of the plan is to focus the research effort and eliminate unnecessary data collection. The market research process outlined in Exhibit 3.1 begins with a set of research goals that clarifies the direction of the research and identifies problems the brand wants to fix. Next, marketers typically form specific questions that guide the data collection. It may sound strange, but marketers collect secondary data first because these data are readily available and easy to collect. The term **secondary data** refers to information that exists already which was probably gathered for another purpose, but could be useful for the problem at hand. For example, the U.S. Census is a treasure trove of information about the U.S. population, and marketers use these data to help segment and target markets. Other types of secondary data are company or industry reports, information from associations, published studies, or other materials you can find in the library. If secondary sources are not sufficient to answer the research questions, marketers may turn to primary data to fill in the blanks. **Primary data** involve conducting studies that help answer the remaining questions. Some typical tools of primary data collection include focus groups, interviews, surveys, experiments, or even observing people or phenomena.

In the next part of the market research process, marketers design the research by determining which targets to study, take a sample or percentage of the target market to examine, and use one of the research tools to gather information. After marketers collect the data, they analyze the response and make conclusions based on the information.

In planning for social media and mobile research, marketers must understand purchase behavior, social media activities, mobile device penetration and usage.

EXHIBIT 3.1

The Market Research Process

Define the problem and objectives.

Develop the research questions.

Determine the research design.

Identify secondary sources.

Plan primary research.

Sample and collect data.

Analyze data.

Report results, conclusions, and recommendations.

Marketers can find some of this information in secondary sources, but may need to conduct primary research to examine product-, service-, or business-specific consumer behavior. This chapter provides many examples of secondary sources of information that can inform a social media or mobile marketing strategy as well as some techniques for mobile primary research.

One company that used the market research process to develop a social media strategy was Unilever. Unilever's Axe brand saw sales flatten after showing strong year-after-year growth since its introduction. Axe's brand managers knew that a sales decline was likely the symptom of a broader problem that required further investigation. In response to the decline, Axe might have formulated the following research questions:

1. Are there areas where sales have declined versus those that have grown?
2. Have sales declined for all Axe products, or only certain products or lines?
3. What competitive moves affected sales? Is the market saturated?
4. What are the attitudes of the target market toward the product?
5. How do consumers purchase and use Axe?

Axe examined secondary sources of information and found that the brand had conducted a prior study on the Axe Detailer, a handheld scrubber, which would be useful. The study indicated that once people had the Detailer, they stopped buying bar soap, the major competitor. Through some further primary research, Axe determined that men did not believe that Axe had strong cleaning power. The conclusions from the research showed that:

Sixty-three percent of men did not believe that Axe "cleans skin thoroughly."

Though 68% of men had tried Axe, only 30% used it "most often."

The product was viewed as a special occasion item and not for daily use.

Building on the research, Axe set clear objectives for the brand to solve the problem:

- Increase the percentage of men who agree that Axe Shower Gel "cleans skin thoroughly" to 45%.
- Increase the percentage of men who use Axe Shower Gel "most often" to 33%.
- Maintain leadership in the men's bath and body category.

As a result of these goals, Axe executed the "Clean Your Balls" campaign on television, in print, on social media, outdoors, and through cinema to convey the message to 18- to 25-year-old men that Axe cleans effectively. The results were that the percentage of men who agreed Axe "cleans thoroughly" jumped from 37% to 50% and the buyers who said they would use Axe "most often" increased by 20%. Most importantly, dealer sales increased 60% compared to the benchmark [5], the baseline measure prior to running the campaign.

Research is an important component to a social media or mobile strategy because information helps determine the proper customer base and the right executions, and offers a means to evaluate success. Social media and mobile technology provide a number of useful methods for gathering information that people share on social media.

consider this...

COLLECTING SECONDARY DATA

Secondary data are available from public sources and are often free. For example, if you wanted information on the soft drink industry, you could easily do a search on Google. Some of the reports you find may be secondary sources of information you can use to help answer questions about the soft drink industry and competitors. A recent Google search for "soft drink industry" returned the following items:

A GUIDE TO THE SOFT DRINK INDUSTRY: Change Lab Solutions

BEVERAGES—SOFT DRINKS OVERVIEW: Industry Center: Yahoo

INDUSTRY ANALYSIS SOFT DRINKS: College of Saint Benedict

SOFT DRINK INDUSTRY MARKET RESEARCH REPORTS: Reportlinker

REPORTS: American Beverage Association

SOFT DRINKS AND BEVERAGES INDUSTRY AND MARKET RESEARCH: Euromonitor. . .

Some of the above links direct the user to a site to purchase a report, while others provide information to their members who pay dues. Students seeking information for an assignment should use their university's library, which may have free access to some of the reports. Though Google search is a very good tool for locating information, the library may have useful sources as well.

One issue in conducting a Google search is the credibility of the information that comes up. Some sources are more reliable than others, but as a general rule, the well-known reputable companies usually conduct sound studies and research that give sources and information on methods and are more trustworthy than what's available at websites that do not include such background data.

When marketers decide they need a brand strategy, they must have information about the industry, competitors, consumers, marketing environment, potential opportunities and threats or problems that a brand faces. Using some of the sources in Exhibit 3.2, marketers create a document called a situation analysis. In the digital age, a situation analysis includes social media monitoring and incorporates mobile data as well.

ELEMENTS OF A COMPREHENSIVE SITUATION ANALYSIS

A **situation analysis** is a comprehensive research document that guides a company's strategy planning, implementation, and evaluation process. A strong situation analysis provides background information on where the company stands within the industry, which competitors operate in the market, who the customers are and what they want and expect from the firm, what the current strategy has achieved, and where the company might head in terms of future goals. These days, a situation analysis would include the current social media and/or mobile strategy of the firm and an evaluation of such strategies as well as those of competitors. As important as data collection is to the process, marketers must also review the information and analyze the available data to determine the effectiveness of industry strategies. It's a forward-looking document based on prior data and analysis. A good situation analysis requires more than just reporting, it requires true insight.

EXHIBIT 3.2

Sources of Information for a Situation Analysis

	SOURCES
Industry data	Standard & Poor's industry surveys, Euromonitor International industry reports, industry/trade associations, industry-related publications such as magazines and white papers
Market segmentation	*Simmons OneView*; Mediamark Research, Inc.; country census data; Facebook advertising data; LinkedIn advertising data
Current marketing strategies	Observational research, company websites, periodicals
Digital strategies	Alexa, Quantcast, ComScore, Think with Google, Klout
Brand communications	Advertising Age Data Center; Kantar Media SRDS
Social media strategy	Social listening tools such as Social Mention, Radian6, Crimson Hexagon, and HowSociable

The following list includes the major elements of a situation analysis and the questions marketers should consider when researching and writing the document:

I. **Industry Analysis**
    Who are the major players in the industry and what are their strengths and weaknesses? What environmental factors (demographic, economic, technological, sociocultural, political-legal, and global) affect the industry? What are the sales and market shares for the various competitors? What is each competitor's positioning strategy? What major issues face the industry?

II. **Market Segmentation**
    How can the market be divided among groups of consumers? What characteristics drive product category-related behavior? Who is the target market for this product? Describe the target in demographic, psychographic, geographic, and behavioral terms. How do consumers view the product/service? How do consumers use the product/service? What factors influence the purchase decision process?

III. **Competitive Marketing Strategies**
    What are the 4p's of the marketing mix for the brand and competitors? Describe the products/services in detail with the important features. How are the products distributed and transported? Evaluate the pricing strategies of competitors versus the brand.

IV. **Digital Marketing Strategy**
    What is the digital strategy for the brand? Evaluate the brand's website and blog and those of competitors. Evaluate the keyword and SEO strategy for the brands and consider how the brand integrates digital with traditional media.

V. **Brand Communications**
    What are the brand positioning and integrated marketing communications strategies for the brand and competitors? How much money does each brand spend in the various forms of media? Are they reaching the target efficiently?

VI. **Social Media Strategy**
    Evaluate the brand's current social media strategy (and mobile if applicable) in terms of search engine rankings, followers, social media conversations, and content. Use social media to determine brand sentiment, monitor competitors, and track industry trends.

The process of collecting information by scanning information on social media sites is often called **social media listening**. There is a tremendous amount of information available online that people post and share which can help a brand develop effective strategies. The problem is collecting and managing the data to ensure that the insights are useful. For example, a brand could have many Facebook followers who post, but what do the comments mean and do these people represent the customer base?

SOCIAL MEDIA LISTENING FOR INSIGHTS

Do you ever post comments online about products or services, or have you seen comments posted on social media that have influenced you to either buy or avoid a particular item? A study of millennials (those born around the turn of the twenty-first century) found that they are 3.6 times more likely to share content online than other age groups and 2.3 times more likely to click on information that was shared by their peers [6]. Marketers are really interested in what you have to say about them and spend a lot of time and money trying to find out what you think.

Social media listening refers to the act of gathering online data using keywords and phrases to determine social media conversations about a brand, product category, issue, or other area of interest. The purpose is to learn how a brand appears in conversations and how customers and others talk about it [7], so marketers can serve both groups better and reach targets when they are likely to be most receptive to messages.

Marketers can also use many of the tools for social listening to examine competitors in the social media space. A number of sites provide free trials to test out their service and the types of data their searches return. Each has a different algorithm or mathematical calculation for determining social media scores based on data that the sites find via Web crawlers, software that searches the Internet seeking specific pieces of information.

The formulas monitoring companies use to scan are company secrets and the firms do not share them with clients. The fact that the companies do not share their systems makes it impossible to truly evaluate the services they offer, which is a very big limitation of using them. For example, one social media listening firm suggested that its service provided information on a brand's customers. However, the data set did not include customers who did not post online or even those who just chose not to write about brands on social media. The sample of information that the various social media listening tools return is not representative of customers and may not even be representative of social media users. A marketer must be cautious about the data and what the company-generated reports mean, whether or not the client pays a fee for the service. However, the information is still useful and shows what some people are sharing online.

Some social media listening companies offer free data for short specified time periods or for a limited set of brands. The free services do not offer as many bells and whistles as the fee-for-services variety. However, they can be a strong starting point for general information for a brand strategy.

There are a few areas where the free or paid tools can provide useful information. Specifically, marketers can do each of the following:

1. Evaluate brand sentiment.
2. Monitor competitors.
3. Track trends.
4. Analyze keywords.
5. Identify bloggers.
6. Determine site analytics.

When you use the tools to examine a particular brand's strategy, you should watch for three things. First, look to see what kind of information the site provides. Most of the free services give brands scores based on how much people are talking about the brand online and whether the talk is positive or negative. Second, make sure you check the time period to see exactly what time frame you are examining. The free tools are good for snapshots in time, but longer-term analysis may require a paid account. Exhibit 3.3 lists the information provided by some of the free social media listening services.

EXHIBIT 3.3

Tools for Social Media Listening

TOOL	FUNCTION
Social Mention	Provides real-time information on brand mentions across the Internet. Includes sentiment, keywords, and hashtags.
Klout	Scores individuals and companies based on their influence in social media.
Hootsuite and Tweetdeck	Customize a dashboard with relevant brand information from social networking sites and key brand properties.
Trackur	Searches the Web for information on brands or other points of interest and determines sentiment and level of influence for the mentions.
How Sociable	Shows the weekly online activity of a brand on various social media platforms.
TweetReach, Tweepie, and Twazzup	Monitor Twitter for information on the activity of brands, followers, and hashtags.
TrendsMap and WhattheTrend	Indicate what people are talking about on Twitter globally and in specific countries at a given time.
Addictomatic	Searches the Web for trend information from a variety of social media sites based on keywords. This platform includes YouTube, Wordpress, Bing, Delicious, and blogs.

NEGATIVE COMMENTS AND WORD OF MOUTH

Marketers are understandably worried about negative postings, tweets, and online reviews, which can affect a business. Some data suggest that negative reviews are not that common. Positive comments outweigh negative ones by a margin of 8 to 1 and small businesses get more favorable reviews than big businesses. Customers tend to be most positive about food, beverages, and beauty products and less positive (but still skew toward favorable) about health-care firms, financial businesses, and telecommunications companies. Consumers who engage in social media are also more likely to purchase a brand's offerings directly, affecting revenue for a firm. When customers engage in social media with a brand, their involvement also affects their friends' purchases. The additional purchases increase the customer lifetime values of those individuals, bringing more revenue to the firm [7].

Brand managers are understandably nervous about negative comments and discussions and may attempt to mitigate them by controlling online postings. In Facebook, the brand can choose to prevent certain words from appearing in the newsfeed or can monitor each post and delete those that denigrate the brand. However, brands that allow negative posts and address the concerns of customers may build better relationships. When companies intervene in instances of product or service failure, customers feel as if the company is concerned about them and may be more likely to purchase. New customers may also view company customer service positively, which might help attract new clients.

EVALUATE BRAND SENTIMENT

Brand sentiment refers to how people feel about a brand, typically ranging from positive to negative. Marketers can use social media to determine sentiment based on the information that people post and share. One online tool for evaluating sentiment is Social Mention. Social Mention measures how often people discuss a brand and the keywords they enter when searching on Google, and provides a list of recent brand-related posts. The scores can be used to compare brand sentiment across brands or as a benchmark to use before and after executing a strategy. However, marketers must be aware that these tools are limited to the universe of those who choose to post online and do not represent all customers. Exhibit 3.4 describes the Social Mention measures.

Many companies offer tools that analyze online sentiment. The tools differ based on the algorithms for scanning the Web and the way the information is organized for a particular brand. Some of the tools can measure emotions such as

EXHIBIT 3.4

Social Mention Measures and Definitions

SOCIAL MENTION MEASURES	DEFINITIONS
Strength	The likelihood that a brand is mentioned on social media. Specific phrase mentions divided by total mentions in the medium.
Sentiment	Ratio of general positive to negative mentions.
Passion	The likelihood that people repeatedly discuss the brand.
Reach	The number of unique authors relative to total mentions.

happiness, sadness, and frustration. Others will evaluate the relevance of the posting to determine the likelihood that the post will influence a sale. Aiailoo Labs uses text analysis to examine sentiment and intention by examining the words in people's posts. Phrases such as "I want" or "I have to get" suggest that the person is looking to buy something. The company based in Bangalore, India, has two tools to evaluate sentences. The first one is **sentiment analysis** in which a person can input a sentence and the system will analyze it to determine whether the statement is positive, negative, or neutral. The other tool is **intention analysis** whereby a sentence will be analyzed to determine whether the person who wrote it intends to make a purchase. For instance, "I want to own a dishwasher" clearly means that a person is in the market to purchase a dishwasher, while "I have a dishwasher" does not indicate purchase intention. This analysis can be done in a number of languages, including English, Chinese, Spanish, French, German, Indonesian, Hindi, Italian, Portuguese, and Swahili.

One very popular system for tracking brands in social media and creating content for brands is Hootsuite. Hootsuite is a comprehensive social media management tool that allows brands to create a dashboard to monitor key social media tools. Marketing managers can watch their brands' social media activity on a daily basis. For example, a business-to-business company could customize a dashboard with its company blog, LinkedIn, and Google. A company selling to individuals might focus on Facebook, Twitter, and Instagram for their dashboard. Brands can watch their information streams, those who follow them, and who they follow; track instances when the brand is mentioned on social media; and monitor brand tweets and retweets. In addition, the platform reports brand sentiment, with the percentages for positive, negative, and neutral adding up to 100%.

MONITOR COMPETITORS

The tools for analyzing brand sentiment can also be used for monitoring competitors on social media. However, there are a few tools that are particularly useful for providing competitive information or comparing various competitors.

Google Alerts is a very useful tool for monitoring online competitors. Brand managers can input the names of competitors into the search query and tell Google how often they would like to receive email notifications of competitive news, blogs, videos, and discussions. This system allows brands to keep abreast of competitive news and information as it appears online, leading to faster reaction time to competitive threats.

Some services score brands so that marketers can see their performance relative to that of competitors. Klout provides a measure of a brand's social media influence using a score of 1 to 100, with a higher score representing more social media "Klout." One place where you can easily see Klout data for companies is Hootsuite, which provides the Klout scores for the entities a person follows. Though we do not know the mathematical calculation, Klout reports that its algorithm is based on [9]:

- Twitter: retweets and mentions
- Facebook: comments, wall posts, likes
- Google+: comments, reshares, +1
- LinkedIn: comments, likes
- Foursquare: to-do's and tips
- Yammer
- Instagram and Bing

This Tweetreach analysis shows the response to the fifty most recent tweets on the hashtag #socialmediamarketing.

Tweetreach,
www.tweetreach.com

There are a number of tools based on Twitter that provide competitive data. Because of Twitter's open platform, more outside vendors analyze Twitter data than other platforms. For example, Tweepie lets you follow other Twitter users' followers. Tweetreach allows brands to input company names to determine each's reach on Twitter over a specified time period, the contributors who had the highest levels of exposure for the brand, and the most retweeted content. One recent search revealed that Pepsi had a reach of 162,943 with 184,132 impressions. The top contributor was Taste of Country, a country music website. A photo of the filming of a Pepsi commercial featuring LYeolNam was the most retweeted tweet. Coca-Cola had lower levels of reach, at 85,756 with 98,225 impressions. The top contributor, Gatsy Rubio, who also retweeted the top tweet was from Argentina; he tweeted, "Si la Coca-Cola afloja tornillos, la Manaos te borra un tatuaje" [10], which means "If Coca-Cola loosened screws, the Manaus would erase a tattoo."

Pinterest has a treasure trove of information about who is pinning, what they are pinning, and how those pins deliver value to firms. Pinterest Analytics is a platform for analyzing Pinterest data open to commercial Pinterest accounts. Companies using Instagram also have access to an analytics platform and services such as Iconosquare and Squarelovin show the data graphically and help manage posts. Simply Measured provides a free Instagram user analysis report.

KLOUT SCORES FOR COKE AND PEPSI

So, which brand is winning the cola wars in social media? Well, it is impossible to say for sure, but we can compare Klout scores for some major brand properties. By choosing Coke and Pepsi for this analysis, we can see not only that Klout scores provide a measure of social media performance, but also a major limitation of relying heavily on these data. The chart to the right shows Klout scores for Coke and Pepsi. Pepsi has a global branded score, but Coke does not. It instead focuses country by country and on specific promotions like the Coke Zone. The more fragmented strategy for Coke, in addition to the greater number of name variations, makes it difficult to judge its social media presence.

Klout Scores of Cola Terms

BRANDS	KLOUT SCORE
Pepsi	89
Pepsi Canada	51
Pepsi	68
Coke Zone	61
Coca-cola Great Britain	57
Coca-cola Canada	59

www.Klout.com (June 2014)

HowSociable can also provide a competitive analysis. HowSociable's magnitude score provides an indication of the level of activity around a brand during a given week. The range goes from 0 to 10. A score of zero means there is zero or near-zero activity for the brand. A score of 10 means the brand has practically saturated the social Web and will likely be recognized by everyone that uses it. The information comes from one week's worth of social activity.

Data for Coke and Pepsi from HowSociable in a one-week period are summarized in Exhibit 3.5 [11]. Though Pepsi only uses one name, its rankings are lower than those for Coke overall. Though you might be tempted to say that Coke is more "sociable" and more influential, you should exercise caution. After all, at this time, Coke had many more Facebook fans than Pepsi and was spending significantly more money on advertising its flagship brand around the world. The way these measures are useful is to see at one point of time which social media sites are ranking the brands higher and as a method of benchmarking prior to executing a strategy. For example, Pepsi may decide to set a goal to encourage more brand engagement. The brand could use HowSociable's measure of its ranking on Facebook and seek to build that ranking over time. In fact, setting measurable goals for any strategy is a key factor in effective execution.

EXHIBIT 3.5

HowSociable Rankings on Major Social Platforms for Coke and Pepsi

	COCA-COLA	COKE	PEPSI
Overall	5.5	6.1	5.5
Facebook	3.1	3.0	3.0
YouTube	3.5	4.1	3.6
LinkedIn	2.7	2.5	2.6
Twitter	3.6	3.7	3.6

www.howsociable.com accessed March 21, 2016

consider this . . .

DETERMINING TRUE SENTIMENT

Online social media sentiment is difficult to examine because of the language people use to express themselves. People say things that a computer would judge to be negative, but are actually positive. Since our use of language and idiom is constantly changing, computerized content analysis is somewhat limited. The accuracy of online social media analysis is about 60% to 65% [12], suggesting that the data can help provide some directional information, but marketers should evaluate further by looking at the actual text.

Is each of the following statements positive or negative?

"My mom hates on my Chobani."
"How am I supposed to eat Chobani with a fork?"

Another reason for marketers to look at actual customer postings is to address concerns that may come up. Customers have a variety of reasons for complaining, but often they appreciate when the marketer attempts to intervene and solve the problem. In addition, if others see that a marketer responds, they may be more open to purchasing from that business.

TRACK TRENDS

The social media space is a place where trends are widely discussed among broad groups of people and brands can track these trends using many available tools. Companies should first determine the key terms associated with their business that might signify a change in the landscape. For example, Coke and Pepsi might be interested in health trends as some of their products are viewed as unhealthful. A brand manager at Pepsi could type "health and exercise" into Google Trends and determine that interest peaked in 2005 and that the topic has cyclical seasonal searches. In addition, people looked for this term most frequently in Australia, Ireland, the United Kingdom, the United States, the Philippines, and New Zealand. Marketers can also examine multiple trends to discern differences [13].

A social media monitoring system for tracking trends is Trackur. It scans social media to return findings based on keywords or competitors. The results show all the mentions of that keyword or competitor globally on a variety of sites in real time. The system also indicates the level of influence of each result and whether the information is positive, negative, or neutral. Recent searches for Pepsi and Coke were heavily skewed toward Instagram, Google+, Tumblr, and Facebook, suggesting that these properties may be important avenues for consumers to communicate about soft drinks [14].

Many social media platforms as well as news outlets provide information on what is trending on their sites as well as online. For instance, Yahoo, Facebook, Twitter, and Huffington Post provide top trending data. This kind of information can be useful for brands that wish to be on the cutting edge of news and events, and choose to utilize the information to communicate with their target audience. Of course, the target should also be informed on events and news, and be interested in what the brand has to say about them.

For example, TrendsMap indicates the top trending terms on Twitter globally and in various locations around the world. You can examine topics in your location, city, region, or globally. On a particular day in 2016 the following trends were popular in the Northeastern United States:. spring, snapchat, mondaymotivation, bitcoin, and periscope.

Globally, world poetry day and human rights day were trending at the same time [15]. On What the Trend, you can see the trending topics in many countries and even provide your trends or your expertise to explain what trends mean for others.

ANALYZE KEYWORDS

Aside from social media monitoring, another useful analysis is to examine the keywords customers use in searching for the category, brand, or issue of interest to the marketer. The keywords help marketers determine how customers are attracted to the brand and what leads them to purchase online. The analysis can also be useful in evaluating competitive strategies and creating content for a brand. Exhibit 3.6 provides information on some useful keyword analysis tools.

The large search engines offer a number of services that can help a brand determine:

Which keywords are most effective in delivering and converting customers
The successful keywords of competitors

EXHIBIT 3.6

Keyword Tools

TOOL	FUNCTION
Search engine keyword suggestion	Most search engines suggest keywords when users type terms into the search box and marketers can see which terms are most popular with searchers. Google offers an "instant" search that appears as people type characters into the search engine.
Google AdWords keyword planner	Allows users to enter keywords, websites, or product categories to determine the number of global and local (country) monthly searches and the level of competition for each search term. Advanced functions show location, language, devices, and cost. The tool allows users to see different key words for an online vs. mobile search.
WordStream keyword suggestion tool and negative keyword tool	The suggestion tool provides the relative frequency, search volume, and level of competition for a keyword or phrase. The negative keyword tool shows words that often appear with a keyword, but may not be relevant to a brand.
Wordtracker	Provides information for keywords, including volume, competition, number of sites that use the keyword on both their title page and on links within the page, and an effectiveness measure.
SEMrush	Provides information on traffic to websites, countries in which a website ranks in terms of organic and paid search, and the keywords purchased by competitors.
SpyFu	Provides daily keyword advertising budgets for brands and competitors, top keywords used in paid and organic searches, and a list of recent ads posted.

The links to which a website connects

The best keywords to include in the content

Demographic and location data for your customers

SEMrush delivers information on keywords of your brand and competitors. When you search for something on Google, some of the results returned are "organic," meaning that the search engine finds those items and they are not paid for by advertisers. These are the results in the middle of the page. Results that appear on the top of the page (with a symbol indicating it is an ad) are advertisements paid for by advertisers who bid to place the ad on the page when you search a particular term. SEMrush provides marketers with information on the search engine keywords as shown in the screenshot analysis of Pepsi.com. In the Key Word Summary, SEMrush shows data for the exact term entered into its system; in the Phrase Match section, SEMrush provides information on similar keywords; and in the Related Key Words section, the system displays similar keywords as determined by the SEMrush algorithm. The left side of the screenshot lists all the different reports available from SEMrush a marketer could examine, and you can go to its site, type in a brand, and look at some of these. Exhibit 3.7 defines the terms shown on the SEMrush screenshot shown here. Some of the terms may be new to you, but they are important components of digital marketing and you will learn more about them in Chapter Seven.

SEMrush reports are useful for brands that wish to understand how competitors buy their advertising, the words that people use to search for their company and other competitors, and for budgeting purposes. Aside from keyword information, the site also shows actual ads that the brand ran, such as this one for Pepsi [16]:

Explore with Pepsi - pepsi.com
Ad www.pepsi.com
Check out exclusive content from Pepsi & Share the Excitement!

Chapter Seven discusses digital prerequisites for social media and mobile strategies and explains how keyword research can inform search engine strategies.

SEMrush Screenshot Terms Defined

TERM	DEFINITION/EXPLANATION
Keyword summary	Shows the keyword that most often brings people to the Pepsi site.
CPC or cost per click	The average price the advertiser pays when someone clicks on the word "Pepsi."
Com. or competitive density	The level of competition to buy the word "Pepsi" on a scale from 0 to 1. The term Pepsi has a competitive density of .25 out of 1.0.
Volume	The average number of times the term was searched over a twelve-month period.
Number of results	The number of results that could be displayed for that keyword (though most people don't go beyond the first page).
SERP source	If you click on the icon, you will see the actual results returned when someone searches for the keyword "Pepsi."
CPC distribution	Shows the CPC in various countries. In this case, the CPC is $3.30 in Denmark—the highest for Pepsi.
Trend	Shows the CPC over time.

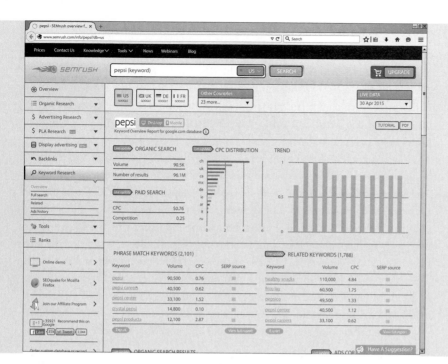

SEMrush provides keyword analysis for brands.

SEMrush, www.semrush.com

Marketers can evaluate keywords in the market and choose those with low levels of competition that are more likely to drive sales. One strategy is to consider longer keyword phrases, simply more words in the search, that hone in on the product, so a marketer can own a particular space without a tremendous amount of competition. For example, if you really want something specific, you might enter more words into Google. Instead of typing "shoes," you might type in "Buy Converse All Star High Top Sneakers." By bidding on the longer search term, Converse would pay less money and be more confident that a pair of Converse high tops is what you want. Buying keywords in search engines is an important part of a **digital marketing strategy** that strongly influences purchase behavior.

IDENTIFY BLOGGERS

Another important avenue for research is to determine the influencers for a particular category. Many industries have **bloggers** who write about products and services in specific categories, but there are also a number of very influential news outlets that have general audiences, such as the Huffington Post or Buzz Feed. Bloggers can spread positive, negative, or neutral information about brands. Therefore, brand managers should be aware of the key bloggers in their categories to monitor news and in order to execute communications strategies through bloggers.

The advantage to marketing through influencers is that consumers value the opinions of others and can be influenced by the recommendations or reported usage of people they respect, such as bloggers, celebrities, or experts. By reaching out to a small cohort of highly connected individuals, a marketer can reduce communications expenses and benefit from the voice of the influencer. An added benefit to reaching out to bloggers and other online content creators is the possibility that their postings will contribute to higher search engine rankings for the brand, meaning that the brand's webpage will earn a higher position in a Google search.

There are a few useful tools for locating bloggers. Most search and identify bloggers based on keywords, such as Twingly, WordPress.com Search, and Meltwater IceRocket. Some, such as InkyBee, report "visibility," a measure of the number of viewers, and "engagement," the degree to which people interact with the blog by posting and sharing. For example, you can find baking bloggers by typing in "chocolate cake and cookies" in the InkyBee search bar. The site returns a list of bloggers such as BlahnikBaker from Syracuse, New York, with a visibility of 70/100 and an engagement of 59/100. Tales of an Overtime Cook had a visibility of 67 and engagement of 60, and Art of Dessert had a visibility of 62 and engagement of 87. A company selling gourmet baking chocolate might target these bloggers and send recipes and noteworthy stories about chocolate cakes.

Exhibit 3.8 describes some of the free tools available for locating category-specific bloggers. In addition, Open Site Explorer can show a marketing manager the sites that link to and from the brand's website (inbound and outbound links), identifying bloggers who drive traffic to the site.

EXHIBIT 3.8

Blogger Sources

Board Reader	Compiles lists of message boards featuring the user's keyword(s). Some of these boards include bloggers who write about topics.
Twingly Blog Search	Identifies blogs using keywords and provides number of links and likes for each post.
Meltwater IceRocket	A search tool for locating blogs on specific topics. Trend data indicate how often keywords are mentioned in blogs.
InkyBee	Searches blogs and posts on the Web based on a keyword and provides a measure of visibility and engagement for each blog.
Open Site Explorer	Examines the authority of a website, its links, and text. The links show which pages link to the site, potentially identifying bloggers.
Blog Catalog	Lists blogs for various categories such as food, entertainment, health, family, and photography. Also lists bloggers in specific geographic areas.

THREE TIERS OF BLOGGER INFLUENCE

Market researchers have developed a method for ranking the influence of bloggers using the set of measures below and creating a three-tiered index to do so.

Blogger Criteria

Viewers per month	The number of visits to the blog per month
Linkages	The popularity of the blog post based on the other pages that link to the blog's content
Post frequency	Volume of posts over a given time
Media citation score	Volume and level of media that cover/cite the blogger
Industry score	The degree to which the blogger participates in events, keynote speeches, and panels
Social aggregator rate	Level of participation in social media
Engagement index	Reader response and quantity of comments
Subject-/topic-related posts	Volume and immediacy of subject-related posts
Qualitative subject-/topic-related posts	Qualitative review of the posts in terms of contribution and sentiment

The model predicts three tiers of blogger influence:

Tier A blogs are news heavy, but have less social connectedness through postings by members of the community than other types of blogs. The community has a large readership and strong contributor base, but tends toward general interest in a broad range of topics.

Tier B blogs are smaller in terms of viewership, but are more social and focused on a particular topic. The content is unique to the blog and features a blogger's perspective aimed at a passionate audience.

Tier C blogs are highly influential on the readership, but have small audiences of very engaged individuals. The topics are very specific and sometimes obscure. The specialized nature of the content shows the expertise of the bloggers who may be sought out for their opinions in other media [17].

TRIBES, TRIBAL NETWORKS, AND NETNOGRAPHY

Netnography is a technique that researchers have used to examine the behavior of consumer tribes and how they affect brand strategy. The term "Netnography" is a combination of the terms Eth*nography* and Inter*net*. **Ethnography** is when researchers deeply analyze consumers by interviewing them in their personal spaces, asking questions about their lives as expressed by their individual environments, their possessions, and homes. Netnographic research is conducted by a researcher who embeds him- or herself within the tribe and interacts with its people to examine issues of interest within the community.

Consumer tribes that form around a product category or brand are important to marketers who seek to understand their behavior and influence their purchases. The participants in these discussions affect the buzz surrounding the brand, and they may directly influence those who seek information online regarding a purchase. In addition, the buzz associated with a tribe of consumers influences search engine rankings through social media and search behavior.

Marketers have to think carefully about how to research tribes and whether to embed themselves in the community and make clear their intentions, or use an outside researcher to examine the issues of interest to the brand within a particular community. One caveat is that consumers view their tribes as personal spaces to share with each other and may not welcome brand participation. Marketers who attempt to influence private tribal groups may encounter negative responses from consumers. Therefore, approaching the tribe honestly and without the intention of selling may be a more effective strategy for collecting data. One place where marketers are free to collect data is on their own company-sponsored social networks. If the brand is clear about its ownership of the network to users, marketing managers may post questions and ask for feedback from the group. Since the customers already know that the site is brand-sponsored, they might not feel as strongly that the brand has invaded their privacy when it pursues research data or attempts to persuade. However, customers may not want to continue to engage with a brand that is always trying to sell something.

DETERMINE SITE ANALYTICS

Marketers who have any Web presence at all can benefit from analytics programs that review the site and provide important feedback for how to improve performance. The most popular tool is Google Analytics. Users sign up for Google Analytics, which provides a code to install on the user's website that will track the activity of the site and report information.

Different websites may have various objectives for their business and Google Analytics is set up to return data related to specific Web objectives. For example, an e-commerce site would want to track sales, while a content site (like a news blog) might want to track page visits or time spent on pages. Google Analytics can measure the goals listed in Exhibit 3.9.

EXHIBIT 3.9

Data Available from Google Analytics

GOALS	EXAMPLES OF DATA SOURCES
Location of a website's audience	Local, global, and country-specific information
Audience engagement	Amount of time spent viewing each page, the number of pages viewed, whether a new or recurring user
Purchase funnel	The pages people viewed and the pages viewed prior to purchase on a site
Trends	Heavy and light traffic over various time spans
Mobile traffic	Visits from types of devices and the operating systems (iOS or Android) accessing the site
Links	Sites that deliver traffic to and receive traffic from the website
Social media	Social media sites and specific posts that deliver hits to the website
Email	Emails that result in traffic to the site
Bounce rate	The percentage of people who leave the site after viewing only one page

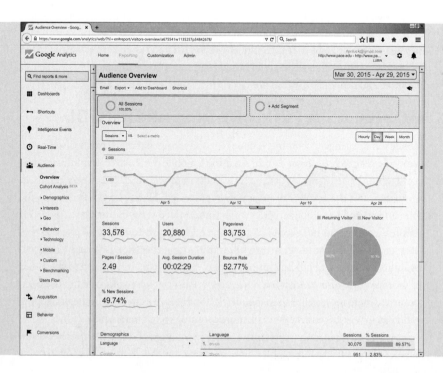

Google Analytics is the platform for providing detailed website data.

Google Analytics, www.google.com/analytics

The screenshot of the Google Analytics page shows the number of sessions on this particular website, the number of unique users who had not visited before, and the total pages that people viewed. On this site, people looked at an average of 2.49 pages for two minutes and twenty-nine seconds and 52.77% of the visitors left after only viewing one page of the site. If you look on the left side of the screenshot, you can see the list of other information available through Google Analytics.

MOBILE DEVICE RESEARCH

Mobile can potentially deliver a significant amount of data that contribute to a brand strategy. Google Analytics can track mobile device information so that these data are also included in reports.

Since people keep their phones with them 24/7, marketers want to track their behavior, so they may influence consumption when people are ready to make a purchase. As such, various market research vendors offer services that track consumers. For instance, Experian provides data on a sample of smartphone users that show what people are doing with their phones throughout the day, such as using the camera, texting, opening apps, sending photos and emails. Experian can also show the smartphone behavior of specific target markets based on their sample of consumers. Since the phone also provides location data, marketers are able to identify where consumers are when they are interacting with their phones. For example, Mazda tracked consumer locations before they visited the Mazda Miata dealership. The goal for Mazda was to determine appropriate venues for location-based advertising. The location data also told the company which people had visited competitive car lots and sent them a message with a prompt to learn more about the Miata. The research company that collected the data did so with satellites that examine 100 × 100 meter physical spaces and device IDs that identify cell phones within those locations [18].

MOBILE AS A PRIMARY RESEARCH TOOL

Mobile is increasingly becoming a venue for conducting market research, also known as **mobile research** (or **m-research**). In using a mobile device to collect information, marketers must be cognizant of time constraints in providing data, connection speed, screen size, and the amount of information requested. Short surveys that are to the point and related to mobile activities will be more effective in generating a response. If response rates are low in Web surveys, mobile might help boost the response and provides something for the target to do while waiting. Consider the customer who is waiting online for a service holding his cell phone. A small incentive related to the brand might encourage him to answer a brief survey. This strategy works well in developed countries where most people have phones, but may also be effective in the developing world where wireless connections are more common than broadband access.

Mobile research only represents a small percentage of all market research and includes both surveys on mobile devices (either by the mobile Web or via text messaging) and telephone surveys using mobile phones. Another application for mobile surveys is to take advantage of the local nature of mobile devices and survey customers as they leave retail locations. Mobile research may be particularly useful among hard-to-reach demographics such as teens or B2B. In addition, there are distinct advantages to using mobile for research, including immediacy and freshness of data, ability to show images, and speed. The disadvantages relate to the small screen, difficulty in downloading using certain devices, and the nonrepresentative sample of people who own cell phones. Marketers who use m-research should ask consumers to opt in, and they must institute a double opt-in process for text message-based research. This means they have to ask the participant to confirm two times that he or she is willing to receive texts from the company doing the research. In any case, it's good marketing practice to get permission to approach someone on his or her mobile device because a phone is very personal to people. Given the restraints in conducting market research via cell phone, ESOMAR, the industry association for market research, and the Mobile Market Research Association (MMRA), publish a set of guidelines for m-research on their sites that includes requirements for disclosure, recruiting, opt-in notifications, data security, and other key aspects of conducting m-research.

consider this . . .

HOW TO CONDUCT A CONTENT ANALYSIS

A **content analysis** is a qualitative research method that is used to judge information. In the case of social media listening research, a content analysis examines statements posted on social media and evaluates the comments by categorizing them. Many social media sites categorize tweets and posts into three categories: positive, neutral, or negative. However, any categories may be used since the process is based on human judgment. For instance, a marketer might listen to online buzz and want to determine the feeling evoked by those statements, such as happiness, guilt, sadness, anger, or anxiety. The marketer could also be interested in categorizing posts into groups of those individuals who are persuasive in their communication versus those who are accepting in their posts. In fact, the process helps whenever the language is ambiguous, which is common in human communications.

The steps for conducting a strong content analysis to determine sentiment from the major social media sites are as follows:

1. Determine which social media sites are relevant to the brand. For example, customers may be using a product category–specific site, such as Trip Advisor, or a general social media site unrelated to the product category, such as Stumble Upon.
2. Choose the sites to examine and set an appropriate goal. For instance, the brand manager might be interested in positive or negative sentiment, certain emotions, or purchase intent language.
3. Select a time frame for examining the social media property. Choose a large enough time period considering the purchase cycle for the brand, any news that could influence postings, and the seasonality of responses. For

instance, a brand manager for a ski company might not choose the summer when people don't ski, the time period following an avalanche, or the Christmas holiday when sentiment may be influenced by external events. However, if such events are of interest to the brand manager, he or she should choose a time period that is long enough to include the event as well as time periods when the event did not influence attitudes. The manager can also choose multiple time periods of the same length to broaden the total population of information to be sampled.

4. Collect all the postings from the time period in each social media property of interest. List and number each posting to generate a complete numbered list. Later, the researcher will sample from that list and judges will evaluate each item.

5. Determine the categories of interest and write clear descriptions of what each category means and provide examples that illustrate postings that would be included in each category.

6. Examine the full list of data and sample by choosing a random starting point (use a random number generator and begin from that post).

7. Train the judges to determine the correct category in which to place each posting. Allow for those postings that cannot be categorized into any group because of ambiguity.

8. Ask the judges to carefully examine each posting and determine the appropriate category.

9. Tally and evaluate the findings from the judges and calculate the degree to which the judges agree. There is a statistical technique for determining the level of agreement among judges. A strong content analysis would have 70% agreement among the judges. The degree to which the judges agree is known as **inter-rater reliability.**

SUMMARY AND REVIEW

CHAPTER SUMMARY

Marketers must conduct research around a brand's current situation before engaging in communications with target markets. As a result of social media interaction, there is a vast amount of information available. The key is to identify appropriate sources and use them to inform a brand strategy. Chapter Three provided many examples of information that can be used to develop a social media or mobile marketing strategy. These tools can help a brand understand consumer sentiment, competitors, trends, keywords, and influencers.

KEY TERMS

bloggers
brand sentiment
content analysis
digital marketing strategy

ethnography
inter-rater
   reliability
intention analysis

mobile research
  (or m-research)
netnography
primary data

secondary data
sentiment analysis
situation analysis
social media listening

SUMMARY REVIEW QUESTIONS

1. Explain the role research plays in developing social media strategy.
2. What is social media listening? What does it achieve?
3. How do marketers conduct secondary research and primary research?
4. Why is it important to analyze the industry competition and market segments prior to executing social media or mobile campaigns?
5. How can mobile devices be used to conduct primary research?

APPLICATION QUESTIONS

1. Choose two competing brands in the same industry and determine which has a stronger social media strategy using Social Mention.
2. Using Klout.com, follow five brands and rank them by their Klout scores.
3. Choose a brand and determine the top followers of the brand. How can these followers help advance the brand's strategy?
4. Examine the data on cola brands in Exhibit 3.5. Which brand is doing better and why? *Hint:* Determine the number of users of each social network site listed.
5. What are the top three trending topics on Twitter? How can a brand use this information? Give an example.
6. How much does Godiva pay to advertise on Google paid search? *Hint:* Use one of the keyword search tools.
7. Using Open Site Explorer, identify three bloggers for a brand you like. Now, find the ratings for each using another data provider.
8. Find three guidelines for mobile research from ESOMAR World Research at ESOMAR.org.

Case Study: Chobani USA

Hamdi Ulukaya, founder and CEO of Chobani, purchased an 85-year-old Kraft yogurt plant in Utica, New York, and began producing Greek yogurt in 2007. The product was new to the U.S. market and only held 2% of the yogurt market share at the time.

By 2012 Chobani's share was 47.3% of the Greek yogurt market in the United States [19] and almost 20% of the total U.S. yogurt market [20]. Sales continued to grow for Chobani. Between March 2011 and 2012, sales increased 144% to $626 million. However, there may have been even more room for growth in the Greek yogurt market as penetration in the United States was lower than in other parts of the world [21].

TARGET MARKET

Only 60% of Americans consumed yogurt at all, but those who did ate an average of four to five 4-ounce cups of yogurt per month. Yogurt was mostly eaten at breakfast or as a snack [21]. Chobani's target consumed five times as much yogurt as the national average. Though yogurt eaters tended to be female, college graduates, moms, and people aged 35–44 [22], Chobani targeted the 60 million men who ate yogurt as well.

Chobani's success was attributed, in part, to its promotional strategy. In 2010 the brand created a national campaign with the goal of not only growing the Greek yogurt business, but also stealing share from the general yogurt category leaders, Dannon and Yoplait. The agency Gotham noticed that the traditional brands focused on health benefits aimed exclusively at women and additionally focused on taste and texture to attract men.

THE CREATIVE

The campaign "Chobani: A love story about yogurt" focused on the employees and customers who felt passionate about the brand. Monitoring social media, the agency found true love stories that customers had posted on Facebook and Twitter, blogged on, or uploaded on YouTube. They further encouraged people to create stories by broadcasting tweets on billboards and giving away free cases of Chobani for the stories that generated the most "likes" on Facebook. Television spots showcased how

far people would go for Chobani and featured real customers, such as the man who biked 80 miles to see the Chobani plant in upstate New York [23].

SEARCH ENGINE STRATEGY

Chobani bought innovative keywords to drive traffic to its website and build impressions for the brand. Like that of other companies, the strategy focused on health, including the words "pro-biotics" and "protein." Open Site Explorer revealed a number of bloggers who discussed Chobani yogurt, as shown in Exhibit 3.10. Though the creative strategy emphasized taste, the company did not buy keywords around the concept of rich flavor, cooking, or indulgence at breakfast (see Exhibits 3.11 and 3.12). The business community was also interested in Chobani, and a number of links discussed the business model and company success.

EXHIBIT 3-10

Chobani's Bloggers

BLOG	DESCRIPTION
Peanut Butter Fingers	Living a life fueled by health food and fitness
The Crispy Cook	Gluten-free with garden and seasons
Blondie and Brownie	Two girls' adventures in food
Serious Eats	"We taste the leading brands to find the distinct differences and rate them with tasting scores."
Sweet Tooth Sweet Life	"In a life of health food, fitness, and fashion, there is always room for dessert."
Food Network Healthy Eats	*Food Network Magazine*
The Craving Chronicles	"I have a sweet tooth and I am not afraid to use it."

EXHIBIT 3.11

Chobani Paid Keywords

probiotics food

low-fat protein

recipes high protein

benefits of eating yo...

list high protein foods

yogurt smoothies

yogurt cultures

probiotic bacterium

yoghurt culture

lactobacillus acidoph...

EXHIBIT 3.12

Chobani Organic Keywords

buy chobani online

chobani

chobani protein

chobani yogurt sale

coupons yogurt

greek yogurt

yogurt brands

yogurt coupon

yogurt coupons

Chobani could have targeted food bloggers who might have been receptive to information on the product and recipes. For example, Grub Street, Delish.com, Foodblogalliance, and the mommy food bloggers, such as $5 dinners, Aggie's Kitchen, Almost Bourdain, Andrea's Recipes, Angry Chicken, and Annie's Eats, all reported on food preparation or eating.

SOCIAL MEDIA LISTENING AND ANALYSIS

In 2015 Crimson Hexagon, a social media listening and research firm, examined Chobani's online conversations over a prior two-year period and found 46% to be positive, 4% negative, and the remainder neutral. The negative comments revolved around a product recall in 2013. During the same time period, Crimson Hexagon found that 37% of the conversations about Chobani were related to cooking and 18% were focused on additional ingredients, such as granola added to the yogurt. Another 8% of the online conversations examined by Crimson Hexagon suggested that people ate the product for breakfast. As a result, the brand launched the #StopSadBreakfast campaign for Chobani oats, pairing the yogurt with oats for breakfast. Crimson Hexagon also determined that Chobani buyers were 4 times more likely to be interested in parenting and 3 times more likely to be moms than average Twitter users. Therefore, Chobani launched Chobani Kids and Chobani Tots (for babies 6 months plus) in January 2015 [24].

EXHIBIT 3-13

Chobani and Competitors

	CHOBANI	FAGE	DANNON OIKOS	YOPLAIT CLASSIC (NOT GREEK)
Klout Score Others Influence Topics	62 18K Yogurt, branding, food	50 3K Yogurt, branding, food	44 <1K Coupons, yogurt	45 1K Yogurt, branding, coupons
Social Mention average time to mention	3 minutes	45 minutes	4 days	20 minutes
Social Mention sentiment	18 to 1	9 to 1	29 to 1	8 to 1
Twitter followers	41,509	35,616	606	47,341
Facebook likes	598K	975K	435K	1 million
YOY growth rate	+144%	+37%	+16%	−8.7 for total yogurt
Greek yogurt dollar share	47.3%	13.9%	19.7%	26.7% total yogurt market

http://articles.chicagotribune.com/2012-03-16/business/ct-biz-greek-yogurt_1_greek-yogurt-chobani-tula-foods
http://www.nutraingredients-usa.com/Industry/Dannon-probiotic-yogurt-sales-up-16-despite-claims-crackdown
http://adage.com/article/cmo-strategy/winning-greek-yogurt-revolution/235206/

However, the competition was strong and present in social media as shown in Exhibit 3.13. All the major brands, including Stonyfield Farm, Dannon, and Yoplait, had Greek yogurt brands. Would the strong brand recognition of the national heavy hitters steal share from Chobani? In spite of competition, Chobani was preparing for growth. The company announced it would grow its market in Asia by shipping from plants in Australia and would use the New York operations to supply Latin America and the Caribbean [25].

QUESTIONS FOR DISCUSSION

1. Describe the competitive landscape in the Greek yogurt industry presented in this case study.
2. Which competitor is best positioned in the marketplace?
3. Are there any external threats to Chobani's market leadership? If so, what are they?
4. Evaluate the keywords Chobani uses based on the information that was supplied here. Are there additional words Chobani should bid on?

5. To what extent can Chobani build on its current social media strategies as it introduces new products? What should the company do differently?
6. Examine the keywords you chose to determine Chobani's competition using the Google Adwords tool. Which terms are the most efficient?
7. Use Social Mention to examine conversations about Greek yogurt and the competitors. What would you recommend for Chobani's social media strategy based on this information?

REFERENCES

[1] Espen, "Dell's Hell: Looking Back with Jeff Jarvis," *BlogCampaigning,* 25 October 2007.

[2] S. Israel, "Dell Modernizes IdeaStorm," *Forbes,* 27 March 2012.

[3] C. Jervis, "IT Pros, Do You Want to Be a Dell Rock Star?," Dell Tech Center, 29 January 2014.

[4] Forrester Research, "Case Study: Dell's Social Media Listening Command Center Builds Customer Relationships," 2011.

[5] Effie Awards, "Axe Cleans Your Balls," 2012 Silver Effie Awards Winner.

[6] K. Abrahamson, "New Consumer Study: Millennials Are 2X as Likely to Purchase Products They Share About," *Share This,* 23 September 2014.

[7] B. Fay, "Turning Negative Conversations into Positive Outcomes," *Forbes,* 18 July 2012.

[8] G. Kumparak, "The Guy Behind the Qwikster Twitter Account Realizes What He Has, Wants a Mountain of Cash," TechCrunch, 19 September 2011.

[9] C. Taylor, "Why Klout Had to Change and Why You Should Not Rely on It," Mashable, 10 February 2014.

[10] TweetReach, http://www.tweetreach.com.

[11] HowSociable, http://www.howsociable.com/.

[12] J. Falls, "Social Media Sentiment Competing on Accuracy," *Social Media Examiner,* 19 April 2012.

[13] Google Trends, https://www.google.com/trends/.

[14] Trackur, http://www.trackur.com/.

[15] TrendsMap, http://www.trendsmap.com, March 21, 2016.

[16] SEMrush, http://www.semrush.com.

[17] N. Booth and J. A. Matic, "Mapping and Leveraging Influencers in Social Media to Shape Corporate Brand Perceptions," *Corporate Communications: An International Journal,* vol. 16, no. 3, pp. 184–191, 2011.

[18] K. Kaye, "Mobile Tracking Drives Consumer Data to Mazda," *Advertising Age,* 5 December 2013.

[19] E. Schultz, "Who's Winning the Greek-Yogurt 'Revolution'?" *Advertising Age CMO Strategy,* 6 June 2012.

[20] D. Natzke, "Chobani Founder Shares Personal, Yogurt Company Story," *Dairy Business,* 22 March 2012.

[21] J. Dudlicek, "Growing a Culture," *Progressive Grocer,* 2012.

[22] Simmons OneView, "Spring 2009 Adult Survey—12 Months," 2009.

[23] T. Forbes, "Chobani Expanding Its Battles on Multiple Fronts," *Media Post,* 21 April 2014.

[24] Crimson Hexagon, "Chobani: Brand Audit, Brand User Behavior, and Campaign Analysis," 2015.

[25] S. O'Holleran, "Chobani Announces Global Expansion, New US Product Innovations," *Food Engineering,* 29 April 2014.

© Shutterstock/Ariwasabi

CHAPTER FOUR

RETHINKING CONSUMPTION

Consumers have become multitasking multidevice operators who have access to real-time product and pricing information for purchase decisions. Consumption patterns are changing and affect the process through which consumers travel on their way to final purchase. As such, marketers must alter the way they examine consumer behavior patterns, media consumption, and postpurchase processes. As consumers adopt new social networking sites, their power in market situations grows. This chapter discusses research in consumption and the evolving purchase decision process, and applies that knowledge to consumer behavior in social and mobile marketing.

LEARNING OBJECTIVES

After reading this chapter, you will be able to:

- IDENTIFY CONSUMER INSIGHTS FROM INFORMATION.

- DEVELOP AND CONSIDER HYPOTHESES OF CHANGING CONSUMPTION PATTERNS.

- OUTLINE THE PURCHASE DECISION PROCESS AS INFLUENCED BY NEW TECHNOLOGIES.

- LEARN THE DOMINANT COMMUNICATIONS METHOD BY SOCIAL AND MOBILE MEDIA.

- EXAMINE WORD-OF-MOUTH COMMUNICATIONS THROUGH OPINION LEADERS.

- MONITOR THE PRODUCT LIFECYCLE FOR SOCIAL MEDIA AND MOBILE TECHNOLOGY.

Some people refer to the Apple iPad as just a big iPhone. Do you agree? The apps available on the iPhone and iPad are almost the same, each has photo and video capability, and both are fairly portable. So, why is more shopping taking place on the iPad than on the iPhone?

Consumers treat their tablets differently from smartphones and laptops, using them for gaming, entertainment, and social activities. People on tablets are also using the device while engaging in other activities, such as eating, listening to music, and cooking [1]. Ninety percent of tablet owners report multitasking when using their tablets at least once a week, and 40% of the time people spend on their tablets, they are also doing something else [2].

A marketer's ability to extract consumption patterns from consumer behavior and predict future purchases is sometimes referred to as **insight**. In the case of tablet devices, usage data can help illuminate insights that marketers consider to develop effective strategies. Exhibit 4.1 shows the secondary activities of people when using their tablet devices [1]. Can you think of a marketer who might be interested in these data?

consider this . . .

MILLENNIALS WATCH AND TWEET

What else are you doing when you watch television? Millennials are much more likely to be emailing, texting, and using social media than other groups while watching TV, presenting an opportunity for shows and their advertisers. Viewers "check in" to shows using location-based services and tweet comments that can be as engaging as the shows. The tactic of promoting content engagement in social media and mobile may help broadcast networks hold viewers during commercial breaks, a major benefit to advertisers. For live events like the Super Bowl, there is an average of 87k tweets per minute and hundreds of thousands of tweets about the ads [3].

Television Shows with High Nielsen Twitter Ratings

Billboard Music Awards

Grey's Anatomy

Empire

Game of Thrones

WWE Monday Night Raw

NBA Basketball

The Voice

Can you believe he said that?

EXHIBIT 4.1

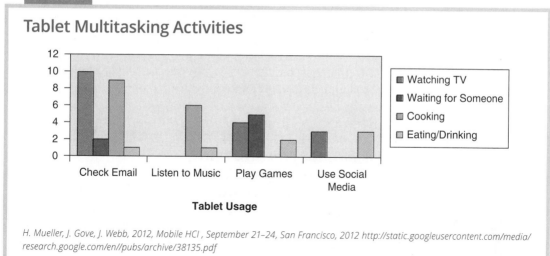

Tablet Multitasking Activities

Tablet Usage

H. Mueller, J. Gove, J. Webb, 2012, Mobile HCI , September 21–24, San Francisco, 2012 http://static.googleusercontent.com/media/research.google.com/en//pubs/archive/38135.pdf

Marketers can use the insights from multitasking to develop strategies to communicate with customers. One insight gleaned from tablet usage is that consumers spend more money when shopping on tablets than smartphones. Tablet users spend almost twice as much per purchase as do shoppers on smartphones [4].

What do you think might explain the differences in spending levels? Marketers formulate testable hypotheses to help explain why consumers behave in particular ways (a hypothesis is a "tentative assumption made in order to draw out and test its logical or empirical consequences" [5]). What are your hypotheses as to why more spending takes place on a tablet than a cell phone?

1. _____

2. _____

3. _____

Sometimes, marketers make assumptions about why consumers behave in particular ways, but it is important to research the reasons behind the actions so that we can understand why people respond to marketing stimuli. Adobe analyzed 16 billion visits to websites of over 150 retailers to determine spending differences. The researchers hypothesized that tablet buyers were a wealthy demographic with high incomes, which could lead to more spending. Another reason might be that tablets offer a richer purchase experience due to the size of the screen. Finally, because tablets are fun, consumers might be excited to try shopping with them, thereby spending more money [4].

consider this . . .

AFFLUENT BUYERS USE MOBILE FOR SHOPPING

Do you need more evidence that purchase behavior differs between tablets and smartphones? One study of affluent shoppers found that smartphones were the preferred method for searching for in-store information, looking up products on the go, and comparing in-store prices, while tablets were better for viewing product information and reading user reviews [6].

THE MULTIMEDIA MULTITASKING CONSUMER

Consumers' relationships with media have already changed with lower newspaper and magazine readership, more mobile engagement, and increasing time-shifted television consumption. There are over 2.55 billion social network users worldwide, representing more than one-quarter of the world's population, and 35% of online adults use social networks at least once a month [7]. Approximately 70% of the global population has mobile phones and a quarter of the world's population owns smartphones [8].

Social media and mobile phone usage have contributed to changing media and consumption behavior. Individuals spend increasingly more time with devices including smartphones and tablets and use these devices for connecting with friends and family through social networks. These new forms of **word-of-mouth communications (WOM)** can spread information faster and further than ever before, leading to opportunities and threats for marketers. For example, Rotten Tomatoes is an entertainment blog featuring movies and television shows. The screenshot here shows a series of reviews written by moviegoers on the site.

Marketers have many opportunities to connect with customers and consumers interact with others who may influence their purchase behavior. This one-to-one and one-to-many set of opportunities for communications complicates the messages that feed into the consumer decision-making process. New media properties also

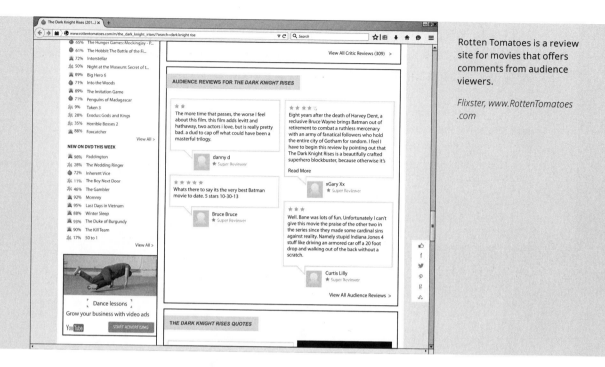

contribute to the amount of data marketers must learn to manage. The environment has become very complex and fragmented. Consumers are interacting with many new forms of media, and marketers are struggling to target the best prospects, reach them through the clutter, and influence their purchase behavior. Then, to complicate matters further, marketers must measure the outcomes of their efforts to reach consumers.

Both new technologies and the variety of media outlets have altered the paths consumers take to purchase. Marketers are very interested in how consumers first consider a purchase and the steps they take as they evaluate options. The path consumers take to purchase is sometimes called the **purchase decision process**, the purchase funnel, or the consumer journey. Whereas the purchase decision process examines buying behavior from the perspective of customers, the **purchase funnel** is from the marketer's view. Specifically, the funnel represents the goals the marketer wants to achieve in moving the consumer down the path toward purchase. For example, the first stage of the purchase decision process is **problem recognition** (or **need recognition**), which takes place in the mind of the consumer when he or she recognizes an unmet need. The marketer can influence the purchase decision process by using social media or mobile strategies. One marketer that uses this strategy is Starbucks, which sends messages to mobile phones as people pass store locations to spark the desire for a coffee drink.

HOW WELL DO PEOPLE MULTITASK?

The answer is that it depends what you mean by multitask. **Multitasking** implies that individuals are doing two tasks at the same time, but in reality often people are running a series of tasks sequentially. The various distractions that compete for attention differ in their interference levels. For instance, you may be able to listen to music while working out at the gym, but unable to study for a difficult exam while playing a video game. Constantly moving between tasks requires the ability to juggle, and by going from task to task, you pay a price in terms of total time spent on the activities. The juggling itself takes time, but some people may be better at the act of juggling multiple tasks than others and practice in multitasking may improve the skill [9].

SOCIAL MEDIA AND MOBILE TECHNOLOGY IN THE CONSUMER DECISION-MAKING PROCESS

Social media and mobile marketing could influence a consumer at any stage of the purchase decision process. For example, a consumer may ultimately purchase a pair of shoes in a store, but was perhaps exposed to all of the following before buying them: television commercials, magazine articles, Facebook posts of friends, media coverage of Fashion Week in New York City, results of an online search, mobile banner advertising, websites of products, and reviews of products online and from friends.

THE PURCHASE FUNNEL AND THE PURCHASE DECISION PROCESS

Marketers graphically depict the purchase decision as a funnel because the bottom section represents a large group of consumers who may experience problem recognition, but a smaller percentage who actually make a purchase toward the top of the funnel. Though the stages of the purchase decision process in the new media environment remain the same, social media and mobile marketing affect each aspect of the purchase decision in profound ways. The purchase decision process consists of five stages: problem recognition, information search, alternative evaluation, purchase, and postpurchase processes.

The purchase funnel uses terms that represent the value of the consumer to the marketer. As such, the purchase decision process is more customer-centric and serves as a good model for understanding how consumers move toward a purchase. Exhibit 4.2 defines the stages in the process and shows them from both the consumer's and marketer's perspectives.

EXHIBIT 4.2

The Purchase Decision Process and the Purchase Funnel

PURCHASE DECISION PROCESS STAGE	CONSUMER ACTION AND MARKETER GOAL	PURCHASE FUNNEL STAGE
Problem recognition	The consumer notices that his or her actual situation differs from an ideal situation that would occur after obtaining a desired product or service. The marketer draws attention to the brand through promotional methods.	Awareness
Information search	The consumer begins by conducting an internal memory search for information related to the need identified and may continue to search external sources for information regarding a purchase. The marketer attempts to build interest and become part of the consumer's consideration set.	Interest/ consideration
Alternative evaluation	The purchaser reviews the various product and brands based on their attributes and determines the best set of brands from which to choose. The marketer convinces the consumer to purchase the product or service.	Intention/ conviction
Purchase	Using a decision rule or heuristic, the consumer chooses a brand and an appropriate outlet for purchase. The consumer executes the purchase transaction and the marketer generates revenue.	Action/ purchase
Postpurchase behavior	After purchase the buyer evaluates his or her satisfaction with the product or service purchased and judges it based on previously determined expectations of performance. The marketer solidifies the relationships and encourages positive word of mouth.	Loyalty/ positive word of mouth

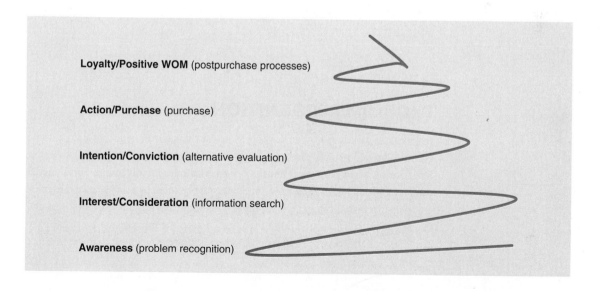

Loyalty/Positive WOM (postpurchase processes)

Action/Purchase (purchase)

Intention/Conviction (alternative evaluation)

Interest/Consideration (information search)

Awareness (problem recognition)

Consumers with significant motivation begin the process and move through the various stages, sometimes completing the process with a purchase and sometimes abandoning the purchase, often to the dismay of marketers. Consumers with high levels of involvement with a purchase decision spend more time and effort, examine more information, and evaluate more alternatives than individuals who are less involved in the process [10]. Social media and mobile can each help marketers retain consumers through the stages of the process, resulting in more purchase behavior. Kohl's loyalty program is built into its mobile application so that customers can easily take advantage of rewards. Customers participating in Kohl's loyalty program made two additional yearly visits to the store and spent an additional $80 a year at Kohl's [11].

consider this . . .

MOBILE BANKING APPLICATIONS

Consider the decision to adopt mobile banking on a smartphone. A relatively small proportion of American consumers use a mobile phone for banking activities. In order for the consumer to begin using a mobile app for banking, he or she must decide that having a mobile banking system would be preferable to his or her current situation of not having access to mobile banking. Once the consumer notices that his or her actual situation differs from the ideal, that person may seek information to solve the problem, but only if the problem is more important than other problems at a particular moment in time. The next step is to search for information to determine whether or not the bank offers mobile banking and to then assess such information in terms of risks. A recent study found that 33% of consumers did not know how secure their mobile banking system was and an additional 33% did not trust the mobile banking technology [12]. As a result, whereas most banks (84%) offer mobile banking services, only 33% of customers use those services over a twelve-month period [13].

PROBLEM RECOGNITION

Individuals are constantly processing events in the environment that may at some point lead to a purchase. The term for when a consumer monitors product category information when he or she is not shopping is **enduring involvement**. Social media can play a strong role in influencing enduring involvement by providing an outlet for engagement with a brand. For example, DC Universe hosts a Facebook Official Game Page that has around 800,000 likes. To keep the interest of players, the page offers photos, contests, tournaments, and opportunities to choose character outfits.

Problem recognition under enduring involvement may occur quickly and lead to a purchase more immediately than when consumers must search for the information at the time of purchase. In this case, mobile marketing may influence the purchase decision process. For example, a consumer evaluating products on the shelf may use a cell phone to access product reviews in the store. A scan-able code could direct customers to store-generated marketing materials, or in-store couponing could be used to compel a consumer to purchase the product immediately, rather than waiting and accessing more reviews of it. Sephora connects customers to product reviews using in-store codes and drives consumers to a loyalty application on mobile devices. As a result of this effort, mobile orders increased 167% and mobile traffic shot up 75% year over year [14].

INFORMATION SEARCH AND ALTERNATIVE EVALUATION

Consumers search for information for products and services in new and varied ways. Influence within the purchase funnel has expanded to include online properties, such as websites; social media, such as Facebook and Yelp; and messaging services, such as Snapchat—all enhance the opportunities for consumers to collect information about products and brands.

Social media and mobile marketing can provide consumers with unique types of information as part of the purchase decision process. With the Qloo app you get recommendations on things you like. The app can advise you in 8 categories including movies, dining, books and travel [15].

Consumers typically seek certain types of information to determine how and what to purchase. The information includes:

- What are the relevant attributes in the purchase/adoption?
- Which brands are available and of interest?
- Which outlets carry the product or service?
- How does each brand perform on each attribute?

Sometimes, it is easy for the consumer to collect and evaluate information about a purchase prior to consumption or usage. This type of attribute is called a search attribute. **Search attributes** are often factual pieces of information available from the marketer, such as the price of an application for the iPhone purchased via iTunes. **Experience attributes** are those that the consumer can only evaluate after using the product or service. An example would be the customer's enjoyment of a song from a new artist purchased through iTunes.

e-readers have search, experience, and credence attributes.

© Shutterstock/Bloomua

Exhibit 4.3 lists some search and experience attributes for e-readers. But not all attributes are identifiable prior to purchase or even after the product has been consumed. Sometimes, using the product or service provides no more insight as to whether the product performed on a particular attribute. For example, with an e-reader, the consumer can never know the effect of radiation from the screen on his or her health. The types of attributes that can never be evaluated by the consumer are referred to as **credence attributes.** Marketers do not typically discuss the negative impact of their products until the information becomes public. However, brand managers can embellish positive credence attributes because consumers are never able to evaluate them, so there is no risk of performance failure. Perhaps Amazon can suggest to Kindle users that they will grow smarter by using the Kindle app?

consider this . . .

EVALUATING SEARCH AND EXPERIENCE ATTRIBUTES

When consumers are online evaluating products, they use different strategies for collecting information. In the case of search attributes, the consumer uses a strategy evaluating many webpages for limited amounts of time. For experience attributes, the consumer does a more in-depth search on each webpage viewed, but visits fewer pages overall. The implication for social media is that marketers have the opportunity with experience attributes to engage the consumer with the brand, using social media tools to help consumers decide. For instance, movie clips on YouTube or on a movie's Facebook page can help consumers evaluate their potential level of enjoyment. In mobile marketing, managers have an opportunity when selling experience attributes to provide fast-loading mobile information that can be deeply examined at the time of purchase [16]. Consumers also differ in how they respond to recommendations on experience and credence attributes. Individuals believe both positive and negative reviews from those with whom they have close relationships for experience attributes, but focus on the negative reviews from friends for credence attributes [17].

EXHIBIT 4.3

Search and Experience Attributes for e-readers

SEARCH ATTRIBUTES OF AN E-READER	EXPERIENCE ATTRIBUTES OF AN E-READER
Price of the reader and materials (such as books and magazines)	Reading comfort
Screen size, weight, and color	Satisfaction with e-reading over time
Items available in the library	Satisfaction with features, lighting, size, and weight

PURCHASE AND POSTPURCHASE PROCESSES

Consumer purchase patterns have changed significantly as consumers adopt new methods for completing transactions. Online shopping is expected to top 3.5 trillion dollars in 2020, representing almost 13% of total retail sales according to eMarketer [18]. M-commerce sales are expected to reach $242.08 million by 2020, but will represent less than 5% of total retail sales [18]. In any case, purchase patterns and behaviors are changing, leading marketers to use new methods to help complete transactions. For instance, Carrefour discovered that consumers engage in meal planning throughout the day and on different devices, so it integrated all platforms to record shopping lists from any device and view the lists in-store at the time of purchase [19].

The purchase decision process does not end until well after the consumer buys and uses the product. In fact, disposal of the product is also part of the purchase decision process. Social media provide consumers with outlets for selling and buying products that they no longer want or need, but would like to pass on to someone else. Online marketplaces like Alibaba, eBay, or Craigslist provide these opportunities for strangers to connect through social commerce.

After the purchase, consumers evaluate their satisfaction with products and services. The opportunity to share positive and negative reactions has grown considerably and marketers must concern themselves with the factors that lead to negative word-of-mouth behavior online. Most online marketplaces provide the opportunity for people to review products, adding value to the purchase process.

ATTRIBUTION IN THE PURCHASE PROCESS

Attribution refers to determining which factors contributed at some point in the journey to a consumer's decision to make a purchase. Attributions can be clear when all the touchpoints are digital, such as website visits or search behavior. However, it is much more difficult for marketers to determine attributions when a visit to a store is part of the mix or a radio ad contributes to a consumer's purchase process. Marketers do have ways to account for real-life events by mapping the schedule of events in real time and matching outcomes to the timing of the events. For example, if sales of eco water bottles in Boston spike after a green marketing event on the Common, some percentage of attribution would be applied to the event. New services also provide more information about consumers' off-line behavior because companies such as Acxiom match consumers based on the email addresses they provide to retailers through their LiveRamp service.

Google is also very involved in determining attributions and provides a tool for examining consumer actions prior to purchase; it is called Customer Journey to Online Purchase. The tool allows one to enter an industry and country

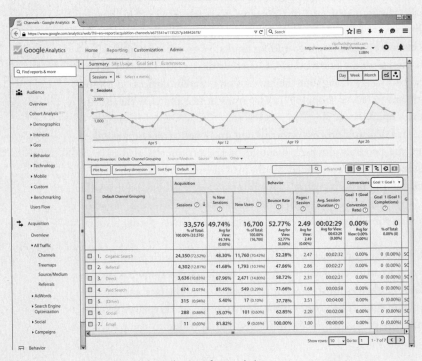

Google Analytics shows last click attributions for a website.

Google Analytics, www.google.com/analytics

and see attributions for email, paid search, social, direct hits, and referrals. The screenshot of Google Analytics shows where a visitor last clicked before coming to the page. In this case, most of the 31,373 visitors to the website came from searching on a search engine by typing keywords into the search bar. Others came by typing the URL into the search bar (direct), and still others were referred from other sites and social media.

GROUP INFLUENCE IN SOCIAL AND MOBILE NETWORKS

Human beings are designed for communication and community. We choose to live together in cities, interact, and relate with one another on many levels. With social networking, individuals are not limited by their geography to connect to like-minded others. These groups or tribes to which we belong influence our purchase behavior and provide us with outlets for entertainment, sharing, and community. Exhibit 4.4 shows some examples of social communities that are aimed at narrow targets, but are not geography-dependent.

Groups exert different types of influence on individuals even within social networks. The influence is greater when members of the group have regular casual contact than when contact is sporadic and more formal. Social networks are a degree removed from face-to-face contact and, all else being equal, should influence individuals less than groups with whom an individual interacts in person.

EXHIBIT 4.4

Highly Targeted Social Networking Sites

SOCIAL NETWORK	DESCRIPTION
Hi5	A social gaming network for creating profiles, communicating, and playing games with other gamers. The network says it exists for meeting new people.
WriteAPrisoner	Connects people with inmates for letter writing as pen pals.
weRead	Community of readers who share favorite books, write ratings and reviews, and take quizzes.
PonySquare	A role-playing site for people (adults, too) who like graphic depictions of ponies, including the toy My Little Pony. Men who are into this are called Bronies.
Elftown	The fantasy and science fiction community members post profiles and share ideas.

Social networks can affect normative behavior, acceptable and unacceptable actions members of the group are permitted to take based on group norms. For example, it is impolite to post in all caps on many social networks, and others sometimes refer to such posts as "screaming." Groups also influence individuals in a value-expressive way, which represents a person's desire to fit in with the group by engaging in certain behaviors. The mobile application Swarm is used by people to connect with friends in the real world. The app, formerly part of Foursquare, allows friends to duel to become the "mayor" of a location and earn stickers. This friendly game is a value-expressive way of connecting with a group. It shows a person's membership in and commitment to the group.

Marketers are particularly interested in the third type of group influence, informational. **Informational group influence** occurs when members share ideas, thoughts, attitudes, and beliefs with one another, sometimes with regard to products or services. Social media enhance the ability of group members to communicate with one another and provide nonmembers the opportunity to view group content. Some social media sites are designed explicitly for product and service reviews, such as Yelp or Angie's List, while others act as a conduit for reviews, whether intended for that purpose or not, such as Facebook or Twitter. Many retail sites also provide opportunities to review products, such as Amazon.com or Overstock.com. Informal networks can affect brand strategy. For example, researchers have examined how Twitter users engage in word of mouth about movies and the result on movie attendance. The findings suggest that there is a strong effect on box office receipts following both positive and negative tweets immediately after a movie's release and lasting weeks past the opening [20].

Consumers have more power in their relationships with marketers than ever. Rather than passively await marketer communications, consumers now develop their own content, critique marketing strategies, and communicate their satisfaction and dissatisfaction to wide networks of friends, family, and strangers. It is lucky for marketers that much of the content is positive. A study analyzing Twitter posts found that over 50% of brand-related posts were positive, whereas only 33% were negative [21].

Content development by consumers is not always positive. When Chevy Tahoe posted advertising images and music for consumers to develop advertising for the SUV, some consumers chose to highlight an environmental message. One ad on YouTube featured the following copy:

> We paved the prairies
> Deforested the hills
> We strip mined our mountains
> And sold ourselves for oil
> To bring you this beautiful machine
> So you can finally drive
> To see what's left of our wilderness

Along with the Chevy Tahoe brand label and symbol, it was displayed prominently on YouTube.

On the other hand, Doritos's annual "Crash the Super Bowl" campaign asks consumers to develop ads that will run during the big game, and many such ads have ranked at the top of the *USA Today* Ad Meter, an unofficial measure of the ads that viewers like. The key is the appropriate management of consumer content, so the brand can benefit from the positive and avoid the negative. Doritos accepts submissions, posts the best ones online, and generates significant page views and viral sharing [22].

consider this . . .

DON'T CLICK ON THAT!

Marketers have to concern themselves with how consumers may respond in social media and be prepared to manage negative sentiment. One interesting feature of negative company information is that one of the drivers of the information is the company employees themselves. When negative news is broadcast online and on social media, the people most responsible for spreading the information and generating higher rankings in search are the company employees who want to read about company dirt. A strategy for managing the crisis would be to instruct employees to avoid clicks on negative information by providing a safe place to air company dirty laundry.

SOCIAL COMMUNICATIONS AND MARKETER INSIGHTS

How often do you participate in social media conversations? You can measure your own personal contribution by signing up on Klout and looking at your Klout score. Online environments present opportunities to track individuals' communications streams and their subsequent influence. A number of services rank people and brands based on their impact in social networks or monitor online conversations to measure buzz. Marketers can now determine which individuals generate the most conversations for a brand and use this knowledge to build relationships with them via social media. If a marketer sees that you are really influential, they can offer you incentives to share with your network. You may be an opinion leader and not even know it.

Marketers have long recognized the value of reaching out to opinion leaders who may be conduits of information to consumers. The **two-step flow of communications** [23], a theory developed in the late 1950s, suggests that ideas from media may reach people through opinion leaders, who may be in a position to influence attitudes. The theory is especially relevant today as the media environment is so fragmented, and reaching people through the clutter is difficult. The notion of communicating via a select few who are highly influential is very attractive to marketers as social groups tend to have some more vocal individuals who share more than others. One research study of Twitter found that people who were more extroverted tended to tweet words such as "bar," "restaurant," and "crowd," while those who were labeled as neurotic more likely tweeted "awful," "lazy," and "depressing." The implication for marketing strategy is that some people may be more effectively influential for a brand than others [24].

consider this . . .

DOCTORS USE SOCIAL MEDIA

The pharmaceutical industry has long relied on doctors to communicate drug information to consumers. A study in the *Journal of Medical and Internet Research* found that 25% of physicians use social media daily for medical information. More than half of the physicians surveyed indicated they found social media beneficial in providing high-quality information and 60% said it improved patient care.

The **basic communications model** involves a source who encodes a message, which is sent through a medium to receivers who decode the message. A simple communications model features two-way communication and feedback to the originator of the message. The traditional communications model includes one-to-many communications in mass media that may occur when the marketer encodes a message in the form of a television commercial and the audience views the message on television. The feedback loop closes when the consumer buys the product, contacts the company, or responds to a survey, though it is difficult for the marketer to determine the origin of the response. Unlike traditional media, social and mobile media can operate as one-to-one, one-to-many, and many-to-many forms of communication between and among marketers and consumers.

EXHIBIT 4.5

Dominant Means of Communication by Medium

	ONE-TO-ONE	ONE-TO-MANY	MANY-TO-MANY
Social networks (Facebook, Twitter)			√
Social coupons (GroupOn, Living Social)		√	
Social encyclopedia (Wikipedia)			√
Social bookmarking (Stumble Upon or Reddit)			√
Mobile SMS (text messaging)	√		
Mobile apps		√	
Mobile websites		√	

FORMS OF COMMUNICATION

Exhibit 4.5 represents social media and mobile properties and the dominant communications system operating among consumer audiences. The form of communication influences marketer strategy. When marketers communicate in the one-to-many category, they have more opportunity to control the message. For example, social couponing sites design the offerings with local businesses without direct consumer input. Even within social networks, there are differences in communications options. Twitter tends to be more of a broadcast medium than Facebook, which offers more engagement opportunities.

In social and mobile properties operating in the one-to-one dominant sphere, the marketer communicates with individuals and receives direct responses. For example, marketers can send SMS texts to customers who must opt in to receive the texts. Such customers are likely highly involved with a brand to elect to receive texts. A marketer must return the favor by abiding by the rules of the game, which include double opt-in and no more messages when the customer types and returns the word "STOP." An SMS campaign is inherently a one-to-many communication and similar to Twitter. That's why Twitter, with a maximum of 140 characters, is often called a **short message service (SMS)**. Similarly mobile apps are one-to-many communication unless the app is specifically designed to be social. Mobile webpages are also one-to-many as many customers may access a mobile site and share the same message.

AND I MEAN STOP!

Two California residents sued Twitter for sending a confirmatory text after the pair had replied STOP to an SMS. According to the plaintiffs, the STOP should have indicated to Twitter to automatically turn off all notifications. The lawsuit was brought as a violation of the Telephone Consumer Protection Act of 1991 [25]. However, the marketers won the suit and are now allowed to return a confirmation.

In **many-to-many communications,** consumers interact with one another to both the benefit and detriment of a brand. Some firms allow open communications on their Facebook pages, while others use the Facebook Admin Panel to control content. In either case, a marketer must consider the degree of tolerance for free-flowing communications, recognizing there are other outlets for customer complaints that may be harder to address elsewhere. For example, a consumer can easily post a review on Yelp or Amazon.com about a product or service. In this case, the marketer has no ability to control the comments once the review is posted. However, if the consumer posts a complaint on the brand's Facebook page, the marketer can address the problem and delete the post.

SOCIAL WORD OF MOUTH

Social networks now play an important role in disseminating information among consumers who may or may not know each other. Potential customers examine review sites prior to purchase, and many access location-specific information to find retailers of products or services. Social media are a form of word-of-mouth communication that can provide information related to a purchase decision. Word-of-mouth marketing, also known as buzz, guerilla marketing, or viral marketing, occurs when marketers intentionally influence communications between and among consumers [26]. These marketer-generated online communications are further influenced by the context in which the communication is viewed by consumers. For example, consumers who are exposed to advertising during violent programming have poorer memory for the ads than those who view the ads embedded in neutral programming [27]. People exposed to social networks vary their emotional states when exposed to positive versus negative information on their newsfeeds. A study of 600,000 Facebook users found that a group who saw fewer positive expressions produced fewer positive posts themselves, and those who were exposed to more negative expressions posted more negatively. The results suggest that social networks can pass on emotional responses [28].

THE INFLUENCE OF BLOGGERS ON CONSUMERS

Researchers studied ninety bloggers who were seeded with information about a new mobile phone. Eighty-four percent of the bloggers mentioned the phone in their blog, though they were not required to do so. The responses of the blog readers differed, depending on the character of the blogger, the types of messages, and the transparency of the communication. The response was hostile to both the communication and the blogger when there was an attempt to conceal the marketing aspect of the message and the emphasis was on the product in a communal setting [26]. Consumers admit that the opinions of friends, family, and others (in contrast to direct advertising) influence their behavior, magnifying the value of positive word-of-mouth communications to marketers. Sometimes, marketers can fool customers and not engender anger. For instance, Budweiser posted videos on YouTube of customers who had been told that the beer they were drinking was a high-end premium brand when it was Budweiser [29].

Early studies of word-of-mouth communications suggested that an elite group of influencers controlled such communications; however, the social Web allows for more communication across populations and more moderately connected individuals are influencing others more than in the past. Because consumers may provide value in their ability to influence, marketers have developed a new measure called "connected customer lifetime value," which considers that a consumer's contributions to a firm's bottom line might be enhanced through his or her social networks [30]. Connected consumers serve as opinion leaders who may influence the purchase behavior of others. People who influence tend to share the demographics of those whom they convince, but often have an elevated status when it comes to knowledge regarding a particular product or service.

CONNECTED MOMMIES

Motherhood is a time when an individual's shopping patterns and behaviors change significantly. Moms in the United States spend sixty-six hours per month online, more than twice as much as the general public, and they are 38% more likely to own a smartphone. Checking Facebook more than 10 times a day, moms can really influence one another [31].

By building relationships with customers, marketers can become part of connected customers' lives and their influence can reach beyond the individual. Consumers recognize when marketing communications are driven by firms with an ultimate goal to influence purchase behavior. Therefore, they tend to trust marketers less than friends and family whom they believe have a greater interest in their well-being.

Social networking tends to take place among and between friends and family members. A study by Pew Internet Research found that friends and family are the most common connections on Facebook [32]. The people with whom individuals connect on Facebook are friends they had in high school (22%), extended family members (12%), coworkers (10%), college friends (9%), immediate family members (8%), friends from volunteer activities (7%), and neighbors (2%). The average Facebook user has over 300 friends who are more likely to influence them than direct messages from marketers [33]. That's why Facebook developed sponsored stories, advertisements that feature Facebook users who "like" products aimed at their own friends.

consider this . . .

FACEBOOK ETIQUETTE?

Facebook users indicate that they dislike the following behaviors most: people sharing too much about themselves, others posting about them without their permission, others seeing posts they were not meant to see, and feeling tempted to post or share more about themselves than they want. Only 5% of Facebook users admit that they log on for "FOMO" or fear of missing out [33].

VIRAL MARKETING STRATEGY

Viral marketing is a type of word-of-mouth communication taking place among individuals on the Web and connected through social networks. Typically, a marketer will start the campaign hoping to build buzz and sharing through a population. Some research on email marketing suggests that people like to pass positive, happy, and enjoyable information to others as well as information about safety and security. These kinds of communications build loyalty and positive feelings among members of a social network for a shared sense of meaning and connection.

What makes people pass along communications in the first place? According to one study [34], there are a variety of reasons:

"It's fun."

"I enjoy it."

"It's entertaining."

"It helps people."

"To let people know I care."

Viral mavens, people who pass along a lot of communications, feel particularly good about sending messages and perceive a reward in doing so. Friends who open viral communications also feel good about receiving communications to stay in touch with the sender. Receivers open such communications when they know the sender and are curious as to what has been sent.

According to the literature, communications are most likely to pass on when there is contact between the parties, the source of the message is credible or favorable to followers, influencers provide useful feedback to reduce the risk to followers, there is some status competition that leads people to adopt to fit in, and social norms support adoption [35]. The second most retweeted tweet is one written by One Direction member Louis Tomlinson: "Always in my heart @Harry_Styles. Yours Sincerely, Louis." It has been retweeted over 700,000 times by One Direction fans [36].

Viral marketing campaigns are very difficult to create because it is impossible to determine the type of message that is likely to go viral. In addition, the message has to be brand-related and appropriate or the marketer risks alienating the customer. There have been a number of very successful viral campaigns and *Advertising Age* tracks the top viral campaigns weekly and annually. The best ones are shared, but also have strong brand meaning that resonates with the target and leads to purchase. For example, one of the most viral campaigns of all time is Blendtec's "Will It Blend" series. Tom Dickson, the company founder, blends various items to demonstrate the power of the blender. He has blended household items and products from major corporations, including the iPad, McDonald's Big Macs, Justin Bieber CDs, and dolls. The viral videos created in-house have generated over 173 million views [37] and Dickson attests to their success in driving sales. The videos are effective because they show the product as the star emphasizing the power of the blender.

SOCIAL MEDIA AND MOBILE TECHNOLOGY ADOPTION

Think about the last time you bought a fashion item. What motivated you to purchase it? There were probably many factors, but emerging social trends, like new products, diffuse through a population following a pattern. We can examine how consumers adopt new social networks and to what extent social connections influence behavior and responses within and between groups of people by examining the adoption process for new products and services. The process also explains how people adopt new mobile technologies and why some happen faster than others, such as mobile games versus mobile banking.

As with all new market entries, both social media and mobile marketing technologies go through an adoption process when individuals begin to purchase or use them. The process can help marketers develop strategies that match the timing of sales and competitive entries into the market. The earliest adopters of new technologies are called **innovators**. These risk-taking individuals adopt new technologies early and are less concerned than other customers with potential negatives that might arise. For example, Vine, the six-second video site owned by Twitter, was made popular by a group of early innovators who were 18 to 24 years old and somewhat more likely to be female [38].

When a target market is technologically savvy, enjoys interacting on social media, and communicates regularly in mobile, marketers should approach it with cutting-edge technologies. Interestingly, an increasing number of consumers trying to find the next cool new thing have joined the race to be early technology adopters [39].

Marketing managers can use technology as a signal to consumers about their brand's technological prowess. Teens are notorious early technology adopters and often move from one social network to the next. Marketers can attract teens by communicating with them using these new platforms. For example, McDonald's and Taco Bell were early users of Snapchat. Even a brand like Band-Aid aimed at children has embraced cutting-edge technology. Band-Aid developed a free app for iPhone and iPad featuring the Muppets. When the app scans a Band-Aid on a child's knee, Kermit the Frog says, "Feeling blue? Not for long, because we're going to have a singalong." He then sings "Rainbow Connection." The effort by Johnson & Johnson was introduced to develop a distinctive advantage over store brands [40].

Opinion leaders, as discussed in Chapter Two, are different from innovators because opinion leaders are more likely to influence the purchases of others. Innovators tend to be on the cutting edge of new technologies and may be inclined to move on to the next cool thing when average people adopt the product. Opinion leaders tend to be more stable, interested in a particular topic or product category, and enjoy interacting and discussing their likes and dislikes with others. They are more socially connected than innovators and are particularly important to marketers [41]. Whereas innovators are adopting new social media sites, opinion leaders pick a site and interact with friends and family there without the need to find the latest and coolest.

THE PRODUCT LIFECYCLE FOR BRANDS CONSIDERING SOCIAL AND MOBILE STRATEGIES

Marketers have long studied the **product lifecycle** to provide information on how products disseminate through a population. The product lifecycle is a graphic representation of a product's sales over time and the stages through which a product passes over its lifespan. The graph at introduction begins sloping slowly upward, then enters a stage of strong growth, levels off in the maturity stage, and may eventually enter the decline stage. The Facebook adoption curve resembles a curved hockey stick and many new entrants into social media have seen rapid growth.

While it is clear that Facebook should consider analyzing the adoption of its network by consumers, other companies and brands should be aware of Facebook's adoption levels over time as well. Marketers make investments in time, content, and information on Facebook and the future prospects for the network affect their businesses. Some social networks may be fads. A **fad** is a product or service that gains strong momentum early in a product's lifecycle by growing very quickly and then dropping off in sales almost as fast.

Several years ago, many companies spent a lot of money building their presence in Second Life, a virtual world where people represented themselves as avatars and interacted with one another. The service was introduced in 2003, but by 2007 there were reports that Second Life was a ghost town and companies were wasting their money on the site [42]. Some of the companies that spent money in Second Life were Coke, Yahoo, Adidas, H&R Block, and Sears. Should Facebook and marketers building extensive pages on Facebook be worried? Maybe, almost half of Americans think Facebook is a fad [43].

The chart in Exhibit 4.6 represents Facebook's adoption curve. The curve moves steeply upward starting in 2009 as more and more individuals join the network [44]. The traditional product lifecycle chart (Exhibit 4.7) shows a growth stage with rapidly rising adoption. If the product lifecycle can predict adoption, we might hypothesize that Facebook's adoption levels would eventually level off and perhaps decline. What is Facebook's global adoption level today?

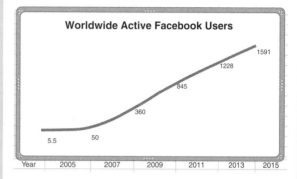

EXHIBIT 4.6

Facebook Worldwide Adoption (millions of monthly users)

Worldwide Active Facebook Users

Statista 2015, Number of Active Monthly Facebook Users Worldwide as of the Fourth Quarter of 2015, http://www.statista.com/statistics/264810/number-of-monthly-active-facebook-users-worldwide/

consider this...

DOES THE PRODUCT LIFECYCLE REALLY REPRESENT A BRAND'S LIFE?

The product lifecycle is only a guide and researchers have not determined definite time periods for lifecycle events. For example, products or services in the decline stage may be rejuvenated by firms as marketing does not operate in the same manner as the biological world, nor do the stages fit a set time frame as human aging does. Most of the research is qualitative in nature, but does provide a means of analysis potentially useful to marketers.

EXHIBIT 4.7

A More Traditional Product Lifecycle

Traditional Product Lifecycle

	2007	2009	2011	2013	2015
	Introduction	Growth	Early Maturity	Late Maturity	Decline

EXHIBIT 4.8

Cost–Benefit Analysis to Adopt *New York Times* Digital Access

COSTS	BENEFITS
Price of monthly service at $35	Ability to get news anywhere
Time to download the app	Views on various devices for varied usage situations
Time to learn the features of the app	Access to digital links
Altered reading experience	Ability to store favorites and bookmark
Requires storage space on a device	Reducing overall paper usage and need to recycle newspapers

Potential customers seeking new products may engage in a simple cost/benefit analysis as shown in Exhibit 4.8 to determine whether to adopt a new product. However, consumer behavior is also influenced by the environment. New products and services are more readily adopted when the following criteria are present:

Relative Advantage—there is a clearly identifiable benefit to the new product relative to current market offerings

Observability—consumers can see others using the product

Trial-ability—people are able to sample or test it prior to adoption

Simplicity of Use—the product is easy to use

Lifestyle Compatibility—usage matches people's lifestyles

Everett Rogers, in his book *Diffusion of Innovations* outlined a set of criteria for evaluating consumer adoption that can be applied to the adoption of social media and mobile technologies [45]. A consumer who considers adopting *The New York Times* app would be more likely to do so if the criteria in Exhibit 4.9 are met.

consider this . . .

WHY DO PEOPLE ADOPT SOCIAL NETWORKS?

An individual's willingness to participate in social networks, as well as his or her likelihood of continuing to use or recommend them and join other social networks, is based on a certain set of beliefs, including [46]:

- **Ease of use**. Does using social networks require effort on the part of the user?

- **Usefulness**. Do social networks improve the way users complete networking tasks?
- **Enjoyment**. Are social networks fun, pleasurable, or entertaining?
- **Social influence**. Does social influence contribute to the use of social networks?
- **Drama**. Do emotional interactions on social networks affect users?

EXHIBIT 4.9

Adoption Criteria for *New York Times* All Digital Access

CRITERION	EXPLANATION	BUYING *NEW YORK TIMES* ALL DIGITAL ACCESS
Relative advantage	There are no available alternatives that provide the benefit at a set level of cost.	News available on multiple devices 24/7.
Lifestyle compatibility	The product or service fits well with a person's daily activities.	Useful information available on the go.
Trial-ability	The consumer can try the product or service prior to purchase.	The newspaper offers a one-month trial period for 99 cents.
Simplicity of use	Adoption isn't complicated. A person can learn the basics quickly without significant time and attention.	The app downloads when the device is turned on and finger swiping is intuitive.
Observability	The consumer can see the product or service in use and the enjoyment of others.	Opportunities to observe others using the app in public spaces.

SUMMARY AND REVIEW

CHAPTER SUMMARY

Marketers have to study consumer behavior in the marketplace to determine the most effective ways to reach and persuade targets. People have widely adopted social media and mobile technologies and have altered their purchasing patterns. These changes present both opportunities and challenges to firms. The key for businesses is to understand how consumers interact in these new ways to better meet people's needs.

KEY TERMS

attribution
basic communications
    model
credence attributes
enduring involvement
experience attributes
fad
informational group
    influence

innovators
insight
lifestyle compatibility
many-to-many
    communications
multitasking
observability
problem recognition
    (need recognition)

product lifecycle
purchase decision
    process
purchase funnel
relative advantage
search attributes
short message
    service (SMS)
simplicity of use

trial-ability
two-step flow of
    communications
viral marketing
viral mavens
word-of-mouth
    communications
    (WOM)

SUMMARY REVIEW QUESTIONS

1. Explain the differences between the purchase decision process and the purchase funnel. How are they related?
2. What are some implications for marketers when consumers multitask?
3. Explain the three types of group influence on consumer behavior and give an example of how social media affect each type.
4. Do the various forms of social media provide different types of connections between marketers and consumers? Explain.
5. Why do consumers pass content to others online and on social media?
6. How does the product lifecycle differ from the human lifecycle?

APPLICATION QUESTIONS

1. Consider the purchase decision process for a product you bought for over $50 and compare to the purchase decision process for a product you purchased for under $50. What were the major differences in your behavior through the process?
2. Evaluate a consumer's decision to purchase and download Angry Birds using Rogers's diffusion of innovations adoption criteria.
3. Go to Adage.com and search for top viral campaigns. Watch the top campaign video and explain why it was successful in going viral.
4. Examine Johnson & Johnson's Twitter feed by typing the company name into the Twitter search bar. Locate one tweet each focused on search attributes, experience attributes, and credence attributes for its products.

5. Choose one of the top blogs online, such as Huffington Post or Mashable. How many posts on a particular day discuss products or brands of companies? Do you trust the product information on the blog? Why or why not?

6. Plot the product lifecycle for a new social network site with which you are familiar. Consider the number of users at various time intervals for your data.

7. Find data on Facebook users in the United States for the past three years. What has happened to the adoption curve? Why?

Case Study Pinterest Joins the Social Media Superstars

New social networking sites spring up daily and marketers must decide whether to invest resources into building a presence on a site or take a wait-and-see approach. In early 2012 some marketers had already jumped onto the Pinterest bandwagon by setting up Pinterest pages and creating "pinable" content for Pinterest users.

Pinterest began in March 2010 as an invitation-only site that allowed users to "pin" images onto personal pin boards at the site. By January 2012 Pinterest had 11.7 million users and brands were flocking to set up pin boards to feature their brand, products, and content. Some companies that adopted Pinterest early on were: Whole Foods, Kate Spade, Domino Sugar, and Kotex. Publications had also flocked to Pinterest, including Mashable, *TIME Magazine,* and the Food Network [47].

THE APPEAL OF PINTEREST

The site was appealing to users because of its visual aesthetics and easy navigation. Users could download pinning buttons for their browsers so that when they visited webpages, the images that appeared could be easily pinned onto their own Pinterest boards. The site encouraged people to "pin" their favorite desired products, thus making the process very attractive to B2C brands and retailers.

B2B marketers of online data and digital client services were enamored with Pinterest since users also pinned data and interesting facts. Infographics, visual depictions of data, grew in popularity because people pinned them and posted them on their boards to share. Websites with infographics such as Marketing-Charts and Kissmetrics encouraged pinning to build relationships with customers and attract potential clients. Many marketing services firms created and shared infographics with their own data, such as comScore and Nielsen.

The social aspect of the site included "repins" so that members could post other people's pins on their own boards, comment on them, like them, or send Tweets about the pins. A member could also follow other members and see their pins as well. Pinterest seemed to take all the positive aspects of social bookmarking, photo sharing, and social engagement and package it together at one visually stimulating site.

The original Pinterest sites were focused on images, with captions below. The captions were limited to 500 characters, but were longer than tweets. Pinterest encouraged users to write their own comments when pinning and repinning.

One big concern was the copyright infringement issue. The problem was that the images people pinned were often copyrighted content for which no one had given express permission to pin. At the time, the Digital Millennium Copyright Act (1998) protected Pinterest from responsibility for the pins of its users, but only the notion of "fair use" prevented those who owned copyrighted material from going after Pinterest's user base [48]. The doctrine of fair use meant that individuals could use small portions of copyrighted works for education, parody, or the creation of something new [49].

COMMITTED TARGET MARKET

Consumers, particularly women 25–54, adopted Pinterest quickly. Exhibit 4.10 shows a chart of the adoption rates of Pinterest from May 2011 through June 2012 and the average minutes spent on the site per user [50].

Growth in unique U.S. users peaked in January 2013, declined a bit in February, and peaked again in April 2013, with 54,200,000 unique users in the United States. By January 2014 the monthly user base flattened, but growth began to pick up in new markets [51]. Pinterest users were spending about an hour a month on the site, which was shorter than the over six hours spent on Facebook.

Pinterest was generating revenue, but the profit model wasn't clear to the users. Originally, Pinterest used Skimlinks to scan links posted on the site to determine whether or not the link led to a retail site. Pinterest made money by dropping a code on the site and collecting a percentage of sales from each

EXHIBIT 4.10

Pinterest Unique Users and Time Spent on Site

	UNIQUE VISITORS U.S. (000)	AVERAGE MINUTES PER USER
May 2011	418	13.7
June 2011	608	20.4
July 2011	1,031	37.8
August 2011	1,270	52.3
September 2011	2,023	93.5
October 2011	3,295	82.7
November 2011	4,855	88.3
December 2011	7,516	80.4
January 2012	11,716	97.8

ComScore World Metrics" March 2012.

EXHIBIT 4.11

Pinterest Unique Users

MONTH	UNIQUE VISITORS U.S. (000)
April 2013	54,200
July 2013	46,900
January 2014	38,580

J. Constine, "Pinterest Will Start Showing Ads as Traffic Keeps Growing but Shifts to Mobile," TechCrunch, 19 September 2013.

purchase [52]. Pinterest was credited with increasing traffic by almost 400% to five specialty clothing retailers in 2011 [52], but those retailers were paying Pinterest a percentage of each sale that originated from users' pin boards. According to TechCrunch, Pinterest dropped the Skimlinks program due to low revenues from the relationship [51].

The early demographics of Pinterest users [53] were different from those of the average technology early adopters:

- 28% had annual household incomes over $100,000.
- 50% had children.
- 68% were women.
- 49% were ages 25–44.

Marketers found the demographic of wealthy women, many of whom were responsible for household shopping and possibly pinning, sharing, and recommending products, irresistible. ComScore reported that users spent more money, bought more products, and executed transactions more frequently online than other social media buyers [54].

By March 2012 Pinterest had 20 million unique visitors [54] and was attracting pinners around the world. In April 2012 Pinterest had 1.3 million users in Latin America, with Brazil leading the pack with demographics similar to those of U.S. users [55]. However, the smaller base of U.K. pinners was about ten years younger, even wealthier, and more likely to be male. Pinterest in the United Kingdom was more about marketing, venture capital, and making money than the U.S. site, which resembled digital scrapbooking [56]. Clearly, the U.K. marketers had noticed the site before the average British mum [57].

PINTEREST'S FUTURE

The plan was to go global and by 2015 the brand was in over thirty countries. Pinterest was still most popular in the United States, but 45% of the site visits originated in other countries. By 2015 the site had 100 million monthly users. [58].

eMarketer was predicting that Pinterest would reach 30% of U.S. social network users by 2019, but the platform had still not generated revenues above expenses for the business. The plan was to make money through "buy buttons" that would run on the site. The goal was to locate potential customers who indicated their preferences for products and services by pinning them on their pages. Pinterest had revenues of $25 million in 2014, but according to leaked documents was looking to grow revenue to $2.8 billion by 2018 [59]. Though companies like Etsy generated over 30% of its business from Pinterest, advertising was not reaching its potential for the firm[60].

COUNTRY	PERCENT OF VISITORS	RANK IN THE COUNTRY
U.S.	45.3	12
India	9.3	17
U.K.	3.8	19
Canada	3.2	14
Spain	2.7	18
France	2.3	39
Mexico	2.0	20
Italy	1.9	32
Australia	1.8	19
Germany	1.8	66

The future looked bright for Pinterest, but the platform still struggled to build a strategy that would attract advertisers and build revenues for the social media underdog.

QUESTIONS FOR DISCUSSION

1. Graph Pinterest's growth over time in terms of unique users and time spent on the site. What stage of the product lifecycle is Pinterest likely in? Should brands have any concerns over the potential for Pinterest going forward?

2. Why is Pinterest appealing to B2C and B2B marketers? Which strategies from the purchase funnel can be used by marketers to promote brands and build revenue?

3. What strategies can marketers employ to encourage pinning of their content? Should the strategies differ by country?

4. Choose an apparel brand and a magazine with which you are familiar. Examine the Pinterest sites for each and evelute them in terms of content, visual aesthetics, and followers. How do the strategies differ?

5. Locate two retailers' Pinterest sites. Which retailer does a better job of enticing potential buyers with content and which has the stronger following?

REFERENCES

[1] H. Mueller, J. Gove, J. Webb, 2012, Mobile HCI , September 21–24,San Francisco, 2012 http://static .googleusercontent.com/media/research.google.com/ en//pubs/archive/38135.pdf.

[2] GFK-MRI, "iPanel Reporter," *Tablets Multitasking,* May 2012.

[3] Nielsen, Twitter TV Ratings Week of 5/16-5/22, 2016, http://www.nielsensocial.com/ nielsentwittertvratings/weekly/

[4] Adobe, "Adobe Study Reveals Tablet Users Were Biggest Online," 2012.

[5] Merriam-Webster's, "Hypothesis," 2012.

[6] eMarketer, "Affluent Shoppers Make Mobile an Essential Stop in the Purchase Funnel," *eMarketer Retail & eCommerce,* 10 June 2013.

[7] eMarketer, "Worldwide Social Network Users: 2013 Forecasts and Comparative Estimates," 18 June 2013.

[8] eMarketer, "Smartphone Users Worldwide Will Total 1.75 Billion in 2014," *Mobile,* 16 January 2014.

[9] C. Dzubak, "Multitasking: The Good, the Bad, and the Unknown," 2007.

[10] J. L. Zaickowsky, "Measuring the Involvement Construct," *Journal of Consumer Research,* pp. 341–356, 1985.

[11] S. Norton, "The Next Step for the Mobile Wallet? Loyalty Programs," *The Wall Street Journal,* 26 January 2015.

[12] A. Carnns, "Consumers Have Concerns About Mobile Banking Security, Survey Finds," *The New York Times,* 17 April 2012.

[13] C. Wilhem, "Mobile Banking Deployment Widespread. Next Challenge: Adoption," *American Banker,* 29 October 2014.

[14] G. Abromavich, "Inside Sephora's Mobile Strategy," 18 January 2013.

[15] E. Price, "Need a Quick Opinion? There's an App for That," Mashable, 8 June 2012.

[16] P. Huang, N. H. Lurie, and S. Mitra, "Searching for Experience on the Web," *Journal of Marketing,* vol. 73, pp. 55–69, March 2009.

[17] L.-Y. Pan and J.-S. Chiou, "How Much Can You Trust Online Information? Cues for Perceived Trustworthiness of Consumer-Generated Online Information," *Journal of Interactive Marketing,* vol. 25, no. 2, pp. 67–74, 2011.

[18] eMarketer, "Mcommerce's Rapid Growth Is Primarily Coming from Smartphones" 4 May 2016, http:// www.emarketer.com/Article/Mcommerces-Rapid-Growth-Primarily-Coming-Smartphones/1013909# sthash.8msQKp1l.dpufhttp://www.emarketer.com/ Article/Mcommerces-Rapid-Growth-Primarily-Coming-Smartphones/1013909

[19] Convertigo, "Case Study: Carrefour Builds Innovative Mobile Commerce Application with Convertigo," http://www.convertigo.com/industries/ case-studies.html.

[20] T. H. Thurau, C. Weirtz, and F. Feldhaus, "Does Twitter Matter? An Investigation of the Impact of Microblogging Word of Mouth on Consumers' Adoption of New Products," *Social Science Research Network,* 11 February 2013.

[21] B. J. Jansen and S. Schuster, "Bidding On the Buying Funnel for Sponsored Search and Keyword Advertising," *Journal of Electronic Commerce Research,* vol. 12, no. 1, 2011.

[22] C. Delo, "Doritos' Latest Super Bowl Ad Contest Storms Viral Video Chart," *Advertising Age,* 12 January 2012.

[23] E. Katz, "The Two Step Flow of Communication: An Up-to-Date Report on an Hypothesis," *Public Opinion Quarterly,* vol. 21, no. 1, 1957.

[24] The Economist, "No Hiding Place," 25 May 2013.

[25] R. Wauters, *Twitter Gets Hit with Bizarre Class Action Lawsuit Over Unsolicited SMS Notifications,* 29 April 2011.

[26] R. Kozinets, K. de Valck, A. C. Wojnicki, and S. J. Wilner, "Networked Narratives: Understanding Word-of-Mouth Marketing in Online Communities," *Journal of Marketing,* vol. 74, pp. 71-89, 2010.

[27] B. J. Bushman, "The Effects of Television Violence on Memory for Commercial Messages," *Journal of Experimental Psychology: Applied,* vol. 4, no. 4, pp. 291–307, 1998.

[28] A. D. I. Kramer, J. E. Guillory, and J. T. Hancock, "Experimental Evidence of Massive-Scale Emotional Contagion through Social Networks," *Proceedings of the National Academy of Sciences of the United States,* vol. 111, no. 24, 25 March 2014.

[29] N. Pillay, "Consumer Fake-out: Budweiser Uses Classic Marketing Tool to Fool Brooklynites," *The Drum,* 18 March 2015.

[30] B. Weinberg, "Connected Customer Lifetime Value: The Impact of Social Media," *Journal of Direct, Data and Digital Marketing Practice,* vol. 12, pp. 328–344, April 2011.

[31] Edison Research, "Moms and Media 2016," The Research Moms.com

[32] K. Hampton, "Social Networking Sites and Our Lives," Pew Internet & American Life Project, 16 June 2011.

[33] A. Smith, "Fact Tank," Pew Internet Research, 3 February 2014.

[34] J. Phelps, R. Lewis, L. Mobilio, D. Perry, and N. Rahman, "Viral Marketing or Electronic Word-of-Mouth Advertising: Examining Consumer Responses and Motivations to Pass Along Email," *Journal of Advertising Research,* vol. 44, April 2004.

[35] M. G. Nejad, D. L. Sherrell, and E. Babakus, "Influentials and Influence Mechanisms in New Product Diffusion: An Integrative Review," *Journal of Marketing Theory and Practice,* vol. 22, no. 2, pp. 185-207, Spring 2014.

[36] E. Linder, "One Direction Pushes President Obama out of the Way in Quest for Most Retweeted Tweet," *MTV News,* 13 January 2015.

[37] B. Shin, "Top 10 Viral Advertising Videos of All Time," *Advertising Age,* 29 August 2011.

[38] S. Bennett, "The Rise of Vine," Mediabistro, 18 April 2014.

[39] J. Wortham, "The Race to Be an Early Adopter of Technologies Goes Mainstream," *The New York Times,* 1 September 2009.

[40] A. A. Newman, "Band-Aids and Muppets Aim to Soothe Child's Scrapes," The New York Times, 22 May 2012.

[41] P. S. van Eck, W. Jager, and P. S. H. Leeflang, "Opinion Leaders' Role in Innovation Diffusion: A Simulation Study," *Journal of Product Innovation Management,* vol. 28, no. 2, pp. 187–203, February 2011.

[42] F. Rose, "How Madison Avenue Is Wasting Millions on a Deserted Second Life," *Wired,* vol. 15.08, 24 July 2007.

[43] S. Murphy, "Is Facebook a Passing Fad? Nearly Half of Americans Think So," Mashable, 15 May 2012.

[44] Statista 2015, Number of Active Monthly Facebook Users Worldwide as of the Fourth Quarter of 2015, http://www.statista.com/statistics/264810/number-of-monthly-active-facebook-users-worldwide/.

[45] E. M. Rogers, *Diffusion of Innovations,* 3rd ed., New York: Free Press, 1983.

[46] R. Lennon, R. Rentfro, and J. Curran, "Exploring Relationships between Demographic Variables and Social Networking Use," *Journal of Management and Marketing Research,* pp. 1-16, September 2012.

[47] "Pinterest," Wikipedia, June 2012, http://en.wikipedia.org/wiki/Pinterest.

[48] K. Falkenberg, "A One Word Fix to Pinterest's Legal Problem," *Forbes,* 15 March 2012.

[49] Stanford University Libraries, "Copyright & Fair Use," 2010, http://fairuse.stanford.edu/Copyright_and_Fair_Use_Overview/chapter9/9-b.html.

[50] ComScore, "ComScore World Metrics," March 2012.

[51] J. Constine, "Pinterest Will Start Showing Ads as Traffic Keeps Growing but Shifts to Mobile," TechCrunch, 19 September 2013.

[52] M. Georgieva, "How to Use Pinterest for Business," Hubspot, 2012.

[53] C. Erickson, "13 Pinteresting Facts about Pinterest Users," Mashable, 25 February 2012.

[54] S. Perez, "ComScore U.S. Internet Report: YoY, Pinterest Up 4000+%, Amazon Up 30%, Android Top Smartphone & More," TechCrunch, 2012.

[55] K. Kaye, "Pinterest Grew Eight Fold in Latin America," *ClickZ,* 15 June 2012.

[56] M. Silverman, "Pinterest: How Do US and UK Users Compare?," Mashable, 14 February 2012.

[57] S. Kelly, "Pinterest Partner: Yes, They're Making Money from Pins," Mashable, 28 February 2012.

[58] E. Griffith, "Pinterest Hits 100 Million Users," September 17, 2015, Fortune, http://fortune.com/2015/09/17/pinterest-hits-100-million-users/.

[59] eMarketer, "Will Pinterest Reach its Potential in 2015?" 25 February, 2015. http://www.emarketer.com/article/will-pinterest-reach-its-potential-2015/1012103.

[60] L. O'Reilly, "Insiders Say What's Going on Inside $11 Billion Pinterest—and It's Not all Good" January 8, 2016, http://www.businessinsider.com/pinterest-worth-11-billion-valuation-revenue-grow-5x-2015.

© Shutterstock/bikeriderlondon

CHAPTER FIVE

DEVELOPING AND DISTRIBUTING

As we've seen, social media and mobile technologies have much to offer each element of the marketing mix. The first and most important marketing function is determining the appropriate products and services to bring to market and developing those offerings. Marketers use social media and mobile strategies to obtain input from employees, consumers, and other constituencies prior to production or, on an ongoing basis, for improvement. Social networks can also help with distribution channels (the P for "Place" in the four P's), for digital products, or even serve as retail spaces for tangible products. Mobile already plays a strong in-store role for consumers, and technological advances are also providing more opportunities for completing transactions. This chapter explores the many ways in which social media and mobile impact product design and distribution.

LEARNING OBJECTIVES

After reading this chapter, you will be able to:

- EXAMINE CROWDSOURCING AS A PRODUCT DEVELOPMENT STRATEGY.

- USE CONSUMER FEEDBACK TO IMPROVE BRAND STRATEGY.

- DEVELOP PRODUCT STRATEGY USING SOCIAL MEDIA AND MOBILE TECHNOLOGY.

- DETERMINE DISTRIBUTION STRATEGIES THROUGH DIGITAL MEDIA.

- EVALUATE RETAIL STRATEGY GIVEN NEW MEDIA OPPORTUNITIES AND THREATS.

Have you ever invented anything? What if you had a great idea for a new product? What would you do? In the past, you would have had to sell your idea to a company or spend your own money to develop your idea and produce it. Today, you can sketch your idea on a napkin, take a picture of it with your iPhone, and upload it to Quirky, a website that facilitates product development. Quirky is a company whose sole purpose is to use social media to develop new products.

The start-up began as an online community and grew to over 300,000 members who evaluated product submissions for commercial viability. By 2015 people had uploaded about 1,500 product ideas a week to the site for potential development [1]. One product, the Pivot Power flexible power strip, earned about $500,000 for the inventor and $50,000 for the developer of the tag line "Flex Your Power" [2].

So, how is this new form of product development working? Though Quirky expected revenues of over $100 million in 2016, the company filed for bankruptcy citing cash flow issues.

The firm had difficulty managing so many diverse products, but had a loyal base of users such that by 2016 a group of investors bought the rights to Quirky[3]. Once again you can bring your ideas to the site and find others to work with you on product development. The advantages of crowdsourcing are that inventors benefit from the crowd's input and a quicker time to market than traditional methods. In addition, even before the company introduces a product, a community has been built up of people who are interested in purchasing the product based on their Quirky experience.

Just as Quirky inventors benefit from knowledge of the crowd, traditional companies can also enhance their offerings by engaging customers in social media long before introducing a new product. Companies may reduce risk by vetting ideas early in the process before management spends money developing them. Social media can really enhance a product development strategy.

consider this . . .

CROWDSOURCING VERSUS PROFESSIONAL PRODUCT DEVELOPMENT?

Who do you think has better ideas for new products, a world renowned team of professional product developers or average customers? To determine the answer, researchers Marion Poetz and Martin Schreier chose the Austrian company BamedMam to participate in a study. BamedMam sells 40 million products in over 30 countries and employs 400 people globally. The firm has won global design prizes and is known for its innovative products.

Seventy customers submitted their product ideas on the company website with the opportunity to earn free products in a raffle. The BamedMam CEO and director of R&D assessed entries from customers and developers using preestablished evaluation criteria. The ideas were grouped by topic and then randomly ordered, so the evaluators did not know who had developed them—a customer or an in-house employee. Each idea was evaluated based on a five-point scale for (1) novelty, (2) problem-solving ability, and (3) feasibility.

The study found that the customer ideas were more novel and more effective in solving customer problems. The professionals scored higher on feasibility, but lower than customers on the overall quality measure [4]. The bottom line is that customers may have better knowledge of their needs and how to solve them than professional developers.

Something for companies to think about, huh?

SOCIAL MEDIA, MOBILE MARKETING, AND THE MARKETING MIX

Social media and mobile marketing influence all four P's of the marketing mix (Product, Price, Place (distribution), and Promotion): the broad strategies marketers use to achieve organizational objectives. These new tools are more powerful in the areas of product development and distribution (Place) than you may realize and have influenced the types of new products marketers develop. Social and mobile media also affect the process by which brand managers plan and create new offerings for their target market and have additionally had a major impact on how a company responds to customers who may be dissatisfied with a product offering. For example, Starbucks has altered product ingredients based on social media feedback. When the company used crushed insects as a food coloring in strawberry drinks, customers posted a petition on Change.org. The customers persuaded Starbucks to use a vegetable-based coloring instead [5]. This example shows how social media affect product decisions, such as the source of ingredients, which in the past would not have included much customer input.

Through social media, consumers may also participate in the marketing of that product or service by contributing to product specifications, evaluating designs, or recommending new features or attributes to marketers. The strategy for marketers differs depending on whether the firm solicited participation versus when customers plan their own involvement. When the company solicits customer participation, management can control the process and to some extent the results by using specified requests and rewarding appropriate consumer input.

PRODUCT DEVELOPMENT IN THE SOCIAL AND MOBILE SPHERES

Firms that wish to minimize their risk in developing new products go through a process that includes testing their new product ideas and executions with customers before making the sometimes substantial investment to bring a product or service to market.

As you have already seen, Quirky's new product development process includes a social component aimed at attracting new inventors. But established firms also take advantage of the social sphere as part of their product development processes. The process for new product development involves a series of steps that are outlined in Exhibit 5.1.

The process may begin when management reviews the firm's current situation and identifies opportunities or threats that may affect the business; often, however, opportunities or threats present themselves when the environment changes and someone in the firm recognizes the situation. A good way for firms to hear about these opportunities in a particular industry, a target market, a geographic region—or worldwide—is to utilize social media tools. Many ideas come from outside the firm, but noticing their value early on can result in a pioneering advantage, the chance to be the first to develop an idea and be known as THE brand in that space. The reality is that most firms are slow-moving relative to entrepreneurs,

EXHIBIT 5.1

Steps in the New Product Development Process

PROCESS	DEFINITIONS
1. Strategy development	Determining the objectives the firm would like to achieve through product development.
2. Idea generation	Using a process to discover ideas for products or services.
3. Concept testing and evaluation	Writing clear descriptions of the ideas and asking potential customers to evaluate them. The firm then selects the most promising option.
4. Business feasibility	Evaluating the ability of the firm to execute product or service development given available resources and capabilities.
5. Model development	Building a representation of the product or service for testing.
6. Product testing	Researching the viability of the product or service model.
7. Production and commercialization	Introducing the product to market.

but they have the resources to acquire new products, so scanning the environment is an excellent way for firms to monitor changes.

Firms can monitor the environment through social listening, using a set of tools that are available online. Chapter Three discussed many of these tools, and they are summarized in Exhibit 3.3. Some companies are experts in leveraging customer feedback to enhance strategy. Gatorade considers itself to be the "largest participatory brand in the world." Marketers monitor the "war room" to determine sentiment for Gatorade product introductions on a daily basis. Similarly, Pepsi created DEWmocracy to include customer opinions on new flavors, with strong sales results [6].

CROWDSOURCING IN PRODUCT DEVELOPMENT

Social media and mobile technology can contribute to a firm's product development process in a variety of ways. In some instances, new technologies bring companies and sources of funding together, while at other times collaboration on ideas occurs virtually. Sometimes, resources are shared or a firm outsources idea development. The term **crowdsourcing,** first used by Jeff Howe of *Wired* magazine in 2008 [7], refers to efforts by a firm to outsource company tasks to groups of people outside the organization. Since that time, the term has been broadened to include people who come together, often digitally, to do something or decide something.

THE WISDOM OF CROWDS

Many books and articles have been written about the fact that large groups of people are often better at solving problems, fostering innovation, and making good decisions than an elite few. James Surowiecki's *The Wisdom of Crowds* was one of the first works to demonstrate this phenomenon across a variety of fields [8]. Surowiecki discussed a number of studies in which groups of people were found to be surprisingly good at collectively guessing correctly. The theory suggests that groups are better at predicting phenomena than individuals, particularly when they are cognitively diverse and independent. Crowds amassed through social media can potentially solve three types of problems:

1. *Cognition*: A group can determine correct right or wrong answers, such as predicting an event or a score.
2. *Coordination*: The group unknowingly works together in patterns of behavior, such as when drivers all follow the same lanes and buyers and sellers find each other in a market.
3. *Cooperation*: People work together even if the behavior is not in their self-interest, such as paying taxes or capping pollution [9].

mPing's mobile weather app.

NOAA National Severe Storms Laboratory, http://mping.nssl.noaa.gov

Some research has even shown that crowds are good at predicting the weather. For example, mPing (Meteorological Phenomena Identification Near the Ground) is a mobile app created by the National Oceanic and Atmospheric Administration and the University of Oklahoma to harness weather data. Users log on from their phones and report on precipitation in their area and the phone locates them using the GPS system. The data help predict severe storms using crowdsourcing enabled through smartphones. You can download your mPing app from iTunes or Google Play and report the weather near you [10].

You have probably searched Google thousands of times and each time you do, your search becomes part of the knowledge base. Crowds contribute to Google's algorithm for locating websites in a search that are appropriate to the searcher. The task is so efficient that 95% of Google searchers do not look beyond the first page of results. So when you search and click on something, you improve Google's search engine by identifying the best results for your search.

Facebook's Graph search helps users find information about the tastes of friends and family members and sort through images by date, individual words, and keywords [11]. These searches are essentially weighted averages based on those hits that users click on the most when searching those keywords [9].

Our need to rely on others for information is based on the notion of social proof, which suggests that if enough other people are doing something, there must be a good reason for their actions. We rely on others to help us make sense of the world around us. Social networking is social proof on steroids. That is why brands must pay attention to trends in social media. After all, their customers are doing so already.

consider this . . .

HOW SUCCESSFUL IS DELL'S IDEASTORM FOR IDEATION?

We introduced Dell's IdeaStorm crowdsourcing platform in the introduction to Chapter Three. A study of IdeaStorm found that over a two-year period most contributors offered only one suggestion, and very few of these were ever implemented. Some of the ideas were as simple as "Use Michael Dell in Dell commercials," or "Advertise on www.Hulu.com." Almost half of the ideas were product-related, suggesting that Dell change style, performance, or hardware, and some ideas had already been implemented by the company. The ideas that Dell most likely implemented were those that were easy or offered a strong financial incentive. Just opening up your site to ideas may not be as productive as a targeted effort to generate ideas with some guidelines for problems that need solving [7].

CROWDSOURCING COLLABORATION

Companies can benefit from several categories of crowdsourcing collaboration: funding, virtual workforce, aggregate knowledge, creative collaboration, locating outside innovation, and employee-based crowdsourcing [12].

Funding

Businesses need funding to help execute strategies and can use social media to locate investors and generate money for investing in areas of potential growth.

Kickstarter is a social financing website. People who want to raise money for a project post their proposal on Kickstarter, and other individuals can invest in the activity in exchange for rewards, such as a copy of the creative output, invitations to performances or mementos. The project runs for a limited amount of time to raise a specified amount of money, and when the activity is fully funded (and only when fully funded), the creator receives the money and must deliver the rewards.

The site is often used by artists to generate funds for artistic expressions. They post videos to explain the task and fans, friends, and family members donate because they are interested in the activity and want to support the effort. A Belgian company created "CHERRY on the bag," a set of high-end leather bags and cases with an embedded electronic tag that can be read by a mobile scanner with NFC technology (near-field communication). When the bag is lost, anyone can scan it and learn the identity of the owner so the bag can be returned. To participate in the project, people invest $99 and receive a leather iPad case with the company's proprietary tracking technology. The inventors hope to raise a total of $70,000 [13].

Some projects have been very successful. The video game developer Tim Schafer made $3.36 million on a new game and musician Amanda Palmer, who asked for $100,000 to create a new album, earned $1 million [14]. The most successful projects are in the area of dance, with the lowest success rate in fashion.

Virtual Workforce

Firms can use social media and mobile technology to locate workers to perform services for customers or complete tasks that do not require specific knowledge. A **virtual workforce** is a set of employees that can be harnessed to perform tasks online.

Amazon's Mechanical Turk is an online site for workers whom firms may hire to complete "human intelligence tasks." The tasks are typically automated, but they still require a person to execute. Some of the tasks include developing products or solving complex problems, while others include writing reviews for products or generating hits for websites. Here are some jobs requesters have posted:

Search Google keyword terms.

Find company contact information.

Write a creative article title.

Categorize products into different candy categories.

Judge the relevance and sentiment of content about Dove, the maker of shampoo, soap, and other products [15].

Many of the "jobs" on Mechanical Turk require a person to identify something that a computer can't or fill out a survey that requires a person's life experience. A similar service called microWorkers.com is aimed at promoting products and brands. The company's website suggests that firms can buy followers on Twitter or votes for YouTube videos. People can place orders to have workers enter contests for them or vote for their contest entries, and businesses can hire Microworkers to write positive reviews or boost rankings on search engines [16]. Businesses can also rate the employees from Microworkers, as shown in the screenshot, below.

Researchers found that using crowdsourced employees is more effective when the task requester provides good examples, annotated subtasks, and clear prompts [17].

Marketers can also access workers in the developing world through mobile text messaging, since text messages are more likely to reach a broader base of potential contributors than smartphones or even the Internet. Many people in the developing world do not have wired connections. A study of mClerk's use in India found that the service is effective for digitizing documents in the local dialect. During the study, 239 workers digitized 25,000 words of text [18].

Employers can rate the employees they hired at microWorker's site.

*microWorkers,
www.microworkers.com*

Aggregating Knowledge

Companies can also leverage social media to pull together individuals and groups to provide information that can help advance product strategies. In this case, the participants are more knowledgeable than the virtual workforce and may have special expertise or information. Scientists can collaborate on experiments, nongovernmental organizations (NGOs) can collectively develop strategies in developing countries, and doctors can discover cures for diseases or assist with surgeries. These are all forms of aggregating knowledge through online social interaction.

For many years, companies have introduced beta versions of software so that people can test it and work out the bugs before full commercialization. With social media, the process can work faster because testers may post responses immediately, work with others to solve problems, and share information with product developers.

For example, when Microsoft needed people to identify bugs in its security software, it used uTest. The company leveraged the knowledge of more than 100 testers around the world and was able to vet the product for global performance in places like China, India, Brazil, and Russia before its release. UTest can complete tasks in as little as 24 hours with more than 33,000 testers in 172 countries. The advantage is that firms only have to pay for specific tests and do not need to hire a staff for this purpose [19].

Another company that uses more advanced professionals is Amazon's Turkomatic. This service is for complex tasks that a requester posts for others to solve in real time. The workers themselves can alter the tasks and solutions to solve the problem without input or the oversight of the requester to allow for creative solutions [20].

consider this . . .

CROWDSOURCING WITH TURKOMATIC

Turkomatic is a crowdsourcing tool that allows users to break down workflow into manageable components so that people can complete the tasks online within Amazon's Mechanical Turk system. The tool asks workers to divide the complex steps of a task into smaller ones until the tasks are simple enough to solve with a simple request. Researchers examining the tool found that the system works, but a more effective method is to include the person requesting the task to participate such that he or she can designate the workflow process. In other words, human direction helps reduce time and error in using Turkomatic [20].

Creative Collaboration

Some social networks use **creative collaboration** to help firms develop ideas by leveraging the power and connections among workers who serve in creative capacities. For example, Tongal is an online social site that allows advertising and media

Tongal crowdsources creative talent for a variety of projects.

Tongal, www.tongal.com

"creatives" to develop videos for major clients, like McDonald's and Procter & Gamble. The site runs as a contest where the top submissions earn money for their creativity. Companies benefit from a wide variety of ideas that can be executed quickly [21].

Locating Outside Innovation

In this type of crowdsourcing, firms open up their companies to individuals who would like to contribute to new product ideas. Unilever, the large consumer products firm, solicits sustainability ideas from universities, design companies, engineers, and environmental groups. These outside contributors are knowledgeable in the area and can contribute technical and creative ideas [22].

"It's not cheating, it's crowdsourcing."

Mark Anderson, www.andertoons.com

Employee-Based Crowdsourcing

Of course, a company's own employees may have specialized knowledge about products or processes. A number of social media sites are aimed at internal employees and are secure, such that only those within the companies have access. These sites are known as "Facebook for Enterprise" and they provide tools to help companies and their employees collaborate. People have started to refer to these tools for companies as "social business" [23].

SOCIAL BUSINESS

The millennial generation is made up of people in the United States born after 1980 who came of age at the turn of the twenty-first century [24]. As young people in the millennial generation begin their careers, companies have had to find new ways to communicate with them to enhance their performance and contributions in the office. Companies have realized that millennials do not use email and instead rely on social networks to learn and share information. Social platforms for businesses like Yammer or Chatter provide a secure space for employees to share best practices and collaborate on developing better products and services [25].

Lingo24 is a U.K.-based language translation service operating on three continents. To help facilitate work processes across the globe, Lingo24 uses Yammer to manage the time zone differences in communications among employees. The company uses Yammer to crowd-source ideas for new graphics on the company website, allowing for contributions from the entire community [26].

PRODUCT OPPORTUNITIES IN SOCIAL MEDIA AND MOBILE MARKETING

Both social media and mobile marketing change the way products are considered by customers and the strategy of the firm. Marketers have new opportunities to influence the consumer's cost-benefit calculation, add value to enhance products and services to improve the customer experience, build business through **complementary products**, that naturally go with other offerings, and fend off the competition by developing unique advantages through social media or mobile technology. The benefits may be tangible or intangible, provided by the company or other customers or channel members, or by the firm itself through a better understanding of the target.

CUSTOMER VALUE

The concept of **customer value** suggests that consumers evaluate product and service offerings by examining the set of benefits provided by the purchase relative to the costs. The common benefits of products or services include both tangible and intangible product outcomes, including the task the product performs, the physical attractiveness of the product, the service performed, and its quality. The intangibles are often in the customer's mind and may be the enjoyment, entertainment value, or image the product or service bestows on the buyer.

EXHIBIT 5.2

Social Media and Mobile Benefits

	TANGIBLE	INTANGIBLE
Social Media Benefits	Limited capability in offering tangible product attributes.	Many opportunities to supplement the product offering by providing customer information and affirmation from social sources.
Mobile Technology Benefits	Capable of providing tangible product benefits, such as in the case of mobile maps and branded gaming apps or on the business-to-business side with mobile payment systems that attach to a mobile device.	Many opportunities to supplement the product offering, such as with location-based check-ins that point toward friends and other customers.

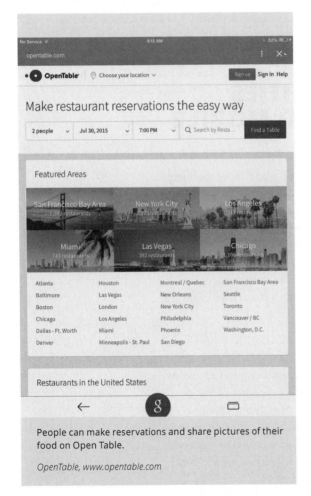

People can make reservations and share pictures of their food on Open Table.

OpenTable, www.opentable.com

The **customer value proposition** is the set of benefits and costs that a marketer offers to consumers. Social media can contribute in many ways to the benefits or the perceived benefits of a product typically on the intangible side of the offering. Mobile is more flexible in that mobile can provide assets that consumers can feel and touch. Exhibit 5.2 presents the tangible and intangible potential benefits of social media and mobile technology.

OpenTable is an online and mobile restaurant reservation system. To enhance the site's service offerings, OpenTable bought the company Foodspotting, which allows customers to search for a restaurant by dish or specialty. Diners share pictures of their meals and their experiences in restaurants on the social media site Foodspotting, and now users of OpenTable can find more information about the restaurants and their product offerings before making a reservation. OpenTable is providing additional intangible value to customers through information that customers want [27]. The company has 3 million photographs of meals from all over the world. Foodspotting also has the capability of providing customer preferences to restaurants to further improve the value proposition to consumers who have unique or special demands [27].

Mobile can also enhance the perception of both tangible and intangible benefits to a consumer

EXHIBIT 5.3

Branded Mobile Applications

COMPANY	MOBILE APPLICATION
Disney	The Parks Mobile Magic app helps customers navigate the park and avoid waiting.
General Electric Industrial	The company's Transformer Monitoring app manages gas turbine inventory and electric transformers globally. The app provides businesses with the opportunity to reduce costs by reducing energy consumption.
General Electric Consumer	The GE Mood Cam allows customers to take pictures of a room and modify the lighting to see the effects. The app adds value by reducing the customer's risk in the decision to purchase lighting and bulbs. GE Brillion appliance purchasers can use the GE Nucleus app to monitor energy consumption of these appliances in their homes.
IBM Industrial	IBM Mobile Systems Remote (IBM Remote) is an application that allows technology administrators to monitor and manage IBM systems (currently, BladeCenter and System x Rack mounted systems via RSA2 or IMM) from the convenience of their mobile device.
Airbnb Consumer	Airbnb enables users to seek out nonhotel travel accommodations listed by other users. The mobile app features an added functionality for travelers on the go. Under the "Search" tab, the "Help! I need a place, tonight!" button helps users find and book nearby apartments that are available at the last minute.

with a mobile application. **Mobile applications** or apps are software programs that reside on a mobile device and perform various functions. The most popular mobile apps connect people to social networks, gaming, or information, such as the weather. Most brands in the Interbrand Best Brands Report have a mobile app in at least one of the app stores (e.g., iTunes or Android) [28]. These apps support the brand and add value to the product in a variety of ways. Exhibit 5.3 lists a variety of branded mobile applications that add value to the customer for increased engagement with the firm or revenue-generating opportunities. You may be familiar with some of these businesses and their mobile applications because they sell to final consumers. Some of these applications are less familiar because they are made for industrial use by companies, rather than by individuals [29], [30].

COMPLEMENTARY PRODUCTS

A brand that has a successful tangible product can offer a new social media or mobile product, building on the brand equity of the name of the original product. For example, Barnes & Noble, a large online seller of digital books, introduced the Nook, a mobile e-reader, to facilitate the sales of digital books. Social media can provide a platform for determining which products consumers may like and how best to design those products. Though the Nook ultimately did not compete well with the iPad or Kindle, social media can signal consumer interest in a product. For example, in the financial arena, customers who hold mortgages with a particular bank may be good candidates for home equity loans or savings accounts.

Social media can help determine which complementary products would add value to the relationship. In addition, marketers can use social media to test new product ideas among a group of loyal customers before investing in an expensive development process.

IMAGE BUILDING

Marketers have used social media to enhance the offering to consumers by providing consumers with desirable connections to a community. BeachMint was a social commerce company that sold products that matched a consumer's personality profile [31]. One of its brands called JewelMint sold jewelry designed by celebrities. Part of the allure of being a JewelMint member was the opportunity to interact with celebrities in the social space or to become a celebrity by earning points for innovating products [32]. The company considered Facebook fans as very valuable engaged customers who were interested in participating in the product development process [33]. BeachMint merged with the magazine brand, Lucky, to combine products with fashion content into The Lucky Group.

COMPETITIVE ADVANTAGE

A company holds a **competitive advantage** when it is more skilled than other companies in a particular business area. Social media can help firms leverage advantages to beat the competition.

Facebook considers "social distance" between users to determine the importance of search queries an individual might make to locate information. In other words, a person will see more content from close contacts than others. For example, TripAdvisor feeds people reviews of those within their Facebook social network. The addition of the intangible knowledge of a person's close relationships may help Facebook offer more value to consumers when they search to help the firm compete with Google in search marketing [34].

Companies who understand the needs of a particular **niche market**, a small market with a highly homogenous target, can compete against larger companies. Snapchat, a mobile app that competes with Facebook, developed its product with a unique feature that Facebook lacks. Whereas images posted on Facebook remain online unless actively removed, Snapchat allows users to take pictures and share them briefly—knowing that the photos disappear after a few seconds [35].

CONSUMER FEEDBACK

Marketers can use social media and mobile marketing to monitor the performance of their products and tweak them to improve their customer's experiences and their bottom line. The YouTube-sponsored *Spangler Effect* is a science show for kids. Google approached Steve Spangler when they saw his interesting YouTube videos and the products that he had developed, such as Color Fizzers and Instant Snow. The original idea for the show was to produce cool science projects that kids could complete at home for amazing effects and then demonstrate how the science project could do something really big. For example, Spangler can make an egg drop into a milk bottle even if it's too big for the bottle's opening and wanted to present a giant version of the experiment on his show. By monitoring audience response, Spangler made a number of changes to the *Spangler Effect*. First, he found that 60% of the audience dropped off when he started with a splashy opening, so he moved that segment to later in the show and added a hook. Another problem was the giant version of the experiment. Viewers dropped off after watching the part they could do at home, so he eliminated that portion of the show, which also cost a lot of money to produce. Now the show is more focused on what the audience wants to see. By monitoring the performance of a product through social media, marketers can improve performance or eliminate unnecessary expenses.

Another example of monitoring products for development is Netflix's show production model. The Netflix original series *House of Cards* was created based on monitoring consumer viewing behavior. Netflix determined that their viewers liked Kevin Spacey and political thrillers, and developed the show to appeal to them [36]. Amazon goes one step further and asks its viewers to vote on pilots to determine which shows the company will produce [37].

SOCIAL MEDIA AND MOBILE DISTRIBUTION AND E-COMMERCE

Social media and mobile technology influence distribution and e-commerce strategies. **E-commerce** represents transactions that are facilitated by Internet connections. Businesses know that people are on their phones 24/7, using their devices to connect on social media and for shopping. Mobile represents close to 30% of e-commerce globally and is growing [38]. **Distribution** refers to the strategies firms use to ensure that consumers can obtain their products and services, and e-commerce is selling through online channels. The **channel of distribution** is the route a product takes from producer to the consumer through a series of intermediaries or companies that assist in the process. Most of the products you use and then throw away are called consumer products because these items are consumed by you, the final consumer. Marketers refer to selling to final users as the **B2C (business-to-consumer) market.** In one type of B2C marketing, **direct marketing,** the producer sells directly to the final consumer with no other businesses assisting within the channel of distribution. Sometimes though, marketers use other businesses or intermediaries to help sell to final consumers or to provide supplies and services. This is referred to as the **B2B** (**business-to-business**) **market.**

Business-to-business marketers were some of the early adopters of social media for generating leads. Most of these companies are suppliers of services, such as marketing communications, technology, or research. B2B marketers develop content strategies, posting articles, case studies, white papers, newsletters, or videos aimed at their business targets. Many suppliers to other firms use LinkedIn to develop their client base and maintain contact with their customers.

There are two common types of marketing channel members, wholesalers and retailers. **Wholesalers** are distributors who may move product from the producer through the channel to retailers, or who may arrange for the product to move through the channel. In marketing physical products, wholesalers are important in storing, assorting, transporting, and delivering products. In the digital marketplace, wholesalers may act as agents arranging for sales. This role is similar to that of a real estate agent in the housing industry who matches a buyer and a seller (but doesn't take ownership of the home him- or herself). Social media have helped wholesalers and agents maintain connections with customers and display their products.

A **retailer** is a member of the marketing channel that distributes products to the final consumer mostly through physical or online stores. Amazon is an example of a retailer that gets products from manufacturers and sells directly to customers. Retailers such as Amazon have embraced social media to engage customers and build loyalty. Amazon's product pages display reviews for products and the site invites purchasers to write reviews. This is a social aspect of the purchase and a major part of the retailer's social strategy, which works even without the use of a big social media site like Facebook.

Social media and mobile technology have affected retailers' businesses by providing opportunities to sell through new outlets, improve transactions, and facilitate sales. However, new threats are also present in the form of customers sharing information with one another and the ability of shoppers to obtain competitive product and pricing information at any time. The next section (and Exhibit 5.4) describes social media and mobile technology usage within the channel of distribution, specifically in wholesale, retail, and mobile transactions.

WHOLESALER USE OF SOCIAL MEDIA

Wholesalers are traditional businesses that have been slow to adopt new social technologies. However, due to the ubiquity of social media interaction and the chance to streamline processes with mobile, wholesalers are starting to consider these options. One group of wholesalers who uses social media extensively is real estate agents. Agents reach out to potential sellers of homes by posting recent home sales on Facebook and Pinterest. Hearing about other sales can help convince potential home sellers that an agent will be able to get the best price for their property

EXHIBIT 5.4

The Channel of Distribution with Social Media and Mobile Influence

Manufacturer   Social Media Product Development and Mobile Crowdsourcing

↓

Wholesaler   Professional Social Media Sites for Best Practices

↓

Retailer   Social Media Store Fronts and Mobile Transactions

↓

Consumer   Social Media Influence in the Purchase Decision Mobile e-Commerce Apps for Product Research

[39]. In the flower business, the American Floral Endowment has developed a *Social Media Guide for Retailers and Wholesalers* that is based on customer and business research in social media habits [40]. And the digital marketing professional community for auto dealers offers blogs; Facebook, Twitter, and LinkedIn sites; videos; and other ways for dealers to connect with each other on common issues and problems. The site indicates that it is the "Social Network for Car Dealers, Automotive Marketing, Advertising and Sales Management Professionals sharing Internet strategies and tactics" [41]. As social media continue to penetrate different professional communities, more and more businesses will see the benefits of making these connections.

consider this . . .

ARE SOCIAL MEDIA GOOD FOR BUSINESS?

Businesses believe that social media are beneficial. According to a study by McKinsey, 69% of companies surveyed said their firms saw measurable benefits from social media in product innovation, marketing, knowledge acquisition, reduced costs, and higher revenues [6]. The companies in the study reported, on average:

- 20% faster time to market
- 20% increased number of innovations
- 20% quicker access to information
- 20% lower development costs
- 15% higher revenues

SOCIAL MEDIA IN RETAIL ENVIRONMENTS

Social media and mobile marketing have strongly affected the retailers who sell to final consumers in the marketing channel. One opportunity for retailers is to set up shop on a social media site, such as Facebook. The industry refers to selling on Facebook as **F-commerce** to mimic the term e-commerce that refers to online selling.

There are a number of Facebook apps that allow marketers to use an existing Facebook presence with the inventory held within a traditional online store. For example, ECWid is a shopping cart for Facebook that allows marketers to feature products for sale [42]. Businesses with under $100,000 in sales and fewer than 10 employees have been more successful with F-commerce than larger firms due to the personal nature of interaction on Facebook. In addition, some of the biggest brands decided to center their strategies on their own websites rather than rely on F-commerce. Some marketers, including Gap, Nordstrom, JC Penney, and GameStop, have even pulled their Facebook stores due to limited sales or simply the desire to have full control of e-commerce on their own company website [43]. One concern is that people are not accustomed to buying on Facebook and trust it less than traditional e-commerce. However, the benefit to firms of selling through Facebook is that the customer spreads the word to friends, family, and others, thus faciliating new sales [44].

Whereas smaller firms led the way in developing Facebook e-commerce platforms [45], larger businesses who have a Facebook presence tend to link to their own websites for e-commerce. For example, FTD florists use shortened website links to drive Facebook traffic to their site when a potential customer clicks on the link associated with an image. Facebook and Twitter feature a "buy" button that people can use to connect to e-commerce options, and Twitter purchased CardSpring to offer mobile coupons to consumers that can be redeemed in-store. With these options, social networks are attempting to be a key aspect of the purchase process [46].

Pinterest is another social network with strong e-commerce potential. The site allows people to post pictures of products they like with strong selling opportunities for companies that market visually appealing products and services. Pinterest has been successful as an e-commerce platform selling products through its site, but the actual execution occurs through links to websites rather than on the Pinterest platform.

Another strategy is to drive sales to the website through social media. Marketers will pay shoppers who post products on their social media sites, such as Pinterest or Twitter. Beso is a company that rewards customers for their buzz. Their motto is: "Everyone should be rewarded for their influence." The Beso affiliate program asks regular people to share their favorite products on Facebook, Twitter, Pinterest, YouTube, Vimeo, Instagram, Google+, and other sites; they then earn rewards [47].

Social media sites have also set up their own retail stores. For example, Facebook added a gift store to encourage social giving when people's birthdays are announced on their timelines. Some of the products include Dean & DeLuca specialty foods and clothing from the Gap. Because Facebook also knows how close people are to one another and their tastes, they can customize marketing messages to encourage appropriate gift giving, a task that is notoriously difficult for the average person. Facebook maintains a warehouse in South Dakota and created tracking software to manage the inventory instead of partnering with Amazon [48].

Online video also drives sales to retail outlets. Consumers can watch video reviews of products and stores, and follow shopping channels. The Srsly videos by Danielle Gibson are an example of retail videos that are distributed to social media and lead to retail sales [49]. There are many new YouTube sensations with strong followings in specific markets. These celebrities often talk about branded products and services, and companies woo them with free products so they will talk about their businesses. Companies also hire online celebrities with large followings for brand advertising in order to influence their base of followers. For example, teenager Tyler Oakley started filming videos in his bedroom and became an online personality, endorsing products such as Taco Bell and providing support to LGBT youth [50].

MOBILE E-COMMERCE AND DISTRIBUTION

Mobile is an increasingly important tool for both marketers and consumers. Marketers use mobile devices for inventory tracking and to execute transactions both at the wholesale and retail levels. Wholesalers can provide mobile application services to their clients that help reduce costs and control merchandising. For example, Benetton offers its retailers a 3D mobile app that helps stores display the company's clothing for maximum profitability. Pepsico's Power4Merch shows PepsiCo merchandisers schedule, store, and display details. The app can also coordinate deliveries so that a product arrives in the store at the right time [29].

Some of these applications simplify the transaction for the customer. Apple stores allow customers to pay for products anywhere in the store by approaching a roving salesperson who executes the transaction on an iPhone. Even smaller companies can use mobile payment systems such as a Square Reader to accept credit cards. The Square device attaches to an iPhone for swiping and reading credit cards.

Marketers can track people's mobile devices in stores to provide services or obtain data. Nomi is a mobile market research firm that follows customers in stores using the customer's mobile devices. Nomi's technology utilizes mobile device IDs (a unique identification consisting of a set of numbers or letters the manufacturer assigns to each device that can be accessed publicly) when people enter stores and monitors their footpaths. Using Nomi, Baked by Melissa, the cupcake store, tested two window displays to determine which was more effective, and Sweetgreen restaurants used Nomi to determine when customers receive their meals to shorten wait times [51].

THEY'RE WATCHING YOU!

How do you feel about being tracked when you walk into a store? Do you think mobile firms like Nomi should be allowed to track you without your consent?

As long as you are over 13, you may be tracked without your permission. There are no laws protecting you from your own cell phone!

Even when purchases are executed online or in-store, the smartphone and tablet can contribute to the sale or alter the selling outcome. Consumers now use their phones in stores to check prices and offerings. Amazon's app allows consumers to scan books in stores and then offers them at a lower price. This competition has significantly altered the way marketers sell books, with many stores closing because of the stiff competition from Amazon. The eBay mobile application includes a built-in scanner so that users can scan products in a store for price comparisons while shopping or scan products they intend to sell. In both cases, the app pulls up all relevant products, so the users can plan their strategy [30].

Many online marketers try to steal sales from physical stores. For example, Groupon offers discounts on a variety of local services by aggregating groups of consumers and offering them a service at a reduced price. Groupon's mobile app is a convenient way for consumers to manage offers, eliminates the need for printing, and can record and store loyalty information [52]. Using it provides a level of convenience, thereby making Groupon an easier option than having to print offers or coupons to present to retailers.

BRICK-AND-MORTAR STORES FIGHT BACK

Traditional retailers, those who operate physical stores, may be threatened by firms such as Groupon and Amazon, but these stores have new opportunities as well. Physical (often called brick-and-mortar) stores can leverage brand loyalty and intervene in the consumer's purchase process. For example, Walgreens's mobile app offers a "Refill by Scan" feature that allows consumers to order drug refills by scanning the barcode on their pill bottle. Users can also receive mobile reminders when prescriptions need to be refilled. The app includes other features that link users to photo printing, coupon information, and a store finder.

WHICH PLATFORM IS BEST FOR GAMING?

Zynga, the online gaming company that partnered with Facebook to deliver games on its platform, was late to the mobile table and suffered a large decline in its stock price when people stopped playing games on Facebook. One very strong opportunity Zynga missed was the chance to offer mobile versions of their games to their users. Instead, other companies stepped in and attracted Zynga's customers. Gamers are a fickle bunch, though, constantly giving up one set of games to try the newest ones. [53].

Businesses operating physical stores have also developed in-store strategies in response to the presence of mobile devices and online competition. Some stores block wireless Internet access or even specific sites inside their stores, while others have eliminated certain products from their in-store offerings. Walmart removed all Kindle products from its stores because management was concerned that customers would browse books in the store and buy online instead. Walmart was particularly worried about the Amazon Kindle Fire, which, if displayed in the store, could allow shoppers to view many competing products or remind customers that they can shop for deals online with their own phones. At the very least, Walmart most likely did not want to help sell a device by Amazon, its major competitive threat [54].

The threat of consumers using the retail store for information related to the purchase and then buying online or through a mobile device has become such a challenge for stores that a term has been coined for it—**showrooming**. To counteract showrooming, some firms replace the bar codes on their products with their own codes so that the customer can't scan them and compare online while they are in the store [55].

TABLETS FUELING ONLINE SALES

Consumers are increasingly using mobile shopping tools and executing transactions on their devices. In Chapter Four, we saw that consumers spend more money on tablets than on their phones. Mobile is poised to grow its share of e-commerce to over 30% of all electronic commerce transactions globally [38]. One reason for the strong growth in mobile is the tablet device, which complements consumers' shopping habits. The touchscreen capabilities offer an easy way for consumers to drag purchases to carts and expand pictures of products for clear viewing. In addition, people can sit in front of the television and shop on their tablet, leading to even higher potential sales for certain product categories [56].

WHAT CONSUMERS WANT: SIMPLICITY

In a Harvard Business School (HBS) study of online shopping motivations, consumers indicated that they engage with brands in social media to obtain a discount, or purchase or review products. The Institute for Business Value found that companies believe consumers follow their brands on social media to learn about new products, get information, and submit opinions. According to the HBS study, consumers are seeking simplicity in their purchases, and the easier it is to make the purchase, the more likely they will do so. Presenting customers with a ton of product information that they need to process before they can buy something online may make the experience so daunting that the customer might not follow through with the purchase. Companies that make the purchase process easy are more likely to drive sales through their channels.

The study examined 7,000 consumers and the factors that influenced consumer **stickiness,** defined as the likelihood of following through on a purchase, buying from a brand repeatedly, and interacting with a brand. Customers overwhelmingly indicated that the ease with which they can gather trustworthy information to confidently and efficiently evaluate the product led to purchase and loyalty [57].

GEOSOCIAL ELECTRONIC COMMERCE

Mobile marketing strategies are often local because the cell phone is carried and used on the go. These strategies include setting up mobile websites, executing mobile advertising, or offering mobile applications. One specific type of mobile strategy that affects retail is called **geosocial** or **location-based marketing,** which leverages an individual's location to offer services. Geosocial marketing has grown as the big social networks such as Facebook and Twitter have integrated location-based technology within their platforms. Whereas, originally, geosocial services focused on the ability to "check in" at particular sites, the concept of identifying one's location was not appealing to most smartphone users. Therefore, the location-based services provide other benefits to users such as notifications and local sites of interest to enhance their offerings. This is where **SoLoMo,** an acronym for social, local and mobile, converges. Offering optimal social, location, and mobile services to enhance consumers' experiences is a goal for many marketers. For example, your phone can send you a notification that one of your friends highly rated the restaurant that is right in front of you [58].

Many marketers use location-based data to enhance consumer experiences. For example, maps use location to provide directions, Booking.com helps people find hotels where they are located, and social apps use location to link people to one another when they are in close proximity. Some of the social media sites, such as Instagram, Snapchat, or Foursquare, are exclusively mobile, thus providing location-based information all the time.

Specialized geosocial services, such as Foursquare's Swarm, encourage people to "check in" at specific locations to indicate their presence there. Originally, Foursquare turned the act of "checking in" into a contest, whereby people competed to become "mayor" of a location. Foursquare ultimately spun off the "check in" component of the business to Swarm and now operates as a review site. Facebook also offers its users a "check in" service and more people use Facebook's interface than apps such as Swarm. In fact, location-based social activities that involve identifying a person's location are not very popular. Whereas over 70% of smartphone owners use their phone to get real-time location-based information, only about 12% have used a service such as Foursquare to "check in." Those 18–29 with incomes under $40,000 are most likely to indicate they use "check in" services with Facebook the most popular [59].

The e-commerce opportunities for geosocial mobile marketing are relatively limited, and few companies have sold through this method. One potential is to use geosocial for connecting people to participate in services that require a group, such as a carpool or team sport. Another option is to provide consumers with incentives to purchase when they "check in" at retail locations. Bars and restaurants could use location-based social data to offer groups of people drink deals to attract them to their establishment, or reward regulars for their patronage.

Retailers can also use a specific type of local service called a geofence to locate customers near their establishments. **Geofencing** is a technological method of identifying the presence of individuals using their cell-connected devices. Retailers can create a virtual fence around certain locations to determine the number of people in the location, its traffic patterns, or even the mobile activities of those within the fence. Since most people carry their phones 24/7, they could receive messages within the fences of particular marketers. However, marketers are limited in their ability to use cell services to track and identify consumers. People must opt in or agree to receive mobile messages.

consider this . . .

CAN YOU USE GEOFENCING TECHNOLOGY?

Marketers are not the only people who want to use geofencing. Life360 is an app that allows members of a family to monitor the whereabouts of one another via a cell network or wireless. The app was so successful that people around the world downloaded it even though the cell component of the service only worked in the United States. Family members can set fences in particular areas, typically, at work and at home, and track the cell phones of family who enter the area [60].

SUMMARY AND REVIEW

CHAPTER SUMMARY

Social media and mobile marketing offer firms new opportunities to harness diverse groups of people to participate in the development process—and this has fundamentally changed how products are created and sold. Social media and mobile marketing have also changed the distribution game in many ways, affecting both wholesalers and retailers reaching customers in business-to-business and business-to-consumer markets.

KEY TERMS

B2B (business-to-business) market
B2C (business-to-consumer) market
channel of distribution
competitive advantage
complementary product

creative collaboration
crowdsourcing
customer value
customer value proposition
direct marketing
distribution

e-commerce
F-commerce
geofencing
geosocial or location-based marketing
mobile applications
niche market

retailer
showrooming
SoLoMo
stickiness
virtual workforce
wholesaler

SUMMARY REVIEW QUESTIONS

1. Explain the concept of crowdsourcing.
2. How does the Google search engine make use of crowdsourcing with regard to the results?
3. Describe how a manufacturer of apparel could use crowdsourcing to develop new designs.
4. Explain the difference between the B2B and B2C markets.
5. What role do wholesalers play in the channel of distribution?
6. List three ways that mobile can influence the purchase decision process.
7. What is showrooming? Have you done this before? When and where?

APPLICATION QUESTIONS

1. Go to Quirky.com and find three products you would consider purchasing. How would you go about purchasing them?
2. Find the top ten downloaded mobile applications and answer the following questions:

   How many of the apps are social media-related?
   How many of the apps are games?
   How many apps are B2B?

3. Find a company-branded application and list three functions for the app. Are these appropriate to the brand? Do the functions help build business, satisfy customers, or reduce costs? Explain.
4. Find one project on Kickstarter and describe it. Report on how much money the project has accumulated and how much is still required before the project is fully funded. What would you get if you donate to the project?

5. Go to Mechanical Turk and click on the HITs tab at the top of the page. What does HIT stand for? List two jobs offered under the HITs tab. Now click on the Qualification tab and explain the concept of qualifications.

6. Using Google, determine the percentage of online sales that are generated by mobile transactions and the total dollar value of those transactions. How much has mobile grown in the past year according to your data?

Case Study: Yammer

Yammer was a social media platform for businesses that connected employees to one another to solve problems, develop products, serve customers, and communicate firm-related business issues. Originally launched as a Twitter-like tool for businesses in 2008, Yammer evolved into a platform more akin to Facebook and included a newsfeed and groups. At the time, "enterprise social networking" was a relatively new way for people to communicate within an organization. Yammer was one such network that integrated other software, such as ERP (enterprise resource planning), HR (human resources), and SPA (sales and purchase agreements). These software programs were already used by many firms to organize business activities. Yammer provided the social component that linked these functions through people [61].

Over 90,000 companies were using Yammer by 2012, with over a million users in 135 countries. At that time, 80% of Fortune 500 companies were running Yammer and Microsoft purchased the company for $1.2 billion.

The system allowed anyone in a company, from the CEO down to the mailroom clerk, to sign up for free, while more advanced features, such as a secure network, were provided on a fee basis of $3–5 per user per month.

Yammer company pages were typically arranged in customizable three-column format with a newsfeed in the center. Users could post any information they chose and were not restricted in the length of the message as on Twitter; they could attach files as well, something not possible to do on Facebook. When people posted, others could "like" or reply to the post.

A study examining the use of Yammer at Deloitte in Australia found that the software was used for sharing information, crowdsourcing ideas, and solving problems with expert advice. As well, Yammer added to relationship building among those in the organization [62].

A diverse set of industries, including industrial, manufacturing, technology, telecommunications, education, financial services, and consumer products, used Yammer for internal communications. However, the client list was proprietary to protect the security of the companies on-site.

THE TYCO YAMMER NETWORK

Tyco was a manufacturer of fire detection and protection systems, home and business security, and safety devices for firefighting and the military. For example, Tyco's American Dynamics division sold video security systems. Bentel Security operated a range of intrusion and fire alarm control equipment to protect property.

The global company with $10.5 billion in sales and 3 million customers used Yammer as part of its strategy to split the company into three units, with Tyco emphasizing the fire solutions and security business. Since Tyco operated globally with a diverse range of employees, effective communications were a key factor in keeping everyone on board. The new mission for Tyco was to "advance safety and security by finding smart ways to save lives, improve business and protect people where they live and work." Tyco had undergone a series of acquisitions and spin-offs, and those outside the United States were not well connected to the North American headquarters in New Jersey. Therefore, the company's new president, George Oliver, considered Yammer to be an integral component of the new Tyco.

The switch to Yammer was generally welcomed by both employees and administrators alike. Tyco's old system provided slow, limited one-way communication, did not allow for posts and publishing, and was not engaging to users. Yammer provided an opportunity to include more people in more aspects of the business, regardless of their time zone, so that units around the world could participate in decisions and share their expertise [63].

The launch of Yammer at Tyco was successful from the first day, when 22,337 employees out of 29,000 logged onto the system and posted 500 items. After that, Tyco continued to see strong usage levels of Yammer throughout the organization. By 2013 57% of Tyco employees were on Yammer and 20% of them were actively engaged on the platform, posting an average of 1,343 items per day. The Tyco Yammer network operated in 50 countries in 1,000 locations, with the top user bases in the United States, United Kingdom, Australia, Canada, and the Netherlands [63].

A number of groups were highly active on Yammer, including Fire and Safety Today, Careers at Tyco, SG Inventory Specialists (Simplex Grinnel division), and Tyco Women's Growth Network.

Tyco used Yammer for a variety of daily tasks, but there were some notable successes with the platform. At Simplex Grinnel, a subsidiary, Yammer coordinated inventories globally so that parts would be more readily available when needed. When Tyco bid for a large contract involving security at soccer stadiums, the client asked for a list of prior work. The request went out on Yammer, and within one week the sales manager had a global list of stadiums utilizing Tyco products. When a Brazilian customer wanted to avoid adding tail-gating (a hinged part) to particular doors, one of Tyco's employees posted the question on Yammer and the solution came from the United Kingdom [63].

YAMMER AT THE ESQUEL GROUP

The Esquel Group produced premium cotton shirts for Ralph Lauren, Tommy Hilfiger, Nike, Hugo Boss, Lacoste, and others with production facilities in China, Malaysia, Vietnam, Mauritius, and Sri Lanka. The supply chain ran from cotton farms, spinning processes, labeling, and trimming to retail. The company started using Yammer to connect operations globally and it later became a morale-boosting and problem-solving entity. Among the most important functions were to percolate ideas from the manufacturing floor to headquarters and to manage complaints. The company viewed Yammer as a means to turn unhappy employees into innovative problem-solvers.

For example, a worker in the garment operation posted that she had to wait in a long line to add value to her staff meal card. The posting yielded forty ideas for solving the problem, and the company decided to install a kiosk that transferred funds from payroll to card [64], [65].

Yammer was also very successful in signing up new companies. By 2014 there were 8 million users worldwide and 85% of Fortune 500 firms were running Yammer. Clearly, word had traveled through social networks that collaboration through Yammer was good for business.

QUESTIONS FOR DISCUSSION

1. How can Yammer help a company that makes security products and a manufacturer of clothing using similar systems?

2. What functions can Yammer facilitate for Tyco and for Esquel?

3. How did Yammer grow so fast?

4. Examine the different businesses discussed in the case. Locate one wholesaler and one retailer. Explain your answer.

5. Is Tyco a B2B or B2C company? How do you know?

6. Consider Esquel's business. How can Yammer help its product development process? What can Yammer do to assist in the supply chain?

7. How has Yammer generated revenue for Tyco and reduced costs for Esquel?

8. The case study paints a very rosy picture of Yammer and its role in two companies. Can Yammer be used in all organizations or industries? Why or why not? Is there a potential negative side to such a system?

REFERENCES

[1] K. Frenkel, "Crowdsourced in the U.S.A.," *Business Week,* 29 June 2012.

[2] D. Fenn, "Quirky Gets Backing From Andreessen Horowitz and Kleiner Perkins," *The New York Times,* 7 September 2012.

[3] S. Lohr, "Quirky, an Invention Start-Up, Files for Bankruptcy" *New York Times,* September 22, 2015. http://www.nytimes.com/2015/09/23/business/the-invention-start-up-quirky-files-for-bankruptcy.html?_r=0

[4] M. K. Poetz and M. Schreier, "The Value of Crowdsourcing: Can Users Really Compete with Professionals in Generating New Product Ideas?," *Journal of Product Innovation Management,* vol. 29, no. 2, pp. 245–256, March 2012.

[5] S. Strom, "Starbucks to Introduce Single-Serve Coffee Maker," *The New York Times,* 20 September 2012.

[6] R. Divol, D. Edelman, and H. Sarrazin, "Demystifying Social Media," *McKinsey Quarterly,* April 2012.

[7] B. Beyus, "Crowdsourcing New Product Ideas Over Time: An Analysis of the Dell Ideastorm Community," *Management Science,* vol. 59, no. 1, pp. 226–244, 2013.

[8] J. Surowiecki, *The Wisdom of Crowds,* New York: Anchor Books, 2005.

[9] J. Surowiecki, "Twilight of the Brands," *The New Yorker,* 17 and 24 February 2014.

[10] National Public Radio, "All Tech Considered," 12 February 2013, http://www.npr.org/blogs/alltechconsidered/2013/02/12/171715999/this-app-uses-the-power-of-you-to-report-the-weather.

[11] National Public Radio, "All Tech Considered," 16 January 2013, http://www.npr.org/blogs/alltechconsidered/2013/01/16/169469050/its-about-time-facebook-reveals-new-search-feature.

[12] E. Markowitz, "The Case for Letting Your Customers Design Your Products," *Inc.,* 20 September 2011.

[13] Gwen and Patrick, "KickStarter," http://www.kickstarter.com/projects/cherryonthebag/cherry-on-the-bag-simply-genuine-smartly-interacti?ref=live [Accessed 6 July 2014].

[14] R. Trump, "Why Would You Ever Give Money Through Kickstarter," *The New York Times,* 8 February 2013.

[15] Mechanical Turk, http://www.mechanicalturk.com.

[16] M. Willis, "Microworkers.com, The Truth," HubPages, 4 July 2014, http://matthewwillis.hubpages.com/hub/Microworkers-The-Truth.

[17] W. Willett, J. Heer, and M. Agrawala, "Strategies for Crowdsourcing Social Data Analysis," in *Proceedings of the SIGCHI Conference on Human Factors in Computing Systems,* Chicago, 2012.

[18] A. Gupta, W. Thies, E. Cutrell, and R. Balakrishnan, "mClerk: Enabling Mobile Crowdsourcing in Developing Regions," in *Proceedings of the Conference on Human Factors in Computing Systems,* 2012.

[19] The Outsourcing Guide, "Meet the Microworkers," 2013.

[20] A. Kulkani, M. Can, and B. Hartmann, "Collaboratively Crowdsourcing Workflows with Turkomatic," in *Proceedings of the ACM Conference on Computer Supported Cooperative Work,* 2012.

[21] R. King, "Meet the Microworkers," *Bloomberg Business Week,* 1 February 2011.

[22] M. Boyle, "Unilever Unveils Online Forum to Attract Outside Innovation Help," *Business Week,* 20 March 2012.

[23] S. Israel, " Will Yammer Hammer Salesforce Chatter?," *Forbes,* 10 April 2012.

[24] Pew Research, "Millennials Confident. Connected. Open to Change," *Social and Demographic Trends,* February 2010.

[25] Digital Insider Podcast, "The $6.4 Billion Social Media Business You Don't Know About," 30 September 2012.

[26] Yammer Blog, 2011, https://blogs.office.com/2011/01/24/spotlight-on-a-customer-lingo24/.

[27] B. X. Chen, "OpenTable to Acquire Foodspotting for $10 Billion," *The New York Times,* 29 January 2013.

[28] S. Perez, "ComScore U.S. Internet Report: YoY, Pinterest Up 4000+%, Amazon Up 30%, Android Top Smartphone & More," TechCrunch, 2012.

[29] Apple, "iPad in Business," 2014,: http://www.apple.com/ipad/business/profiles/ge/.

[30] E. Swallow, "13 Branded iPhone Apps That Enhance Their Company's Products," Mashable, 12 September 2011.

[31] J. Iredale, "Beachmint Adds Beauty in Latest Growth Pitch," *Women's Wear Daily,* 1 September 2011.

[32] Hispanic PR Pro, "Beachmint Brings Commerce and Celebrity Curation to Facebook," *Hispanic PR Pro,* 1 July 2012.

[33] R. Fisher, "BeachMint's Fresh Take on Celebrity-Backed Brands," *Talentzoo,* 2010.

[34] S. Sengupta, "For Search, Facebook Had to Go Beyond 'Robospeak,'" *The New York Times,* 28 January 2013.

[35] J. Worthham, "A Growing App Lets You See It, Then You Don't," *The New York Times,* 8 February 2013.

[36] S. Spangler, Social Media Examiner Podcast, 7 February 2013, Interview.

[37] T. Spangler, "Amazon Studios to Bow 5 Pilots in Third Pilot Wave," *Variety,* 11 August 2014.

[38] Criteo, "Criteo State of Mobile Commerce: Growing Like a Weed," 2015.

[39] J. Fox, "5 Real Estate Social Media Marketing Resolutions for 2013," 26 December 2012, Available: http://www.jasonfox.me/5-real-estate-social-media-marketing-resolutions-for-2013/.

[40] American Floral Endowment, *Social Media Guide for Retailers,* 2013.

[41] Automotive Digital Marketing, 6 July 2014, http://www.automotivedigitalmarketing.com/.

[42] Facebook, 2014, https://www.facebook.com/ecwid.

[43] A. Lutz, "Gamestop to Penney Shut Facebook Stores," *Bloomberg,* 17 February 2012.

[44] E. Zimmerman, "Small Retailers Open Up Storefronts on Facebook Pages," *The New York Times,* 25 July 2012.

[45] T. Geron, "What Is Facebook's Future as an Ecommerce Platform?," *Forbes,* 12 April 2011.

[46] V. Goel, "Coming Soon to Social Media: Click to Buy Now," *The New York Times,* 17 July 2014.

[47] Beso, 2014, http://www.beso.com.

[48] S. Sengupta, "With a Billion Birthdays on File, Facebook Adds a Gift Store," *The New York Times,* 27 November 2012.

[49] M. Angelo, "Women Who Take Their Shopping Very 'Srsly'," New York Times, 2 September 2012.

[50] D. Rushkoff, "Generation Like," *PBS Frontline,* 18 February 2014.

[51] K. Kaye, "Startup Nomi Tracks Shoppers by Their Mobile Phone Signals," *Advertising Age,* 11 February 2013.

[52] Nielsen, "Which Shopping Apps Do Savvy Shoppers Use Most?," A.C. Nielsen, 2012.

[53] D. Streitfeld, "Zynga at a Crossroads in Mobile Quest," *The New York Times,* 5 February 2013.

[54] S. Clifford and J. Bosman, "Walmart Is Deleting the Kindle from Stores," *The New York Times,* 20 September 2012.

[55] S. Clifford, "Luring Online Shoppers Offline," *The New York Times,* 4 July 2012.

[56] C. C. Miller, "Do People Actually Shop on Their Phones? The Answer Is Decidedly Yes," *The New York Times,* 9 January 2013.

[57] P. Spenner and K. Freeman, "To Keep Your Customers, Keep It Simple," *Harvard Business Review,* May 2012.

[58] M. Ballve, "Beyond Check Ins: How Social Media Apps Are Driving a Boom in Location-Based Data," Business Insider, 5 August 2013.

[59] Zickuhr, K. "Location Based SErvices, Pew Research Center, September, 12, 2013. http://www.pewinternet.org/2013/09/12/location-based-services/

[60] K. Fitchard, "The World Gets the Geofencing Bug: Life360's Family Locator App Explodes Overseas," 2 July 2013, http://gigaom.com/2013/07/02/the-world-gets-the-geofencing-bug-life360s-family-locator-app-explodes-overseas/.

[61] J. V. Grove, "How Yammer Won Over 80% of the Fortune 500," Mashable, 21 October 2010.

[62] K. Riemer, P. Scifleet, and R. Reddig, "Powercrowd: Enterprise Social Networking in Professional Service Work: A Case Study of Yammer at Deloitte Australia," Working Paper, Business Information Systems http://ses.library.usyd.edu.au/handle/2123/8352, 2012.

[63] Yammer, "The Tyco Yammer Network," 2013.

[64] Yammer Blog, "Esquel: Social Technology Weaves an Enterprise Together," 12 June 2014.

[65] Esquel Group, 2014, http://www.esquel.com.

© Shutterstock/Annette Shaff

CHAPTER SIX

PRICING AND PROMOTING

Chapter Five examined the influence of social media and mobile marketing on the first two elements of the marketing mix: product and place. We will now look at the final two components of the marketing mix: price and promotion. Consumers use social media to determine price–value relationships by reading online reviews and judging the expected performance of products and services relative to transparent prices that are readily available online. Mobile further allows people to acquire pricing information from any location, disrupting retail environments. Social media and mobile marketing influence each element of a promotional strategy, including sales promotions, sponsorships and events, public relations, and personal selling, affecting how people receive and interpret messages from companies.

LEARNING OBJECTIVES

After reading this chapter, you will be able to:

- DESCRIBE THE CHANGING NATURE OF PRICING STRATEGY AND PROMOTIONAL TECHNIQUES DUE TO SOCIAL MEDIA AND MOBILE MARKETING.

- DEVELOP PRICING STRATEGIES TO ACHIEVE ORGANIZATIONAL GOALS.

- EXAMINE CONSUMER RESPONSE TO PRICING AND PROMOTIONAL METHODS.

- EVALUATE PROMOTIONAL TECHNIQUES TO ENHANCE COMMUNICATIONS STRATEGY.

- DETERMINE SOCIAL MEDIA AND MOBILE INFLUENCE ON SALES PROMOTION, SPONSORSHIPS AND EVENTS, PUBLIC RELATIONS, EXPERIENTIAL MARKETING, AND PERSONAL SELLING.

- REVIEW COMPANY STRATEGY IN SOCIAL MEDIA AND MOBILE MARKETING RELATED TO PROMOTIONS.

Astrong marketing strategy includes all four elements of the marketing mix. Brands may augment a strategy with intelligent pricing methods or smart promotions that boost consumer response and encourage purchase at a particular time and place. Sometimes, the task is as simple as reminding consumers to purchase. Since most people already know what to do with an Oreo cookie, all the brand has to do is tell consumers to purchase the product. Therefore, Oreo uses a broad range of pricing and promotional strategies to reach its customers around the world.

Oreo has strong brand awareness among consumers who love the product and want to be part of the team. The task for the brand is to stimulate purchase behavior when consumers need a sweet snack and are receptive to its message. The strategy in the United States is focused on childlike wonder over the crème cookie filling with no real need to say much about the product itself because it is so well known [1].

Not only is Oreo loved in the United States, but Kraft has penetrated emerging markets with the chocolate cookies, and the brand currently nets $1.5 billion in global annual revenues. Oreo, "America's Best Loved Cookie," launched in China in 1996. Chinese consumers are not big cookie eaters, so Kraft did some market research to determine their tastes and preferences. The consumers complained that the cookies tasted "too sweet and too bitter" and that the price was high. The brand altered the formula and offered smaller packages for sale at a reduced price. Though the Chinese had no experience pairing cookies with milk, the messaging worked to increase sales in areas where Kraft's "dunking" campaign ran.

Kraft also recognized that India was a completely different market with a strong preference for cookies and a large volume of sales by competing brands. Oreo launched in India under the already well-known Cadbury brand with small packages and a sweeter formula for the Indian palate. The theme in India is "togetherness," and the launch included a Facebook page paired with a bus tour to build togetherness among families in 9 cities and 450 smaller towns. The tour generated content for the Facebook page, and now Oreo can claim 30% of the cream biscuit market in India [2].

In the United States, the target for Oreo is moms, who are active social media users and constantly connecting on their mobile devices. As such, the Martin Agency chose to use social media to highlight the fascination people continue to have with the brand. To encourage active social media engagement on Twitter, Oreo sent street teams out in Oreo t-shirts with the Twitter hashtag #wonderfilled. On the day that Oreo launched its new jingle, singers in Oreo shirts descended on New York City's Union Square to encourage tweets. On Social Mention, a social media monitoring site, Oreo achieved a 50% reach, representing the number of unique authors of posts in social media divided by the total number of brand mentions in social media. Sentiment, the ratio of positive to negative comments, was 17 to 1 for #wonderfilled.

Oreo also succeeded in taking advantage of the thirty-minute power outage that occurred during Super Bowl XLVII in New Orleans. During the blackout, the cookie maker's social media team cleverly tweeted, "Power out? No problem," with an image of a barely lit solitary Oreo and the caption, "You can still dunk in the dark." With many sports fans now using several screens when watching big events, this tweet was an instant hit, with over 15,000 retweets. The post also earned 20,000 likes on Facebook in one day, and was posted on Tumblr and Digg [3]. Social media sometimes require thinking on one's feet and taking advantage of opportunities.

Both the U.S. positioning and the Indian launch strategy relied heavily on social media. The brand leveraged traditional media as well to make strong brand connections that were authentic and resonated with the appropriate target markets. However, brands must consider and review all aspects of the marketing mix before launching a campaign. Pricing strategy and outside promotions can make or break a relaunch or an initial market entry strategy. Without a reduced-price package size, the brand would not have penetrated markets in the developing world.

THE IMPACT OF SOCIAL MEDIA AND MOBILE TECHNOLOGY ON PRICING STRATEGY

The Internet has already changed marketers' abilities to manipulate prices within the marketplace. With information widely available regarding the prices of products and services in many categories, marketers can no longer price by outlet and must justify instances when prices differ. Consumers search for pricing information online and may use social media to evaluate the product to determine appropriate prices and thresholds.

Determining the proper price for a product or service is a difficult task for marketers. Brands must consider consumer demand, competitors, costs, and profitability. Social media and mobile make many pricing elements more transparent to buyers, thereby limiting price premiums that brands have long enjoyed.

The power struggle between consumers and companies began even before the advent of social media or mobile communications. Consumers had already begun researching prices online and comparing prices at various outlets. When Amazon entered the market, the potential for determining the lowest price on any item grew with Amazon's increasingly large

ShopSavvy is a mobile shopping assistant with a price-matching service that uses a barcode scanner.

ShopSavvy, www.shopsavvy.com

product offering. Today, it is easy for consumers to get competitive pricing information at the moment of purchase. People can download the Amazon Price Check app to use in stores to scan products for Amazon prices. Not only is it easy to obtain price information, but customers can also get reviews by scanning barcodes once they've downloaded "Purchx," a mobile application.

consider this . . .

PRICE COMPETITION FOR AMAZON?

Amazon will experience some very hefty competition as Alibaba enters the U.S. market. As described in Chapter One, Alibaba is a Chinese social media and e-commerce company with $160 billion in sales. The company sells to both intermediaries and final customers, but its revenue comes from advertising. Alibaba makes money when people browse the site, even if they do not buy. The company also has very low labor costs and benefits from China's lower corporate income tax. Amazon earns revenue by selling products and accepting very low margins to compete against retail stores. In the end, however, Amazon may not be able to compete with the zero margins of Alibaba [4].

Consumers search for prices when they view the task as easy and when they perceive that the prices have a large range—leading to the potential of obtaining a better price. Services that make the process easier help consumers navigate through the maze of potential prices and find deals. These services identify the best options at any given price level, allowing customers to make informed trade-offs between price and quality. One example of a service that provides pricing and quality information is TripAdvisor. A study examining how consumers choose hotels online found that the dominant decision factor driving choice was the strength of the reviews. A review that described a superior experience could convince a consumer to pay more for a particular hotel [5].

consider this . . .

TRAVELERS POST AND COLLECT EVIDENCE

One type of information that consumers evaluate on travel sites is pictures posted by travelers. Some travelers are more likely to post photos of their trip than others. Researchers discovered that those people who post photos like to provide evidence of their experience. As a result, these travelers are also more likely to give souvenirs as gifts to friends and family, purchasing local specialty items at destinations as additional evidence of their experience [6].

Another important factor, use of mobile devices for shopping, has further increased the tension between marketers and consumers, particularly at the retail level. Consumers use mobile to search for prices at home, at work, and on the go. Sometimes, consumers are just price searching, but often these searches trigger desirable outcomes for marketers. According to Google, three-quarters of mobile searches lead to follow-up actions on the part of consumers, such as a phone call, store visit, social sharing, or purchase [7]. Consumers around the world are increasingly using shopping apps in stores to compare prices. A **shopping app** is a mobile application that guides consumers in retail establishments by providing information during a store visit. Mobile users are increasing the amount of digital time they spend using applications and shopping apps are growing in popularity [9]. The content areas where people spend the most time are shown in Exhibit 6.1. As you can see mobile app usage is dominated by photo and messaging services, but retail apps are also used.

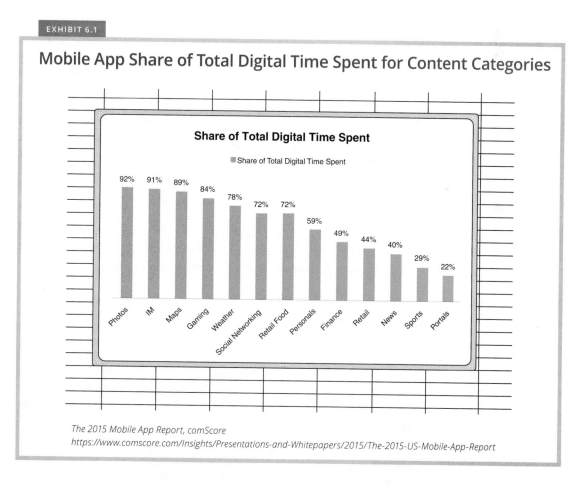

EXHIBIT 6.1

Mobile App Share of Total Digital Time Spent for Content Categories

The 2015 Mobile App Report, comScore
https://www.comscore.com/Insights/Presentations-and-Whitepapers/2015/The-2015-US-Mobile-App-Report

PRICING CONSIDERATIONS

Pricing has always been complicated for marketers. In order to price well, marketers must evaluate various factors, some of which are difficult to quantify. These include internal factors, which are determined within the company, and **external factors**, set by the environment. The **internal factors** are the costs for the product or service and the mechanisms in the organization for offering prices to customers, such as sales commissions, along with the objectives guiding the firm, such as the desire to maximize profits or build market share. The external factors are consumer demand for the product or service and the competition, which a firm can't control.

Pricing strategy to some extent depends on the elements of the marketing mix determined by the brand. With regard to the product, social media and mobile technology can potentially provide an additional level of quality. For example, mobile apps may offer convenience for which consumers may pay more. Promotion through social media to build engagement may help solidify relationships with customers who would pay a higher price or at least remain loyal in the face of product or service failure. Some research has suggested that when consumers have relationships with firms, they are more accepting of failures. Finally, how and where marketers distribute products or services affect the price. For example, you would probably pay more for cosmetics sold in a fancy store than at your local drug store.

The ability of consumers to price shop through social media and mobile affects demand—sometimes leading to narrower margins for firms. For example, airline margins have been squeezed by travel sites that show the lowest fares. As a result, airlines assess fees for various products and services, unbundling what was previously included in a fare, such as baggage handling. In addition, airlines run fewer flights and fill them to capacity to remain profitable.

Competitors can access the same information available to consumers to learn about industry pricing strategies online. Some companies have taken advantage of transparent pricing by undercutting the competition to attract cost-conscious customers.

Since competitors often have similar cost structures within an industry, transparent prices could result in price compression, which occurs when prices for particular goods and or services converge, eliminating premiums.

Environmental factors also affect how a brand can price. During times of economic recession, marketers tend to hold prices steady rather than try to raise them as consumers buy less and rely more on home inventories. When manufacturers raise prices after a recession, their sales volumes do not necessarily recover because people are accustomed to the recession pricing [10].

consider this . . .

SOCIAL AND MOBILE BUNDLE PRICING IN GHANA

A young Ghanian woman named Monica told me that she regularly used Facebook to communicate with her friends. Many young educated Ghanians are active social networkers using wireless connections on smartphones to communicate with their vast groups of friends. That may explain why the local cell provider offers free unlimited use of Facebook, Twitter, and WhatsApp as part of the mobile cell plan in Ghana.

Cell tower in Beyin, Ghana.

Randi Priluck

PRICING METHODS

Internal and external pricing factors are the basis for three categories of pricing methods: cost-based, competition-based, and demand-based. **Cost-based pricing methods** require that a marketer determine the cost to produce or offer a particular product. Then the marketer simply adds on an additional amount for the profit. Social media and mobile marketing do not have a very strong impact on cost-based pricing, except perhaps because these marketing efforts may reduce overall marketing costs, if social media or mobile efforts are more cost-effective than traditional advertising. However, that would have to be determined by the particular brand and strategy.

Competition-based pricing methods are more influenced by social media and mobile because marketers can obtain exact pricing information and determine their price relative to the competition. For example, Chipotle prices differently depending on location. A competitor could determine location-by-location prices and decide to price at parity, or above or below Chipotle's price, to appear more exclusive or to compete more directly on price. Though not directly a pricing strategy, competitors could use mobile couponing to offer deals to consumers to give them more value. (Couponing is a promotional technique discussed later in the chapter.)

The final type of pricing is demand-based. **Demand-based pricing methods** start from the perspective of the consumer and seek to determine how much customers may be willing to pay for a product or service, setting the price accordingly.

For example, with a **price skimming** strategy that is often used for specialized products, such as new electronics, the marketer offers the product for sale at a very high initial price to attract those customers who demand the product so strongly they are willing to pay the highest price to purchase the product when it comes out. Over time, the marketer then lowers the price and with every price drop attracts more of the market. Apple has used this strategy to introduce products that have very strong initial demand, such as the iPhone. Social media can boost a price skimming strategy by encouraging sharing of information about the product and developing people's desire to own it as the product's features are shared through social networks. Price penetration is another strategy that may benefit from social media. When marketers use **price penetration**, they offer the product or service at a low initial price in the hopes that people will become loyal to the product and continue to buy it as the price goes up over time. This strategy requires a strong large base of customers that develop a loyalty to the product. Social media can help solidify this strategy as people share their love for the product with others and provide reasons to continue to purchase the product even as the marketer raises the price. Some digital properties that were originally free began charging fees for services, such as the *New York Times* digital edition and SugarSync, an online and mobile application for storing and accessing files on one's various devices. The goal of these firms is to get you hooked and then keep you as a customer. The more you share positively about their offering, the more others hear about and try the product.

The company's marketing strategy became increasingly sophisticated.

© Shutterstock/Cartoonresource

SOCIAL PRICING WITH UBER

Have you ever requested a car from Uber? Uber's business model relies on demand-based pricing. The company uses surge pricing, raising prices when demand is high so that more drivers have an incentive to be out on the road when people need them. The company has come under criticism for raising its prices during natural events, such as snowstorms and hurricanes, and now caps the price at 2.8 times its usual fare during declared states of emergency [11].

CONSUMER RESPONSE TO PRICING STRATEGY

Smart marketers understand that pricing influences consumer behavior, but what can marketers do to influence purchase response? The first step is to understand how consumers think about prices and what they signify. Often when products are priced above market levels, consumers perceive that the products are higher quality. However, when consumers are faced with multiple prices in a category, they may respond to the marketer's pricing cues, particularly when buyers do not have clear prior expectations of price.

To understand how consumers respond to prices, it helps to consider the concept of framing. **Framing** refers to the consumer's perception of price relative to his or her expectations or knowledge regarding prices within a product category. Marketers can influence consumers' perceptions by framing the price of a product or service for the customer. For example, a marketer of mobile apps would like to sell a game for $1.99. However, consumers expect a price of 99 cents for the typical mobile gaming app. The marketer can reframe the context by showing a variety of price options as follows:

Option 1: Basic service with no features and limited play . . . 99 cents

Option 2: Enhanced service with all features and unlimited play . . . $1.99

Option 3: Superior service with all features and special options . . . $3.99

Which option looks like the best deal? In this case, the marketer can encourage consumers to pay $1.99 by providing a higher-priced option that makes people more comfortable choosing the middle option.

When marketers provide a middle-of-the-road option for only a small additional outlay, people tend to choose the midrange. The higher-priced version makes the middle price acceptable to customers.

In general, consumers prefer lower prices for products and services, so reducing the base price and later adding on fees for extras can help retain marketer profitability at a lower price point. The same strategy can also be effective if the marketer breaks down the price into a cost per day. For example, a virus protection software company may tell consumers that their laptops will be protected for less than $1 a week, rather than give the full price of $49.99, which may seem like a good deal to protect your data.

Before prices became so accessible online, consumers tended to be fairly ignorant of prices, putting the marketer at an advantage in framing. Consumers today can frame their own prices and potentially know the value of all offerings. The challenge for consumers is to figure out which model is offered at a particular price as marketers change these numbers frequently to make the task of matching a price to an offering harder for customers even with their mobile devices. In lieu of an actual search, consumers use reference prices for decision-making. **Reference prices** are the expectations of price that consumers hold in their minds. These prices are typically lower than actual prices—presenting a problem for marketers. **External reference prices** are those supplied by marketers to frame the context in an advantageous way to enhance profitability [12].

consider this...

WHO APPRECIATES A GOOD DEAL?

Which group of people is more likely to believe that warehouse clubs offer brands comparable to national brands and that warehouse clubs offer quality products?

1. Households earning 150k or more
2. Households earning 100k–149k
3. Households earning 50–74k
4. Households earning less than 25k

People with the highest incomes appreciate the warehouse club more than others and consider such stores to be a good value—even if they don't need the discount. Forty-four percent of the highest-income households compared to only 27% of the lowest-income households hold positive attitudes toward warehouse clubs [13].

consider this...

UTILITARIAN VERSUS HEDONIC CONSUMERS

Consumers engage in online price search behavior to obtain better prices, but also because they enjoy the process of online shopping. In a study of apparel shoppers, researchers identified two groups of online customers: utilitarian shoppers and hedonic shoppers. **Utilitarian**

shoppers seek products with a purpose, carefully consider prices, and do not tend to buy impulsively. **Hedonic shoppers** prefer the sensory experience that marketers can encourage in online shopping and are more prone to unplanned purchases [14].

PRICING STRATEGIES FOR SOCIAL MEDIA AND MOBILE PROPERTIES

Social media sites use a variety of pricing methods to generate revenues. The most common is to offer the service for free to customers and sell advertising to firms. Both Facebook and Twitter use the free-to-consumer model and have positive revenue streams generated by advertising, particularly mobile. Facebook and Twitter make a majority of their revenues from mobile ads [15], [16]. Other popular sites that use the free model with ad support are Tumblr, Pandora, and Snapchat in the United States; Sina Weibo in China; and VKontakte in Russia [17]. Originally, Pinterest's revenue model included collecting a percentage of sales when consumers made purchases through Pinterest links. However, Pinterest moved to the advertising model as well, citing limited revenue streams from links as the reason [18].

Mobile-only properties are less likely to rely solely on advertising revenue because there is a dearth of advertising space in mobile that remains unsold, pushing prices down. Mobile games offer a free initial download to consumers followed by a series of potential in-app purchases that consumers buy to make the game more exciting or to continue to play. Some games also charge initial download fees for the game, occasionally as low as 99 cents, but offer opportunities to purchase add-ons as well.

Some social media sites offer an initial basic level of service for free and charge for premium services, such as Yammer or Spotify. Since Yammer's customers are companies that would purchase the service for a very specific purpose, revenue generation has been relatively easy. Once they purchase the service, companies invest time and money in training for their employees, so they are reluctant to switch to a new service. The music streaming business is different: customers are individuals, there is a lot of competition, and customers only need to worry about their own use of the application—so it's relatively easy for them to switch brands. About 20% percent of Spotify's customers pay for premium advertising-free services. Both social media and mobile sites can earn revenues by selling data. Facebook is able to mine data to determine very specific pieces of information about consumers that marketers wish to target. Mobile apps have access to the other apps on a customer's phone and can access location data, contacts, and other information.

SOCIAL AND MOBILE PROMOTIONAL STRATEGY

A good portion of this text is devoted to communications strategy using social media and mobile technology. Many marketers seek to achieve organizational objectives by persuading customers or other businesses to purchase their products and services using integrated marketing communications (IMC), a set of methods for reaching the target with appropriate messaging in the right media. Before marketers used the term IMC, they called communications strategy promotion. Promotion included advertising, sales promotion, personal selling, and public relations. Chapter Eight covers methods for strategy planning in IMC with an

EXHIBIT 6.2

Definitions of Integrated Marketing Communications Tools

Advertising	A nonpersonal paid form of persuasive communication aimed at target markets through various forms of media by identified sponsors.
Sales promotion	A short-term incentive offered to consumers or the trade to induce purchase.
Sponsorships	A form of nonpersonal communication in which marketers seek brand attention by purchasing naming rights to an event, entity, or activity that they do not own.
Experiential marketing	A set of product- or service-related activities designed for consumers to directly interact with a product or service in real life.
Public relations	An indirectly paid form of communication in which marketers seek to gain media attention in order to persuade people, without paying for media time.
Personal selling	An interpersonal form of one-to-one communication about a product or service designed to persuade.

emphasis on advertising, while this chapter focuses on the tools that support the brand message—sales promotion, sponsorships, experiential marketing, public relations, and personal selling (see Exhibit 6.2)

Whereas marketers often establish an initial price for products and services, there are opportunities to alter the price. **Sales promotion** refers to a communications strategy in which the marketer adjusts the price-value proposition for a product or service. In this case, the official price remains the same, but discounts, deals, or adjustments result in additional value for the customer. Marketers can aim sales promotional efforts at either intermediaries (the trade) in the channel, such as wholesalers or retailers, or at final consumers. In both cases, the goal is to influence the purchase cycle such that the target buys more quickly.

COUPONS AND OTHER SALES PROMOTIONS

The most common form of sales promotion in the United States is a coupon; over 80% of consumers report using coupons regularly. The goal of the coupon is to provide an incentive to consumers to purchase when they might otherwise wait. The offer pushes the consumer to act earlier than he or she would otherwise purchase. Though most people have used coupons, 31% tend to use them in some situations and not in others [19]. For example, the prior research indicates that when customers plan a shopping trip, they are more likely to use coupons than on an unplanned trip. Mobile distribution may make coupons more readily available, but consumers often fail to redeem coupons even when they are in the store or on the package itself.

There are over 3 billion coupons distributed annually in the United States and coupon issuing has been increasing at a 3% annual rate. Currently, digital coupons represent less than 1% of the total coupon market, but digital distribution is expected to increase [20].

consider this . . .

CROCS USES MOBILE COUPONS

When the global shoe company Crocs wanted to call attention to the Croslite material in their shoes, management used in-store mobile coupons delivered via text message. Approximately 185 stores posted the following call to action:

"What is a foot's best friend? Find out and save 15 percent today! It is as easy as one, two, three."

1. Text CROCS 1234 to 63103
2. Receive a 15% off coupon code and
3. Show the code at check out.

Crocs had 94,000 coupon requests in the first month of the campaign [21].

In addition to coupons, marketers also offer samples to encourage a purchase and to help reduce the risk in buying a product or service. Marketers sometimes offer gifts, also called **premiums**, which represent additional products that add to the value of the offering. In retail environments, sellers can offer promotions at the point of sale when consumers are completing transactions. Finally, loyalty programs are promotions because they provide incentives for customers to maintain ties with a brand. These loyal customers represent the bread and butter of a business and must be treated with care. Some research suggests that for many product categories, customers who are heavy users represent 80% of the revenues of a brand. Therefore, rewarding their loyalty is a good way to retain them.

A very popular promotional technique to execute via social media is a contest. A **contest** is a promotion in which people compete to win prizes based on skill or merit and are then evaluated based on objective criteria. Sometimes, marketers ask the participants to perform certain actions to win. For example, Activia, a brand of yogurt, ran a campaign in Slovenia that required players to complete tasks on Facebook, such as uploading videos of themselves eating and enjoying Activia, and posting pictures that represent how they feel when they eat

Activia. The promotion led to social sharing and one lover of Activia won a trip to Indonesia. Contests provide people with something meaningful to share with their friends and family, which increases the **reach**, or the number of viewers who see the campaign. The content, the pictures, videos, and other materials that the contestants create is called **user-generated content (UGC)**. User-generated content is important to marketers because some research has found that UGC is more persuasive than materials created by the marketer. In essence, UGC is an endorsement of the product or brand with the unique creative input of customers. As such, the efforts are more believable to others. Not only that, but UGC can be shared. Warby Parker asks customers to try on glasses and post the results on Twitter with the hashtag #WarbyHomeTryOn. The screenshot shows one video blogger who also did the at-home try-on and posted on her YouTube channel.

A study of user-generated content versus **marketer-generated content (MGC)** in the apparel industry found that social media participation led to increased purchases and that UGC had a significantly stronger effect on purchase behavior than MGC [23]. Nevertheless, marketers still develop promotions to influence consumers. Exhibit 6.3 describes a number of different types of sales promotions for various marketers: coupons [24], samples [25], gifts [26], point of sale [27], loyalty [28], and contests [29].

On YouTube, Leigh Ann showed her glasses on to over 600,000 followers.

Leighannsays, www.youtube.com/ leighannsays

EXHIBIT 6.3

Types of Consumer Promotions

	EXAMPLES
Coupons	Valpak, the company that delivers coupons by mail to people's homes, now has a mobile app featuring local businesses. To attract a young target, 16 Handles, a frozen yogurt chain, ran coupons on Snapchat that disappeared in ten seconds. The brand asked customers to take a picture of themselves at 16 Handles and send it to "Love16Handles" on Snapchat to obtain coupons offering 16%–100% off their next purchase. The only catch? You had to redeem the coupon in 10 seconds.
Samples	Facebook allows brands to send samples to target markets through its site. For example, Unilever used Facebook to distribute samples of its Marmite Cereal Bar to mothers and young adults. An ad ran on Facebook with the headline "Free Marmite Cereal Bar" and listed the names of friends who had received free samples. Not only did Unilever deliver 33,000 sample vouchers in two weeks, but the campaign generated 21.5 million impressions, meaning millions of people were aware of the campaign and the brand.
Gifts/premiums	When Spotify launched its service, users could download a free app that would play songs which friends shared on Facebook with just one click.
Point of sale	Marketers can offer deals to consumers at the point of purchase on a mobile tablet payment device. The tablet can be used to upsell customers at the point of purchase or add on features that may not be included in the base price, such as insurance. Tully's Coffee encourages customers to buy a $40 coffee card by offering $44 of coffee on its card. The cards could be offered via mobile to increase the likelihood that people would buy them and commit to Tully's.
Loyalty	Tesco's Club Card program is 100% digital and mobile. The company no longer has to ask for cards that people often leave at home. Instead, the loyalty program is available all the time on a customer's mobile device.
Contests	Lands' End ran a successful "Pin It to Win It" campaign on Pinterest. Customers competed by creating pin boards using Lands' End products, and each of the best boards won its creator a $250 gift voucher.

TRADE PROMOTIONS

Sales promotion aimed at intermediaries is also called **trade promotion**. Trade promotions include special sales and discounts to wholesalers or retailers if they agree to buy a large amount, merchandise the product in a particular way, or participate in joint marketing efforts. In the case of trade promotions, social media are not strongly developed, but mobile provides a number of opportunities for firms to offer promotions to dealers. For example, a manufacturer could run a mobile barcode contest with stores to determine which one sells the most product via mobile and test varying executions in the process.

MONITORING TRADE PROMOTIONS

Which are more effective, e-mail or mobile text message coupons? Researchers sent a mobile coupon either via email or text message to a group of Germans who had agreed to receive communications from a software company. The team examined 37,000 offers of a 67% discount on downloadable PC software and found that mobile yielded a stronger conversion rate. Though the coupon sent via email had higher initial response rates, mobile text customers were more likely to buy the software, yielding higher revenues [22].

The management consulting firm Accenture offers software to help companies manage their trade promotions. The software, known as the Trade Promotion Management and Optimization program, tracks consumer promotion at the retail level to provide information for planning, execution, and evaluation purposes. Accenture can help firms model the best promotional strategies that deliver the highest returns. One successful strategy has been to segment retailers to offer the optimum promotions on a store-by-store basis to deliver stronger returns. For instance, a dollar coupon may be more effective than a bonus pack in some locations.

RESEARCH ON CONSUMER RESPONSE TO SALES PROMOTIONS

The role of sales promotion is to support other communications strategies and is not usually the lead medium of a campaign because offering deals to people does not help build brand identity or image. Sales promotion achieves more short-term sales-related goals, such as encouraging people to purchase earlier than they might otherwise have bought or buying more than they planned. Researchers have long studied the influence of promotions on consumers. People who are frequent users of promotions are price sensitive, are receptive to brand information, are brand switchers, and are often heavy users of a category. Brand-loyal customers tend to be confident in their knowledge of price, while brand switchers are more influenced by external pricing cues [19].

One great concern for marketers in creating promotions is that customers can become "deal-prone." That means they wait for the promotion and expect to get a price reduction whenever they buy the product or service. There are two kinds of deal proneness: passive and active. **Passive deal-prone customers** stockpile the product, so they can respond whenever there is a deal, and **active deal-prone customers** switch brands to get the deal whenever available. Marketers need to take care in limiting scheduled promotions to avoid a de facto price reduction on their product or service. If consumers become too accustomed to getting a deal, they may always refuse to pay full price.

In order for sales promotions to be effective, consumers must be convinced that the marketer is offering an incentive rather than simply getting rid of old merchandise. Very large discounts can be counterproductive because consumers become suspicious unless they know the brand very well. However, promotions can alter the value of the brand to a customer without denigrating the consumer's perceived quality of it [19].

SOCIAL MEDIA FOR EXECUTING SALES PROMOTIONS

The major social media sites offer marketers the means to execute promotions via their platforms, and new types of promotions spring up regularly. The sites help marketers by encouraging people to share the offers with friends and family to build buzz around the promotions. For example, Twitter offers a #FlocktoUnlock hashtag to facilitate social sharing, and when enough people retweet the offer, everyone gets the deal. A hashtag is a searchable term on Twitter that uses the symbol # to aggregate comments using that hashtag. Brands can use these hashtags, so consumers can search for them or share them easily on Twitter. Bonobos is a large online men's clothing company that offered a series of #twixclusive deals over a 24-hour period on Twitter. When the sale began, @Bonobos (the company's Twitter handle) tweeted an exclusive deal for $49 chinos. However, in order to get the deal, customers were required to share the deal by retweeting a cumulative forty-nine times across Twitter. The deal unlocked in less than 10 minutes and those lucky customers got $88 pants for $49. The offer was only available through Twitter and only for 24 hours. The offers can take place in any country with a Twitter presence [29].

consider this . . .

PEPSI IN ARABIA

Promotional strategies using social media are truly global. Pepsi ran a Twitter campaign in Saudi Arabia to engage customers in naming their new beverage. Teaming up with Bader Saleh, a celebrity YouTube personality, @7UP-Arabia asked people to vote on one of three names: Lemo, Lamoon, or Squeeze. The brand used promoted tweets and the hashtag بـدر_وسـاعد_صـوت# (note Arabic reads right to left). The brand tallied votes from Twitter, a Facebook application, a microsite, YouTube videos, SMS, and a toll-free number so that everyone could participate. The results were 3,137 new Twitter followers and a 200% increase in mentions of the hashtag. Which name do you think won? Pepsi now markets Squeeze, a new lightly carbonated lemonade, in Saudi Arabia [30].

Facebook's Power Editor helps marketers run promotions by offering call-to-action buttons that can be added to posts. When people click on the call-to-action button, they can receive an offer, a coupon, or a free download. Twitter's format now also encourages clicking on promotions, as landing pages (pages to which you are taken when you click) show up within the tweet so people can see the offer, rather than just a shortened URL. Similarly, all the major social sites offer mechanisms for marketers to use the network to share various types of promotions.

Snapchat is another social media site on which brands run promotions, particularly coupons and deals. One company based in Manchester, England, The Co-operative Electrical, targeted students, offering them a coupon code for a £30 reduction on the price of any laptop in the store. To get the deal, all students had to do was to add the electronics retailer as a Snapchat friend [31].

Coca-Cola ran a successful campaign on China's social media site Sina Weibo. The cola company offered consumers a special promotional opportunity on the social site to customize their own Coke bottles for 20 yuan a piece, payable through Weibo Wallet. Each day of the campaign, more and more bottles sold with the help of promotion through Sina Weibo and a set of celebrities who posted their own customized bottles [32].

Sales promotions are part of an integrated marketing communications strategy and must be managed so that the efforts are in sync with other messages. For instance, a marketer would not want to offer a deep discount on a product on a regular basis or customers might come to expect the discount. A marketer would also not want to offer larger discounts than necessary to retain the profit margin. Small discounts may be enough to stimulate a response from consumers and still make money on the sale.

DAILY DEAL SITES

Pricing and promotion have been significantly affected by the emergence of daily deal sites, such as Groupon, LivingSocial, and Scoutmob. These social platforms originally offered large discounts (as much as 50%) for a particular product or service by aggregating customers for the offer and encouraging people to share the deals with friends through social media. Daily deal sites have been criticized for requiring steep discounts from vendors and generating strong revenues at their expense. For example, Groupon makes an 88% margin on the deals and 20% on Groupon Goods, resulting in over $3 billion in revenues annually [33].

Brands have been successful generating business with deals. A study of 641 small- and medium-sized businesses that ran daily deals found 55% to 61% were profitable for the merchant. The businesses that had the most success with these promotions were the most experienced in running the deals and had the most positive attitudes toward them. The study also found that the most successful businesses were spas and salons and health and fitness firms. Restaurants and retailers had the lowest rates of success with daily deals [34]. The businesses that ran profitable Groupon promotions had higher levels of repeat purchase and increased spending by customers over the value of the deal than those with unprofitable deals [35].

consider this . . .

GROUPON AND CUSTOMER SATISFACTION

A study by MIT found that the Groupon deals that generated high levels of customer satisfaction were the ones most likely to be negative for the merchant's level of profitability. In general, when customers are extremely happy, they are getting a very good deal on the service. As such, the companies offering the deep discounts lose money, but the deals attract strong levels of demand. The researchers estimated that the four categories in which they noted a relationship between satisfaction and lost profits represent 50% of Groupon's volume [36].

Groupon, the first daily deal site, launched in November 2008, and by January 2011 it was valued at $15 billion. A number of competitors entered the market and the business model was called into question by many of the vendors who offered their services on the site. Several years later, daily deal sites are popular only among a niche market of consumers [38]. Only about 10% of U.S. consumers participate in daily deals, and a full 40% have never even heard of such offerings. In a survey of daily deals, customers overwhelmingly preferred Groupon's deals, but only 16% agreed that, in general, the deal sites offer good value. The most popular daily deals are in [39]:

Food and beverages

Shopping

Events and activities

Travel and getaways

Marketers have found success using daily deal sites, but should be careful about how they use the service. As with any strategy, targeting the market and setting goals for the activity will help clarify the customers of interest and how they will be served by the marketer's offering. The timing of the deal and the number of deals available during specified times help marketers manage the potentially large influx of new customers and provide for mechanisms to convert daily dealers to regular customers, such as asking for contact information. Interestingly, marketers may not need to offer such large discounts to attract customers. Constant Contact, the email marketing company, found that its customers succeeded in attracting clients with discounts of as little as 10%.

DAILY DEALS FROM THE CUSTOMER PERSPECTIVE

A study of 655 daily deal customers found that the people who purchased eleven or more deals were the most enthusiastic about the sites. These daily dealers regularly checked the deal sites, preferred Groupon over the other offers, did not view themselves as on the fringe, but were interested in trying new things, liked to influence others, and enjoyed getting a deal [37].

Social Media versus Daily Deal Customers

While daily deal customers expect a discount, people who engage with a marketer through social media tend to interact in ways that are more advantageous to the marketer. One study found that when customers participate in social media, they increase their visits, buy premium products, and show lower price sensitivity. These customers who do not demand deals provide higher levels of profitability for brands [40].

DAILY DEALS AND COUPONS

Brands can also issue coupons via daily deal sites. LivingSocial, the second most popular deal marketer, offers coupons on 3,000 retail businesses. Bloomin' Brands, owners of Outback Steakhouse, offered a LivingSocial deal that was claimed by 52,000 people, who also shared it 5,000 times on social media [41].

ENHANCING SPONSORSHIPS WITH SOCIAL MEDIA AND MOBILE

Sponsorships are an effective method of promotion that can help build brand awareness and favorable associations for a brand, rather than lead to an immediate sale. A **sponsorship** involves a brand purchasing naming rights to an entity (such as a stadium), an event (such as a concert), or activity (such as a sport). Companies use sponsorships to create an association in the minds of consumers between the brand and the sponsored entity, activity, or event. Social media and mobile technology can enhance the sponsorship strategy by building buzz around the event to further tie the two together and provide a means for sharing the connection. For example, Barclays Bank sponsors the English professional football's Premier League. The league is very successful, with 4.7 billion cumulative television viewers worldwide, 212 global territories, stadium visibility, and a strong social media presence. Barclays uses social media to measure the impact of the sponsorship by examining online buzz about the brand associations. The bank found that about 1 in 4 posts about the Premier League mentioned Barclays. A study of the brand in the Middle East showed that although the UAE (United Arab Emirates) and Saudi Arabia had the strongest buzz surrounding the league, people in Kuwait were far more likely to mention Barclays on social networks. Marketers are particularly enamored with sports sponsorships, even when the relationship between the product and the sport is unclear, as demonstrated by the "Consider This . . . Kia and the Australian Open" feature.

consider this . . .

KIA AND THE AUSTRALIAN OPEN

Kia, the Korean automobile manufacturer, annually sponsors the Australian Open. In order to further solidify the connection between Kia and the Open, the brand leveraged social media. The goals were:

Engage tennis fans in new and interesting ways.
Amplify Kia's brand messages.

The strategy was to develop interesting and engaging content for Kia related to the Australian Open sponsorship. The campaign began with the "Kia Big Shot," a Pong-like game hosted on Fandango that people could play with their Facebook friends. The more they played, the better the chance to win a Kia car on the final day of the matches. The "Kia-Tie-Break" encouraged people to bet daily on the players they expected to win, gaining more opportunities to earn prizes. Kia tweeted live from the tennis stadium using the popular tennis blogger, The Aussie Word, for legitimacy, and using the hashtag #kiaAO and a Tweetwall to screen the Twitter action. The results showed increased social media activity for the brand and hashtag, with 28 million impressions in all social channels and 12 million via #kiaAO alone. One hundred thousand people visited the Kia-related contest sites, and the brand earned 6,000 additional "likes" on Facebook [43]. The only question remaining is: Did the effort increase sales of Kia?

PUBLIC RELATIONS AND SOCIAL PROMOTION

Public relations (PR) is an indirectly paid for form of promotion aimed at building reputations and relationships for firms. The purpose is to persuade, but the persuasion is indirect, often coming from a third party. The PR industry, consisting of firms that help other companies manage their relationships with stakeholders, has recognized that its business has changed significantly with social media. In the past, the dominant tool of the PR practitioner was the press release, a document that contains news and information about a company that is distributed by the brand to media entities, such as television networks, radio stations, and news organizations. Companies issued press releases in the hope that the media would cover the story and help the firm achieve its goals, such as brand recognition, reputation for expertise, or to attract investors or other partners. Though PR could not be completely controlled by a firm, the media coverage was often favorable toward business because companies were also larger advertisers in traditional outlets such as television, print, and radio, providing revenue for media companies.

Today, there are many more media outlets with which to engage. Aside from traditional media, there are myriad digital properties, websites, and blogs that influence conversations about products and brands, and PR strategy has changed as a result. Since a major goal of PR is to influence others, the industry has turned to social media to reach influential people. Brands can follow celebrities, pundits, and industry experts to interact with them via social media and comment on their blogs and postings. Another important role of PR is to help manage digital communications, particularly company blogs.

Like any form of communication, public relations must be planned and integrated with other firm strategies. Integration across many communications providers, such as ad agencies, the firm's employees, promotion companies, and

PR firms, can be complicated. Therefore, brands must set PR goals and communicate the strategy within the company and to all the partners working on the strategy. Most PR professionals agree that firms must have social media policies and training for employees, research the social media landscape, set goals, determine targets and stakeholders, review available content and messaging, and measure results. A study of PR practitioners found that social media provided new ways to communicate with both internal and external audiences using a variety of networks. The most frequently used platform for PR was Twitter followed by Facebook, LinkedIn, and YouTube. Eleven percent of PR practitioners spent more than 50% of their day on social media and mobile, and 21% spent 26%–50% of their time there. Only about half of PR firms reported that the brands for which they worked measured the results in social media [44].

Blogging strategy is a key element in public relations because many stories covered more broadly in media begin as blog posts and with influential bloggers. Reaching these people is important to a social media strategy to build a rapport and to encourage buzz about a brand. Chapter Nine, "Executing Strategy," will discuss these public relation techniques in more detail.

EXPERIENTIAL MARKETING AND NEW MEDIA

Experiential marketing takes place in the real world with person-to-person interaction surrounding a brand and the offering. In this type of marketing, the consumer has the opportunity to try the product and obtain product and purchase information. Each experience is unique to a brand, but should be part of an integrated strategy by supporting the brand image and message. Garnier's strategy in China harnessed experiential marketing by dressing up Jeannie Chan and Katy Wong, Garnier's celebrity spokespeople, as schoolgirls. The two then ran a competition to determine which of three moisturizer essences was softer on the skin. People in the streets were asked to put the moisturizers on their skin and stick their hands into bowls filled with polyurethane balls to see how many stuck as a measure of tackiness. As you can imagine, the task was pretty engaging and directly related to the brand and product characteristics.

During the campaign, the celebrities interacted with 100 passers-by and 14 bloggers on a brand-related task to build awareness and positive attitudes toward the product. There was a strong social media component to the campaign to leverage the experience and increase the reach of the strategy. The agency filmed the experience and posted it on YouTube and Facebook. Unfortunately, in spite of this effort L'Oreal pulled Garnier from the Chinese market due to low sales levels [45].

SOCIAL SELLING

Personal selling is the interaction of salespeople with potential customers to sell products and services on a one-to-one basis. Like other sales methods, personal selling has been strongly influenced by social media over the past few years. According to one study of B2B marketers, 90% of salespeople used Facebook, 53% used Twitter, and 47% harnessed LinkedIn to generate leads and communicate with customers. Another study of 1,000 sales professionals in the United States, United Kingdom, Brazil, and China found that social media had a strong influence on purchase behavior, with 49% of sellers agreeing that social media were important to their businesses—particularly among the most successful closers. Sales professionals in Brazil were more likely to receive social media training from their companies than in the United States, and 38% of Chinese sales reps use personal blogs as an aid in selling, compared to only 3% in the United States.

Social media have turned the one-to-one relationship into more of a conversation with many involved parties such that the buyer has more information in the purchase process. However, selling is still about connections between people and salespeople can use social media for relationship building. Most personal selling happens on a B2B basis because industrial products are expensive and require a more targeted approach than consumer products. Business-to-business marketing differs because theoretically the decision is logical rather than emotional, there are higher costs, the sales process takes longer, multiple people may be involved, and businesses may have specific processes at work for buying. Social media can help salespeople navigate some of these issues with their clients.

IBM is one company that decided to jump into social media full force to reach its customers. As the world's largest IT consulting company, IBM found that its core IT customers had turned to social media for product research. To help sell its Public Cloud services, IBM set two major objectives: (1) generate many good-quality leads and (2) advance leads from engagement to sales.

The strategy emphasized Twitter and LinkedIn to "listen and respond" to IT people in social media. IBM empowered the workforce and trained them to engage in conversations with potential customers in social media and answer their questions to demonstrate their expertise. IBM developed a database of key information to share online to support their staff members.

The task involved monitoring the environment for key topics, developing meaningful content to resonate with clients with appropriate and universal hashtags for Twitter, with the goal of driving leads to salespeople's personal sites for conversion. The result was that 19% of leads were attributable to social channels and these leads were generated at a reduced cost. In addition, IBM noted a

55% increase in Twitter followers, more retweets, and 2,000 clicks to sites that drove sales of Owly and SmartCloud [46].

Though most salespeople are on Facebook, more leads are generated on LinkedIn, which is a social site for business contacts. The selling process is multi-faceted with many steps because of the long time frame. Sales representatives may develop relationships over a long period of time before realizing a sale. The discussion in the "Consider This . . . How Do You Sell a Welded Steel Tank" shows how Fisher Tanks uses social media to bridge the time challenges of selling an industrial product.

The sales process includes a number of steps, each of which can benefit from social media or mobile technology. First comes **prospecting**, or seeking out potential customers. These targets may be on social media. A very good way to use social media to attract prospects is to develop content that interests them and link it to your website. Attracting prospects with your content so that the prospects contact you is called **inbound marketing**. The quality and relevance of the content matter so that the company can establish expertise in a sales area. Firms may also publish their beliefs and values, which may help identify like-minded customers. Of course, invitations and offers help salespeople engage clients as well.

The next step, **qualifying**, refers to determining whether the prospect has the ability and willingness to purchase so that the salesperson doesn't waste his or her time. Online research can provide a salesperson with information about a prospect (see Chapter Three). Specifically, LinkedIn profiles list job titles, so a sales rep can determine who the decision-makers are in various companies. Reps can also connect with partners who may have worked with a client and can provide information. People constantly signal their intentions with a keyword search, blog readership, and other content consumption. Smart salespeople can use the various research techniques to locate and qualify leads. IBM examined the language IT buyers used in their searches and created a set of how-to videos building on the word streams and tagging them exactly to match the keyword search entries.

Once the marketer qualifies the prospect, it is time to present the product or service to the potential customer. At this point, the salesperson should also conduct research to determine the information available to the consumer online and in social media to prepare a presentation that is persuasive and addresses key issues, customer needs, and potential concerns.

After the presentation of the product or service, the salesperson handles any objections on a one-to-one basis. Communications may take place on social media, in person, or by telephone. The end result is that the seller addresses all the issues of the customer and closes the sale. Of course, after the close, the seller continues to maintain a relationship with the buyer, perhaps via social media.

HOW DO YOU SELL A WELDED STEEL TANK?

Fisher Tanks, an employee-owned company in Chester, Pennsylvania, makes giant waste water, pulp and paper, and fuel tanks for industry. The company, which has been in business over sixty years, primarily used cold calling and referrals from clients for lead generation. But a social media campaign increased its Web traffic by 119%, with a 4800% increase from social media sites. Over the length of the campaign, the company increased leads by 3900%, requests for quotes by 500%, and qualified new sales leads by $3.4 million. What did the company do to achieve these goals? It improved its website and created a content strategy with a blog and social sharing with free downloads. Most of the blog includes information about how to reinforce tanks, tank construction, and reading safety labels, which is probably not of much interest to the average person, but that's how you sell a steel tank [47].

SUMMARY AND REVIEW

CHAPTER SUMMARY

The elements of the marketing mix—product, price, place, and promotion—work together to create an image for a product or service. Social media and mobile technology can enhance that image when used properly as part of an integrated communications strategy. Pricing and promotional activities signal important cues to consumers who may respond by purchasing, sharing information, or demonstrating loyalty. Marketing via social media or mobile can help facilitate desirable brand-related consumer responses that help firms meet organizational objectives.

KEY TERMS

active deal-prone customers
competition-based pricing methods
contest
cost-based pricing methods
demand-based pricing methods

experiential marketing
external factors
external reference prices
framing
hedonic shoppers
inbound marketing
internal factors
marketer-generated content (MGC)

passive deal-prone customers
personal selling
premiums
price penetration
price skimming
prospecting
public relations (PR)
qualifying

reach
reference prices
sales promotion
shopping app
sponsorship
trade promotions
user-generated content (UGC)
utilitarian shoppers

SUMMARY REVIEW QUESTIONS

1. Explain the difference between internal and external pricing factors.
2. Consider a product with which you are familiar. What is its price? What external and internal factors did the marketer of your product have to consider in determining that particular price?
3. What might a consumer think when a brand raises its price? What if the brand lowers the price?
4. What has been the influence of consumer price shopping on retailers? Manufacturers?
5. How do most social networks make money?
6. Explain the purpose behind sales promotions and why marketers use them.
7. What is the danger in using sales promotions from the marketer's perspective?
8. How can marketers use social media to enhance their sponsorships and their experiential marketing campaigns?

APPLICATION QUESTIONS

1. Do some research online to determine the original price of a 50-inch Samsung flat screen television. How much does a similar model cost today? Explain the brand's pricing strategy.
2. Using your smartphone, download a price-scanning application (consider Amazon's or type shopping application into Google). Scan a product and report the information that the app provides for the item. Might the information be helpful in your decision to buy the product?
3. Visit the websites of Amazon and Alibaba and compare the two sites on product variety, prices, and the social aspects of the site. Which do you prefer for buying?
4. Locate a #flocktounlock promotion on Twitter by typing the hashtag into the Twitter search bar or using a search engine. What is the offer and does the deal enhance the brand's image?
5. Consider an event that you see advertised, such as a concert, sporting event, or cultural event.

Are there any sponsors? If so, how many? Discuss the degree to which one of the brand's messages matches the sponsorship. Is there a brand that would be better suited to sponsor your particular event? Which one?
6. Examine the Twitter hashtag for the event you mentioned in Question 5. How often is the brand mentioned when you look at a stream of twenty tweets?
7. Locate one brand event on YouTube that shows experiential marketing. Describe the activity and the brand's message.
8. Go to McDonald's.com and describe one of the promotions. Is it integrated with McDonald's message?
9. Type a company name into Google and the words "news release." Who published your release? Now, type the title of the news release into Google. Was the information picked up by other media outlets? If so, what did the media say about the company?

case study The Social Cola Wars

Who won the cola wars? The rivalry between Coke and Pepsi had been fought since Pepsi followed Coke's introduction in the late 1800s. Throughout their history, Coke and Pepsi have gone head-to-head in terms of their products, targets, messages, and positioning strategies. Both brands have tried to dominate the global beverage market by securing higher market shares with large advertising budgets. The fight then moved to the digital arena as both Coke and Pepsi used social media to engage customers, build loyalty, and execute promotional strategies.

Between 2013 and 2018, the global soft drink market was expected to grow 4.5%. The trouble for Coke and Pepsi was that sales had been steadily declining for carbonated soft drinks as people, particularly in North America and Western Europe, turned to healthier alternatives such as water and juice. The U.S. market appeared to be saturated, with only 0.3% growth in soft drinks expected through 2018 and a high per capita consumption of 260.9 liters a year. Exhibit 6.4 reports the global sales of various beverages. Colas continued to dominate the market overall, but still bottled water was catching up.

Both brands operated in the global market. Coke's largest markets were the United States, Japan, and Mexico; Pepsi's were the United States, Russia, and Mexico [48]. The two brands were often fighting on the same turf and would continue to try to gain share in the developing world, which had higher predicted growth through 2018 than the developed world. Exhibit 6.5 shows overall soft drink sales by region [49], and Exhibit 6.6 reports volume and per capita consumption levels.

In 2014 the total global soft drink market was 548,531.2 million liters [49]. Coca Cola controlled 48% of the global carbonated beverage market, compared to Pepsi's 20.5% [50]. These numbers made it appear that Coca-Cola was winning the cola wars. In addition, Coke was more committed to maintaining its flagship business, as evidenced by higher levels of global media spending. Coke outspent Pepsi $3 billion to $2 billion between 2009 and 2012 and had plans to increase spending by an additional $1 billion by 2016 [51]. Whereas carbonated beverages represented more than 75% of Coke's business, Pepsi also sold snack

EXHIBIT 6.4

Global Dollar Sales of Beverages

	GLOBAL VALUE (IN U,S.$)
Cola carbonates	$104,275
Noncola carbonates	78,813
Still bottled water	70,597.5
Still RTD tea	45,313.7
100% Juice	42,604.5
Juice up to 24%	34,862.7
Energy drinks	25,549
RTD coffee	22,994.2
Nectars (25%–99% juice)	20,945.4
Sports drinks	20,049.7

Source: Euromonitor, "Soft Drinks in the US," March 2015.

foods in its Frito-Lay division [52]. Half of Pepsi's revenue was generated from food products, and unlike soft drinks, the snack food market was growing [53].

Carbonated drinks were popular among global teens and both companies targeted young people; 56.7% of youth ages 16–24 reported drinking a carbonated beverage at least once a week. The only drink that teens were more likely to consume was a dairy beverage. The countries with the highest carbonated beverage consumption among teens were Brazil, the United States, and the United Kingdom. In addition, the battleground for messaging emphasized the youth market, and focused on music, sports, and celebrity [48]. Exhibit 6.7 shows the beverages that teens consumed most.

DIGITAL STRATEGIES

Each brand experimented with digital strategies. By 2014 Coke had over 83 million fans on Facebook, compared to Pepsi's 32 million. On the other hand, Pepsi had chosen to emphasize Twitter more heavily with its strategy of reaching out to the youth market and had more followers than Coke. Pepsi had 2.58 million Twitter followers and Coke had

EXHIBIT 6.5

Soft Drink Dollar Sales by Region

REGION	OFF-TRADE (RETAIL) SOFT DRINK SALES (MILLIONS OF LITERS)
Asia Pacific	160,068
Australasia	4,114.2
Eastern Europe	34,494.5
Latin America	95,373.5
Middle East and Africa	60,898.9
North America	89,915.5
Western Europe	86,965.5

Source: Euromonitor, "Market Sizes," Passport, 2015.

EXHIBIT 6.6

Volume and per Capita Consumption

COUNTRY	OFF-TRADE VOLUME (MILLIONS OF LITERS)	PER CAPITA CONSUMPTION (LITERS)	GROWTH 2013–2018
USA	82,540.7	260.9	0.3%
Brazil	20,871	104.2	5.5
Russia	12,295.9	85.8	3.0
India	11,548.2	9.3	17.0
China	76,685.4	56.7	9.7

Source: Euromonitor, "Market Sizes," Passport, 2015.

EXHIBIT 6.7

Youth Consumption of Various Beverages

	PERCENTAGE OF HIGH SCHOOL STUDENTS WHO DRANK ONE OR MORE OVER A ONE-WEEK PERIOD
Water	72%
Milk	42
Fruit Juice	30
Soda	24
Sports Drink	16
Other Sweetened Drinks	17
Coffee or Tea	15
Diet Soda	7
Energy Drink	5

Source: Centers for Disease Control (CDC), "Physical Activity Levels of High School Students - United States, 2010," Morbidity and Mortality Weekly Report, June 7, 2011, http://milk. procon.org/view.resource.php?resourceID=004361.

2.5 million, though each brand had a number of Twitter accounts for each country.

To reach teens, Coke decided to test an all-digital strategy with its "Ahhh" campaign. The brand set up a website with unique experiences such as videos and games. The site garnered 5 million visits, 70% of which were from organic search. Additionally, engagement was strong, with each visit lasting more than two minutes, much longer than a typical thirty-second television spot. After the first year of the campaign, Coke decided to use more traditional media to boost engagement with the campaign and added a television spot to the mix [54].

The most watched video of the "Ahhh" campaign was a music video featuring teen Internet and television stars such as Kurt Hugo Schneider and Zendaya of the Disney Channel. One of the singers, Kina Grannis, was the winner of the Doritos's (a Frito-Lay brand) Crash the Super Bowl contest. In addition, Coke appeared to be taking a page from the Doritos playbook by asking teens to film their Ahhh moments and tweet them at #thisisah, as part of a contest to promote the brand. By this time, Doritos had been running ads during the Super Bowl with user-generated content for over five years [55], [56].

For its cola brand, Pepsi ran the global "Live for Now" campaign featuring music, entertainment, and pop culture since 2012. The Pepsi Pulse site ranked pop culture trends and encouraged visitors to participate in challenges posed by celebrities such as Beyonce and Nicki Minaj.

PROMOTIONAL OFFERS

A key element of the marketing strategy for both brands was promotional items. Coca-Cola introduced My Coke Rewards in 2006, which offered customers the opportunity to earn points toward prizes and sweepstakes by entering codes found on Coke products. The codes could be found on bottle caps for fifteen Coca-Cola products or on cardboard packages of multipacks. Participants registered at the My

Coke Rewards.com website and could track their points and earn bonus points. The program was integrated with offers from partner companies, such as Royal Caribbean Cruises, Dunkin' Donuts, Visa, Sony PlayStation, and Game Stop, a video game retailer. Coke offered music downloads and streaming through Spotify, one of its partners. In an appeal to its older audience for Diet Coke, the brand also offered an opportunity to use the points for school donations and paying down a mortgage.

In 2013 Pepsi took the rewards program to the next level in an attempt to build social media interaction, developing the Pepsi Experiences Points program. Pepsi's rewards were tied to actions consumers could take, rather than to product codes. Specifically, users could share something on Facebook for 25 points, follow Pepsi on Twitter for 300 points, visit Pepsi.com for five points, and sign up for emails from Pepsi for 500 points. Pepsi points earned consumers prizes such as a Pepsi digital camera or cooler, chairs, and other branded items. Pepsi was criticized for having an unexciting and small rewards site, as compared to Coke's [57].

The My Coke Rewards and Pepsi Experience Points programs were separate from the merchandise stores available on each brand's Facebook page. Coke's merchandise strategy was integrated on the Facebook page, offering consumers a link to the Coke Store for branded items. However, these promotional products, such as soccer balls, cups, and hats, were offered for sale rather than for redeemable points. Pepsi also offered items for sale on its Facebook page. rather than offering point redemptions.

OTHER PROMOTIONAL STRATEGIES

Coke experimented with other promotional strategies to build sales. Specifically, Coke originally launched the "Share a Coke" campaign in Australia. Coca-Cola determined the most popular first names in the country and printed those names on bottles of Coke sold in stores. The campaign included television spots with photos of people sharing the same name, celebrities and influencers uploading photos of their names on bottles, opportunities to text message names to billboards, and personalized virtual cans of Coke that were shared on Facebook. There was also significant buzz in major news outlets surrounding the campaign. Some 65,000 people requested that their names be added to the campaign, so Coke released 50 new names. The results were that consumption of Coke products increased 7% during the campaign and it garnered 18,300,000 media impressions. Traffic grew 870% on Coke's website and 39% on the brand's Facebook page [58].

The Australian campaign was so successful that Coke launched it in the United Kingdom and later in North America. The U.K. campaign used the most popular 150 names and promoted the bottles through traditional advertising, such as television, billboards, and the Twitter hashtag #shareacoke. People could also have their name inscribed on a custom bottle through a traveling Coca-Cola tour [59].

The results of the U.K. program were that consumer perceptions of Coca-Cola, Diet Coke, and Coke Zero improved among those who were exposed to the "Share a Coke" television spots, particularly among the core target of 18- to 24-year-olds. Similarly, those exposed to the "Share a Coke" social media campaign registered more positive views of Coca-Cola than a control group. Among people exposed to the campaign on Facebook, their positive perceptions of Coke products increased by 18% (see Exhibit 6.8). The measures were [59]:

- **Buzz:** Over the *past two weeks,* which of the following brands have you heard something *positive/negative* about (whether in the news, through advertising, or talking to friends and family)?
- **Impression:** Which of the following brands do you have a generally *positive/negative* feeling about?
- **Recommend:** Which of the following brands would you *recommend/tell a friend to avoid*?
- **Consideration:** When you are next in the market to make a purchase, which brands would you consider?

Both Coke and Pepsi continue to share the same target and attempt to convince young people around the world that their brand is the superior one. Exhibits 6.9 and 6.10 provide Klout scores and HowSociable data to help you further analyze the situation. Will the cola wars continue and who will win? You be the judge.

EXHIBIT 6.9

Klout Scores for Cola Brands

BRANDS	KLOUT SCORE
Pepsi	89
Pepsi Canada	51
Coke Zone	61
Coca-Cola Great Britain	57
Coca-Cola Canada	59

www.klout.com

EXHIBIT 6.8

Perceptions of the Share a Coke Campaign

	CONSUMER PERCEPTIONS* (YOUGOV)
18- to 24-year-olds	+28%
25- to 34-year-olds	+21%
35- to 44-year-olds	+13%
45- to 54-year-olds	+12%
Nationally representative sample (control)	+9%

Brand index survey of fifteen metrics.
Source: http://cdn.yougov.com/cumulus_uploads/document/u7gltkr717/Share-a-coke-report.pdf

EXHIBIT 6.10

HowSociable Rankings on Major Social Platforms for Coke and Pepsi

	COCA-COLA	COKE	PEPSI
Overall	7.2	8.0	8.2
Facebook	6.1	6.4	6.8
Youtube	4.6	4.8	4.8
LinkedIn	2.7	3.8	4.1
Twitter	5.2	5.7	6.3

www.howsociable.com

QUESTIONS FOR DISCUSSION

1. Compare Coke and Pepsi's market shares to their media spending levels. Does additional media spending appear to lead to increased sales? Explain.

2. Examine the rewards programs of each brand. What were the different goals of the brands when they established their rewards strategies? How does each brand meet its goal?

3. To what extent should Coke and Pepsi use social media to communicate with customers and potential customers? What are the advantages and disadvantages to using social media and mobile for Coke and Pepsi?

4. The case suggests that the U.S. market is saturated, but Coke intends to spend an additional billion dollars on advertising. What would you recommend Coke do with that money?

5. Evaluate the metrics for the "Share a Coke" campaign in Australia and the United Kingdom. Which metrics are meaningful in the long term?

6. Should Coke expand the "Share a Coke" campaign further? What would the limitations of doing so be for the brand? Can the program be adapted to other countries using social media or mobile? Explain.

7. Who won the cola wars?

REFERENCES

[1] R. Hallman, "Biz Buzz: The Martin Agency Pushing New Oreo Campaign," *Times Dispatch,* 4 June 2014.

[2] S. Clements, T. Jain, S. Jose, and B. Koellmann, "Smart Cookie," *Business Today,* 31 March 2013.

[3] A. Watercutter, "How Oreo Won the Marketing Superbowl with a Timely Blackout Ad on Twitter," *Wired,* 4 February 2013.

[4] J. P. V. Sampere, "Alibaba: The First Real Test for Amazon," HBR Blog, 21 January 2014.

[5] K. A. McGuire and B. M. Noone, "Pricing in a Social World: The Influence of Non-Price Information on Hotel Choice," *Journal of Revenue and Pricing Management,* vol. 12, no. 3, September 2013.

[6] B. B. Boley, V. P. Magnini, and T. L. Tuten, "Social Media Picture Posting and Souvenir Purchasing Behavior: Some Initial Findings," *Tourism Management,* pp. 27-30, August 2013.

[7] Google, "Mobile Search Moments," *Think with Google Newsletter,* March 2013.

[8] Nielsen, "The Mobile Consumer," 2013.

[9] The 2015 US Mobile App Report, comScore, 2015, www.comscore.com

[10] Acosta, "AMG Strategy Advisors," 2012.

[11] J. Crook and R. Lawler, "Uber Will Cap Surge Pricing During NorEaster," TechCrunch, 26 January 2015.

[12] L. Perner, "The Consumer Psychologist," http://www.consumerpsychologist.com.

[13] J. Loechner, "High-Income US Households Find Quality at Warehouse Clubs," *MediaPost,* 25 July 2014.

[14] E. J. Park, E. Y. Kim, V. M. Funches, and W. Foxx, "Apparel Product Attributes, Web Browsing and eImpulse Buying on Shopping Sites," *Journal of Business Research,* vol. 65, pp. 1583-1589, November 2012.

[15] T. Peterson, "Facebook Now Makes 62% of Its Ad Money in Mobile: What the New Earnings Mean," *Advertising Age,* 23 July 2014.

[16] Z. Stambor, "Mobile Ads Account for 81% of Twitter's Ad Revenue," *Internet Retailer,* 29 July 2014.

[17] S. Shcheglova, "FOCUS: Vkontakte to Focus on High Growth Strategy since Durov Remains CEO," 7 Prime Business News Agency, April 2014. http://www.1prime.biz/news/0/%7BDC0F5610-B52B-40C3-8924-704571EAE8CF%7D.uif?layout=print

[18] iResearch China, "Sina's Weibo New Advertising Model Marks Monetization of the Long-Tail Marketing Strategy," *iResearch,* 2 April 2014.

[19] P. Chandon, "Consumer Research on Sales Promotions: A State-of-the-Art Literature Review," *Journal of Marketing Management,* vol. 11, no. 5, pp. 419-441, 1995.

[20] Valassis, "Coupon Facts Report Reveals Evolving Media Mix and Marketing Strategies," *Marketing Weekly News,* 15 March 2014.

[21] Electronic Retailing Association, "Crocs: A Case Study Using Mobile to Engage Shoppers In-Store," 11 August 2010.

[22] P. Reichart, C. Pescher, and M. Spann, "A Comparison of the Effectiveness of Email Coupons and Mobile Text Message Coupons for Digital Products," *Electronic Markets,* pp. 217-225, September 2013.

[23] K.-Y. Goh, C.-S. Heng, and Z. Lin, "Social Media Brand Community and Consumer Behavior: Quantifying the Relative Impact of User- and Marketer-Generated Content," *Information Systems Research,* pp. 88-107, 14 January 2013.

[24] T. Wasserman, "Is Snapchat the Next Frontier for Marketers," Mashable, 2 January 2013.

[25] Facebook, "Unilever Case Study," 2012.

[26] R. Bostrom, K. Byrne, B. Chakraborty, J. L. Ugarte, and S. Yagi, "Playing the Social Tune," *Business Today,* 24 November 2013.

[27] Heartland Payment Systems, "Tully," 2013.

[28] S. Vizzard, "Tesco Looks to End Frivolous Promotions with Pounds 200m Price Investment," *Marketing News,* 25 February 2014.

[29] L. Fisher, "5 Case Studies of Brands Using Niche Social Sites (and Why You Should Too)," *Simply Zesty,* 12 January 2012.

[30] Twitter, "7-Up Arabia," *Twitter for Business,* 2012.

[31] T. Hunt, "The 5 Best Snapchat Campaigns," *Postano,* 17 January 2014.

[32] Sabrina, "Case Study: Coca Cola's Weibo Marketing," *China Internet Watch,* 26 July 2013.

[33] E. Griffith, "Counterpoint: Groupon Is Not a Success," *Fortune,* 20 March 2015.

[34] U. M. Dholakia, *How Effective Are Groupon Promotions for Businesses,* Working Paper Rice University, 2010.

[35] U. M. Dholakia, *How Businesses Fare with Daily Deals as They Gain Experience,* Working Paper Rice University, 2012.

[36] T. Keiningham, S. Gupta, L. Aksoy, and A. Buoye, "The High Price of Customer Satisfaction," *Sloan Management Review,* 18 March 2014.

[37] U. M. Dholakia and S. E. Kimes, "Daily Deal Fatigue of Unabased Enthusiasm? A Study of Consumer Perceptions of Daily Deal Promotions," Working Paper, Rice University, 11 September 2011.

[38] K. Bradford, "Groupon Guide: How to Save Money with New Deals Every Day," *Laptop Magazine,* 1 February 2011.

[39] Morpace, "Omnibus Reports: Deal of the Day," 2013.

[40] R. Rishika, A. Kumar, R. Janakiraman, and R. Bezawada, "The Effect of Customers' Social Media Participation on Customer Visit Frequency and Profitability: An Empirical Investigation," *Information Systems Research,* pp. 108-127, 20 December 2012.

[41] LivingSocial, "Living Social Offers Increased Flexibility for Merchants," *Marketing Weekly News,* p. 180, 5 October 2013.

[42] E. Crook, "How Sports Sponsorships Benefit Brands," *Brand Watch,* 2 May 2013.

[43] "Case Study: Kia at the Australian Open," *Marketing Magazine,* 27 May 2013.

[44] D. Wright and M. Hinson, "Examining How Social and Other Emerging Media Are Being Used in PR," *Public Relations Society of America,* 22 July 2014.

[45] A. Lam, "Garnier Digitizes Experiential Marketing," 25 July 2014, http://www.marketing-interactive.com/garnier-digitise-experiential-marketing/.

[46] "IBM Social Selling Case Highlights," 5 March 2013, http://www.b2bmarketing.net/knowledgebank/social-media-marketing/case-studies/case-study-ibm-turns-its-sales-staff-social-media-.

[47] R. Peterson, "15 B2B Case Studies Prove Social Media ROI," *Barn Raisers,* 24 May 2014.

[48] Euromonitor, "Soft Drinks in the US," March 2015.

[49] Euromonitor, "Market Sizes," *Passport,* 2015.

[50] J. Fox, "Still Sweet on Coke and Pepsi?," *Bloomberg View,* 21 January 2015.

[51] N. Zmuda, "PepsiCo Announces Millions in Additional Ad Spend, Plans to Trim Agency Roster," *Advertising Age,* 9 February 2012.

[52] M. Esterl, "Coke Sticks to Strategy While Soda Sales Slide," *The Wall Street Journal,* 9 April 2014.

[53] V. Wong, "Pepsi's Snack Business Is Coming in Handy," *Business Week,* 17 April 2014.

[54] C. Stromann, "Digital Campaign for Coca Cola Wins at Engagement Marketing," *Fast Horse,* 9 September 2013.

[55] T. Wasserman, "Coke's All-Digital 'Ahh' Campaign Prompts 4 Million Visits," Mashable, 20 August 2013.

[56] L. Thompson, "The Ahh Effect Expands to Explore More Dimensions of Coca Cola's Delicious Refreshment," *Business Wire,* 20 March 2014.

[57] traveldealexpert, "Pepsi Experience Points," *FlyerTalk,* June 2012.

[58] Marketing, "Share a Coke Campaign Post Analysis," 22 June 2012.

[59] The Drum, "Case Study: What Coke Share a Coke Campaign Can Teach Other Brands," 28 January 2014.

CHAPTER SEVEN

DIGITAL IMPERATIVES

Before executing a social media or mobile strategy, marketers must consider the brand's digital presence, which includes a website, search engine marketing, and email executions. Marketers have readily adopted search marketing and search engine optimization strategies because of the extent of search as an integral part of shopping behavior. Many communications strategies drive consumers to websites that marketers design to achieve specific organizational objectives. A Web presence also provides a mechanism for monitoring the success of social media and some mobile strategies because analytics programs can track consumers' digital journeys. This chapter covers elements of digital marketing and direct marketing through a brand's Web or Internet presence, which is important to social and mobile strategies.

LEARNING OBJECTIVES

After reading this chapter, you will be able to:

- APPLY INTERNET RESEARCH TO SOCIAL MEDIA AND MOBILE MARKETING

- EVALUATE WEBSITES AND MOBILE SITES USING EFFECTIVENESS CRITERIA AND USE CASE SCENARIOS

- EXAMINE CULTURAL DIFFERENCES IN RESPONSE TO INTERNET MARKETING

- LEARN THE BASICS OF SEARCH ENGINE MARKETING AND SEARCH ENGINE OPTIMIZATION FOR INTERNET AND MOBILE SEARCH

- REVISIT EMAIL MARKETING AS A MOBILE STRATEGY

- CONSIDER DIRECT MAIL TECHNIQUES FOR SOCIAL AND MOBILE STRATEGIES

With a U.S. audience of close to 500 million monthly and reaching close to 90% of active desktop users [1], Google's properties are an important marketing tool. The company owns YouTube, Google Drive, Google Maps, Chrome, Doubleclick, Android, Gmail, Blogger, and Scholar, but search remains Google's biggest business and revenue generator. Search represents nearly 50% of Internet advertising revenues [2] and Google's engine runs over 65% of Internet searches, though its share in the United States is declining [3].

Consumers engaged in search behavior around the world are often looking for products and services to research, sample, plan to buy, or actually purchase. The influence that Google wields in the purchase process is significant, particularly since most searchers do not look beyond the first page of search results for information. Not unexpectedly, marketers attempt to manipulate the search results to get their brand a top ranking.

In the early days of search when consumers typed the name of any household product into the Google search bar, a particular retailer came up most often. The search, even for a specific brand name within a category, such as for Samsonite luggage or Martha Stewart bedding, landed the same retailer at the top.

Who was the retailer? Not Amazon who sells many household items online, but JC Penney. Penney came up first for luggage, bedding, area rugs, table cloths, and furniture. The store also came up first for skinny jeans and a host of other items. How did JC Penney get to the top of the Google search results for so many items? The simple answer is search engine optimization as accomplished by the firm SearchDex. To optimize search, SearchDex created links from the JC Penney page to sites all over the Internet with product-related content. It sounds like a great strategy, but when Google found out, it dropped JC Penney past the 70th position on the search page, essentially making the company invisible to most searchers [4].

Is gaming the Google search engine a good strategy for a marketer? While it might be advantageous to have your brand name on the first page of a Google search, it's not likely worth the effort. First, Google's algorithm, its mathematical model for ranking results, is constantly changing and requires that a site build content links with meaningful information to make it eligible to rise to the top. Second, search engine optimization (SEO), the task of achieving high search engine rankings, requires a budget and an agency to manage the task. A search engine optimization firm creates links to content and stays on top of Google's algorithm alterations to benefit clients. Third, if the search engine finds that your brand is artificially highly ranked, it could lower the ranking.

A better strategy would be to focus on the long-term business goals of the brand by building relationships with customers, providing meaningful information, developing loyalty, and generating positive word of mouth. Getting to the top of a Google search alone will not achieve those goals.

This chapter focuses on a company's Internet or website presence and aspects of digital marketing that firms must consider in planning for social media and mobile technology. Because many strategies drive traffic to the website, it is important to have a strong website. Along with the website goes a plan for **keyword optimization** in search engines and an SEO strategy. Many of the concepts that researchers have studied in Internet marketing are applicable to social media and mobile marketing. In particular, this research provides information on online effectiveness in site design and email marketing, two areas that greatly affect social and mobile strategies.

THE INTERNET AS A PREREQUISITE FOR SOCIAL AND MOBILE STRATEGIES

The advent of social media and the growing influence of mobile technology make digital marketing even more crucial to a communications strategy. Social media platforms are Internet-based and many of the same concepts from online search, Web design, Internet analytics, and e-commerce can be used for planning social media. Many mobile strategies also take advantage of Internet platforms. For example, mobile websites are forms of traditional websites (though they may not look the same) and operate on the same basic principles. Consumers have acclimated to using the Internet to search for products and services and regularly buy online, making digital marketing a key element of a marketing strategy and important to social media and mobile executions.

A brand manager must consider overall digital strategy before executing any social media or mobile campaign and, ideally, these elements would be planned together as an integrated marketing communications strategy. Whereas **Internet marketing** refers to all the elements of the marketing mix used to attract and sell to people online, the term digital strategy tends to focus more specifically on communications. **Digital strategy** consists of **search engine marketing (SEM)**, SEO, website development and management, and email marketing campaigns as well as the social media and mobile strategies outlined in this book.

The most important prerequisite to any digital campaign is a website. Usually, social media and some mobile strategies deliver people to a brand's website in order to achieve firm objectives. If the site is an e-commerce platform, the main goal is a sale. For a media site, a successful outcome might be that the visitor views an advertisement on the site. In either case, having a website allows the brand to monitor and evaluate the success of digital communications strategies because the brand can track people's click-stream behavior and determine how visitors arrived at the site.

Aside from the major objectives set by a company, another important factor that brands should take into account is how their site ranks with the various search engines, such as Google, Bing, and Yahoo. These search engines often deliver a significant amount of business to a website and brands must appear on the first page in order to be seen by a large proportion of customers. Most online searchers do not look past the first page of search results.

THE IMPORTANCE OF SEARCH IN MARKETING

Search engines represent close to half the digital media spending of brands [2]. Marketers love search engines because frequently consumers are searching with the direct goal of making a purchase. The opportunity to persuade consumers as they collect purchase information is irresistible.

ORGANIC SEARCH

To understand the impact and potential of social media and mobile marketing, you must have some knowledge of search engine marketing (SEM). SEM is an umbrella term that covers paid advertising on search engines and search engine optimization (SEO). Search engine optimization refers to the effort to raise a website's **organic ranking**, the unpaid ranking that appears in the center of the page when people search key words or phrases, so that the site appears on the first page when the engine returns results to a searcher. Marketers can boost their rankings by altering their sites to rank higher in the search engine's results returned by that search engine's algorithm. Search engines do not sell organic results listings to advertisers. So, advertisers attempt to game the system to get their brands top rankings.

consider this . . .

GLOBAL SEARCH ENGINE GIANT

When it comes to search engines, Google is the behemoth, running over 85% of all desktop Internet searches worldwide. The other search engines don't even come close. Bing is the next largest, but only has a 4.5% share of searches with Yahoo close behind at 4%. The largest search engine in China, Baidu, runs less than 1% of all global searches because people in most countries use Google [5]. Google's global mobile share is even higher—at over 90%—of all mobile Web searches. That is why brands consider Google as the key to their search engine optimization strategies. But, Google's dominance is waning in the US and that might mean brands will have to optimize for other search engines as well.

PAID SEARCH

Another type of search engine marketing that marketers use to influence potential customers is paid search. **Paid search** refers to the sponsored keyword advertising that appears above and to the side of organic results' listings. In a paid search, advertisers bid in an auction against each other to buy keywords or phrases that lead their ads to appear on the searcher's page. Google provides assistance to brands looking to bid on keywords through its Keyword Planner platform. The platform shows the number of searches, level of competition, and suggested bids for certain keywords and phrases.

The Google AdWords auction operates as a second price auction. In this type of auction, the advertisers each bid the maximum they are willing to pay, but in the end, the highest bidder only pays the maximum price of the next highest bidder. For example, if one advertiser bids $4 and another bids $3 for the keyword, the highest bidder would only pay $3 for the advertisement. However, Google also runs a secondary process in determining which advertiser should place highest in a search. Using Ad Rank, Google also evaluates the expected click-through rate for the advertisement, the quality of the landing page experience associated with the ad, and the ad's relevance to the searcher. A landing page is the website page that users see when they click on an advertisement; Google wants to ensure that the pages are high-quality, useful, and secure. Google also gives preference to ads that provide more information, such as phone numbers,

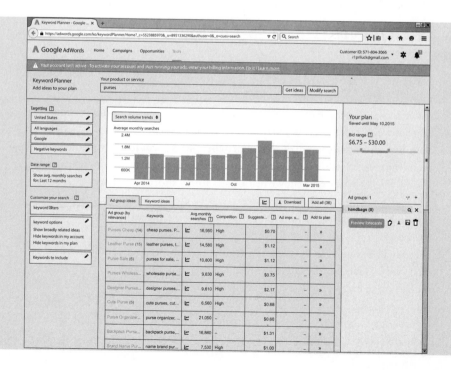

Google's Keyword Planner with suggested keywords, monthly searches, competition, and suggested bid levels for those words.

Google AdWords, www.google .com/adwords

product pictures, and prices. Google uses all these factors to create a score or Ad Rank that determines ad placements. An advertiser with a high bid, but a low Ad Rank, may not show on a page at all as a result of Google's system. On the other hand, an advertiser with a strong Ad Rank score can pay less for the ads because of its ranking [6].

When advertisers use AdWords, they may also elect to use Google's display network. In this case, an advertiser can bid for advertising space on nonsearch websites in the Google network and can request certain types of pages or targets. Ads may appear on Google-owned sites such as Gmail, YouTube, or Blogger. The Google display network includes over a million websites, mobile applications, videos, and blogs. The network reaches 80% of all Internet users worldwide in 30 languages and 100 countries [7].

In search engine marketing, each advertiser first must determine the method of payment for the advertisement. Marketers can pay on a cost-per-click, cost-per-impression, or cost-per-acquisition basis. If the advertiser buys **pay-per-click** ads, the company (or individual person) pays each time a searcher clicks through to the site from Google's search page. An advertiser who pays on a **cost-per-impression** basis pays for each person who views the ad when it comes up on the search engine page, even if the viewer does not click through. Finally, a marketer can choose to pay only when the person actually completes an action, known as a **conversion**, which could be downloading a free report or buying a product. Which do you think costs more for the advertiser?

CHOOSING THE BEST PAYMENT METHOD

Different types of businesses benefit from using various payment methods. For some, it is more efficient to only pay when people buy something, rather than for each viewer. However, those advertisers with very strong websites that really convince people to buy may benefit from using cost-per-impressions at a much lower bid price. When marketers buy on a cost-per-click basis, people see their branded ads even when they don't click, which could deliver some cheap branding opportunities. Advertisers control how much they spend over a time period that they set and they can run ads for as short or as long as they like. The AdWords platform allows advertisers to create their own ads and track the clicks, impressions (number of times people see the ad), cost per click, and total cost.

An ad designed for Google AdWords must meet certain requirements established by Google. The company is constantly updating and adding features to the system to encourage searchers to click on ads. For example, Google advertisers have the option of including product pictures and prices in ads, and the Knowledge Graph feature posts company information when people search the company name.

BECOME A GOOGLE ADWORDS EXPERT

Google AdWords certification offers people a course in designing ads for Google AdWords. By taking a test at the end of the program, you can become AdWords Certified. The program involves learning the requirements for Google AdWords ads. If you are ambitious, you can also get certified for Google Analytics and learn the platform that websites use to evaluate performance.

DO PAID RESULTS INFLUENCE ORGANIC SEARCH?

Since both organic and paid search are shown on the same page, the two influence each other. Specifically, brands achieve higher click-through rates on organic search when employing a paid search strategy. One study found that the dual strategy increased conversions, click-through rates, and revenues [8].

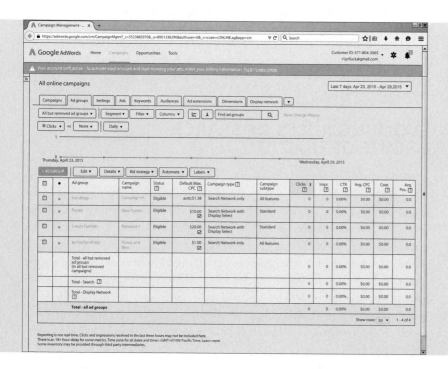

The Google AdWords platform with campaigns for certain keywords in both search and display networks.

Google Adwords, www.google.com/adwords

SEARCH ENGINE OPTIMIZATION

You type queries into the Google search bar regularly, but do you know why certain items show on the first page, while others may be on page 52? Google's algorithm is a closely guarded secret, but a whole industry has popped up in an attempt to influence the rankings. Search engine optimization firms help companies improve their rankings first by monitoring the changes Google makes and then figuring out how such changes will affect client's rankings. Marketers have two terms for the tactics that search engine optimization firms and companies use to game the search engines. **Black hat tactics** are those that take advantage of questionable means of improving rankings by linking to a variety of unrelated sites, paying to have people share content, or creating useless content for links. The more acceptable methods are called **white hat tactics** because they build on the strengths of the search engines to improve rankings by creating strong content and sharing the information in appropriate ways or tweaking a website to perform better.

Google (along with other search engines) is constantly changing its search **algorithm**, the mathematical equation that determines the links that will be listed for a particular keyword search by a particular individual. The rules are constantly in flux as the search engines try to improve their services.

In one year alone, Google made 890 updates to its search engine, leaving brands scrambling to figure out their new rankings. Sometimes, the changes help businesses, but they can also devastate a site even when the site has strong content. Metafile.com, a website whose users posted interesting articles and answers to questions, was dropped from the first page of Google search results to the third page in one day. The site lost 50% of its leads and never recovered [11].

EVOLVING RULES OF SEARCH ENGINE OPTIMIZATION

In the past, marketers would fill their web pages with keywords meant to trigger search engine algorithms to pick up their sites in a search. Many firms put entire backgrounds of keywords to influence the rankings. Later, when companies figured out that Google placed a high level of importance on links, companies tried to link their sites to every possible type of website on the Web regardless of the quality of the content to improve rankings. Content developers sprung up to fill the need with useless articles about nonsense to provide links to companies. Google responded by updating the algorithm to punish links to "spammy" sites and reward firms that had good-quality content which was widely shared by others. Companies are in a constant race to keep up with the latest algorithms.

GOOGLE PANDAS, PENGUINS, HUMMINGBIRDS, AND PIGEONS

Google regularly updates its algorithms, making changes that are meant to improve the user experience, but updates often derail marketers' attempts to rank high in Google searches. When Google found that too many organic searches were listing low-quality links that made it to the first page of an organic search the company issued updates. For those businesses engaged in SEO, first the "Panda" update and then the "Penguin" update threw major wrenches into their strategies. Many top-ranking sites lost ground because they did not meet Google's new standards [9]. Google then changed the engine with its "Hummingbird" update that focused on semantic (language-based) search in an effort to better answer longer queries. Next, Google changed local search with the "Pigeon" update. Google rolled out the Pigeon update in the United States, testing it extensively, and then expanded the update to Canada, the United Kingdom, and Australia [10]. These are just some of the hundreds of updates that Google implements annually. The company will continue to update the algorithm and marketers will likely respond to optimize their listings.

It's important to remember that search engine firms like Google serve both searchers and advertisers. According to Google, the updates improve the search engine results for people who are searching and Google does not accept advertising dollars in exchange for rankings. They change the algorithm so that advertisers do not control the organic listings. On the other hand, Google makes billions of dollars of revenues from advertisers and must consider the most effective strategies to deliver business to websites.

GREGG'S BAKERY

Google regularly updates and changes its algorithm, sometimes affecting companies in strange ways. Gregg's Bakery in the United Kingdom experienced a major headache with Google's Knowledge Graph, a program that automatically brings up company information on the search engine page when someone searches for the company's name. In August 2014 people searching for "Gregg's Bakery" found a fake slogan posted under the company logo that read, "providing sh*t to scum for 70 years." The logo and fake slogan had come from a website called Uncyclopedia that satirizes the Web. Luckily, Gregg's caught the error and contacted Google, which offered to take down the slogan in exchange for a sausage roll [12].

EXHIBIT 7.1

Search Engine Optimization Recommendations from Google

1. Marketers should use title tags in their HTML documents. The title tag tells search engines what the page is about and shows up as titles in search results.

2. Title tags should be unique for each page, brief and descriptive.

3. Use descriptive meta tags, which are part of a webpages' head section, that are different for each page

4. URLs should be simple and descriptive and contain words related to the page.

5. Make the site easy to navigate and provide links to move users around the site.

6. Generate a site map for search engines.

http://static.googleusercontent.com/media/www.google.com/en//webmasters/docs/search-engine-optimization-starter-guide.pdf

TIPS FOR SEARCH ENGINE OPTIMIZATION

Google may control the search business, but it also offers some recommendations to companies for search engine optimization. Some of these tips require a rudimentary understanding of HTML, the computer language for websites, but even without knowledge of HTML, it's important to be aware of these basics, which are summarized in Exhibit 7. 1. These are not exhaustive, but they do illustrate the kinds of issues a webmaster must consider in designing an effective site [19].

A free resource for managing search engine optimization is Google Webmaster Tools, which allows webmasters the opportunity to test out their sites to determine whether search engines can find the site, broken links, keywords that lead to search engine rankings, links to the site, and site statistics.

WEBSITE DESIGN FOR ACHIEVING GOALS

As noted above, marketers must consider designing their websites so that search engines locate the pages and rank them high when potential customers search for keywords or phrases related to the company's business. But an effective website must also be designed to move visitors through the pages in a way that will lead a firm to achieve its objectives.

Ascend2, a market research firm, conducted a study of over 270 marketing professionals from its database of 50,000, asking companies about their website marketing objectives. Exhibit 7.2 presents the most important objectives firms hope to achieve in attracting visitors to their sites [13].

EXHIBIT 7.2

Company Objectives for Website Marketing

OBJECTIVES	PERCENT OF RESPONDENTS INDICATING THIS AS MOST IMPORTANT
Increase lead generation	58%
Increase conversion rate	48%
Improve brand awareness	44%
Increase measurable ROI	42%
Improve data/lead quality	40%
Increase website traffic	27%
Increase sales attribution	17%

Source: Ascend2, "State of Digital Marketing Survey Report," March 2016.
http://ascend2.com/home/wp-content/uploads/State-of-Digital-Marketing-Survey-Summary-Report-160307.pdf

Though marketers use social media sites for communication, they do not own or control the third party platforms. That is why marketers must have their own site that they manage to serve as the primary interface for the brand and to use for evaluating strategies.

To design a good website, marketers must first determine what they want people to do when they go to the site. The best sites are those that people find useful, are easy to navigate, are entertaining, and match the brand experience [14]. Two other factors, interactivity and perceived risk, also influence people's usage and satisfaction with websites.

INTERACTIVITY

Websites are different from social media sites in the interactivity they offer. Generally speaking, people prefer social media sites that are interactive and offer the ability to communicate with others, where they have control over information they share, and where they have opportunities to share at convenient times. At a website, most people just want to get things done and do not want the distractions of social interaction. That's why marketers really have to understand why people come to their site and what they hope to accomplish there. Types of interactivity in websites are summarized in Exhibit 7.3.

EXHIBIT 7.3

Definitions of Interactivity in Websites

Active Control	Desired participation in a network and the ability to control behavior to obtain benefits.	The degree to which individuals share personal information on LinkedIn is dependent on their active control, provided they are aware of the privacy settings.
Two-Way Communication	The ability for members to communicate with online entities and one another and complete transactions.	Individuals comment, write reviews, and seek information for local purchases on Yelp, a social media site.
Synchronicity	Compatible timing of information transmitted and received based on the responsiveness of the system.	Comments on YouTube videos are posted and are accessible immediately for users.

A consumer's response to interactivity depends on his or her cognitive nature, the purpose for engaging in online behavior, and his or her expectation of the experience [18]. There are some people who tend to prefer to interact more than others, but the task matters. Consider a person who is leaving on a business trip the next day and needs to buy a charger for her laptop. The business traveler will not likely want to chat with an online operator to execute the sale. In this case, interactivity is not desirable. Now, consider the stay-at-home dad who is seeking healthy snacks for his children who are at school. He may be looking for interactivity at a website to connect with other parents for new menu ideas and support in encouraging healthful eating. The same is true for social media sites. A person using LinkedIn to search for employment information is in a very different mindset than a person who is taking a picture of his or her meal and posting it on Facebook. The difference provides some explanation as to why U.S. consumers are reluctant to engage with brands on Facebook. The reason for using Facebook is to connect with friends and share day-to-day life issues, not to shop or connect with companies.

PERCEIVED RISK

When people feel that using a website is risky, they tend to limit their use of the site. Individuals perceive that an activity is risky when the outcome can't be predicted [15]. For example, in online or mobile shopping, the consumer expends time and effort to search for a product online, make a purchase decision, research the product and the marketer, go through the checkout process, and agree to shipping terms. A person may feel uncertain about when the product will arrive, the quality of the product, the fit of the product, the return policy, the shipping terms, or the credit card security system.

EXHIBIT 7.4

Potential Risks Associated with Websites

Social	Uncertainty over how information is stored and broadcasted. Concern for who will see the information and how it will be used.
Financial	Costs or potential future costs for participating in the network.
Time	The amount of time that information will be retained by a third party.
Performance	Serving as a conduit or receptor for advertisers and the changing privacy agreements of networks.

In social media, individuals may perceive uncertainty over how information they post is used by others and the possible consequences. Exhibit 7.4 outlines the potential risks in using the Web [16].

In social networking, privacy plays a role in perceptions of the network's risk level, further influencing the decision to continue to use the site [17]. People have legitimate concerns regarding privacy in social networks. Marketers often alter privacy agreements with long detailed legal documents that would require significant time and effort on the part of the consumer to read and understand.

The concern goes further as social networks attempt to monetize their offerings. At one point, Facebook users who "liked" a brand or product could have been featured in "Sponsored Stories" with the information advertised to the person's network of "friends." When a Facebook user liked a post, a notification may have gone out to his or her network of "friends" and "friends of friends," depending on the person's privacy settings. Many people didn't appreciate this aggressive sharing of their likes and habits.

When people examine websites they often scan pages and strong websites help people hone in on the information they need. Good Web design enhances the scanning capabilities of individuals and includes clear headings, bullet points,

strategically placed tabs and buttons, and a layout that contributes to the ability to find information. From a business standpoint, good Web design drives users to revenue-generating activities. The designer has to achieve the dual goals of ease of use for the individual and profit maximization for the marketer. Some other elements of good design are search boxes, call-to-action buttons, easy-to-use shopping carts, quick checkout processes, pleasant graphics, fast loading pages, and a meaningful URL, so people can find the site.

The Web Marketing Association grants WebAwards to the best websites of the year. One winner, U by Kotex, won an award for its Ban the Bland site. The site allowed customers to design feminine hygiene pads using a special design tool. The site was attractive with bold graphics and an interactive design feature. Designing a good site requires research to know the habits of the target, the strategies of competitors, and the key revenue-generating elements of a business. When companies are reviewing their websites to improve the design, they can follow the steps in Exhibit 7.5 to guide their efforts to maximize effectiveness [20].

EXHIBIT 7.5

Build a Better Website

1. Analyze site metrics.	Look at number of users, bounce rate (measure of those who leave the site), conversion rate, and search engine keywords.
2. Set clear goals.	Build awareness, generate traffic, drive users to particular pages, obtain email addresses, generate revenue.
3. Retain key revenue-generating site elements.	Determine where the sales are generated and maintain the elements of the site that contribute to income.
4. Examine competitive sites and benchmarks.	Review what competitors do well and where you might find an opportunity to improve on industry strategies.
5. Leverage a unique selling proposition.	Use your website to build a competitive advantage.
6. Present personas of customers on your site.	Allow prospects to get a sense of whether the site matches their lifestyle and personality.
7. Optimize the site.	Use SEO strategies to rank high in searches.
8. Include calls to action.	Give clear instructions to consumers on how to navigate toward revenue generators.
9. Plan an ongoing content strategy.	Consider the content to provide to customers and when to deliver it.
10. Use buttons and tabs to connect to social media.	Add a blog, RSS feed, and social media buttons to the site for connecting.

DEVELOPING WEB AND MOBILE USE CASE SCENARIOS

You love surfing the Web because it provides information, entertainment, and products and services 24/7. However, because the interaction occurs on a screen, it differs from real-world face-to-face connectedness. Marketers have adopted their practices to make the interaction online as meaningful and real as possible. For example, Zappos.com shows multiple views of a pair of shoes online and has video demonstrations, but must allow the shopper an easy return because trying on the actual shoe is still impossible online.

A **use case** describes how a person interacts with a system and the functions that the system will perform [21]. The designer must consider the business purpose, the user interface, and the technical requirements of the task to create a favorable user experience, while achieving company goals.

Use cases are different depending on what the customer is looking for and the device from which he or she accesses information. Consumers seeking answers from mobile phones are inherently different from those sitting at their desktops. Most mobile customers are looking for local information that they can access quickly, such as the name of the store that sells those cool gadgets.

Many types of businesses have to consider how to design the customer experience and determine how users will interact online and on mobile devices. Initially, mobile sites were just extensions of websites and looked much the same. Later, companies realized that mobile sites should have their own design because the screens were smaller, and so they created dedicated mobile websites to better meet consumer needs. Currently, firms are moving to **responsive design**, which seeks to give users a pleasant interface and easy navigation over a wide range of devices. In responsive design, the Web experience and the mobile experience are similar. For some businesses, using responsive design might make for a seamless experience for the users. For instance, a news organization might want to have a similar look and feel on mobile as in the desktop version. However, sometimes, companies benefit from a more nuanced approach, recognizing that people access information on different types of devices for varied purposes.

The opposite of responsive design is **adaptive design**. In adaptive design, marketers consider how people's use is different, depending on the device they are using. One company that optimizes the online and mobile experiences for its customers is JetBlue. In order for JeBlue to design a strong mobile experience, the company has to figure out when and why people use their mobile devices to access the airline's information. Think about when you might use your cell phone to connect to an airline. Would it be to buy tickets? Would it be to check schedules and information? Would you want to check in for your flight using your phone? Might you check gate information? Since these answers are often different for Web users than mobile users, JetBlue designs its various websites with different goals and interfaces.

EXHIBIT 7.6

JetBlue Web Presence

| Plan a Trip | Manage Flights | Where We Jet | Flying on Jet Blue | Travel Information | TrueBlue |

Hi.

Buy.

The Web version of Jetblue.com is focused on trip planning. The interface shown in Exhibit 7.6 makes the task of finding and booking flights easy, with clearly visible buttons for planning trips. JetBlue also makes it very easy to BUY tickets—the major revenue-generating website goal.

Whereas the use case for JetBlue's online experience focuses on researching and purchasing a trip, their mobile experience is quite different—because of the different mindset of the mobile user. JetBlue's mobile site offers the options shown in Exhibit 7.7.

The mobile site is clearly geared for people on the go who need information about the flights they are about to take. That's why the mobile site emphasizes flight status, check in, and travel alerts. Brands that have both an online and mobile presence should consider the information consumers require from the different types of devices and create experiences that match their needs.

EXHIBIT 7.7

JetBlue Mobile Presence

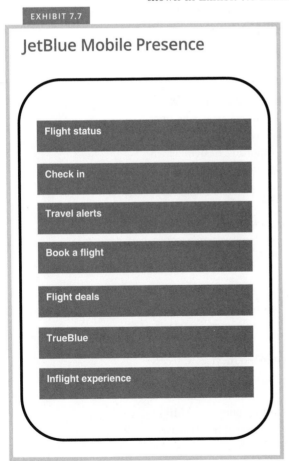

Flight status

Check in

Travel alerts

Book a flight

Flight deals

TrueBlue

Inflight experience

CULTURAL FACTORS IN WEB DESIGN

A brand thinking about Web design may need to consider how people in different cultures respond to strategies. Many brands have multiple sites due to language differences around the globe, but often the differences are deeper than simple translation.

Researchers have found that people's response to marketing communications differ by culture. For example, people who live in cultures that are collective, where people consider the needs of the group, tend to be more risk-averse than those whose cultures are more individualistic. People from individualistic cultures are more likely to respond to a person's use of a product depicted in messaging, while those in collectivist cultures are more concerned with trust [22]. Therefore, it is important in developing digital executions to work with a local agency that has country-specific knowledge. Simply translating a page or a strategy into another language is not likely to work globally. To manage a global strategy, many advertising agencies operate offices around the world. For instance, DDB, based in Chicago and the agency of record for McDonald's, operates offices in 90 countries. Tribal DDB, the digital arm of the agency, operates 56 offices in 38 countries.

Though designing country-specific websites is more expensive than standardizing (creating one global site), studies have found that company websites tend to be localized (designed for specific countries). Brands seek to make their websites consistent with the needs of the users, and websites that match a culture tend to be more useful and easy to navigate so that users have better experiences and more positive attitudes [23]. That's why many companies develop and manage many different country-specific sites. For example, IKEA operates multiple websites with different elements across the globe. On one representative day, Iceland's site featured flowering plants, Italy's site showcased multicolored furnishings, the United Arab Emirates (UAE) was having a sale, Malaysia and Turkey's sites displayed images of kitchens, Russia's site had pictures of children, Japan's site depicted a closet containing only white clothes, and Canada's showed closets with beige and brown clothes (see Exhibit 7.8) [24].

IKEA has relationships with ad agencies around the world, including Mother London, Forsman & Bodenfors in Sweden, DDB Germany, and Crispin Porter + Bogusky. The brand is known for cutting-edge campaigns. Its agency Cake developed a mobile app that allows customers to take pictures of their homes and place IKEA products in their rooms electronically [25]. As a global brand, IKEA recognizes the importance of appealing to consumers in different countries with a local strategy.

EXHIBIT 7.8

IKEA's Websites

COUNTRY	FEATURED IMAGE ON WEBSITE
Iceland	Flowering plants
Italy	Multicolored furniture
France	Bedrooms
Malaysia and Turkey	Kitchens
Russia	Children
Japan and Canada	Closets
Israel	Books and shelves
Kuwait	A transparent chair
United States	Entertainment centers and sofas

MOBILE SITES

Aside from planning a Web-based strategy, marketers often require a mobile Web presence to serve customers who search for company information from mobile devices. Since cell phones and tablets are different sizes and people use these devices in different ways, marketers must carefully consider the strategy for presenting mobile websites to their customers.

People use their mobile devices to search the Internet at home, in the office, and on the go. Mobile devices are easily accessible anywhere, and sometimes people find it more comfortable to kick back and search on a mobile device than power up their desktop. These days, people spend more time on their mobile devices than on their computers and use cell phones and tablets for a variety of tasks. The consumer behavior of mobile users differs from that of desktop users as mobile seekers may make quick decisions in transit [26]. Brands that can attract consumers at the moment of decision have the opportunity to sell their products and services to receptive searchers.

According to Google, only 17% of mobile searches are conducted on the go, but people expect those searches to deliver timely and useful information [27]. The busiest day for mobile search is Friday, when people are getting ready for the weekend and looking for entertainment and activities [26]. Since mobile lends itself to local searches and Friday is the end of the week, people may be leaving work early to shop and meet. Mobile is the tool many use to find their way. As such, some of the most searched businesses on mobile devices are restaurants [28].

Mobile users are more likely than online searchers to click on top search results and are more likely to seek geographically close locations. However, mobile search is often less satisfying to customers because of slower download speeds and the more limited data that are returned [29]. Therefore, marketers must consider the mobile experience and the goals that searchers are trying to achieve in mobile to simplify their mobile websites to provide the answer quickly and in fewer clicks. Some research has shown that people will abandon a shopping cart if the site is not optimized for mobile and that people expect mobile sites to load in less than thirty seconds [30]. When executing a mobile Web strategy, brands should consider the recommendations in Exhibit 7.9 [31].

Just like a website, a mobile site should be optimized for search engine listings. Most mobile consumers conduct their mobile search through Google, which runs 90% of mobile searches [32]. The results are displayed specific to the device accessing the site and may differ by carrier, phone, or browser. In any case, there will be fewer results in mobile, so strong business listings (particularly in Google) are essential [32].

Optimizing for search means researching the keywords that mobile customers search, which may differ from desktop searches. Mobile keywords are more likely to include misspelled names and location-related terms, so marketers have to prepare multiple strategies. In addition, mobile phone users tend to download more content than post information when out and about, suggesting they demand information [29].

EXHIBIT 7.9

Mobile Web Tips for Marketers

- Evaluate potential strategies for mobile Web versus online.

- Broaden the scope of search keywords and find high-volume terms.

- Local strategies are the way to go.

- Use mobile functions such as click-to-call and location-based information.

- Target immediate consumer needs in the market.

- Have a mobile site that loads quickly and navigates well.

EMAIL MARKETING AND THE MOBILE OPPORTUNITY

Email marketing is an important digital tool that people sometimes overlook next to cooler social media options. Often though, email marketing can be more effective in driving desirable results at a lower cost to execute. People still use email more than social media—though some demographics have reduced email usage in favor of social media, such as teens. Not only is email used by 92% percent of online adults in the United States, but people expect to receive marketing messages via email since they have opted in to receive communications. Email marketing, like other communications, should be part of an integrated strategy, clearly designed with the target in mind and with strong subject lines that lead people to conversion [33].

Relatively little academic research has been conducted in the area of email marketing despite its wide-scale usage among practitioners. According to the Internet Advertising Bureau, email marketing represents less than 1% of total digital ad spending [2], but the figure does not represent its true usage because email marketing is inexpensive to execute. Email marketing campaigns deliver strong value to firms, with returns estimated to be 50% higher than the typical return on investment (ROI) for other digital strategies [34]. According to Hubspot, marketers are increasing email spending, with over 75% of marketers reporting they are using more email than in the past. A report by ExactTarget found that 68% of marketers indicate that e-mail marketing is a key component of their business and 88% find that email produces a positive return on their investment [35].

Aside from the advantages in terms of ROI, email is gaining new attention because of its ability to deliver response throughout the day and the purchase cycle. People check their email regularly on mobile devices and marketers can reach people at key decision-making moments. For example, Uber, the car service, can send emails during people's commutes to encourage them to try its service.

In one execution, Uber argues that a ride with it is less expensive than a taxi and presents fare comparisons in emails to prospective customers [36].

Email is an important customer relationship management tool and many marketers use email to acquire, inform, and relate to customers. A good strategy can drive traffic to a website, encourage information search, remind consumers to purchase, offer incentives, provide information, and persuade. On the back end, email is measurable, testable, and customizable. AT&T used responsive design to create an email campaign that would look equally good on a desktop as on a phone. The message was "Treat Yourself. Add a line, get a lot" and included both "call now" and "shop now" buttons to facilitate the purchase. These kinds of calls to action can be very effective in encouraging people to interact when the message is top of mind [36].

One important aspect of successful email marketing is that the person on the receiving end should opt in to receive the email and have a desire for the product, service, or information provided. Spam is undesired email and spamming may reduce a brand's value in the eyes of consumers. The rationale for an opt-in strategy is that those who give permission to receive market-related emails will be more receptive to communications because they desire the information. Therefore, permission-based marketing has become a standard for legitimate marketers. However, marketers do their best to make it difficult for people to unsubscribe from their email lists, and very often emails continue to arrive once someone has unsubscribed. Since email is so inexpensive, there is little incentive for firms to remove

consider this . . .

THE CAN-SPAM ACT

CAN-SPAM stands for the Controlling the Assault of Non-Solicited Pornography and Marketing Law, enacted in 2003 and intended to regulate online commerce. Here is what the CAN-SPAM act says [37]:

An Act to regulate interstate commerce by imposing limitations and penalties on the transmission of unsolicited commercial electronic mail via the Internet.

Be it enacted by the Senate and House of Representatives of AFFIRMATIVE CONSENT when used with respect to a commercial electronic mail message, means that:

(A) the recipient expressly consented to receive the message, either in response to a clear and conspicuous request for such consent or at the recipient's own initiative;

(B) if the message is from a party other than the party to which the recipient communicated such consent, the recipient was given clear and conspicuous notice at the time the consent was communicated that the recipient's electronic mail address could be transferred to such other party for the purpose of initiating commercial electronic mail messages.

email addresses from lists even when the law demands those removals. The U.S. CAN-SPAM Act is summarized in the "Consider This" box that follows.

WHEN TO CHOOSE AN EMAIL STRATEGY

Marketers should consider their email strategies and determine when email delivers the best response because too much email can repel a potential customer. In general, people are receptive to email messages when they provide desired information and dislike email that doesn't add value. For example, a study of college students and emails related to online dating found that students who were single and seeking a relationship were more likely to open an email and purchase matchmaking services than students who were already in a relationship [38]. This is not at all surprising as people are much more likely to respond to personally relevant communications and purchase services that they want and need.

In email marketing, the offer is the benefit that the marketer promises to the customer. Due to the large number of emails people receive that include marketing messages, awareness of the offer is a key attribute in determining a response to the email. Once the consumer becomes aware of the offer, another factor that influences response is urgency. Offers with limited time frames may lead to higher levels of response than less urgent emails [39]. Exhibit 7.10 provides recommendations for optimizing email strategies [40].

Though consumers hold negative attitudes toward spam and are more positively inclined toward permission-based emails, people do not always remember they opted in to receive emails. Another limitation of email marketing is that a person might be so overwhelmed by the daily barrage of emails that he or she neglects to open some of them. The subject line should either drive the consumer to open the email or communicate enough to achieve the goal, such as a brand identification.

EXHIBIT 7.10

Recommendations for Strong Email Marketing Campaigns

DO	DON'T
Integrate email with brand strategy.	Buy third-party lists to avoid opt-in.
Maintain a strong targeted list.	Hide the subscriber box to force permission.
Encourage unsubscribers to stay at a reduced commitment.	Prevent unsubscribing.
Maintain contact.	Send undesired emails.
Examine appropriate analytics.	Maintain a strategy that doesn't work.

STRATEGIES FOR COLLECTING OPT-IN EMAILS

One challenge of permission-based email marketing is obtaining the necessary permissions. Those who opt in are likely better targeted prospects with more of an affinity for a brand. Marketers can encourage opt-in by providing easy access or incentives, but a technique that has become popular from B2B marketing is providing compelling content for free and collecting email contact information. A content marketing strategy is often used to collect email addresses for further follow-up. For example, Hubspot, a company that helps firms manage email and social media, offers free reports, ebooks, and white papers to small businesses to guide them in digital marketing. In order to read the reports, the user must provide an email address.

In the world of social media, email competes with a number of other marketing strategies. Opt-in email may take a back seat to marketers' attempts to build Facebook likes, Twitter followers, check-ins, or repins. Removing email campaigns from the mix may be short-sighted, as having email addresses and approaching customers directly may be more useful than asking users to visit yet another social media site representing the brand. Email is still an inexpensive, viable, and effective method to reach customers with relevant and timely messages.

Mobile marketing presents an opportunity for email marketers. People with smartphones now have access to email on the go and when they are in-market. The challenge is to time the information, so it is available at the moment of purchase. One strategy is to offer an incentive through email that encourages users to open the email in-store. Marketers should consider that emails may be opened from a mobile device and consider the mobile use case scenario for the brand. Providing a link to a mobile website in an email can help facilitate mobile usage. For instance, Toys "R" Us uses email as part of its strategy to encourage holiday shopping.

Mobile email is a good way to distribute coupons. Marketers simply have to remind consumers who are shopping in the store that the coupons are available on their phones and be ready to accept the coupons in the mobile format. One easy method for coupon verification is a code in the email. That way, even a store without strong information technology can accept a coupon via email.

consider this . . .

A BUSINESS-TO-BUSINESS EMAIL MARKETING CASE

Email can drive measurable results. Crowe Horwath, a public accounting and consulting firm, was looking to generate leads for its service. Before choosing a strategy, the firm set its target audience, researched business drivers, and determined topics of interest to potential clients.

The target market was C-suite executives, including chief financial officers, chief risk officers, and chief operations officers in large financial institutions with at least $1 billion in assets. These financial companies could benefit from Crowe Horwath's expertise in four areas: compliance with the Dodd-Frank Wall Street Reform Act, money laundering legislation, improving business processes, and evaluating core banking systems.

The firm identified a list of 4,000 executives to whom they sent email offers once every four weeks on each of the various topics. Those recipients who downloaded three pieces of content became viable leads. Crowe Horwath examined the data from those who downloaded the content and categorized each person, so that such an individual would receive more content that was specific to his or her interests. The scoring led to better open rates and after 12–18 months the program resulted in an ROI of 133%. The emails resulted in 33% of the invite executives joining the opt-in email program and a 75%–85% open rate [41].

EMAIL RETURN ON INVESTMENT

Marketers work with budgets, so determining the impact of one strategy relative to another helps marketers evaluate the success of different programs and make decisions on how to move forward. One metric that can be used across a variety of strategies is **return on investment (ROI)**—the measure of the cost of a strategy relative to the benefit to the firm. In email marketing, ROI is often strong because the costs are low. Even a little bit of money earned from an execution can lead to a positive return. To calculate ROI, marketers use the following formula:

$$\frac{\text{Return} - \text{Cost of the Investment}}{\text{Cost of the Investment}} \times 100$$

The cost of the investment in email marketing is the money a firm would pay to an email marketing company if it uses a vendor, or the cost of developing the email and sending it out to prospective customers. The return is the money earned that can be attributed to the email, such as sales resulting from people who have been directed to the website via the email or have redeemed coupons delivered in an email.

In order to calculate ROI, email marketers should understand the basic terms listed in Exhibit 7.11.

EXHIBIT 7.11

Email Marketing Terms

1. Number	How many emails were sent?
2. Bounce Rate	What percentage of the emails came back undeliverable by the server?
3. Open Rate	What percentage of emails was opened by the customers?
4. Conversion	What percentage of customers purchased based on the email?
5. Net Revenue	How much, on average, does the marketer earn per conversion?

DETERMINING ROI FOR BELLAGIO PIZZA

An email list for a local restaurant, Bellagio Pizza, consists of 200k opted-in email addresses. In one campaign, the restaurant sends a standard email message to its entire list. The deal is a lunch special at 11:00 a.m. to encourage visits to the restaurant. The meal deal costs $4.99 and includes lunch consisting of a personal pan pizza, small salad, and a beverage. It costs Bellagio $1.50 to provide the meal. The bounce rate is 1%, the open rate is 20%, and 5% of those who read the email come to the restaurant and ask for the meal deal (with a code identifying the email received). What is the ROI for this email campaign?

In the case of Bellagio Pizza, the ROI is

Customers who receive the email = 198,000
Customers who read it = 39,600
Customers who convert = 1,980
Profit per customer from the deal = $3.49
Total revenue = $9,880
Total cost = $2,970
ROI = 9,880 – 2,970/2,970 = 232%

Of course, a number of customers might have visited the restaurant anyway, and there is some unaccounted for cost in creating the email and sending it out, but the return based on this analysis is a very strong 232%.

LESSONS FROM DIRECT MARKETING

Direct marketing has long been an important form of communication for marketers, and years of research in this area provide insights on how consumers respond to offers and direct appeals from marketers. Direct marketing has been defined as "any activity whereby you communicate directly with your prospect or customer and he or she responds directly to you" [42]. Therefore, direct marketing encompasses many online activities, including email and social media and mobile marketing strategies. Direct mail was the traditional method of making direct contact with customers, and some of the widely studied techniques of direct mail can be applied to email marketing, social and mobile efforts.

The key elements of direct mail include the quality of the list of prospects or customers, the offer, the message, a call to action, and testing. Exhibit 7.12 describes the major factors in developing a successful direct marketing campaign, and Exhibit 7.13 provides some of the best practices of direct marketing that a marketer can apply to email, social media, or mobile campaigns.

EXHIBIT 7.12

Elements of Direct Marketing

ELEMENT	EXPLANATION
The List	A strong correct mailing list with targeted prospects or current customers.
The Offer	Must attract the customer and results in an action desired by the firm.
The Message	A personalized tailored message that builds a relationship.
A Call to Action	A clear ask of the desired response.
Testing	Numerous in-market tests of copy, layout, offers, terms, prices, premiums, or content.

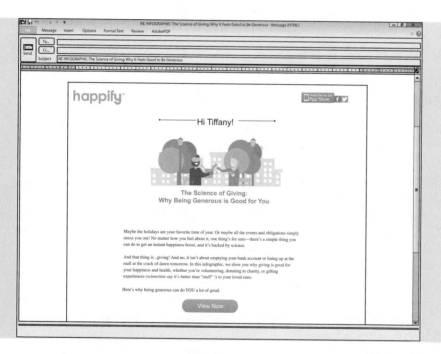

Happify provides a great subject line, interesting data, and a shareable infographic in its email campaign, with links to download the app.

Happify, www.Happify.com

The final stage in a successful direct mail campaign is testing. Through testing, the marketer can determine the optimum setting for each element of a campaign. In direct mail, marketers can send different letters to different samples of prospects to determine which of two offers leads to higher conversions or the preferred wording of a call to action (see Exhibit 7.13) [42].

EXHIBIT 7.13

Lessons from Successful Direct Mail Campaigns

- The call to action should ask for the order.
- Personalize the message, not just the salutation.
- Long copy sells more. If someone is going to read it, you may as well give that person the information he or she needs.
- Integrate campaigns rather than plan strategies in individual forms of media.
- Repeat winning strategies. Don't worry that people have seen it before if the strategy works.
- Optimize offers by testing, recombining, and testing again.

SUMMARY AND REVIEW

CHAPTER SUMMARY

There are many important lessons to be learned from the digital marketing arena and the years of research preceding social media communities and mobile technology. Many of the behaviors and attitudes studied are applicable to emerging strategies in social and mobile. Certainly, a website presence is important for firms as social media and mobile strategies often drive traffic to a website. Understanding how consumers use websites and the strategies that make them successful will deliver results from online marketing strategies. Mobile phones will invigorate email marketing and access to the mobile Web will continue to grow. Students of social media and mobile marketing must have a strong understanding of digital strategies to execute successfully integrated campaigns.

KEY TERMS

adaptive design
algorithm
black hat tactics
conversion
cost-per-impression
digital strategy

internet marketing
keyword optimization
organic ranking
paid search
pay-per-click
responsive design

return on investment
  (ROI)
search engine marketing
  (SEM)
two-way
  communication

use case
white hat tactics

SUMMARY REVIEW QUESTIONS

1. What are the major forms of digital advertising and when would a marketer prefer each type?

2. Explain the concept of interactivity and how it affects Web usage.

3. Should websites and mobile sites look the same to users? Why or why not?
4. What are some ways to rank high in a Google search?
5. What is the difference between an organic search and a paid search?

6. What is email's role in mobile marketing? Is it effective?
7. Which aspects of direct mail are useful in social media marketing?

APPLICATION QUESTIONS

1. Go to http://adwords.google.com and sign into your Google account (or create a new account). Click on the "CAMPAIGN" tab and open the drop-down menu. What are the major types of campaigns you can run on Google Adwords? Enter data for all the fields and create your own advertisement for your favorite clothing store. Use the URL of the store, and you can see how your ad will look.

2. Conduct a search for the term "Europe" on Google and Bing, and then on a mobile device. What are the biggest differences in the organic or paid results?

3. Go to the website of a retailer from whom you have bought items online by typing the URL directly at the http:// prompt. Next, set your browser to private viewing. You can learn how to do this by typing your browser name and "private viewing" into Google. Now, compare and contrast the experience of shopping using the two methods. What is the difference? Which would a consumer prefer? Why?

4. Sign up for email alerts from your favorite charity. Log the days, dates, and times that emails arrive in your in-box. Evaluate the charity's strategy. Did the emails come at the right time for you? What would have been more effective? On which subject lines were you the most and least likely to click?

5. Examine two competitive websites based on the criteria for good design. What is the major goal of each site? Which site is better and why?

6. Using SEMrush, evaluate one brand's keyword strategy. Which keywords does it buy? How effective is the brand's SEO and are its ads appropriate? Would you recommend any longer keyword phrases?

7. Find a brand that uses responsive design and one that uses adaptive design on its mobile site. Why do these two brands differ in their strategies? Consider a use case.

8. Evaluate the email marketing strategy of a brand that sends you a lot of emails. Which are most effective in driving a response? Why?

case study Screwfix's Digital Strategy

Screwfix was a U.K. retailer specializing in the do-it-yourself and building contractor markets. The company operated over 350 stores in the United Kingdom, Northern Ireland, and Germany with revenues of £557 million. Its parent company, Kingfisher plc, was heavily invested in the building materials market both in retail stores and online. Aside from Screwfix, the company owned B&Q stores in the UK, China, and Ireland, Castorama home and garden stores in France, Brico Dépôt in France, and Koçtas in Turkey.

Screwfix's product line included power tools, kitchen and bathroom fixtures and accessories, electrical equipment and lighting, plumbing supplies, and outdoor and gardening products. Early on, the company mastered digital marketing with a strong e-commerce website and digital communications campaigns in a variety of media. The retailer ran display advertising, paid search, email marketing, social media, and mobile strategies to drive both online and in-store sales.

The market for building materials had shifted by 2014. Through 2008 home stores benefited from homeowners who had renovated their own houses, but these customers were aging and were no longer inclined to climb ladders to paint or plaster. After 2008 the DIY market declined 22%, and companies like Screwfix chose to target tradesmen, a profession growing at a rate of 10% in Great Britain. A good portion of the revised strategy was to leverage digital media and build strong relationships with contractors. Kevin O'Byrne, Screwfix's CEO, stated at the time: "We are revisiting how and where we spend our marketing. It doesn't need to be clever, it needs to be effective. The point is to drive footfall . . . and put a trading drumbeat into the business." He indicated that the company would adopt clear and simple messaging, impactful promotions, larger displays in-store, and high levels of stock [43]. The plan was to relaunch the website to improve conversion rates [44].

WEB STRATEGY

Screwfix was strategic in considering the professional target market and customizing online experiences. The various ads directed tradesmen to different homepages based on their professions so that plumbers saw a different Web interface than electricians. Both sets could customize shopping lists for regular materials and order online or on a mobile device, while on a job. The supplies would then be available for pick-up from a nearby store in less than fifteen minutes. Professionals sought the best brands and prices, and the task of the site was to make the process as easy as possible, without a lot of hand holding [45].

Disaster struck in early 2014, though, when a pricing glitch on the Screwfix website set everything—including expensive power tools and lawnmowers—at a price of £34.99. Before the company became aware of the problem and had a chance to shut down its site, word spread on social media, and through the site HotUK-Deals, early morning online shoppers placed their orders, and customers began showing up at the store to demand their purchases. Screwfix decided to honor those purchases that customers came to pick up or that had already shipped, but not those orders that had yet to be processed. Customers were given refunds for those transactions. At the time, the site had 1.3 million visitors a week, and with discounts as much as £1800 on certain items, the company would have gone bankrupt very quickly. But it weathered the storm by reacting quickly. Customers who got the deals were very happy and shared their joy on social media [46].

ORGANIC SEARCH AND SEO

Screwfix optimized its website, leading to a consistent set of keywords that generated organic listings. The top keyword was Screwfix, followed by some popular products and the term "rated people," a British expression for building contractors. The U.K. website www.ratedpeople.com was where Brits went to seek out the best contractors for home improvement jobs. The keywords in Exhibit 7.14 put Screwfix in the top rankings on Google's U.K. page [47]. The columns show the position screwfix.com earned on Google's search engine page when the word was searched, the number of monthly searches executed by users for that term, and the cost that the brand would have to pay to purchase the word in a paid search.

The chart in Exhibit 7.15 indicates that in an organic search, a number of competitors shared common search terms and results.

EXHIBIT 7.14

Organic Keywords for Screwfix

ORGANIC KEYWORDS	POS	VOLUME (12 MONTHS)	CPC
screwfix	1(1)	1,830,000	0.39
screw fix	1(1)	60,500	2.43
radiators	1(1)	49,500	2.93
rated people	2(4)	110,000	0.30
kitchen taps	1(1)	22,200	1.72

www.SEMrush.com

EXHIBIT 7.15

Competitive Keywords

COMPETITORS IN ORGANIC SEARCH			
DOMAIN	COMPETITION LEVEL	COMMON KEYWORDS FOR WEBSITES*	SE KEYWORDS BRINGING USERS TO WEBSITES FROM TOP 20 SEARCHES
wickes.co.uk	High	30.5k	59.3k
diy.com	High	37.8k	93.6k
toolstation.com	High	12.7k	10.8k
homebase.co.uk	High	26.5k	98.3k

Number of words shared with another company.
www.SEMrush.com

The competitors were strong and also engaged in search engine marketing. As a result, DIY.com, Homebase, Wickes, and Toolstation overlapped on a significant percentage of paid search words [47].

Screwfix used SEO techniques with the goal of improving search engine rankings. As a result of its efforts, Screwfix ranked high on a variety of searches. Of course, so did Screwfix's competitors. Therefore, Screwfix had to have a strong listing and paid strategy so that when people looked at the search engine results, they would choose Screwfix.

MOBILE SEARCH AND SEO

Screwfix also operated a mobile website (m.screwfix.com) that ranked no. 1 on Google's search engine when searchers entered the company name on a mobile device. The address of the site suggested that Screwfix had a dedicated mobile page that was optimized for mobile devices. M.sites were popular in the early days of mobile commerce because the pages loaded more quickly on devices than full websites. These sites offered a pared-down experience for users, without the full functionality of a website. However, by 2014, many brands had moved away from dedicated m.sites and developed sites using responsive design. Brands chose more complicated interfaces because people spent a lot more time on sites with more functionality, the load time for responsive sites improved, and Google no longer ranked m.sites highly [48].

However, the mobile search listings for the brand name were highly favorable toward Screwfix and included the Screwfix company listing on Google, Screwfix's Facebook page, the Screwfix bathrooms landing page, the Wiki site for Screwfix, Careers at Screwfix, the Screwfix appliances landing page, and Screwfix's Twitter feed [49]. Exhibit 7.16 shows the sites that delivered organic traffic to screwfix.com.

PAID SEARCH

An important aspect of the digital strategy was buying Google AdWords, so when people searched for building-related products, ads for Screwfix would display on the Google search page. First, the company purchased its own name and paid $.39 when searchers clicked on Screwfix ads. In 2014 the volume of searches for the keyword Screwfix was 1,830,000 in the United Kingdom. In August 2014 Screwfix spent about $45,000 monthly on paid search, but that figure increased to $54,000 in September [47].

Google's search engine generated 70% of the brand's search business. As a result, Screwfix analyzed responses to its executions by copy-testing messages. The brand found a 25% difference in responses to strong versus weak ads and ran the ads most likely to deliver strong click-through rates. Screwfix also collected data based on the time of day to determine when to bid on AdWords, aiming for times when people were more likely to buy than simply browse. The brand altered budgets and ads daily to respond to the analysis of the prior day's campaigns [50].

The keywords bringing users to the website via a Google paid search in August and September 2014 appear in Exhibit 7.17 [47], and the actual text of the ads run by Screwfix and their competitors are presented in Exhibits 7.20–7.23.

Domains Delivering Organic Hits to Screwfix

POS (TYPE OF DOMAIN)	DOMAIN	URL
1	screwfix.com	www.screwfix.com/
2	screwfixbathrooms.com	screwfixbathrooms.com/
3 Parent company	kingfisher.com	www.kingfisher.c...d%3D36
4	wikipedia.org	en.wikipedia.org/wiki/Screwfix
5	facebook.com	www.facebook.com/Screwfix
6	youtube.com	www.youtube.com/user/Screwfix
7	screwfixcareers.com	www.screwfixcareers.com/
8	twitter.com	twitter.com/Screwfix
9	apple.com	itunes.apple.com...mt%3D8
10	screwfixlive.com	screwfixlive.com/
11	screwfixappliances.com	www.screwfixappliances.com/
12 News organization	telegraph.co.uk	www.telegraph.co...9.html
13 Jobs website	reed.co.uk	www.reed.co.uk/j.../p3394
14	screwfixwardrobes.com	www.screwfixwardrobes.com/
15 Manchester's event space	eventcity.co.uk	www.eventcity.co...-live/
16 Personal finance news	thisismoney.co.uk	www.thisismoney....e.html
17	indeed.co.uk	www.indeed.co.uk/Screwfix-jobs
18	hotukdeals.com	www.hotukdeals.c...ix.com
19	easy-greendeal.com	www.easy-greende...x.html
20	moneysupermarket.com	www.moneysuperma...259/1/

www.SEMrush.com

EXHIBIT 7.17

Paid Keywords, August and September

AUGUST PAID KEYWORDS	VOLUME	CPC
kitchen sinks	14,800	0.87
table saw	9,900	0.56
mitre saw	9,900	0.51
screwfix promo code	9,900	0.56
dehumidifier	60,500	
SEPTEMBER PAID KEYWORDS	VOLUME	CPC
cooker hoods	18,100	1.26
kitchen sinks	14,800	0.87
oil filled radiator	9,900	0.92
screwfix promo code	9,900	0.56
toilet cistern	6,600	1.24
cooker hoods	18,100	1.26

www.SEMrush.com

Screwfix also purchased product listing ads that showed specific Screwfix products and their associated prices to searchers in the advertising section of Google's search page. The product ads were very effective in generating clicks. The company found that using product listing ads led to:

Conversion rates 49% higher than those for standard AdWords listings
A 55% higher return on ad spending compared to text ads
A 39% lower cost per acquisition rate versus the simple text-based ads

EXHIBIT 7.18

Sample Screwfix Ad in Tribute to Yuri Gagarin

Out Of This World Deals
Whether You're Building A Rocket or A House We Have The Tools You Need
www.screwfix.com

In addition, Screwfix was strategic when considering buys on Google. For instance, the brand would create ads related to the Google doodle and to the day's news because people tended to search for those items. Consider an ad that Screwfix ran when Google paid tribute to Yuri Gagarin, the first person to enter outer space. When people searched "google doodle," up came the Screwfix ad in Exhibit 7.18 [51].

SOCIAL MEDIA

Screwfix had an advanced social media strategy that included a number of third party platforms and its own online community. The strategy was aimed at giving the brand a unique personality that was fun and irreverent, thus engaging more people. The target of DIY enthusiasts and tradesmen were not typical social media users, so Screwfix found an entertaining way to become the authority for the target market with competitions, conversation, and banter, rather than many overt selling messages. See Exhibit 7.19 for competitive social media data [52].

EMAIL STRATEGY

Screwfix used segmented email to reach customers depending on how long it had been since their last purchase. The brand developed emails with messages such as "we're sorry" and "was it something we said?" aimed at lapsed buyers. By using specialized emails, Screwfix saw open rates 60%–70% higher and conversions 60%–85% higher than obtained with standard blast emails. In this way, the brand segmented based on a variety of criteria to offer targeted emails to their customers [53].

CONCLUSION

Screwfix used a number of digital strategies to drive online and in-store sales. The combination of those strategies resulted in strong visibility online. According to *Marketing Magazine*, Screwfix was the most visible U.K. building retailer online with a consumer voice index score

EXHIBIT 7.19

Competitive Social Media Data

UNITED KINGDOM	FACEBOOK LIKES	TWITTER FOLLOWERS	YOUTUBE VIDEOS	GOOGLE PLUS
Screwfix	127,074	22,700	1,823 subscribers	1,096 followers, 1,742,563 views
Homebase	127,287	16,400	1,121 subscribers	1,267 followers, 231,962 views
Wickes	21,645	14,800	2,308 subscribers	520 followers 22,981 views
DIY.com (B&Q)	95,388	160,000	18,062 subscribers	1140 followers 159,541 views

Source: www.Facebook.com, www.Twitter.com, www.YouTube.com, www.googleplus.com

of 53% compared to 21% for Wickes, 15% for Homebase, and 11% for B&Q. In 2016 Kingfisher, the parent company of Screwfix and B&Q, announced that it would continue to grow sales with a large investment in its digital strategy. Apparently, digital, aimed at an increasingly tech savvy customer, was driving significant results for the brand [54].

EXHIBIT 7.20

Sample Paid Search Ads for Screwfix, August

Fencing At Screwfix	Lighting	Karcher At Screwfix	LED Lights
Buy Fencing Supplies At Screwfix. Trade Prices—Free Delivery. www.screwfix.com/ Garden Supplies	Buy Internal And External Lighting. Free Next-Day Delivery Over £50. www.screwfix.com/ Lighting	Buy Karcher Products At Screwfix. Free Next-Day Delivery Over £50. www.screwfix.com/ Karcher	Buy LED Lights At Screwfix. Free Next-Day Delivery Over £50. www.screwfix.com/ Lighting
Keywords: 398 Kitchen Splashbacks	Keywords: 377 Screwfix Interior Doors	Keywords: 368 Mira Showers	Keywords: 247 Radiators At Screwfix
Buy Splashbacks At Screwfix Trade Prices—Next-Day Delivery. www.screwfix.com/ Kitchens	Wide Range Of Interior Doors. Free Next-Day Delivery Over £50. www.screwfix.com/ Interior Doors	Buy Mira Showers At Screwfix. Trade Prices—Next-Day Delivery. www.screwfix.com/ Mira	Buy At Trade Prices. Free Delivery or Order Online—Collect In Store. www.screwfix.com/ Radiators

www.SEMrush.com

EXHIBIT 7.21

Sample Paid Search Ads for Screwfix, September

Cooker Hoods - Screwfix.com_ Buy Cooker Hoods at Screwfix. Free Next Day Delivery Over £50 www.screwfix.com/ Kitchens	Kitchen Sinks - Screwfix.com_ Wide Selection of Kitchen Sinks At Screwfix.com - Trade Prices www.screwfix.com/ Kitchens	Oil-Filled Radiator - Screwfix.com_ Oil Filled Radiators at Screwfix. Trade Prices - Free Delivery www.screwfix.com/ OilFilledRadiators	Screwfix.com - Screwfix: Great Savings_ Power Tools, Plumbing & Electrical. Trade Prices - Free Delivery www.screwfix.com/

www.SEMrush.com

EXHIBIT 7.22

Sample Paid Search DIY Ads, September

Do It Yourself
Inspirational Ideas for Kitchens, Bathrooms & Much More Online
www.diy.com/

B&Q Dulux Paint - Quality Dulux Paint at Low Prices - diy.com Free Delivery On Orders Over £50! www.diy.com/Dulux-Paint	B&Q Mirrors Buy Quality Mirrors online at B&Q. Low Prices & Great Savings www.diy.com/Mirror	B&Q Wallpaper Quality Wallpaper at Low Prices Free Delivery On Orders Over £50! www.diy.com/Wallpaper

www.SEMrush.com

EXHIBIT 7.23

Sample Paid Search Ads for Wickes, September

Buy Concrete - Extensive range of Concrete Buy online from Wickes today! www.wickes.co.uk/Concrete	wickes.co.uk - Doors at Wickes - Wide range of Doors Order online from Wickes. www.wickes.co.uk/Doors	Kitchen Worktops - wickes.co.uk Buy Kitchen Units at Wickes & Get 1/3 off! View Our Range Now www.wickes.co.uk/KitchensUnitsSale	Wickes - Doors uPVC - wickes.co.uk Visit Wickes and buy from our great range of Doors uPVC. www.wickes.co.uk/Doors_uPVC

www.SEMrush.com

As long as the building contractor market continued to grow, Screwfix could expect to drive professionals to the stores and the site [52].

QUESTIONS FOR DISCUSSION

1. Should Screwfix buy competitor names in paid search? If so, what is likely to happen?
2. Why does Screwfix use Google Plus?
3. Which elements of Screwfix's strategy are most and least successful?
4. Evaluate Screwfix's paid search ads versus competitors.
5. Is there a way for a brand to distinguish itself in this space? How?
6. Visit the Screwfix website. Evaluate the ability of the site to convert do-it-yourselfers and tradesmen? Who is more likely to feel comfortable with the site?
7. What is the role for email at Screwfix? Explain why email is an effective strategy to drive a response for Screwfix relative to other options.
8. Do paid advertisements influence response from organic searches? How?
9. Should Screwfix continue to run an m.site or consider other formats?
10. Go to Google's UK search engine and type in key words for a search related to home building supplies. What comes up? Is Screwfix's strategy working? When?

REFERENCES

[1] Quantcast Top Sites, United States https://www.quantcast.com/top-sites, May 2016.

[2] Internet Advertising Bureau, "Internet Ad Revenue Report," 2015.

[3] R. Hof, "Why Google's Search Market Share Loss to Yahoo Means Pretty Much Nothing," *Forbes,* 8 January 2015.

[4] D. Segal, "The Dirty Little Secrets of Search," *The New York Times,* 12 February 2011.

[5] Statista, "Worldwide Share of Search Engines," July 2014, http://www.statista.com/statistics/216573/worldwide-market-share-of-search-engines/.

[6] Google, "The Ad Auction," 2014, https://support.google.com/partners/answer/1704431?hl=en&ref_topic=2799732.

[7] Google, "Display Network," 2014, https://support.google.com/partners/answer/117120?ctx=glossary.

[8] S. Yang and A. Ghose, "Analyzing the Relationship Between Organic and Sponsored Search Advertising: Positive, Negative, or Zero Interdependence?," *Marketing Science,* vol. 29, no. 4, pp. 602–623, 2010.

[9] M. Moog, "One Year Later: How Google Panda Changed Our Business," TechCrunch, 3 March 2012.

[10] Site Visibility, "Local SEO Tips & Google Pigeon with Greg Gifford," Internet Marketing Podcast, 1 April 2015.

[11] TLDR, "How Google Is Killing the Best Site on the Internet," On the Media, NPR, 3 June 2014. http://www.wnyc.org/story/tldr-27-how-google-killing-best-site-internet/

[12] A. Gestenhues, "Google Knowledge Graph Proves to Be (Brief) PR Nightmare for Major UK Brand Greggs Bakery," *SearchEngineLand,* 19 August 2014.

[13] Ascend2, "Inbound Marketing Research Summary Report," August 2014.

[14] E. T. Loiacono, R. T. Watson, and D. L. Goodhue, "WebQual: A Measure of Website Quality," in *Proceedings of American Marketing Association Winter Educators' Conference*, Chicago, 2002.

[15] M. Conchar, G. Zinkhan, C. Peters, and S. Olavarrieta, "An Integrated Framework for the Conceptualization of Consumers' Perceived Risk Processing," *Journal of the Academy of Marketing Science,* vol. 32, no. 4, pp. 418–436, 2004.

[16] M. Laroche, J. Bergeron, and C. Goutaland, "A Three Dimensional Scale of Intangibility," *Journal of Services Marketing,* vol. 4, no. 1, pp. 26–38, 2001.

[17] X. Tan, Q. Li, Y. Kim, and J. Hsu, "Impact of Privacy Concern in Social Networking Websites," *Internet Research,* vol. 22, no. 2, pp. 211–233, 2012.

[18] D. Sohn, C. Ci, and B.-K. Lee, "The Moderating Effects of Expectation on the Patterns of the Interactivity-Attitude Relationship," *Journal of Advertising,* vol. 36, no. 3, pp. 109–119, Fall 2007.

[19] "Google Search Engine Optimization Starter Guide." http://static.googleusercontent.com/media/www.google.com/en//webmasters/docs/search-engine-optimization-starter-guide.pdf

[20] J. Meher, "10-Step Checklist for Your Next Website Redesign," Hubspot, 2012.

[21] E. Gottesdiener, "Use Cases: Best Practices," IBM, 2003.

[22] M. de Mooij, *Consumer Behavior and Culture,* Thousand Oaks, CA: Sage, 2004.

[23] F. Vyncke and M. Brengman, "Are Culturally Congruent Websites More Effective? An Overview of a Decade of Empirical Evidence," *Journal of Electronic Commerce Research,* vol. 11, 2010.

[24] IKEA, 3 June 2012, http://www.ikea.com.

[25] Z. Rogers, "Ikea's Digital Work: Often Oddball, Always Clever," *ClickZ,* 17 May 2011.

[26] L. Johnson, "Mobile to Outpace Desktop Local Search by 2015," *Mobile Marketer,* 20 April 2012.

[27] Google and Nielsen, "Mobile Search Moments: Understanding How Mobile Drives Conversions," 2013.

[28] MobiThinking, "Global Mobile Statistics," 2012.

[29] A. Ghose, A. Goldfarb, and S.-P. Han, "How Is the Mobile Internet Different? Search Costs and Local Activities," 2011.

[30] I. Mills, "Five Reasons You Absolutely Must Optimize Mobile," 16 April 2014, http://www.huffingtonpost.com/ian-mills/5-reasons-you-absolutely-_b_5122485.html.

[31] 360i, "Mobile Marketing Playbook," 2010.

[32] Sterling, G. "Google's PC Market Share Off Its Peak, Yet Company Seeing More Searches Than Ever," Search Engine Land, October 17, 2015. http://searchengineland.com/googles-pc-market-share-off-its-peak-yet-company-seeing-more-searches-than-ever-233780

[33] Pew Research Internet Project, "Search and Email Still Top the List of Most Popular Online Activities," 9 August 2011, http://www.pewinternet.org/2011/08/09/search-and-email-still-top-the-list-of-most-popular-online-activities/.

[34] O. K. Pavlov, N. Melville, and R. V. Price, "Toward a Sustainable Email Marketing Infrastructure," *Journal of Business Research,* vol. 61, no. 11, pp. 1191–1199, 2008.

[35] Z. Stambor, "58% of Marketers Plan to Boost Their E-mail Marketing Budgets This Year," *Internet Retailer,* 30 January 2014.

[36] G. Soskey, "HubSpot," 31 October 2013, http://blog.hubspot.com/marketing/email-marketing-examples-list.

[37] Controlling the Assault of Non-Solicited Pornography and Marketing Act, 2003.

[38] J. Fogel and S. Shlivko, "Singles Seeking a Relationship and Spam E-mail for Romantic Relationships or Matchmaking," *Journal of Internet Business,* vol. 8, pp. 41–60, 2010.

[39] R. C. Hanna, P. D. Berger, and L. J. Abendroth, "Optimizing Time Limits in Retail Promotions: An Email Application," *Journal of the Operations Research Society,* vol. 56, no. 1, pp. 15–24, 2005.

[40] M. K. Anderson, "The Complete Guide to Optimizing Email Marketing for Conversions," Hubspot, 2012.

[41] A. Sutton, "Email Marketing: 133% ROI for B2B's First Ever Nurturing Program," *Marketing Sherpa,* 21 January 2014.

[42] K. Roman and J. Maas, *How to Advertise,* New York: St. Martin's, 1992.

[43] S. Vizard, "B&Q Shifts Marketing Focus as It Aims to Be Market Leading Not Just Market Leader," *Marketing Week,* 25 March 2014.

[44] The Economist, "Down Tools Home Improvement," 8 March 2014.

[45] Marketing Week, "Personal Shopper," 15 March 2012.

[46] R. Sayid, "Bargain Hunters Cash In after Screwfix Website Glitch Slashes Thousands off Price of Products," *The Mirror,* 21 January 2014.

[47] SEMRush, "ScrewFix Search," 2014.

[48] T. Everts, "Six Reasons to Ditch Your M.site in 2014," *radwear,* December 2013.

[49] Google, "Google UK Search," 2014.

[50] B2B Marketing, "Case Study: ScrewFix Search Campaign," 17 August 2009.

[51] S. Phil, "A Surefire PPC Brand Exposure Tactic for AdWords Advertisers," 13 April 2011, http://www.steviephil.wordpress.com/.../a-surefire-ppc-brand-exposure-tactic-for-ad.

[52] DIY Week, "News," 15 March 2013, http://www.diyweek.net.

[53] S. Young, "Relighting the Flame Tested Email Strategies to Win Back," DMA Email Marketing Council, 2011.

[54] D. DuPreez, "Kingfisher Announces Huge Digital Investments and Appoints ex-Amazon Director", Diginomica.com, January 25th, 2016. http://diginomica.com/2016/01/25/kingfisher-announces-huge-digital-investments-and-appoints-ex-amazon-director/.

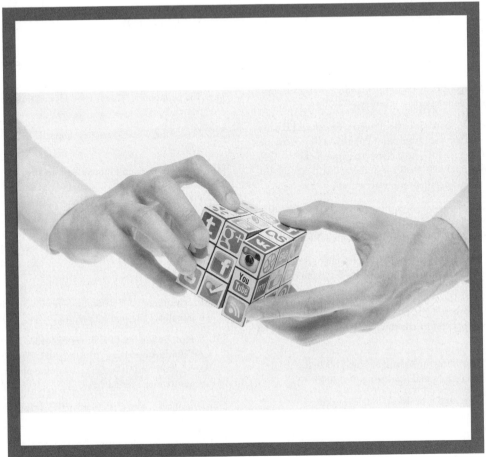

© Shutterstock/Bloomua

CHAPTER EIGHT

PLANNING COMMUNICATIONS

The process of formulating effective integrated marketing communications campaigns that incorporate social media and mobile marketing includes goal setting and budgeting. We'll see in this chapter how marketers use different types of content in digital strategies and the role of the advertising agency in assisting firms in promotional activities. The key element in the communications process is integration.

LEARNING OBJECTIVES

After reading this chapter, you will be able to:

- OUTLINE THE ADVERTISING PROCESS.

- EXPLAIN THE CONCEPT OF INTEGRATED MARKETING COMMUNICATIONS WITH DIGITAL MEDIA.

- DESCRIBE COMMUNICATIONS WITH VARIOUS TARGET AUDIENCES.

- SET CLEAR, QUANTITATIVE, AND MEANINGFUL PROMOTIONAL OBJECTIVES FOR SUCCESS.

- DETERMINE THE SOCIAL MEDIA AND MOBILE MARKETING VEHICLES AND THEIR ADVANTAGES AND DISADVANTAGES.

- CONSIDER THE ROLE OF THE ADVERTISING AGENCY IN PROMOTION.

McDonald's is one of the world's largest advertisers, spending $200 billion in advertising annually. With a budget that size, it is not surprising that McDonald's uses a variety of integrated marketing strategies to reach targets around the world. You have probably seen ads for McDonald's since you were a small child, but you probably did not see the kinds of executions that McDonald's emphasizes now. Today, McDonald's reaches out through many social media platforms to engage and deliver its message to customers around the world.

However, McDonald's Corporation has seen some tough times. Sales slumped 21% at the end of 2014 with net income dropping 15%, largely due to millennials who were choosing healthier alternatives in the fast-food category. To prevent continued decline, McDonald's decided to build on its "I'm Lovin' It" slogan with a new game, Pay with Lovin' Instant Win Game. Participating McDonald's restaurants were given 100 "prizes" (which consisted of a free meal) to distribute to customers over a two-week period. Unofficial winners (chosen based on being the first to walk through the door at random times predetermined by the store's "Lovin' Lead" manager) were asked to perform a random act of Lovin' also designated by the store's manager. The "Lovin' Acts" included things that could be done right away, like calling a loved one on the phone, blowing a kiss, or asking someone to dance. Customers who completed that act to the Lovin' Lead's satisfaction were named official winners—and received their orders for free. The brand ran big-budget ads that showed people sharing the love, but additionally promoted the ads on YouTube. The company announced that it would listen and monitor social media more to interact with customers [1]. The question was whether a little love could bring millennials back to McDonalds. The share of monthly McDonald's visitors aged 19–21 has dropped 12.9 percentage points since 2011, and visits by 22- to 37-year-olds have remained flat [2]. Unfortunately for McDonald's, the campaign generated some buzz, but did not result in significantly improving people's ratings of the brand's image [3]. What turned out to be more successful was offering all day breakfast and by 2016 same store sales jumped 5.7%. Social media can help boost a strategy, but the underlying marketing mix must be strong [4].

Social media and mobile marketing open up new avenues for communication between companies and customers, and among the customers themselves, and many companies are being creative about the ways they use these new channels. Social media and mobile marketing are different from other media formats and require specific strategies, new methods of monitoring and measuring success, and, in some cases, new mindsets on the part of marketing managers.

THE IMPORTANCE OF INTEGRATED MARKETING COMMUNICATIONS

McDonald's spends a lot on advertising and you have likely seen multiple messages from the company. Can you think of all the ways McDonald's tries to communicate with you? Maybe you have seen television ads or a disappearing ad on Snapchat, passed by a store and saw the golden arches, or downloaded one of McDonald's gaming apps. These are just some of the ways McDonald's executes its integrated marketing communications strategy.

As we've seen in previous chapters, **integrated marketing communications (IMC)** is the process that marketers use to communicate with consumers through various touchpoints with the intent to persuade, remind, or otherwise influence attitudes and behavior. Communications are integrated when the different forms of media all focus on the same message for a given target market or reflect a particular concept, idea, or theme on which a marketer can build a brand's personality. For instance, consider the brand Nike and write down the thoughts that come to mind when you think of it. Is there a particular idea or theme that jumps off the page? Nike's message is integrated around the notion of performance.

Typically, when consumers think of Nike, some of the following come to mind: the swoosh, Tiger Woods, sports, running, comfort, motivation, "Just Do It," victory, sneakers, Nike Air, sweatshops, Michael Jordan, athlete, Venus Williams, expensive, and cool.

Nike's promotional strategy supports the performance positioning and tries to limit people's thoughts of the negative aspects of the brand, such as "sweatshops." Though Nike maintains a Facebook presence, the company developed its own social media site called Nike+ to directly interact with customers. Athletes join the site to connect with others who share their sport and can train, challenge, compare, and advise others in the network. Nike is a social brand and builds relationships with a strong integrated global marketing communications effort. Each message supports the general theme of high performance.

consider this . . .

ENCOURAGING RUNNING IN SHANGHAI

Running is not a very popular sport in China and few runners can be seen on the streets. Clearly, Nike has an uphill battle to encourage the sport that will help it sell shoes and apparel in a giant potential market. With the agency AKQA, Nike created the "Run For" campaign employing Chinese social media sites to get Chinese runners to talk about why they run by creating their own personalized videos on running. Nike's microblog account on Sina Weibo housed a number of professional videos for inspiration. The campaign also featured an experiential component, a series of "Lunar Runs" (named for the Lunar Glide running shoe) in Beijing, Shanghai, Guangzhou, and Wuhan with coaches, music, and celebrities to highlight the fun aspect of running, day or night [5]. Nike hosts nine different accounts on Sina Weibo to localize its strategy and has seen much more engagement on social media than its nearest competitor, Adidas [6].

PROMOTIONAL OPPORTUNITIES ABOUND

Before the term "integrated marketing communications" was used, marketers referred to the promotional process as the **promotional mix.** The components of the promotional mix are advertising, public relations, sales promotion, and personal selling. The concept has evolved because brand messages are everywhere, and consumers come into contact with the messages through many varied forms of media. Try conducting an experiment. During the next hour, count how many marketing communications you see and note where you saw or heard them. What kinds of media reached you the most?

You might see an advertisement in a bathroom stall or on a billboard on the street, a television commercial on a show you are watching on your desktop the day after it ran on TV, a video on YouTube that played before the video you really wanted to see, an ad delivered to your phone that disappeared in twenty seconds, a spot on an Internet radio station you listened to on your mobile phone, a text ad that appeared as you were surfing the net, or even signs in stores directing you to products. Because of the vast opportunities to connect with customers, integration is more complex than ever before and reaches people in so many places. These places and spaces where marketers interact with customers are called **touchpoints.** Exhibit 8.1 illustrates the opportunities for a brand to deliver messages to customers through a variety of touchpoints, such as when

EXHIBIT 8.1

Consumer Touchpoints

PRODUCT TOUCHPOINTS	RETAIL ENVIRONMENT TOUCHPOINTS	TRADITIONAL MEDIA TOUCHPOINTS	NEW MEDIA TOUCHPOINTS	EXPERIENTIAL TOUCHPOINTS
Features	Store atmosphere	Television	Websites and online advertising	Events
Packaging	Salespeople	Print	Online search and display advertising	Sponsorships
Quality	Merchandise assortment	Radio	Social media platforms, videos and pictures, advertising and blogs	Demonstrations and trials
Co-branding	Checkout	Direct mail	Mobile text messages, Web, apps	Trade shows
Product mix and extensions	Loyalty programs	Telemarketing	Email	Experiential marketing

people engage with the product, a retail environment, traditional media, new media, and experiential media.

CHOOSING THE RIGHT STRATEGY FOR THE RIGHT TOUCHPOINT

IMC does not mean that the advertising message is exactly the same in all forms of media; instead, it suggests that there is a synergy in matching the communications strategy across the consumer touchpoints for a given target market. For example, Geico's strategy in the United States involves a number of different advertising executions that deliver the same message of low prices. The brand is represented by a talking gecko, has featured cavemen who save money on car insurance, and even a couple who lives in a mini-house to save money. All executions reinforce the same low price message. This is quite different from State Farm, which "like a good neighbor . . . is there." State Farm pledges to take care of you in an emergency. The commercials show people making wishes for a variety of things and State Farm

consider this . . .

GEICO'S U.S. SOCIAL MEDIA STRATEGY

Promotional spending in the automobile insurance industry has been rising, with Geico leading the pack, spending almost $1 billion annually [7]. The Gecko's "Journey Across America" was the brand's social media campaign with the goal of getting the Gecko out from behind his desk, where he saves customers money, to see America. Fans could follow the Gecko on both Facebook and YouTube to see which places he visited after leaving Geico's Maryland headquarters [7]. The Gecko visited major tourist sites and got himself into some trouble, just to make it all interesting and funny. However, the big question that marketers must ask is whether the campaign reached the target and achieved the brand's promotional goals. With all of Geico's advertising spending, one might think the company controls the market.

However, the brand is a solid no. three in the U.S. auto insurance market, with both State Farm and Allstate the share leaders [8].

The Gecko is the Geico company mascot.

© iStockPhoto/Lanier

EXHIBIT 8.2

Media Spending by Format

FORM OF MEDIA	PERCENTAGE OF GLOBAL MEDIA SPENDING 2016
Television	36.9%
Internet	30.7%
Newspapers	9.4%
Radio	9.2%
Magazines	8.5%
Outdoor and cinema	5.3%

EXHIBIT 8.3

Global Ad Spending by Brand

COMPANY	GLOBAL ADVERTISING SPENDING (IN MILLIONS OF U.S.$)
Procter & Gamble	$10,615
Unilever	7,413
L'Oréal	5,643
Toyota	3,310
General Motors	3,206
Coca-Cola	3,029
Nestlé	2,987
Volkswagen	2,971
McDonald's	2,693
Pepsi	2,470

Advertising Age, "Advertising Age Fact Pack," 2014.

delivers. Both the Geico and State Farm campaigns are humorous, but the messages are very different, each focused on the central theme of the brand. Geico is about low prices, while State Farm focuses on reliability. The unique brand messages are integrated to resonate with the appropriate target market.

ADVERTISER SPENDING IN THE GLOBAL MARKET

The opportunities for marketers to interact with consumers have grown considerably with social media and mobile properties. Though marketers still engage in traditional promotional strategies such as sales promotion and public relations, digital marketing commands a greater percentage of the overall advertising dollars spent globally. According to eMarketer, digital will represent over 30% of total global advertising spending by 2020 [9]. Though advertisers will spend more in digital media than in newspapers, radio, or magazines, television remains the dominant medium around the world as shown in Exhibit 8.2 [9].

As a student of social media and mobile marketing, you should know a few facts about the advertising business. Here is a little quiz to get you started:

1. *Which industries spend the most money on advertising?*
   Think of the products that you see advertised the most—especially on television. These also tend to be the kinds of companies that spend the most on advertising in all forms of media. The product categories with the highest spending levels are personal care, automotive, food, drugs, and entertainment.

2. *In which country is the most money spent on advertising?*
   Where do advertisers want to spend their advertising dollars? In places where people have

the money to buy products and services. The United States is the world's largest advertising market, representing over 30% of global advertising spending [10].

3. *Which companies spend the most money on advertising globally?*
The two biggest global spenders are Procter & Gamble and Unilever, both selling personal care, hygiene, and food items. The rest of the top global spenders are listed in Exhibit 8.3, and you can also see how much money they spend in millions of dollars. These numbers are somewhat deceiving because they represent media spending for all the brands that the company advertises globally and include data for brands as diverse as Ariel, Gillette, Olay, and Pampers [10].

STEPS IN THE MARKETING COMMUNICATIONS PROCESS

Because of the growth in promotional opportunities, a brand manager's job is more complicated than in the past. There are more decisions to make on how, when, where, how often, and with whom to connect. Advertising has been the traditional communications method for brands, but the word "advertising" now encompasses a variety of traditional and digital strategies.

Traditional advertising media such as television, radio, or print represent mass media that connect brands to people on a one-to-many basis. For most mass media, the marketer creates a message and blasts it out to consumers who do not have the opportunity to respond. In traditional media, the brand buys media time or space and has control over the message within certain parameters set by the media companies. In the past, feedback from consumers came in the form of sales, complaints, or market research data. Currently, the communications come from many different places both online and off-line, and consumers expect marketers to respond to their communications.

Marketers still face the challenge of determining whether traditional media are successful in driving response. One of the great advantages of digital is that marketers can monitor response and determine which strategies led to particular online behaviors. That is one of the reasons why brands have shifted marketing budgets toward digital media—the results really show. The world's biggest advertiser, Procter & Gamble, cut its spending and workforce to focus more heavily on digital marketing after the success of the Old Spice campaign featuring Isaiah Mustafa. The company continued to reduce spending while maintaining customer engagement by boosting mobile marketing and social media strategies [11].

IMC planning means that marketers see value in using various forms of media to reach out and engage customers. And, some research even suggests that people

Steps in the Integrated Marketing Communications Process

1. Conduct a comprehensive situation analysis.
2. Set objectives.
3. Segment and target the market.
4. Evaluate current integrated strategy.
5. Determine budget.
6. Outline potential marketing strategies.
7. Integrate with current strategy.
8. Select media.
9. Test online advertising executions.
10. Execute.
11. Evaluate the campaign.

are more attentive to messages when they come in different formats. So, marketers want to use a mix of media to reach targets. For example, Unilever sponsors YouTube's "Young Hollywood Network" channel hosted by R. J. Williams, and Toyota is sponsoring channels aimed at moms. Both brands are still heavily invested in traditional media and use a mix to reach a variety of targets for different products. Since moms tend to be highly digital and mobile, it makes sense for Unilever to communicate with websites, apps, and search engine marketing. Moms also watch television, so advertising during hit TV shows can also be effective in generating brand awareness.

Consumers have shifted their media consumption habits and marketers have responded by reaching them with highly targeted online properties that also deliver in terms of metrics, so marketers can directly measure success based on organizational objectives. A clear integrated campaign development process can help marketers create effective messaging strategies aimed at targets that achieve measurable organizational objectives. Exhibit 8.4 outlines these steps, and each of the steps is discussed in more detail below.

SITUATION ANALYSIS

A **situation analysis**, a comprehensive review of the current issues facing a brand, is the document that critically examines each brand element and is an important prerequisite for developing a campaign, as discussed in Chapter Three. The situation analysis is the starting point for setting goals because the research contained in the report provides a baseline of performance.

An important aspect of the situation analysis is evaluating the current brand communications strategy. Established brands are likely to already have a message and should examine the methods they use to reach consumers. The customers of most established brands already have a set of associations, attitudes, and beliefs. Marketers should research customer perceptions and then build a strategy to position the brand with the ultimate objective of achieving its goals.

In order to evaluate the brand's current communications strategy, the marketer should answer each of the questions below:

1. What is our current communications strategy?
2. How do consumers think about and talk about the brand?

3. Do consumer attitudes differ by target market?
4. Are the target markets distinct enough for different messaging?
5. What are the current media vehicles?
6. How is each vehicle contributing to established goals?

These questions provide a base of knowledge for the marketing team. If the prior messages are strong and favorable, the brand can consider building upon the associations. If the team determines that the messages are weak, off-base, or not achieving goals, it can revise the strategy with full knowledge of the current customer's mindset.

For example, in a deep brand analysis, H&R Block found the company was losing share to other tax preparers with lower fees. But, when H&R Block lowered its fees, market share continued to drop. That is when the brand decided to go for the high road and highlight H&R Block's expertise in tax preparation. Because consumers had prior feelings about the brand, H&R Block had to determine precampaign attitudes. Without that knowledge, H&R Block may have continued with the losing price-reduction strategy. The "Never Settle for Less" campaign highlighted the tax expertise of the firm in generating a higher refund than other brands for the taxpayer [12]. Exhibit 8.5 shows how H&R Block used strategic thinking to achieve its goals.

EXHIBIT 8.5

H&R Block's Communications Strategy

COMMUNICATIONS STRATEGY	MEDIA VEHICLES	GOAL ACHIEVED
"Second Look" promotion for consumers asked them to bring their tax returns filed by another preparer to H&R Block to determine how much money could be saved with H&R Block's tax professionals.	Information and results on the website Neversettleforless.com.	Improved taxpayer agreement with the statement "H&R Block reduces taxes and saves you money" from 63% to 65%.
Prepared tax returns for residents of Greenback, Tennessee, and calculated the size of the refund on revised returns.	Seven television spots ran during tax season, website content.	Increased agreement with the statement "H&R Block tax pros have expertise in taxes" from 70% to 74% of taxpayers.
Showed additional footage of people receiving larger tax refunds with H&R Block.	Longer-form videos for YouTube.	Defended H&R Block's share of the tax preparation market at 15.6%.
Preparing one free tax return per person.	Public relations through earned media.	"H&R Block offers value for the money" increased to 65% of the target agreeing, from 64% before the campaign.

SETTING ORGANIZATIONAL OBJECTIVES AND GOALS

Marketers communicate with customers to achieve organizational objectives. **Organizational objectives** are broad and tend to focus on maximizing profits, dominating markets, or reducing costs. A few firms hold more lofty ambitions, such as social or environmental responsibility. These firms are more likely to operate for the greater good of society, rather than for shareholder profit, and aside from communicating about their products, these firms also want to be known as environmentally friendly organizations.

Goals are hurdles or guideposts a firm surpasses on the way to meeting the **corporate mission**. Since most firms are profit-driven entities, marketing managers are expected to generate sales increases when executing promotional campaigns. That is why sales results are a common goal of advertising and are almost always included as part of the goal-setting process. Goals that are clearly stated, measurable, and achievable are a prerequisite for any campaign. They are important for a number of reasons. (1) Setting goals ensures that the brand and its agency (or groups of agencies) are in agreement over the strategy, with each working toward a common end. (2) Goals provide an important method to measure success and evaluate the outcomes of a campaign. (3) Achieving a set of goals or failing to do so provides important information on how to proceed with the next promotional campaign. (4) The goals may help determine compensation for the agency if they are paid by performance and their ability to achieve the stated goals.

Social media and mobile marketing could help marketers achieve a variety of goals that ultimately lead to sales, but also can be measured at an earlier point in time to guide the strategy. These intermediate achievements are referred to as interim goals, which are described in the next section. Exhibit 8.6 shows how firms have used social media or mobile to achieve interim goals, such as awareness, trust, education [13], loyalty, persuasion [14], or to remind [15].

Brands should always set financial goals for a strategy to ensure a positive return on investment. However, it may take time before a strategy delivers a measurable financial return. Therefore, brands also set interim goals, sometimes measured by **key performance indicators (KPIs)** to guide the strategy and to check in to make sure the brand is headed in the right direction. For example, Bayer may have a goal of increasing sales for its signature product, but set an interim goal of building customer engagement. The KPI may be an increase in social media activity, as measured by a social media listening platform such as Radian 6's. Bayer hosts a social media room online with health and nutrition topics [16] and can track site usage using Google Analytics. A smaller brand could use Google Analytics or one of the free services that scans the Web to evaluate brands, such as Social Mention or HowSociable. These platforms are described in Chapter Three.

EXHIBIT 8.6

Brands Achieving Goals with Social and Mobile Strategies

GOALS	BRANDS ACHIEVING GOALS WITH SOCIAL AND MOBILE STRATEGIES
Awareness	Hyundai created an iPhone driving app that ran on the giant screen in Times Square in New York City. People could control the onscreen car with their phones.
Trust	Procter & Gamble joined the BlogHer conference aimed at female bloggers to "engage with a group of smart women, who are consumers themselves." The company promoted Tide, Cover Girl, Pantene, Charmin, Bounty, and Downy among other brands. The purpose was to generate conversations for P&G brands by trusted influencers.
Education	General Electric created the Six Second Science Fair. Participants use Vine to create a short science video to share on Twitter with the hashtag #6secondsciencefair. The goal is to show GE's leadership in technology with the slogan "Follow as we explore the changing worlds of science and technology."
Loyalty	The Apple Passbook loaded onto iPhones can hold loyalty card information from various vendors. Users simply download loyalty apps from the app store and organize them with Passbook.
Persuasion	John Deere hired Chip Foose to design a tractor for a giveaway contest and supported the effort with YouTube videos, each with a clear call to action. "Win a classic 4020 tractor customized by the legendary Chip Foose! Register to Win at your local dealer." The videos received over 13,000 views in the first hour and thousands of people entered to win the tractor.
Remind	Ariel brand detergent set up an interactive glass installation in Central Station, Stockholm, Sweden, where users who were invited through Facebook could control a robot to stain shirts. Later, the shirts were washed using Ariel Actilift and sent to the players' homes.

Interim goals and KPIs provide insight on how the campaign is proceeding before a brand can measure sales results, because sales may lag ad exposure. Campaigns involving social media should set intermediate goals to help guide the strategy. For instance, Athleta, the work-out clothing brand, advertises on Pandora and encourages its customers to develop "Power to the She" work-out music stations. Athleta should set goals for the number of people it intends to reach on Pandora and how many times a person will be exposed to the message (reach and frequency). When the campaign is over, the brand would also measure return on investment and compare the result to the expected level of return by examining sales data.

Goal Setting in Action

Unilever's Canadian division set the goals listed in Exhibit 8.7 for Dove Nourishing Oil Care. Take a look at the three goals set by the brand and evaluate

EXHIBIT 8.7

Dove Nourishing Oil Care Goals

DOVE NOURISHING OIL CARE GOALS CANADA

Launch the new Dove Nourishing Oil Care line and achieve 0.3% dollar share of the hair category within the first six months of launch.

Grow overall sales of the Dove hair care line +2% at the expense of Pantene in the first year.

Increase online conversations around Dove hair care from 1% to 20% of online conversations within six months of launch.

Dove's goals based on the criteria for setting successful goals. Is each goal measurable, time-specific, and reachable?

Prior to setting these goals, Dove did some research and determined that there were relatively few online conversations about hair care, and that with some effort, Dove could own the online conversation space and become the leading voice in the category. The strategy was to show that the product worked in real-life settings and to then spread the brand's story through social media. Dove invited fourteen women to perform the song "Singing in the Rain" in the outside rain to show how their hair held up under conditions that would normally cause frizz. Through online videos and bloggers, their performances were passed along in social media. In the end, Dove did increase its share of the hair care conversation (as measured by Radian 6) to 29% and earned 8 million Facebook impressions. Dove's share in hair care grew +4%, while the category grew only 1% and the major competitor, P&G's Pantene, lost almost 3 share points. Dove also increased its sales by $1.7 million. The above goals were stretches for Dove as it usually hit targets of 1% sales growth [17].

Dove's goals do not specify social media or mobile properties as part of the goal-setting process. Though the brand intended to increase conversations, many different possible strategies could have achieved the same goal. A strategy is an action that a firm might take in pursuit of a goal. Typically using Facebook, Twitter, Instagram, Mobile Games, Spotify, Stumble Upon, or bloggers is an element of a strategy. Therefore, a marketer would not set goals such as increase Facebook "likes" by 20% or grow Twitter followers to 5,000. Strong goals are broader and business-oriented, not social media- or mobile property-specific.

SEGMENTING AND TARGETING THE MARKET

One of the most important decisions to make prior to developing a communications strategy is determining the target market. The new media market is highly fragmented, with consumer eyeballs in many different places, often simultaneously. Each technology product or service offers consumers new ways to divide their time and attention. The challenge for marketers is to locate the consumers when they are ready to receive communications and ideally when customers are in the mindset to purchase something. Digital media can provide insight on the moment when people may be ready to buy by identifying keywords used in searching for products and services. Clearly, marketers would be highly interested in persuading such ready, willing, and able customers at the moment when they are making their purchase decisions.

Some of the keywords people search are purchase-related, while other keywords are information-oriented. Though Bing's Commercial Intent tool no longer exists, the concept is still important for marketers. That tool indicated the keywords that were likely to lead to a purchase versus those words that signified some other demand for information that was not purchase-related. Marketers want to identify the keywords that result in purchases as those prospects are more likely to buy. For example, if a consumer searches for "wide-screen televisions," she may be in the market to buy one, but if she types "viewing instructions for wide screen televisions," she wants information and not products. The distinction can help marketers optimize their search marketing strategies.

Marketers must also determine how targets use media differently. Younger consumers are heavy users of digital media, and reaching them via Twitter, Snapchat, or Kik might be possible. Older consumers may still be consuming content in traditional media, and marketers can reach them efficiently with television and newspapers. However, marketers would benefit from a more nuanced

Lady Gaga has one of the top Twitter followings in the world.

© Shutterstock/Jaguar PS

consider this . . .

REACHING TARGETS WITH CELEBRITIES

Some brands want to reach people who follow celebrities, and some stars have large followings that pay attention to their tweets. Lady Gaga has over 27 million followers, Justin Bieber has over 25 million, and Katy Perry has over 23 million followers according to Twittercounter. To reach celebrities, brands often send them free products, reach out to their publicists, and even pay for sponsorship. Marketers should determine which celebrities will best reach the target, meet the creative needs of the message, achieve the goals of the campaign, and integrate with prior messaging in order to provide a return on the investment for the strategy.

view of media consumption, recognizing that people view media in a variety of locations or contexts and on various devices. A **cross platform strategy** in which multiple forms of media distribute the message may lead to important synergies. For example, targeting television viewers who also tweet during *Real Housewives* could lead to direct hits to a website for a handbag worn by one of the show's stars.

Social media generally skew young and female. One exception is LinkedIn, which has a larger proportion of men. People who use social media tend to be educated, with above-average incomes, but marketers should be aware of the demographics of the platforms they choose for reaching their targets. Exhibit 8.8 details the demographic composition of the major social networks among U.S. adult Internet users [18]. Exhibit 8.9 describes the general mindset of the users of various networks and the advertisers who try to reach them there. Specifically, Samsung reaches consumers using Facebook [19], agencies are increasing their use of Twitter for their clients [20], LinkedIn is heavily into B2B [21], B2C brands love Pinterest [22] and Instagram [23], and BMW is using Google+ among others to build reach.

When developing a social media strategy, marketers must understand the demographics and psychographics of the media vehicles they consider to effectively reach the target. Demographic criteria are those that define population characteristics, such as age and gender, and psychographic groups are those defined by people's activities, interests, and opinions.

Each social media site provides opportunities to hone in on psychographic groups of people with paid advertising. Though it might be tempting to reach out to everyone, good marketers know that it is more important to reach the right people. Consider LinkedIn paid advertising. Marketers can select targets based on people's company, position, work tenure, schools attended, and locations. Facebook's targeting can reach people who are fans of a town's local soccer team.

The Importance of Consumer Attitudes in Strategy Planning

Marketing managers should establish a baseline of consumer attitudes from which to build a communications strategy. Consumers are not blank slates without prior thoughts and feelings about product categories, brands, competitors, and the environment. Each individual has likely developed a complex pattern of behavior for a product or service that already meets his or her needs. Rarely do marketers have an opportunity to invent a product that is completely new to the world, and even when a revolution occurs, people have prior attitudes that will influence their view of that product. Therefore, marketers can increase success by researching the attitudes of current and prospective customers (see Exhibit 8.10).

EXHIBIT 8.8

Social Networking Demographics*

ONLINE U.S. ADULT USERS	GENDER	AGE	RACE	EDUCATION	INCOME	HOUSING
Facebook	Women, 77% Men, 66%	18–29, 82% 30–49, 79% 50–64, 64% 65+, 48%	White, 70% Black, 67% Hispanic, 75%	Graduate HS, 71% Some College, 72% College+, 72%	Less than $30k, 73% $30–49,999k, 72% $50–74,999k, 66% $75,000+ k, 78%	Urban, 74% Suburban, 72% Rural, 67%
Twitter	Women, 21% Men, 25%	18–29, 32% 30–49, 29% 50–64, 13% 65+, 6%	White, 20% Black, 28% Hispanic, 28%	Graduate HS, 19% Some College, 23% College+, 27%	Less than $30k, 21% $30–49,999k, 19% $50–74,999k, 25% $75,000+k, 26%	Urban, 30% Suburban, 21% Rural, 15%
Pinterest	Women, 44% Men, 16%	18–29, 37% 30–49, 36% 50–64, 24% 65+, 16%	White, 32% Black, 23% Hispanic, 32%	Graduate HS, 25% Some College, 37% College+, 31%	Less than $30k, 24% $30–49,999k, 37% $50–74,999k, 41% $75,000+k, 30%	Urban, 26% Suburban, 34% Rural, 31%
LinkedIn	Women, 25% Men, 26%	18–29, 22% 30–49, 32% 50–64, 26% 65+, 12%	White, 26% Black, 22% Hispanic, 22%	Graduate HS, 9% Some College, 25% College+, 46%	Less than $30k, 17% $30–49,999k, 21% $50–74,999k, 32% $75,000+k, 41%	Urban, 30% Suburban, 26% Rural, 12%
Instagram	Women, 31% Men, 24%	18–29, 55% 30–49, 28% 50–64, 11% 65+, 4%	White, 21% Black, 47% Hispanic, 38%	Graduate HS, 25% Some College, 32% College+, 26%	Less than $30k, 26% $30–49,999k, 27% $50–74,999k, 30% $75,000+k, 26%	Urban, 32% Suburban, 28% Rural, 18%

*Percentages of people in each group who use the network.

EXHIBIT 8.9

Social Networking Psychographics and Advertisers

MEDIA VEHICLE STATISTICS IN THE U.S. MARKET	PSYCHOGRAPHIC TARGET	EXAMPLES
Facebook	A broad base of users around the world with varied interests.	Samsung is one of the largest advertisers on Facebook, estimated to spend about $100 million on the platform. The goal is to leverage loyal Samsung customers to compete effectively against Apple.
Twitter	Top trending Twitter topics are sports and music, with an occasional world news disaster.	WPP Group, one of the "Big Four" advertising conglomerates, announced it would spend more money on Twitter ads. The company's clients include Gillette and Ford, two very large global advertisers.
Pinterest	For those interested in crafts, hobbies, interior design, fashion, and fashion design.	Lowe's, the home improvement store, has close to 4 million followers with boards such as Grillin' and Chillin' and fifty projects under $50. Martha Stewart Living has over 600,000 followers and 20,000 pins with home fashions and design.
LinkedIn	Career and job networking for firms and seekers.	Some of the top advertisers on LinkedIn are Citigroup, Prudential, Microsoft, Philips, and Chevron. Cathay Pacific used LinkedIn to find executives likely to book a business flight. 70% of the members reached through the campaign were planning a flight within twelve months.
Instagram	Young people with a passion for documenting their interests in a visual medium.	Levi's, Ben & Jerry's, and Taco Bell were some of the earliest Instagram advertisers seeking to connect with young people. Luxury brands such as Starwood and Burberry use the platform to show their style in pictures.
Google+	Populated by young working professionals.	BMW has over 4 million Google Plus followers—though not all of them are in the target market for the product.

Prospective customers differ from current customers in their attitudes and brand knowledge, relationships to competitors, loyalty levels, and even the ability of the marketer to reach them with marketing messages. More importantly, current customers already purchase the product, suggesting more positive attitudes toward the brand. Since they support the product with their spending, any strategy must consider their attitudes and behaviors. A strategy that is distasteful to a brand's customer base can result in disaster, with customers defecting for competitors if they are offended or angry.

EXHIBIT 8.10

Differences between Current and Prospective Customers

	CURRENT CUSTOMERS	PROSPECTIVE CUSTOMERS
Purchase attitudes and behaviors	Brand-specific attitudes and behaviors. More likely to be positive or neutral.	Neutral or product category attitudes and behaviors. May be positive, negative, or neutral toward the brand.
Competitive positioning	The brand currently represents the best of competitive offerings.	The customer may or may not purchase the product category or may purchase a competitor's product. People consider competitive offers.
Brand loyalty	Possible brand loyalty or high switching costs.	May be loyal to a competitor or perceive high switching costs.
Communications	Relatively easy to reach with communications and more open to information.	More difficult to locate for communications purposes and may be more resistant to arguments.

consider this . . .

INTEGRATING MEDIA AT STATE FARM AND GEICO

Social and mobile media can be used on their own to achieve brand communications goals, but they are often seen as supporting strategies or as integrated components of a broad-based brand strategy. State Farm's Pocket Agent mobile app is a good example of an integrated support strategy that builds on the notion that "like a good neighbor State Farm is there." The app that is available on State Farm's website helps customers pay bills, manage the process of making a claim, document witnesses, and fill out paperwork; Geico's app has similar functionality, but the concept is not as well integrated with the low-price strategy. Geico's limited attempt to integrate featured the caveman (one of Geico's mascots) using the mobile app in an instructional video. The hairy hand is humorous (like many of Geico's commercials), but the message of low prices gets lost in this execution. Another example of this lack of focus was Geico's other mobile app, "Help the Guinea Pigs Get Away!" The game had nothing to do with the strategy of offering low prices for car insurance and the app is no longer available from Geico. Marketers who do not integrate well end up spending more money to drive home their message. Geico's strategy of using many humorous themes and characters to break through the clutter and deliver the low-price message requires repetition and high levels of media spending. Rather than waste money on apps that don't match the message brands should build on prior campaigns and the base of customer knowledge for more efficient marketing communications development and spending.

State Farms has business-related applications for customers.

© Shutterstock/James R. Martin

consider this . . .

ACHIEVING BRAND SYNERGY

"What Happens in Vegas, Stays in Vegas"

An IMC strategy can achieve synergy when the whole is greater than the sum of the parts. Each component of the communication can help achieve part of the overall goal, but together, the message is stronger because there is a central theme that is reinforced through multiple touchpoints. A truly well-integrated strategy results in clear brand associations in the minds of the target market. For example, the Cosmopolitan hotel in Las Vegas used multiple media to introduce travelers to the hotel. The quirky brand message "Just the right amount of wrong" built on the larger Las Vegas theme, "What happens in Vegas stays in Vegas," to integrate the hotel's message with the broader destination message. Research had shown that Las Vegas was perceived by visitors as predictable and the Cosmopolitan wanted to update this image. The campaign ran on television and billboards; in newspapers, magazines, and interactive display ads; and via emails with a consistent message for the upscale target market. The campaign was successful in achieving higher occupancy rates for the Cosmopolitan than competing brands [25].

Marketers should always remember that current customers are more valuable than prospective customers. A brand's base provides revenue and positive word of mouth, and those customers should never be sacrificed to attract newbies. What do you do when your target is aging and disappearing? Cadillac has this problem with sales declines on its traditional sedans. But, rather than give up on its customers, the car maker will target the luxury market and develop super-high-end cars that will enhance its image [24].

DETERMINING THE BUDGET

When considering how much to budget for various forms of media, marketers consider a number of factors, including the reach of a particular medium, its cost, and creative requirements. They must also consider any executional prerequisites for the brand, such as use of logos and legal statements. For example, prescription drug advertisers must disclose a significant amount of information on side effects, product usage, warnings, and other factors. Therefore, it is difficult to advertise prescription drugs in a banner ad on a mobile device.

In recent years, a number of brands have decided to budget more for digital media than for traditional media. Social media are popular among brands because

Media Spending by Three Major U.S. Brands

PROCTER & GAMBLE		DOLLARS SPENT IN THE U.S. (MILLIONS)	PERCENTAGE OF TOTAL SPENDING
Magazines		1,082.9	31%
Newspapers		280	8%
TV		1,852.6	53%
Radio		11.5	0%
Outdoor		4.7	0%
Internet		234.4	7%
Total measured spending	3,466.1	3,466.1	69%
Total unmeasured spending	1,524.9	1,524.9	31%
Total P&G's media spending		4,991	

(Continued)

EXHIBIT 8.11 (Continued)

Media Spending by Three Major U.S. Brands

JP MORGAN CHASE		DOLLARS SPENT IN THE U.S. (MILLIONS)	PERCENTAGE OF TOTAL SPENDING
Magazines		46.7	12%
Newspapers		17.6	4%
TV		225.3	56%
Radio		20.4	5%
Outdoor		33	8%
Internet		59.2	15%
Total measured spending	402.2	402.2	21%
Total unmeasured spending	1,476.60	1,476.60	79%
Total JP Morgan's media spending		1,878.8	

AMAZON		DOLLARS SPENT IN THE U.S. (MILLIONS)	PERCENTAGE OF TOTAL SPENDING
Magazines		43.4	13%
Newspapers		9.2	3%
TV		217.5	66%
Radio		1.5	0%
Outdoor		2.6	1%
Internet		54.9	17%
Total measured spending	329.1	329.1	23%
Total unmeasured spending	1,106.10	1,106.10	77%
Total Amazon's media spending		1,435.20	

Advertising Age Data Center, 2015.

of their seemingly low cost, but they do require significant investments in staff to manage and execute the strategy. Exhibit 8.11 shows traditional and digital spending for a number of brands [26]. The "measured media" are the forms of media listed from magazines to the Internet, while the "unmeasured media" reflect other spending the brand incurs, including costs for social media, Web development, apps, and public relations. From consumer products, to computing to banking, brands are favoring digital. Can you believe how much spending is in unmeasured media?

Many brands have jumped into social media executions expecting to reap large returns because of the low barrier to entry in developing a social media strategy. While developing an initial presence in social media is inexpensive, managing the task is very important and requires a very expensive resource—people.

Some brands have decided to make small initial investments in social media to test the waters. For example, Procter & Gamble's investment in the Old Spice "Red Zone" campaign showed the company the benefits of a digital strategy. P&G has now committed to more social media and mobile strategies for many brands, taking away some of the budget from traditional television, particularly daytime programming, to spend on digital [11].

The biggest advertisers can afford to take a small percentage of the advertising budget to spend on social media or mobile and still maintain traditional executions. However, smaller brands have to evaluate the cost versus the benefits of social media or mobile prior to execution to ensure that current customer needs are met. Smaller firms must make choices as to which forms of media drive the best responses by looking at Google Analytics or other programs that track response and examine the traffic flows to their website and other entities.

OUTLINING POTENTIAL MARKETING STRATEGIES

Situation analysis provides significant information as a baseline for strategy development and for writing a creative brief. A **creative brief** is a short document written in outline form that highlights the key requirements for the brand's communications strategy. The creative brief covers the background research, goals, problem statement, target market, brand positioning, advertising executional elements, and key brand requirements to guide the creative team in campaign development. The traditional advertising agency model paired a copywriter, the person who wrote the words of the ad, with an art director, the one who managed the ad visuals. This two-person team used the creative brief to brainstorm and create ads for a brand to reach its established goals. Though many agencies

FROM CREATIVE BRIEF TO PRINT AD FOR KIWI

A creative brief gives art directors and copywriters a guide as they create the advertising. The Richards Group creatives used their creative brief to develop print ads with the headline "Unpolished shoes are the open fly of footwear." The ad featured a product shot on a red background.

Unpolished shoes are the open fly of footwear.

still use the traditional team model for creative strategy development, other firms use larger teams to build a strategy. In either case, the creative brief remains important; it ensures everyone is in agreement over the strategy and sets the tone for how the creative team, such as copywriters, art directors, digital planners, and producers, approach the challenge.

The agency for Kiwi Shoe Polish, The Richards Group, used a creative brief to communicate the most persuasive idea that would sway consumers to purchase the product. The central theme was that although people don't look down at their shoes, other people see their shoes. Since shoes can make an impression, they should be shined. The goal was to encourage consumers to polish their shoes more often than just for special occasions [27]. In this case, the goal would deliver people to the Kiwi brand because the category of shoe shining products is small—encouraging polishing would lead to increased sales for Kiwi. Creative briefs can focus on the message solely or consider data on the target, quantitative goals, and other details that relate to the brand.

Another important consideration on social media and mobile marketing is whether the brand requires a content management strategy. These days, many brands produce content, such as white papers, podcasts, blogs, tweets, videos, or photos. These materials serve to engage customers and encourage online sharing often through social networks. A content management strategy has become important to firms who wish to communicate with current and potential customers and to raise search engine rankings.

IDENTIFYING AND DEVELOPING CONTENT

You may have heard the saying "Content is king." This statement refers to all the materials that people and firms create to share on the Internet. Without content, there would be nothing to share to engage audiences. An important part of a digital strategy is developing or curating content that people can post online through social media and send to family, friends, and acquaintances. For many brands, content:

1. May represent valuable information that people want.
2. Establishes a brand's or company's expertise.
3. Engages and attracts customers.
4. Boosts search engine rankings when it is shared.
5. Provides an avenue for collecting customer information—such as email addresses.
6. Shows a company's willingness to participate in the broader community.

In some cases, marketers have been forced to become publishers in order to be successful in the digital marketplace. Even marketers who sell products or services can benefit from a content strategy that is executed in various forms of online media, including social and some mobile properties. For example, Johnson & Johnson has a very successful website full of content aimed at moms and moms-to-be. Though J&J sells consumer products, the company is also an online publisher. J&J's Baby Center reaches almost 33 million people monthly, 62% of visitors are in the US and 83% view on a mobile device [28]. The site provides general parenting information, but also weaves in its products and advertising to influence people to develop favorable attitudes toward J&J brands.

Content development is a key aspect of social media strategy. Marketers who wish to be effective with a content strategy should begin by determining the content that already exists or can be easily created by the brand team. The next step is to set goals for each piece of content that the brand managers intend to share. In addition, marketers should create a schedule for releasing content to various forms of media and a strategy for evaluating the content once it has been released. Smart companies also consider the keywords that attract people to the brand on search engines and include this language in the content to increase search engine rankings.

EXHIBIT 8.12

Steps for Planning a Content Strategy

Identify goals for the content.

Research the tastes of the target and competitive content.

Determine the currently available resources within the firm.

Develop ideas for new material, keeping the target in mind.

Create and review the content.

Publish the materials in appropriate vehicles.

Link and connect the materials to related sites.

Evaluate the strategy and improve the content.

consider this . . .

POSSIBLE GOALS FOR CONTENT

1. Build online conversation around a product, service, or brand.
2. Deliver pertinent information to customers and prospects.
3. Add value to a sale by providing additional desirable materials.
4. Grow the reputation of a firm as the expert in a particular arena.
5. Cultivate a strong email list of current and potential customers.
6. Increase the likelihood of ranking high in search engine rankings.

Though it seems like it would be easy to simply shoot some photos or a video, or write a blog, a content strategy requires a solid plan. Companies that want to establish a content strategy should consider the steps enumerated in Exhibit 8.12, which help reduce the risk in executing a content strategy, while ensuring that the results will be useful for the firm.

Business-to-Business Content Strategies

Business-to-business marketers were the pioneers in developing content strategies to attract and engage clients. These firms created blogs, white papers, e-books, podcasts, and reports that they offered for free online to anyone who provided an email address. One example of a company that has been successful using content to attract an audience is Social Media Examiner, the online social media news site. The site offers articles, information, white papers, and a weekly podcast to business owners who want to improve their social media presence. There is no advertising on Social Media Examiner. Instead, the site makes money by running social media seminars and advertises through a strong email list that it collected by giving away free content. Social Media Examiner has established itself as an expert in the social media sphere by delivering well-written, pertinent content to users for free online. As a result, the seminars are well attended, at a price of $597 per person. In addition, the seminars are virtual, reducing costs and leading to strong margins [29].

Content Management Systems

Marketers who develop content strategies can ease the task by using a content management system. A number of companies offer software to help manage scheduling, posting to a variety of sites and evaluating the outcomes. The content created in one forum can be retooled to automatically feed to other platforms. For instance, a Facebook status update can appear on Twitter. Most of the content management sites integrate with many social media platforms and multiple accounts, track mentions of the brand in the social space, schedule postings, provide reports and analytics, and mobile access. Some of the more popular content management systems are listed in Exhibit 8.13.

A content management system is useful to small businesses and other organizations with limited budgets. Bigger brands usually work with an advertising agency to manage their brand personality and most agencies can manage social or mobile content campaigns. One of the most popular content management systems is Hootsuite. You can use Hootsuite to simultaneously post on a variety of social networks and schedule the postings. You can also monitor your blog, those who mention your blog, people who message you, your followers, or your messages.

EXHIBIT 8.13

Content Management Providers

SITE	DESCRIPTION
WordPress	A blogging platform that can act as a hub for social media executions. Bloggers can publicize their content through Facebook, Twitter, and Google Plus among others.
HootSuite	A complete system for inbound marketing that integrates with numerous social platforms.
TweetDeck	A free service that arranges information for each examination and includes information from various sites organized by the user.
Sprout Social	A site for monitoring and managing conversations, keywords, and social channels.
Crowdbooster	A method of locating influencers, analyzing messages, tracking engagement, and interacting with followers.

The author can use Hootsuite to monitor her blog, mentions in other blogs, those she follows on Twitter, and her scheduled tweets.

Hootsuite, www.hootsuite.com

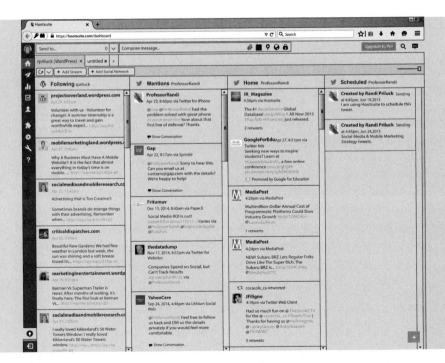

Content Development and Management Strategies

The most important piece of content is the brand's website. Marketers should store proprietary materials on the brand's site rather than use third party platforms, such as Facebook or YouTube, so the firm controls the material. A good website has a clear menu-driven interface with clean graphics, offers a search function, and drives viewers to revenue-generating opportunities when appropriate. The pages of websites are searchable by search engines, and Web content with strong links will rank higher when the keywords are present in a meaningful way.

Marketers can create a wide variety of content, depending on their brand personality and product and service offerings. The content should build the reputation of the firm by featuring expert advice on the brand's product or service area. For example, a catering business would blog about food nutrition, quick and delicious meals in under twenty minutes, or the best place in town to find crepes. Conversely, an accounting firm would provide tax advice to businesses and information on audits. Presented here are some different types of content that brands can create and examples from firms who use such a strategy to build their businesses. Exhibit 8.14 lists examples in the following categories: blogs [30], pictures [31], newsletters, case studies [32], white papers [33], interviews, articles, e-books, podcasts, infographics, videos [34], press releases, contests [35], and portfolios.

Selecting Media for a Communications Strategy

Marketers have many potential media options when they want to reach consumers. Of course, there are traditional media such as television, radio, and print and there are digital media such as email, social networks, mobile websites, and mobile applications. A strong strategy involves evaluating the various media options to select those that most effectively and efficiently reach the target at the right time with the appropriate message. This sounds easy, but it is actually challenging to decide which elements of a strategy will deliver the highest returns. A good analysis involves looking at the target market's media usage patterns and determining the costs associated with each strategy. Chapter Nine discusses methods for evaluating digital media options and Chapter Ten covers traditional media.

Testing Online Advertising Executions

One reason why marketers are so keen on digital media is because the results are easily measured. A marketer can receive immediate feedback on the success of a strategy by looking at the website metrics via Google Analytics or through some of the social media sites that provide data. One very useful tool in Google Analytics is the Multi-Channel Funnels report that tells a marketer which websites the

EXHIBIT 8.14

Examples of Content

CONTENT	EXAMPLE
Blogs	The European Paper Company, an online stationery store (oddly based in Boulder, Colorado), has a blog with brand-related content, creative art, planner information, interior design, notebooks, paper and pens, and writers/authors. For example, one post has examples of photographs of glass art in public places.
Pictures/images	Benefit Cosmetics used Instagram to find real people who use their mascara. Fans submitted 11,900 selfies with the #realsies hashtag.
Newsletters	Samsung's monthly newsletter features new products, promotions, news, and videos.
Case studies	InMobi, a large mobile advertising network, features case studies on GM, Intel, Reebok, Sony Ericsson, and Yamaha describing the challenge, the solution, and the results achieved through mobile advertising.
White papers	Euromonitor International published the "Top 10 Consumer Trends" white paper to demonstrate its research and reporting skills to potential clients. The white paper discusses selling to millennials and consumers' growing concern about privacy.
Interviews	"The Six Pixels of Separation" Mirum podcast by Mitch Joel features interviews with social media experts. The goal is to provide expertise regarding digital strategies to build business for his agency.
Articles	1. Charles Schwab, the financial services firm, publishes articles and provides expert insight on investing and personal finance. 2. Standard & Poor's, a leader in financial market intelligence, publishes research articles on its website.
E-books	Both Radian-6 and Hubspot have a series of how-to-books on social media. These firms offer services in social media listening and inbound marketing to businesses.
Podcasts (audio or video)	Netflix's podcasts tell you whether a movie is worth watching.
Infographics	Kissmetrics posts a series of infographics to highlight its expertise in online data.
Videos	Zappos uses video to drive sales. The videos describe and demonstrate products with real Zappos's employees and not models or actors. The videos have a sales impact of 6%–30%.
Contests	Wikipedia launched a photo contest called "Wiki Loves Monuments" to encourage people to photograph monuments "of historic and cultural relevance," upload them to Wikimedia Commons under a free license, and allow Wikipedia to use them. Judges determined the best photo submissions, narrowing them down to the top ten finalists and a grand prize winner.
Press releases	Nielsen, a leading global provider of information and insights into what consumers watch and buy, publishes press releases on its website.
Portfolios	BBDO, the global advertising agency, presents a portfolio of its work on its website.

target market visited prior to coming to the site. The system can also attach a dollar value to a strategy by tracking conversions that take place on a website. A conversion is the ultimate goal a brand wants to achieve, which is often a sale. Tracking website data allows marketers to evaluate strategies to see if they are working.

Marketers can also run specific tests to compare one strategy with another. For example, Burger King can send two groups of people different email coupons for lunch specials and examine which works better when people redeem them. Other methods for testing digital marketing strategies are described in Chapter Twelve.

Executing Strategy

Once the brand managers are clear on the goals for a brand and have outlined the strategy, it's time to put these plans into action. Smaller firms typically execute social media strategies on their own, but likely already have a website for conducting business and perhaps also an agency that assists with digital matters such as search or SEO. Mobile strategies are more expensive to execute and require more technical expertise to develop and are usually managed by an agency, though some executions are possible with a limited budget and available free tools. For example, a brand can set up an inexpensive mobile website using a template from Wix.com, Squarespace, or other such vendors who specialize in the mobile Web.

Most large advertisers hire advertising agencies to help manage their communications strategies and execute them in the various forms of media. The agencies provide specialized expertise in creating advertisements that meet the requirements of media companies. For example, television advertising requires that a brand hire a production company, actors, writers, and editors. The agency may also evaluate the legality of the ads or ensure that the brand meets the network's requirements for running commercials.

The advertising business consists of a set of advertising agency conglomerates that own a variety of advertising agencies. The "Big Four" holding companies control most of the advertising agencies and work with the world's largest clients. Exhibit 8.15 lists the global agency conglomerates, their revenues, the largest agencies, and clients [10].

Some of the agencies are full service and provide all marketing services, including creative, media services, research, production, digital, social media, mobile, public relations, direct marketing, and promotions. The companies also hold smaller agency brands that specialize in specific services such as creative houses or direct marketing. Of course, there are also independent agencies that serve specific niche markets.

EXHIBIT 8.15

The Global Advertising Conglomerates

	INTERPUBLIC GROUP	OMNICOM	PUBLICIS	WPP GROUP
Worldwide revenue	$7.12 billion	$14.58 billion	$9.23 billion	$17.25 billion
Major agency networks	McCann World Group, FCB Lowe and Partners, IPG Media Brands, Deutsch, Hill Holiday, R/GA	DDB Worldwide Communications Group, BBDO Worldwide, TBWA Worldwide, Omnicom Media Group, Fleishman-Hillard, Ketchum, CDM Group, Marketing Arm, Media Specialist Communications, LLNS	Leo Burnett Worldwide, DigitasLBi, Saatchi & Saatchi, Starcom MediaVest Group, ZenithOptimedia, Zenith Healthcare Communications Group, MSL Group, Razorfish	Y&R, J. Walter Thompson Co., Grey Group, Geometry Global, United Network, GroupM, Tenthavenue, WPP Digital, Ogilvy & Mather
Largest clients	GM, J&J, Microsoft, Unilever, Verizon Communications	McDonald's, Pepsi, Skansa, Visa, General Electric, Nestlé, Volkswagen, Nissan	American Express, Coca-Cola, L'Oreal, All State, Kraft, Honda	British American Tobacco, P&G, Ford, Colgate-Palmolive, Microsoft, Unilever

Advertising Age Data Center, 2015

ADVERTISERS AND AGENCY ROLES AND RELATIONSHIPS

The relationship between advertisers and agencies is often close because agencies are responsible for an important part of the firm's marketing mix, namely promotion. In addition, the agency handles funds for the client and has a fiduciary duty to manage the client's funds properly. However, sometimes there are conflicts and advertisers may decide to review their agencies. That may lead to an agency search on the part of the advertiser, as the company seeks a new agency for a brand.

The process begins when a client decides to hire an agency or replace a current agency on its roster. The client announces the search or hires a firm to manage the search to avoid unsolicited requests. Usually, the client will ask agencies to complete a questionnaire and then choose four to five agencies to participate in a more comprehensive pitch, in which the agencies develop creative content for the client and present their ideas.

The Association of National Advertisers publishes guidelines for an agency search to set the ground rules for ethical and fair behavior on the part of both clients and agencies. The guidelines cover how to manage a search, when to conduct a search, which types of agencies to consider, issuing requests for proposals (RFPs), and choosing finalists. There are also best practices for agencies to follow, such as how to respond to an RFP and expectations in the pitch process.

When it comes to the social media or mobile part of the digital execution, the large agency conglomerates have digital agencies to which they can refer clients. Today, because social media and mobile executions are so important to advertising, these strategies are often part of the advertising plan right from the start. Most agencies are well versed in executing digital as well as traditional strategies and can merge the two when necessary.

EVALUATING THE CAMPAIGN

Finally, after the campaign runs, marketers must evaluate the success of the effort. Though not all campaigns lead to sales immediately following execution, brands should examine the metrics associated with the interim goals, such as net new followers and website hits. A more in-depth, long-term analysis should indicate whether additional followers and Web visits led to conversions. Of course, some brands can see sales increases immediately following campaigns and attribute those results to a particular strategy. For example, people can go out and easily purchase a Coke after watching a viral video. Marketers can evaluate these campaigns in a relatively short time span. A purchase of an automobile takes more time, and the results from related campaigns take longer to evaluate due to the long buying cycle. A variety of techniques for evaluating social media and mobile marketing strategies are discussed in Chapter Twelve.

SUMMARY AND REVIEW

CHAPTER SUMMARY

An integrated communications strategy is the key to successful brand messaging. By integrating strategy, a brand delivers more effective communications, taking advantage of the synergies among the various forms of media. IMC also allow marketers to reach a target and reinforce the message in various ways. Social media and mobile marketing are newer forms of digital marketing, but marketers should still evaluate their contribution to the total message and consider the role of content in attracting and engaging audiences. An important part of a digital strategy is developing content to share online, which builds engagement and may help boost search engine rankings for brands.

KEY TERMS

content development
corporate mission
creative brief
cross platform strategy

integrated marketing
  communications
  (IMC)

key performance
  indicators (KPIs)
organizational
  objectives

promotional mix
situation analysis
touchpoints

SUMMARY REVIEW QUESTIONS

1. Describe advertiser spending trends in the global market. Which form of media commands the highest percentage of global media spending? Which industries spend the most money on advertising?
2. Name some of the largest global advertising companies.
3. What are the steps in the IMC process?
4. What is a creative brief and why is it important?
5. List three types of content and indicate whether the format can be used by business-to-business firms, business-to-consumer firms, or both.
6. Explain how brands can manage their content at various sites.
7. What are the advantages of an integrated communications strategy?

APPLICATION QUESTIONS

1. Go to Pinterest.com and locate IKEA's pins (type Ikea in the search box). Examine the pins, and record the number of likes and repins. What would you recommend to IKEA with regard to its Pinterest strategy based on your data?
2. Choose an advertiser with which you are familiar. Examine the Twitter feed, the Facebook page, and the YouTube strategy for one of its brands. Next try to determine the goal of each strategy.

Are all the executions meant to achieve the same goal? Discuss.
3. For the same advertiser, list all the types of content that the brand creates. Which are most effective for reaching current customers? Which are most effective for reaching potential customers?
4. Find an example of a B2B firm using content and a B2C firm using content. Describe every individual piece of content. What is the difference in the content that each firm distributes?

5. Go to Hubspot.com and find the list of available e-books. Which titles would help you most in developing a social media strategy?
6. Using Alexa.com, determine the demographics for a new social media network. How do the demographics compare to those for Facebook and Twitter?
7. Find an infographic online. Evaluate the credibility of the content. Does it provide sources? If so, are they legitimate?

case study Porsche's Social Media Planning

Owning a Porsche is a dream for many and a reality for a few wealthy automobile enthusiasts with the incomes to afford a high-performance sports car. Porsches were designed for speed with a style that had always turned heads. But, even with such prestige and performance, Porsche has had its ups and downs in selling cars in the United States.

After the economic downturn in 2008, Porsche faced a difficult market. Car buyers concerned with a deep recession stopped buying new cars. The luxury market was especially hard hit. The target market of consumers who could buy a Porsche was still financially able to do so, but did not feel good about buying a car they would only drive occasionally. Even as the economy improved, people were reluctant to spend on luxury items, especially those with big tickets that were highly visible. However, by 2015, the sports performance automobile market recovered and Porsche set its sights on rebuilding its U.S. business back to its prerecession levels.

THE COMPANY AND U.S. SALES

Porsche Automobil was a German company marketing cars under the brand names Volkswagen, Audi, Skoda, and Porsche. Porsche Cars North America, a subsidiary, marketed Porsche cars in the United States. As a small niche player in the U.S. market, Porsche sold about 20,000 cars annually, less than 1% of the total cars sold in the U.S. light vehicle market [36].

The U.S. car market was large, but susceptible to fluctuations in the economy. Automobile sales were a leading indicator of a potential recession in the United States, and policymakers and automobile manufacturers watched the automobile sales figures for signs of weakness in the economy. If consumers felt confident about their prospects, they were more likely to buy cars than if they were worried about losing their jobs. The automobile industry contracted after the 2008 recession, and by 2013 sales had still not recovered to prerecession levels. Exhibit 8.16 shows U.S. automobile sales 2008 through 2014 [37].

Porsche's sales followed the general market trends, dropping in 2009 and heading toward recovery by 2013. Exhibit 8.17 represents Porsche's sales in 2009, 2013, and 2014 by model. People commonly purchased preowned Porsches, reflecting their quality and long-term value to potential customers. The most popular new Porsches were the Cayenne and the Porsche 911. According to *Motor Trend,* the Cayenne's MSRP was $52,600 and the 911 base price was $84,300 [38].

U.S. Automobile Sales in Units

YEAR	U.S. CAR SALES IN UNITS
2008	6,796,107
2009	5,400,890
2010	5,635,432
2011	6,089,403
2012	7,243,654
2013	7,780,710
2014	7,918,601

Wards BEA, 2014.

THE PORSCHE TARGET MARKET

Only very wealthy consumers could afford to purchase a Porsche sports car. The profile of the consumer who spent more than $50,000 on a vehicle was an educated 35- to 64-year-old male with a career in management, business, or finance; a household income of over $150,000 annually; and a home worth over half a million dollars.

The Porsche target was interested in business news and sports and traveled often. These customers were also early Internet adopters, accessing sites for news, entertainment, and information. Owners of cars over $50,000 were heavier than average users of online news sites such as Fox News and the New York Times, as shown in Exhibit 8.18 [39]. However, as other demographic groups began to use the Internet more frequently, the indices for the target market declined.

Porsche Sales in Three Years

PORSCHE MODEL	2009 U.S. SALES	2013 U.S. SALES	2014 U.S. SALES
Boxter/Cayman	3,875	7,953	7,292
All 911	6,839	10,442	10,529
All Cayenne	7,735	18,507	16,205
All Panamera	1,247	5,421	5,740
Macan			7,241
Total	19,696	42,323	47,007
Preowned	6,658	7,953	11,843

Motor Trend, "New Porsche Cars," 2015.

EXHIBIT 8.18

Profile of Luxury Automobile Owners

INDICES FOR OWNERS OF AUTOMOBILES OVER $50,000+	2009 INDEX	2012–2013 INDEX
Wall Street Journal	216	183
Users of Gmail	152	101
iTunes	174	131
Wikipedia	156	102
Facebook	132	101
Google Maps	174	104
Weather.com	142	121
YouTube	128	91
Twitter	333	75
LinkedIn	326	207
WebMD	152	130
Spotify		133
WSJ.com	316	151
NYTimes.com	177	149
NFL.com	107	150
Expedia.com	149	161
Tripadvisor.com		204

MediaMark Research & Intelligence., "Product Automotive," Fall 2013.

RECESSION HITS PORSCHE

In 2008 Porsche saw a 22% decline in U.S. sales followed by a further decline of 27% in 2009. The recession had reached the luxury automobile market. The problem was not that the target market could not afford to buy a Porsche. The nation's wealthiest 5% of households accounted for about 37% of consumer spending, according to Moody's Analytics. Porsche's customers still had high incomes and could afford to purchase. The recession had not hit high-income individuals very hard [40].

However, Porsche was facing a new type of consumer, one who did not want to flaunt his or her wealth as was comfortable prior to 2008 [41]. Even those individuals who could afford super-luxury vehicles wanted to show respect for those whose lives had been affected strongly by the downturn. Luxury car marketers noticed a shift in consumer values, with people indicating they were happier with fewer material possessions and more concern for relationships and values (see Exhibit 8.19) [40], [42].

The challenge for Porsche was to convince its customer base that is was indeed acceptable to buy a Porsche and provide solid proof points for the assertion. However, before setting out on a social media strategy, the company set clear goals for the brand:

1. Improve the value proposition for potential buyers.
2. Drive consumer purchase consideration and dealer inquiries.
3. Increase sales levels.

The campaign's message was that Porsche cars were designed for everyday hard driving, but

Luxury Car Buyers

AGREEMENT AMONG THOSE EARNING 100K+	Q1 2009	Q4 2010
"I like it when others recognize me as wealthy."	30%	40%
"I feel guilty buying luxury goods in this economy."	54%	42%
"It doesn't feel right to wear expensive flashy brands."	59%	47%

Effie Awards Silver Case Study Winner Porsche, 2012
https://www.effie.org/case_studies/case/2126

with a special magic. The agency decided to move away from showing the car in beautiful environments as they had done in the past and to feature everyday situations.

The website http://porscheeveryday.com featured interviews with Porsche owners such as Jack and Ginny Case, who had purchased their first Porsche in 1955. Well past their seventies, they used their Porsche for daily shopping. Janet Mullins bought her car when she was pregnant with her second child, an atypical time to buy a Porsche. To help execute the strategy, the company sent flip cameras to owners in the Porsche Club of America and asked them to post their stories online. Porsche also leveraged dealerships to support the "everyday magic" message by showing model cars with groceries and ski racks. Dealers offered test drives to potential customers that included stopping by Starbucks to pick up a coffee. On Facebook,

Porsche created a photo mosaic with owners' faces and posted over 300 videos on YouTube, including one video of a Porsche built with the names of Facebook fans written all over it [43].

To drive targets to the www.porscheevery day.com site, Porsche bought both magazine and mobile advertising, leveraging business publications and reaching people who had interacted with Porsche ads in the past. Billboards and digital outdoor boards ran in airports supported by radio spots. Porsche spent $25 million in advertising in 2010 [44].

The campaign generated positive results. By 2011 GfK brand monitor indicated that the car was "for every day," "worth its price," and "comfortable," with supporting customer statements that the brand was "fascinating" and made "driving fun" (see Exhibit 8.20) [44]. Dealer traffic increased 51% between 2010 and 2011; website traffic tripled; and dealer webpage views increased 144% over the same period. Finally, sales increased +19% for the 911, market share increased +14%, and overall sales of two-door Porsches increased +6%.

PORSCHE IN 2015–2018

The environment for luxury car buying was very different in 2015. The recession was over, unemployment in the United States was only 5.5%, and people were again buying big-ticket items [45]. Luxury sales were expected to continue to grow. The U.S. luxury market was the largest in the world, three times the size of Japan's luxury market. Cars selling for over $40,000 represented more than 10% of the automobile market in units and close to 20% of the market in terms of dollar value. These figures represented a significant opportunity for Porsche.

EXHIBIT 8.20

Perceptions of Porsche

PERCEPTIONS/ METRICS	2010	2011
For every day	11%	29%
Comfortable	23%	36%
Worth its price	39%	53%
Fascinating	55%	61%
Driving fun	75%	83%
Considering Porsche	30%	45%
Website visits	547,000	1.1 million
Car configurator usage	1.3 million	1.6 million
Average time on site	4:48	12:25

Effie Awards Silver Case Study Winner Porsche 2012
https://www.effie.org/case_studies/case/2126

After a few years of running the "Engineered for Magic Everyday" campaign, the brand resurrected its famous "There is No Substitute" slogan. The goal was to increase sales within the luxury segment that was poised for growth. The everyday positioning was no longer necessary or relevant to the brand.

To further capitalize on the growing market and grow significantly by 2018, Porsche introduced the Macan SUV. The new vehicle showed strong initial promise [46]. To further emphasize the unique nature of Porsche, the company ran a campaign associated with Le Mans, the oldest active sports car endurance race, which took place annually in France and was widely considered the most prestigious. Clearly, Porsche was no longer talking about everyday life and instead had shifted to presenting the good life. How will Porsche continue to create and deliver relevant content, impress its target market and reclaim its luxury positioning?

QUESTIONS FOR DISCUSSION

1. What are the characteristics of well-written goals?
2. Evaluate Porsche's goals prior to running the 2010 campaign. Do these goals meet the criteria of well-written goals?
3. What was Porsche's strategy for the brand developed in 2010?
4. Write three new goals using the criteria for well-written goals.
5. Why did Porsche fail to set proper goals and metrics for the campaign in advance?
6. Was the Porsche "everyday driving" strategy risky at all?
7. Which is a better positioning for Porsche? "Everyday driving" or "no substitute"? Explain.
8. Given the data presented in this case study, how would you recommend Porsche proceed with a communications strategy? Should Porsche include social media and mobile? What is the role for traditional media?
9. How did Porsche use content in 2010? What types of content should the brand consider now?
10. How did consumer attitudes change between 2008 and 2015? Could Porsche have used social media to determine customer sentiment over that time period? How?

REFERENCES

[1] McDonald's, "McDonald's U.S. Announces New Brand Vision," *Newsroom,* 2 January 2015.

[2] K. Bachelder, "I'm Not Lovin' It, McDonald's," *The Wall Street Journal,* 3 February 2015.

[3] C. Morran, "McDonald's Pay with Lovin Campaign Doesn't Result in Any Actual Love for Company," Consumerist.com, 18 February 2015. http://consumerist.com/2015/02/18/mcdonalds-pay-with-lovin-campaign-doesnt-result-in-any-actual-love-for-company/.

[4] P. La Monica, McDonald's Sales Sore Thanks to All Day Breakfast, CNNMoney, January 25th, 2016, http://money.cnn.com/video/investing/2016/01/25/mcdonalds-earnings.cnnmoney?iid=EL.

[5] Advertising Age, "Nike Faces Marketing Challenge in China: Making Running Cool," 21 October 2011.

[6] D. Xu, "Nike Utilizes Local Social Media to Maximize Chinese Market Reach," East West Center Blog, 9 March 2015.

[7] L. Schism and E. Holm, "Geico Spends Nearly $1 Billion on Ads as Car Insurers Battle," *The Wall Street Journal,* 25 June 2012.

[8] T. Wallack, "State Farm Stays Out of Mass," *Boston Globe,* 26 November 2011.

[9] eMarketer, "Total U.S. Ad Spending to See Largest Increase since 2004," 2014.

[10] Advertising Age, "Advertising Age Fact Pack," 2014.

[11] N.Tadena, "P&G Cut Traditional Ad Spending by 14% in 2014," March 18, 2015, Wall Street Journal, http://blogs.wsj.com/cmo/2015/03/18/pg-cut-traditional-ad-spending-by-14-in-2014/.

[12] Effie Awards, "H&R Block, Finance North America, Silver Award," *Effie Award Winner Showcase,* 2012.

[13] General Electric, "Six Second Science Fair," 2015.

[14] N. Fergie, "John Deere Lead Generation Success," Successful Marketing Blog, 11 May 2013.

[15] The Bees Awards, 2012.

[16] Bayer, "Social Media Room," 2015. http://www.bayer.com/en/social-media-channels.aspx.

[17] Effie Awards, "Dove Singing in the Rain," Bronze Effie, 2012. tps://effie.org/case_studies/by_category/64/by_year.

[18] Pew Internet Research, "Social Network Usage," January 9, 2015. http://www.pewinternet.org/2015/01/09/demographics-of-key-social-networking-platforms-2/.

[19] J. Edwards, "Here Are Facebooks Five Biggest Advertisers," *Business Insider,* 6 May 2014.

[20] A. Taube, "The World's Biggest Advertising Company Will Double Its Spending on Twitter," *Business Insider,* 20 June 2014.

[21] J. Edwards, "This LinkedIn Deck Shows the ROI for 8 of Its Biggest Ad Clients," *Business Insider,* 3 August 2012.

[22] J. Rampton, "Pinterest Marketing Tips: What You Can Learn from the Top 20 Brands," *Entrepreneur,* 5 September 2013.

[23] G. Sloan, "Instagram Video Ads Are Coming Soon," *AdWeek,* 27 April 2014.

[24] A. M. Kessler, "Cadillac Makes Big Plan to Woo Luxury Market," *The New York Times,* 19 September 2014.

[25] Effie Awards, 2012, Silver Award, Cosmopolitan Hotels, Just the Right Amount of Wrong. https://effie.org/case_studies/by_category/64/by_year.

[26] Advertising Age Data Center, 2015. http://adage.com/datacenter/.

[27] M. Baker, "Respect the Brief: The Art of Creating a Smarter Creative Brief," Creativity Central, 8 May 2011.

[28] Quantcast, 24 March, 2016. https://www.quantcast.com/babycenter.com?country=US#cross PlatformCard.

[29] M. Stelzner, "Social Media Examiner's Business," Social Media Examiner Podcast, 2012.

[30] European Paper Blog, http://europeanpaper.com/blog/.

[31] R. Gilette, "How the Most Successful Companies Dominate Instagram and You Can Too," Fast Company, 22 April 2014.

[32] InMobi, "InMobi Case Studies," 2 April 2015.

[33] Euromonitor International, "White Paper: Top 10 Consumer Trends 2015," 15 January 2015.

[34] M. R. Robertson, "Video Demos Increase Sales Conversions at Zappos.com," ReelSEO, 5 December 2009.

[35] A. Lee, "Wikipedia Photo Contest Expected to Be World's Largest," Mashable, 5 September 2012.

[36] The Wall Street Journal, "Auto Sales Market Data Center," 2 April 2015.

[37] Statista, "U.S. Car Sales 1951–2014," 2015.

[38] Motor Trend, "New Porsche Cars," 2015.

[39] MediaMark Research Inc., "Product Automotive," Fall 2013.

[40] G. Strauss, "For the Wealthy, a Return to Luxury Spending," *USA Today,* 21 February 2011.

[41] Forbes Insights, "Automotive Outlook Report," 2012.

[42] C. C. Berk, "Why Holiday Sales May Hinge on How 'The One Percent' Feels," CNBC, 18 November 2011.

[43] C. Lake, "Seven Reasons Why Porsche Is Winning the Social Media Game," eConsultancy, 17 February 2011.

[44] E. Tegler, "Porsche Puts Dollars Behind Sports Cars Again After Pushing SUV, Sedan," *Advertising Age,* 18 April 2011.

[45] Bureau of Labor Statistics, "Labor Force Statistics from the Current Population Survey," in *Databases, Tables & Calculators by Subject,* 5 May 2015.

[46] Porsche, "Porsche Reports May Sales," May 2014. Press release.

CHAPTER NINE

EXECUTING STRATEGY

Once a marketer has determined that social and/or mobile media should be part of the brand's marketing strategy, he or she can plan and execute a strategy. A typical social or mobile plan includes owned, social, paid, and earned media. Marketers must determine the most appropriate combination of tools to use to engage customers and achieve goals. This chapter describes specific social media and mobile strategies for attracting and engaging global audiences.

After reading this chapter, you will be able to:

- IDENTIFY PAID, OWNED, SOCIAL, AND EARNED MEDIA

- DEVELOP STRATEGIES FOR EFFECTIVE BLOGGING

- REACH AND ENGAGE AUDIENCES WITH DIGITAL MEDIA

- UNDERSTAND PROGRAMMATIC BUYING AND REMARKETING

- UTILIZE SOCIAL AND EARNED MEDIA TO INCREASE SEARCH ENGINE RANKINGS ven as Facebook's growth in the United States slows and Americans leave for other social platforms [1], Facebook's growth in other countries is on the rise. For example, people in India are adopting the social network like crazy. By 2017 India is expected to have the highest number of Facebook users, at 277.8 million people, compared to 180.5 million in North America (see Exhibit 9.1) [2]. Marketers in India have significant opportunities to reach their target audiences through Facebook's mobile platform as 70% of India's population accesses the Internet via mobile devices [3]. The average Indian mobile Internet user spends almost three hours a day using the mobile Internet and over two hours a day on social media, making Indians some of the most active Internet users in the world. Internet users in India are also very involved online with brands, following an average of ten brands on social media [4]. That is why when Kiehl's opened its Mumbai store, the brand turned to social media to build buzz among consumers. The goals of Kiehl's marketing communications plan were:

- Engage with the right audiences.
- Build an insightful connection to the brand.

The strategy was to leverage influential consumers using a series of contests to build buzz on social media. The execution included a daily Twitter contest, exclusive weekend contests, and opportunities to tweet about the

EXHIBIT 9.1

Projected Facebook Growth

REGION (2016 DATA FOR CALCULATING GROWTH)	USERS IN 2017 (MILLIONS)	GROWTH
North America	180.5	3.6%
Western Europe	182.7	29.3%
Central and Eastern Europe	-166.4	9.5%
Latin America Brazil	307.1 103.9	29.5% 66%
Asia-Pacific India	616 277.8	34.4% 17.7%
Middle East and Africa	318.9	31.8%

http://www.emarketer.com/Article/Emerging-Markets-Drive-Facebook-User-Growth/1009875

#needtousekiehls. The brand found a lot of engagement midweek and in the middle of the day, peaking at 5 p.m. In response, the brand ramped up the efforts at those busier times, right before people were leaving the office and considering a shopping excursion. Kiehl's drove contest winners directly to the store to pick up goodie bags, leading them to tweet even more. To go along with the Twitter campaign, the brand started a Kiehl's meet-up with giveaways and skin-care demonstrations. The result was that Kiehl's grew Twitter followers, influencers tweeted about the campaign, and Kiehl's trended on Twitter for three days in a row during the store launch. The brand also reported a +42% conversion rate for key opinion leaders [5].

Twitter allowed Kiehl's to engage people with contests on their mobile devices. But how successful was this campaign? What additional information would you want to know in order to judge the success of Kiehl's Mumbai introduction?

THE EVOLUTION OF MEDIA IN DIGITAL MARKETING

Social media and mobile technologies have changed the conversation about marketing in both digital and traditional media. In the past, marketers would develop strategies for television, radio, direct mail, and public relations as part of an integrated marketing communications plan. The new lingo in the digital arena refers to brands developing presences in *owned, social, paid,* and *earned media*. In digital, brands can create and manage their own sites (owned media), use social networks to engage customers (social media), buy media space on various platforms (paid media), or benefit from people who pass along company information (earned media). These terms are defined further in Exhibit 9.2.

EXHIBIT 9.2

Definitions of Owned, Social, Paid, and Earned Media

MEDIUM	DEFINITION
Owned media	Channels or platforms that brands create, manage, and control.
Social media	Platforms that brands use for communication, that are owned and controlled by other companies.
Paid media	Advertising that brands run on the platforms of other companies.
Earned media	Brand impressions or mentions by people online as a result of social sharing.

EXHIBIT 9.3

Relationships among Digital Media

Owned Media

Earned Media

Paid Media

Social Media

Owned media are valuable to a brand strategy because the company sets them up and manages them—and thus controls every aspect of the interface with customers. Marketers may also use social properties, such as social networks, bookmarking sites, or content aggregating sites, to communicate with customers, but they must abide by the rules set by the sites. Many brands use Facebook, Snapchat, Kik, Pinterest, among others. Marketers can also use paid media to communicate with targets by buying advertising time on social media sites. Finally, when people share content with others, companies register brand impressions akin to word-of-mouth marketing. These impressions, or mentions in media, are collectively referred to as **earned media**. The new language highlights the opportunity marketers see in using social media to build conversations around their brands that will resonate across the Internet. Exhibit 9.3 shows the relationships among the different forms of media and how owned, paid, and social media interact to encourage earned media.

The discussion of Kiehl's strategy at the beginning of this chapter reveals that Facebook users in the United States and United Kingdom may be abandoning the

consider this . . .

LAUNCHING A PRODUCT EXTENSION WITH DIGITAL

Can a marketer successfully launch a new product with digital as the lead medium? Hershey's thought so and used Facebook to introduce the new Minis brand of peanut butter cups to its loyal customers. The goals were to break through the holiday clutter to gain awareness for the new product, engage existing customers to generate buzz for the launch, and reward brand loyalists by letting them be the first ones to know about the Minis.

The brand used a teaser campaign titled "A Love Story with a Happy Little Ending: Told in

10 Posts and a Tab" to slowly unveil the new product to over 6 million Facebook fans. The story about two peanut butter cups falling in love, meeting, their first kiss, their engagement, their dance, and their honeymoon all appeared on the page in the form of posts that fans could share. The cups' baby announcement was a fan's first exposure to the new product. The full side tab saw high levels of fan engagement on the first day, with over 40,000 tab views and 13,000 clicks from the wall post. In all, 750 people commented and 284 shared the news [7].

https://www.facebook.com/reeses/posts/10150111624615412.

site; it's possible that people are growing bored with the Facebook platform [6]. Though the trend toward social media adoption appears strong, different media platforms become popular for a while and then others take their place. However, in India, Kiehl's found a successful avenue for launching its products using Facebook, a popular platform there.

OWNED MEDIA AND SOCIAL MEDIA

A brand owns certain properties that marketers use for communications purposes. When a medium is "owned," it is controlled and paid for by the brand. The most common forms of owned media are websites and company blogs. Exhibit 9.4 outlines the major forms of digital media and some of the issues faced by marketers [8].

With owned media, the brand decides the long-term strategy for the medium and the content. Anything posted on the site belongs to the company, as do any data that are generated from the users. For example, a third party site such as Facebook or Twitter could restrict access to customer information such as email addresses or usage statistics. With owned media, the company controls every aspect of the experience and maintains the data. For instance, Facebook does not allow businesses to send direct messages to the individuals who "like" their brand. This limitation prevents companies from spamming, but also reduces the communications power of Facebook for a company.

EXHIBIT 9.4

Forms of Digital Media

MEDIUM	OWNERSHIP OF THE CONTENT	EXAMPLES	ISSUES
Owned media	The company or the brand	Websites and mobile sites, blogs on company platforms	The company owns and controls all content and data forever, but the platform does not have a natural audience to view it. Customers may be skeptical of company-sponsored content. There are costs associated with setting up and managing the technology.
Social media	The platform itself	Facebook, Twitter, Pinterest, Tumblr, and Instagram pages	These platforms have large audiences, but a brand does not own its posted content or the content posted by users. The platforms do not share data with companies and some are not accessible by outside programmers. Companies pay to develop content, but do not pay for media time directly.
Paid media	The company owns the content of the message, but the medium limits the format.	Television commercials, magazine ads, banner ads, preroll video ads, promoted tweets, billboards, and mobile banner ads	Paid media have preexisting audiences and companies can create messages within the network's parameters. Companies have to pay for both media time and content development.
Earned media	The content exists on various platforms and is owned by its creators.	Reviews, user-generated content, posted comments, blog posts, customer retweets, pins, photos, and viral videos	The company benefits from Internet traffic that results in higher search engine rankings, but companies can't control the content. The company pays to develop original content, but not for content created by others unless requested expressly by the firm.

consider this . . .

AN OPEN API

The acronym API refers to the **application protocol interface,** a term that specifies a set of routines for how a type of software interacts with the user onscreen. An open API allows developers to write programs for the platform and access data. For example, Twitter offers a few open API's: including one for accessing core Twitter data and another for search and trends data. YouTube's API allows developers to integrate YouTube videos

In the last chapter, we learned about the various types of content (including articles, videos, and images) brands can create as well as strategies for developing the best content to display on their owned and social media. The most common place for marketers to store their content is on their websites. Smart marketers will host content on their webpages to make it clear that they own the content and use that space for interacting with target markets. Another advantage to hosting owned content on a website is that the marketer can track analytics on each element of the site using Google Analytics or other providers. Though Facebook Insights provides some analytics, a marketer can delve more deeply into the meanings of the analytics and the relationships among various strategies to determine which elements of the website drive conversions when their customers interact with their owned media. By contrast, when posting content on social media such as Twitter, Pinterest, or Facebook, brands may own their content, but they no longer control it because the terms of service on many sites give the platform a global royalty-free license to use it. In addition, brands must operate within the rules of the sites, which may change without much notice to brand managers. For example, when Facebook rolled out its Timeline format, marketers had to adapt to the change whether or not they were prepared to do so. In addition, Facebook controls the posted content as well as information about and access to the brand's followers.

BLOGS ARE OWNED MEDIA FOR BRANDS

A blog is a website on which individuals and companies can post their content to share with others. Blogs can become the central repository for many online strategies because they are owned media, they can support many types of content, and because people can read, share, and comment on them. Brands can use blogs to build relationships with customers that may lead directly or indirectly to sales. In one study, 80% of Internet users indicated that blogs either somewhat or very much affected their purchase decisions [10]. Another important consideration for blogs is the inbound and outbound links associated with them. Inbound links are websites that post a blog's URL or link on their page, and outbound links are the URLs of other sites posted by the blog itself. A brand should consider the linking strategy of the blog and connect to related content and highly trafficked sites to help boost search engine rankings. The Google algorithm examines links to determine the importance and ranking of a blog.

consider this . . .

BLOG READERSHIP STUDY

One study of 1,000 computer, e-reader, and device owners from a national U.S. panel found that blogs are popular among Internet users. Specifically, 80% of the sample read five or more blogs, read blogs at least once a week, and did so first thing in the morning (most at 10 or 11 a.m.). Another study by the same author found that blogs with the words "insights," "analysis," "answers," "questions," and "advice" receive the most views. Other words earn more links from other blogs and sites, including "recent," "insights," "soon," "answers," and "analysis" [10].

Setting Goals for Blogs

Marketers should be clear on their goals for the blog. Specifically, the blog may be viewed as a destination for engagement, a way of directing people to a website, or a strategy for improving search engine results. The specific goal would then dictate what, when, and how to post as well as with whom to link. Some studies have shown that bloggers are more likely to link to websites very early in the day, while people view blogs in the later morning. The reason for the early links is that bloggers who wish to link are seeking content early in the morning, whereas regular readers are reading and commenting when they get to the office [10]. However, each blog is unique and viewership varies. Marketers should review their own blog data and test variations to maximize efforts to reach their goal. Patagonia uses Tumblr to host a series of blogs about climbing, snow, surfing, and fly fishing among other activities, but also blogs about various sports on its website to reach different audiences.

A brand's blog can provide marketers with a number of important benefits within the owned media realm. Content in the form of a blog is versatile in that marketers can use text, video, graphics, or multimedia presentations that customers, potential customers, bloggers, influencers, and the broad media can follow. The blogging platforms also facilitate sharing online through a website, social media, and mobile. New brands with small budgets can start out with small blogs on social platforms and move to blogs with more features and capabilities as they grow. For example, Wordpress, a popular blogging platform, can host content on a blog's page or provide the interface for content hosted elsewhere, such as on YouTube. A blog on Wordpress can also link to other social media sites such as Twitter and Google Plus for sharing when the blog is scheduled to appear.

When marketers create and contribute to blogs for their brands, they benefit by creating shareable content that search engines can index, so the content ranks high in a search. Brands can include valuable content and keywords within the

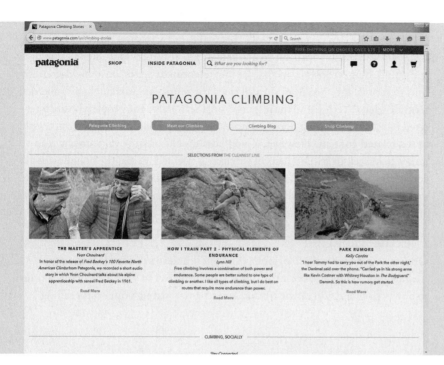

Patagonia's climbing blog hosted on the company website is known for its great content.

Property of Patagonia, Inc. Used with permission.

blog posts that boost organic rankings for certain types of brand- or product-related searches. As we saw in Chapter Seven, organic search is more trusted by customers than paid search, thus providing an important benefit for the brand. Not only that, but research suggests the position of the results matters. People are more likely to click on the first ad that appears on the search page, and 33% of clicks are on the first position [11]. Exhibit 9.5 reports click-through rates by position on search engine pages [12].

EXHIBIT 9.5

Ad Click-Through Rates by Position on Search Engine Pages

	DESKTOP	SMARTPHONE	TABLET
First position	3.2	4.9	4.3
Second position	1.9	2.2	2.0
Third position	1.5	1.9	1.6

J. Loechner, "First Position Ads Dominate Click Throughs," MediaPost, 9 October 2014.

Blogs maintain permanent links that make it easy to share posts in their original form and remain available to marketers and customers long after a campaign ends. Since blogs are owned media, the marketer can drive response and encourage calls to action, and then he or she can track the results of individual posts and determine what exactly drove the response, or lack thereof. The people who are interested in a blog are strong potential leads for business because they interact with brand-related content. However, a blog post should provide value to the reader, rather than seek to sell products or services. As owned media, the brand owns all comments on the blog and any email addresses it collects on the site. As a result, marketers can build an email list to follow up with those engaged with the blog and to offer subscriptions to readers [13].

Effective Blogging

One strategy for effective blogging is for your brand to show itself as the expert in the category, giving important advice and information to people. When it is time to buy, your brand will be the trusted source, a very strong position for selling.

consider this . . .

OPTIMIZE YOUR BLOG

One tool that can help a marketer improve a blog post's search engine optimization (SEO) is Rainmaker. The platform analyzes the post's keyword potential, making suggestions for improvements. The result may be higher search engine rankings for a blog that incorporates keywords which will drive business.

Executing a blogging strategy takes time and effort. In terms of aesthetics, a brand's blog should be professional-looking, with its own URL. Since people enjoy interacting with images and video, a good blog will include items that relate to the brand which attract the eye. In addition, it is important for a brand to stay current in updating the blog, regularly writing with passion in an appropriate voice for the brand that will engage the audience and encourage sharing. To optimize for SEO, the blog should use keywords in titles and in the body, link to related blogs and comments, and share posts from other blogs.

THE DEVELOPMENT OF SOCIAL NETWORKS

Social networks are a set of online services that individuals use to create profiles, to define a set of others with whom they connect, and to interact with those connections in a variety of ways [14]. The original social media sites connected people with each other and were not intended for commercial purposes. Users of the services were accustomed to interacting on the sites without advertising and may view such communications as intrusive. Marketers would have to tread carefully when engaging with customers online.

Over time, social media sites had to support their expenses and have done so in a number of ways. Some sites have developed their own advertising platforms, others have opened up their sites to third parties to allow advertising or tracking of customer behaviors and data, some charge fees or request donations, and investors fund other sites, hoping to reap future financial rewards.

The major online social media properties control brand advertising on their sites based on their revenue models. Each site has different rules and requirements for how information will appear on the site. For example, Wikipedia, the social encyclopedia, is an informational social medium and does not allow marketers to control the messages, though Wiki sites rank high when consumers use search engines. The information on Wiki for brands is not always positive. For example, recently the Wikipedia entry on Coke included a section at the end titled "Criticism of Coca-Cola," and a separate page lists Coke's "adverse health effects, its aggressive marketing to children, exploitative labor practices and high levels of pesticides in its products" among other things [15].

Internet users around the world have embraced social networking to stay in touch with friends and family. As a result, marketers have increased efforts to communicate with customers through social and other digital media at the expense of traditional media, particularly newspapers and magazines.

SOCIAL MEDIA AROUND THE WORLD

The average social media penetration today approaches 30% of the world population [16]. Globally, mobile has surpassed desktop as the primary means of accessing the Internet and mobile penetration continues to grow. Over 80% of Facebook's global users access the platform via mobile [16]. Thus, a firm with a global market for its products should include the leading social media and mobile networks as elements of their integrated marketing communications strategy. Determining which social media networks are popular and which ones are growing in popularity is an important first step. Whereas China and Eastern Europe prefer their own local social network sites, Facebook is the dominant platform in 130 of 137 countries [17]. The remaining top social networks are listed in Exhibit 9.6.

Consider the Chinese social media market, one where Facebook is not dominant. 47% of the population use social networks, that represents over 600 million people, a population larger than that of the entire United States [18]. More than half the population has a smartphone and they are active Internet users. Chinese

EXHIBIT 9.6

Leading Global Social Networks

	ACTIVE USERS (IN MILLIONS)	COUNTRY USED MOST
Facebook	1,550	USA
WhatsApp	900	India
QQ	860	China
Messenger	800	USA
QZone	653	China
WeChat	650	China
Tumblr	555	USA
Instagram	400	USA
Twitter	320	India
Skype	300	USA
Baidu Tieba	300	China
Viber	249	Russia
Sina Weibo	222	China
Line	212	Japan
Snapchat	200	USA
YY	122	China
Vkontakte	100	Russia
Pinterest	100	USA
BBM	100	Indonesia
LinkedIn	100	USA

S. Kemp, "Digital in 2016," We are Social, http://wearesocial.com/uk/special-reports/digital-in-2016, January 27, 2016.
Alexa, The Top 500 Sites on the Web by Country, 2016, www.Alexa.com

users are more likely to log onto social media sites via mobile than from desktops and use messaging sites [18].

Sina Weibo, the Chinese microblogging site with twice as many users as Twitter, reaches more than 35% of the Chinese Internet population. The site is popular with celebrities for connecting with fans. But, Chinese Internet users are more likely to use instant messaging than microblogging [19], [20].

Russian Internet users log onto Vkontakte (meaning "in touch") for social networking more often than Facebook. The site was launched in 2006 and grew rapidly before Facebook introduced its Russian language site in 2008. Vkontakte offers certain advantages for Russian users, such as allowing users to watch full-length movies and host audio and video files within groups and personal pages. The features go beyond Facebook's limited interface, offering something more like a blog for the Russian market [21]. Russians are very active social networkers, indexing higher than the global population on social networking activity, visits to social networks, and time spent on social networks.

Marketers have a vast array of options available to them for reaching out to customers, sending messages, and engaging people online all over the world. To make the task manageable, it's important to go back to the basics and determine the right target market and the objectives prior to executing a strategy in any country.

Sina Weibo is popular in China.

© Shutterstock/Gil C

STRATEGIES FOR SOCIAL MEDIA

Strong integrated marketing communications planning requires that brands consider the most efficient means of reaching targets to achieve goals. The strategy may include traditional media, digital media, social networks, or mobile marketing. The various elements work together to create messaging for a brand that resonates with targets and influences behavior.

In general, when it comes to social networking, brand managers who wish to engage with users should post relevant, interesting content that is search engine-optimized and will lead to sharing. Search engine-optimized means that marketers include keywords that potential customers use to search for the category, within the content. Each property operates slightly differently, and brands have unique issues and opportunities in using each of these forms of media. Smart marketers will experiment with various strategies and examine the outcomes relative to their established goals. Exhibit 9.7 indicates potential goals for social media and various methods for achieving those goals. Many of the methods can help a marketer achieve more than one goal or be used in tandem to influence target markets.

EXHIBIT 9.7

Goals and Strategies for Brands

POTENTIAL GOALS FOR BRANDS	STRATEGIES FOR ACHIEVING GOALS
Sales "Increase sales by 5% over the next 5 years." "Build Web conversions by an additional 2% year over year."	Bid on keywords with commercial intent. Advertise in traditional media to persuade and remind. Use mobile to drive store visits.
Search Engine Rankings "Rank number one on the Bing search engine for the 10 most searched industry terms." "Raise our ranking to the top three for our brand name."	Target bloggers with content. Link back to bloggers with related topics. Post content on social media sites. Encourage online sharing.
Brand Equity "Increase the percentage of people who recognize our brand name in the next 3 months." "Raise levels of brand loyalty among our customers."	Run ads in a variety of media. Buy social media and mobile paid media. Develop a mobile website. Host online reviews.
Engagement "Build customer engagement on our website by 10% this year." "Grow online brand comments by 50% over last year."	Post videos and images on key sites. Ask engaging questions in social media. Respond to questions and comments. Conduct customer service activities online.

PAID MEDIA

As we learned earlier in the chapter, **paid media** refers to the purchase of media time or space to run commercial messages. The forms of media advertisers buy may be traditional or digital and include television, magazines, radio, websites, search engines, social media sites, or billboards. Advertisers pay for the time or space within the medium. In television, the space is commercial time (minutes), and in magazines, the space is the page or portion of a page. Online advertisers buy banner ads, preroll videos, keyword search terms, website sponsorships, and other formats that audiences view when they are online. In mobile, marketers can reach people with mobile banner ads and ads on mobile websites and within mobile applications, such as games or geosocial sites.

As with all other advertising, marketers must set goals for paid media and seek out the right target markets. Since advertisers have control over the message, brands can use the media space or time to engage, persuade, remind, or build awareness. To determine effectiveness, brand managers should evaluate the advertising or the campaign using appropriate metrics for the channel.

PAID PLATFORMS

A variety of social media advertising platforms are available to marketers to reach target markets. Most social networking sites offer advertising platforms for marketers who wish to reach the people engaged on particular social sites. Each platform runs advertising around the general content, with some ads more integrated into the site than others. For example, Pandora runs audio ads after the user listens to a predetermined number of songs, while Twitter runs promoted tweets in the feed. Advertisers can buy ads on Snapchat that disappear after a certain amount of time, matching the platform's general format. Exhibit 9.8 lists the most visited social networking sites in the United States [22]. Marketers can use these platforms to reach a broad base of potential customers and then target specifically within the site to connect with those most likely to engage with the brand. The largest social networking site, Facebook, can reach 2 billion users globally and represents 60% of the social networking visits in the United States [18].

Advertisers pay on a cost-per-click or cost-per-impression basis and can target ads based on information users have provided to the site, or based on data that the networks have mined to find out about users. OkCupid, the dating site, has stated very publicly, "We experiment on human beings," and uses their data to inform its own business decisions [23]. The site also publishes research on dating so that users can date more effectively. For instance, OkCupid examined the racial profiles of users to determine the degree of interracial dating [24]. This kind of spying may make you nervous, but you should know that anytime you use a website, mobile site, or application marketers are tracking you and possibly manipulating what you see.

Paid advertising helps amplify a social media campaign and encourages social sharing because marketers can use paid advertising to generate awareness of interesting content. For example, Charles Schwab created a series of articles, videos, and infographics on investing and used Facebook-sponsored posts with messages to attract customers such as "Thinking of investing in tech? There may be some good signals for tech companies this year" and "Wondering what to do with that 401k from your employer?" Charles Schwab's agency, 360 Degrees, found that using these sponsored posts increased interaction with the customer, while the costs to reach customers decreased [25]. Another financial services company chose mobile paid media to build mobile Web traffic. Specifically, ING Bank used Google AdWords in Turkey to increase the number of inquiries via mobile. The campaign quadrupled consumer loans, while it reduced the cost to reach the target [26].

consider this . . .

FACEBOOK EDGERANK

Facebook's EdgeRank is an algorithm that determines which posts go to the newsfeeds of those who like a brand. EdgeRank evaluates posts based on three factors and sums those factors to determine placements as shown in Equation 9-1, below.

The formula determines to what extent an individual engages with someone else's content, their attitudes toward the content, and other users' interactions with the content [27].

$$\sum U_e W_e D_e$$

U = affinity, W = weight, and D = time decay
Equation 9-1

Another reason for using paid social media to reach customers is to ensure that posts are seen by potential customers. Marketers may think that when they post news, information, and offers on Facebook, all those who "like" the brand will automatically see the information in their newsfeed. However, Facebook controls the newsfeed distribution using its proprietary algorithm, EdgeRank (see the "Consider This . . . Facebook EdgeRank" box); some estimate only about 2% of brand content goes to newsfeeds with 500k or more followers [28]. Running paid advertising on Facebook assures marketers that their content will be shared with their customers.

EXHIBIT 9.8

Top U.S. Social Websites by Total Weekly Visits

	WEEKLY VISITS (IN MILLIONS)	SHARE	PAID PLATFORMS
Facebook	1,645	44%	Newsfeed and domain (right side of the page) ads
YouTube	830	22%	In-display ads (thumbnails of suggested and recommended videos) and in-stream ads (video preroll)
Reddit	204	5%	Self-service campaign dashboard
Twitter	189	5%	Promoted tweets, promoted accounts, and promoted trends
Instagram	62	2%	Sponsored images and video
Pinterest	61	2%	Promoted pins
LinkedIn	55	1%	Profile page, homepage and inbox ads, talent solutions, sales solutions, and targeted status updates. Search results and group ads.
Tumblr	50	1%	Sponsored posts, Radar posts, and trending blogs
Yahoo! Answers	41	1%	Domain ads (right side of page)
Yelp	33	<1%	Yelp ads

http://www.experian.com/marketing-services/online-trends-social-media.html, week of March 19, 2016

consider this . . .

FACEBOOK TREADS ON GOOGLE TERRITORY

Facebook's Atlas platform uses data mined from Facebook users to serve them ads across the Internet on other sites they visit and within mobile applications. Since Facebook has data on people's unique and specific preferences and tastes, the ads can be highly targeted. For instance, Facebook can target fans of particular television shows. Pepsi was one of the earliest adopters of the Atlas service—taking advantage of the opportunity to find Pepsi drinkers [29].

SELF-DIRECTED PAID PLATFORMS

The largest social networks offer advertisers self -directed platforms on which to create and run ads. The advertiser chooses the target market, writes the basic text of the ad, specifies the maximum price the brand will pay for the ad, and indicates where a click on the ad will lead—usually, a website or dedicated landing page. On Facebook and Twitter, advertisers also indicate the goal they wish to achieve and the system recommends particular ad formats. For example, the goals on Twitter are:

Tweet engagements

Website clicks or conversions

App installs or app engagements

Followers

Leads on Twitter

On Google Plus and LinkedIn, advertisers do not specify goals, but instead select target markets from a very specific set. For example, on LinkedIn, marketers can target people based on where they went to school, their specific occupations, and their locations. These options are useful for reaching professional audiences.

The various social networks offer large advertisers more attention, dedicated sales representatives, and specialized products to assist in ad management and delivery. Large advertisers on Facebook, defined as those spending more than $25 a day, receive assistance from Facebook staff. Advertisers can also take advantage of Power Editor, a program that helps manage multiple campaigns on Facebook. Using Power Editor, advertisers can create overall ad campaigns and ad sets within those campaigns to examine separate results and track conversions (by inserting a snippet of code on the webpage). Large advertisers can also negotiate for better page positions and specific types of ad formats.

consider this . . .

FACEBOOK-SPONSORED STORIES

"Sponsored Stories" was a Facebook ad platform that incorporated people who "liked" a brand into actual Facebook advertisements. According to the Facebook terms of service, "liking" a brand gave permission to the marketer to use that person's image in ads aimed at his or her connected friends on Facebook. These stories were controversial because they used an individual's profile picture to promote a product in an ad that the user had not specifically approved. Some Facebook users were very unhappy about lending their names and faces to marketers for promotional purposes. Facebook promoted "Sponsored Stories" to advertisers in this way:

> If someone likes your Page they are saying they are interested in being connected to you and it can be interpreted as an endorsement of your brand or service. People may see when their friends like your Page, but because there is a lot of activity in news feed, they may miss it. When you create sponsored stories, you're increasing the number of people who will learn about you through the actions of their friends. [30]

Eventually, Facebook dropped the service after receiving many complaints from users, but not before calling attention to the fact that Facebook controls people's content.

REVIEW SITES

Another potentially useful set of social platforms for advertising are the various review sites that customers examine to determine which products and services to buy. These sites are attractive to advertisers because viewers are likely seeking to make a purchase when they examine these sites. Exhibit 9.9 lists the most visited review sites in the United States [31], [32], [33].

Advertisers have a strong incentive to encourage reviews, and some companies pay people to write positive reviews. Sites such as TripAdvisor and Yelp have protocols in place to limit false reviews. For example, TripAdvisor requires that reviewers verify their reviews through an email address and that reviewers provide detailed comments. Yelp simply erases reviews that it deems false based on its procedure for identifying fraud. Yelp erases about 20% of the reviews on its platform [34].

Generally speaking, consumers trust other customers more than marketers, so reviews from independent parties can benefit a marketer's business [35]. Reviews are particularly important in service businesses because they address many different aspects of the consumer's experience. Which of the review sites that you visit do you think provide the most credible information? According to a study by Survey Monkey, 28% of respondents trust Google most, 24.9% trust Yelp most, and 16.8% trust Angie's List most [36].

A strategy to consider for building reviews is to ask customers to write the review immediately following the service and ask them to post it online in

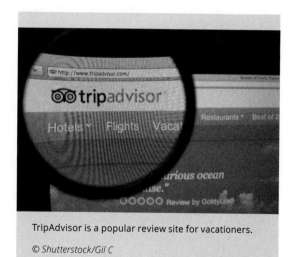

TripAdvisor is a popular review site for vacationers.

© Shutterstock/Gil C

EXHIBIT 9.9

Most Visited Review Sites in the United States

INDUSTRY	SOCIAL REVIEW SITE	NO. OF UNIQUE MONTHLY VISITORS
Travel	TripAdvisor is the largest global travel information and advice site with more than 200 million reviews and opinions, covering hotels and attractions.	315 million
Local	Yelp has over 72 million reviews of local businesses in a variety of cities around the globe.	135 million
Local businesses	Google My Business allows businesses to register with Google, at which point they'll be listed on Google Maps as well as show up in Google search results with extended information and data available at a glance.	Monthly visitors on Google.com: 175,756, 484
Local businesses	Citysearch provides local business listings, user tips, and reviews.	874,030
Local businesses	Angie's List charges a membership fee for users to read and post reviews, though listings are free for companies.	3,905,134
Career	Glassdoor.com is a website that provides information on what it's like to work at a particular company with ratings, reviews, and salaries.	9,448,756
Products	Epinions is a service of Shopping.com, Inc., a provider of comparison shopping services. Epinions covers millions of products and services in over 30 different categories.	352,827

TripAdvisor, "Fact Sheet TripAdvisor," 2015; Yelp, "Overview Press," 2015; Millward Brown, "Compete," 2015.

exchange for a small gift, insider status, or special offer. A marketer must make certain that the customer base will be open to writing reviews and, most important, the business has to deliver the kind of customer service that leads to strong reviews. Of course, offering to address any concerns at that moment might help to reduce the likelihood of negative reviews. This strategy highlights again the importance of an integrated strategy around all four components of the marketing mix. A great YouTube channel or Pinterest page can't make up for poor product or service performance. Each element of the strategy must be strong and contribute to the overall brand image.

consider this . . .

PROGRAMMATIC BUYING, REAL-TIME BIDDING, AND REMARKETING

Marketers can also buy advertising through automated networks, a process known as **programmatic buying**. According to Ad Age, every automated paid media system is considered programmatic buying, including those ads marketers can purchase through Facebook or LinkedIn platforms [38]. In programmatic buying, the price may be managed as an auction, negotiated with advertisers, or fixed at certain levels. The inventory of ads may be reserved, in which advertisers choose particular ad spaces, or unreserved purchased either through an open auction or offered at a fixed price [39].

The most popular type of programmatic buying is called **real-time bidding (RTB)**. Originally, RTB sold remnant advertising inventory that most advertisers did not want, but now the largest publishers offer RTB. In RTB, advertisers set criteria on which customers to target and an advertising network delivers the ads to the requested target market based on the bid amount offered by the brand. The ad networks or exchanges allow advertisers to target individual people in real time to serve an advertisement as a result of a particular customer's action. Before RTB, each person who visited a website, such as Yahoo! Finance, saw the same advertisement. RTB uses customer data to determine people's demographics

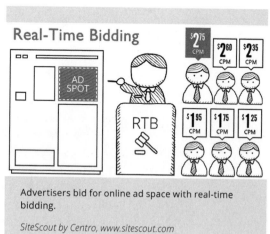

Real-Time Bidding

Advertisers bid for online ad space with real-time bidding.

SiteScout by Centro, www.sitescout.com

and tastes and serves each individual person an ad that is tailored to the data. For example, a 50-year-old premium traveler would see an ad for the luxurious Tauck tours to international destinations, while a 20-year-old athlete would see an ad for a local CrossFit studio, even though they both visited the same website. According to eMarketer, RTB will see double-digit growth through 2017 and represent over 50% of total digital display advertising [40].

Remarketing is a technique for finding customers who have interacted with a brand's website. In remarketing, the marketer serves consumers who visited the site and may or may not have taken certain actions, such as buying a particular item. You have probably been targeted yourself for this type of campaign if you shop online. Have you ever noticed the ads on webpages for items you looked at and did not buy from the online store? For example, Kelly may have put a book into her shopping cart and then abandoned the cart. Amazon can then remarket to Kelly and offer her the book when she visits other websites or send her an email offering a special deal on the book. Google's AdWords platform offers remarketing to advertisers who want to reach those who interacted with their websites through Google's search page or display network. Marketers can also remarket using email by targeting those customers who visited the site and then abandoned their carts.

Both Facebook and Twitter offer paid advertisements to marketers who wish to remarket to people who have visited their websites. A social media site can alert its advertiser partners when a particular user with the partner's cookie visits Facebook or Twitter, so the ad partner can bid to target the user with its ad. The idea is that the user is already favorable toward the marketer as he or she has visited the partner's site, resulting in a cookie being left on the prospect's computer. The marketer may be in a good position to subsequently sell the prospect products or services by showing the person a relevant advertisement.

Programmatic buying and remarketing are also useful tools in mobile paid advertising. Advertisers can buy mobile banners through advertising networks and via RTB platforms to target sites with particular content, such as sports, consumer interests, or specific demographic groups. For example, in mobile RTB, a marketer can target individuals who have searched locally for stores or restaurants and feed them an ad for a hamburger at lunch time. Ideally, the marketer would like to target those people who are receptive to advertising from it at a particular moment in time.

Mobile offers a number of other opportunities for marketers to buy media space. Mobile banner ads can run on the mobile websites of a variety of

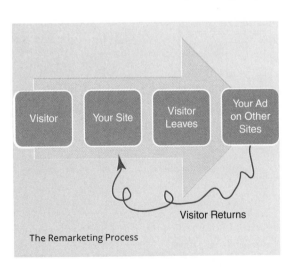

The Remarketing Process

entities, such as TV and movie sites, gaming sites, and information sites like the Weather Channel mobile site. Another avenue for mobile advertising is in-app advertising. Applications designers sell ad space within their apps to outside advertisers. For example, aside from buying an ad on the Weather Channel's mobile website, an advertiser can buy an ad within the Weather Channel app and even specify that it will run the ad only when it is raining in a particular market.

Earned Media

One of the best reasons for a brand to engage on social media is to generate responses from others that reverberate around the Internet and build positive buzz. Earned media refer to efforts by a company to build online conversations that result in positive comments, higher search engine rankings, and potential increased sales of products or services. Earned media consist of comments, shares, and postings by customers and content shared or created by bloggers and traditional news outlets, which may pick up material from brands' social media pages. The material could be in the form of reviews, videos, comments, pins, articles, photographs, or shares and could appear in any social media network, within blogs, on social bookmarking or answer sites, on a video- or photo-sharing site, or elsewhere on the Internet.

Marketers "earn" media because the company doesn't directly pay for ads, but instead people share information about the brand with others through social media. Earned media are similar to public relations in that marketers cannot fully control the content that people share online, but can help generate buzz with their content. As with public relations, earned media are paid for indirectly, but still cost money to execute effectively. Ultimately, the goal is for earned media to work with a brand's paid media and owned media to communicate effectively.

Social media sharing can influence a brand's ranking on search engines. Annually, Searchmetrics examines Google rankings and provides correlation data for the various tactics brands can use to boost their rankings. A correlation is a measure of the degree of relationship between two items. The numbers run from 0 to 100, with higher numbers indicating stronger relationships.

Exhibit 9.10 lists the top eight factors that lead to high rankings on Google's search engine according to Searchmetric's annual survey [41].

EXHIBIT 9.10

Search Metrics Google Rankings Correlation Analysis

	CORRELATION
Click-through rate	.67
Number of website backlinks	.28
Domain visibility	.26
Google+	.31
Facebook	.28
Pinterest	.23
Twitter	.23
Relevant terms	.15

http://www.searchmetrics.com/wp-content/uploads/Ranking_Correlations_EN_print.pdf.

The most important factor that leads to a high ranking is the click-through rate on the link related to the specific search term. When a lot of people click on something, it must mean that it was the "right" answer. The next item is "number of backlinks," the number of other sites that link to a website. The backlinks are a measure of the popularity and quality of a site.

Third is domain visibility, the average ranking for a website by a search engine. The higher the ranking, the more weight the site gets in future rankings for keyword searches. The next four items of the list refer to the social sites that, through sharing, can boost a website's ranking. These social sites include Google+, Facebook, Pinterest, and Twitter. Finally, "relevant terms" are important, suggesting that brands should continue to include terms related to their business in their content [41].

consider this . . .

THE POWER OF "LIKE"

One form of earned media is the buzz associated with Facebook postings. When a brand hosts a Facebook page and a post appears in a person's newsfeed, his or her friends may also see the post. ComScore and Facebook conducted a study to determine the impact of earned media for certain brands. The company divided people into test and control groups, and both fans and friends of fans who were exposed to brand posts increased their purchases by 38% more than those in the control group not exposed to the brand post. A similar research study reported 21% higher sales both in-store and online among the test group exposed to Facebook posts for Target. According to Facebook, 70% of brand campaigns have a 3 to 1 return on investment and almost half have a 5 to 1 return. Of course, this was before Facebook began severely limiting brand content in newsfeeds via EdgeRank [42].

BLOGGER OUTREACH

An important avenue for generating earned media is through bloggers. Brands can reach out to people who write blogs, encouraging the bloggers to write about the brand and share their thoughts with their followers. Bloggers boost earned media by linking to a brand's website and through social sharing. As suggested by Exhibit 9.8, backlinks and social sharing influence Google's search engine rankings.

There are numerous bloggers online who may relate to a brand's business product, location, or target market. Reaching out to bloggers with interesting content they would want to share with their followers can be a useful strategy for reaching the target. Blogs are written by individuals and organizations on a variety of topics. Some of the more popular areas are news, technology, parenting, sports, food, and entertainment (see Exhibit 9.11) [43]. For example, marketers may want to reach out to the mommy bloggers who cover pregnancy and infancy topics. It is a potentially lucrative strategy because new moms buy a lot of stuff in preparation for their baby and what will be needed after his or her birth. These moms take recommendations seriously and are heavy social media and mobile users. According to Nielsen @plan, 81.1% of people expecting a child access the Internet from their cell phones, while only 58.9% of the overall 18+ population does. This target also checks email (70.8%), interacts on social networking sites (63.5%), and buys at Amazon (shopping) [44].

A successful blog strategy relies on interesting content and focuses on the most relevant blogs with strong audiences that match the target. To implement its strategy, a marketer should draft a personalized note to the blogger tailored to the blog's content and tone—recognizing the unique contributions of the blogger—that asks the blogger to use the content if it is of interest. To help ensure that a blogger does publish the requested material, marketers can follow the blogger, comment on the blog, link to the blogger's content on his or her website, retweet tweets from the blog or "like" content and otherwise build a relationship. In addition, the brand should provide the blogger with a fully completed communication with images and videos to make it easy for the blogger to include it within his or her blog. To further sweeten the deal, the brand can offer bloggers exclusivity on information or special opportunities or discounts for the blog's readers.

EXHIBIT 9.11

Top General-Interest U.S. Blogs and Top Mom Blogs

GENERAL BLOGS	MOM BLOGS
Huffington Post	TotallyHer.com
TMZ	Busy-at-Home
Business Insider	Have U Heard
Mashable	Mom Blog Society
Gizmodo	From Dates to Diapers
Lifehacker	MomDot
Gawker	Princess Hairstyles
Daily Beast	Imperfect Parent
TechCrunch	Radical Parenting

consider this . . .

BLOGGERS OR AMBASSADORS?

Another effective strategy for brands is to focus on influencers. When American Express wanted to reach millenials, it decided to sponsor the music festival Coachella and give members prizes and VIP tickets. The brand also turned a set of top Instagramers into #AmexAmbassadors to post photos. The campaign earned 15 million impressions 75x more than those who attended the concert. http://mediakix.com/2016/04/marketing-case-study-coachella-2016/#more-7226

Of course, a blogger may choose to ignore the content or review it in an unfavorable way. This strategy is similar to some public relations efforts with the objective of generating media coverage. The coverage may hurt the brand more than it helps. Marketers should read the blog to see how similar products, brands, and topics are covered.

Bloggers themselves and/or a blogger's organization carry great influence with readers, and an endorsement can be a business builder. Advance research on the blog and blog writers should help mitigate some of the risk in the strategy.

Marketers are not permitted to pay for content to appear on a blog, and bloggers must disclose their brand connections. However, marketers have been successful in dolling out free merchandise and other perks to important bloggers. For example, after hearing the outcry when announcing the company would no longer make plus-sizes readily available, Target invited three leading bloggers to corporate headquarters to review its new AVA and VIV plus-size collection and encourage positive coverage of the brand [46].

SOCIAL NETWORK ENGAGEMENT

Marketers earn media when others share their content. Each social site has different rules of engagement that lead people to participate in the network and share with others. Each brand must determine the best content to achieve the goal and the optimum time and place to post it. Each site has its own features and usage behaviors that brands should research, so their communications fit with the network. However, there are some general guidelines that apply to many of the social sites on which marketers seek to engage audiences [47], [48]:

1. Research the target's usage rates and habits in social media and for the various networks.
2. Post relevant brand-related content.
3. Ask that people "like," "follow," "retweet," "repin," or comment.
4. Question using the terms "who," "what," "where," and "when." Do not ask "why"?
5. Include photos, videos, and links to attract people.
6. Stay active and post regularly, but don't flood the networks.
7. Use hashtags to help people find your content.
8. Choose the most efficient and effective networks to reach the target.

Marketers wishing to engage customers use a variety of techniques in the various social networks. Each network has its own aesthetic, and smart marketers wishing to reach targets using those networks can develop fairly creative strategies. Exhibit 9.12 describes how some marketers have leveraged Instagram [49], Pinterest [50], YouTube [51], and Facebook [52] to build engagement.

EXHIBIT 9.12

Examples of Social Media Engagement Strategies

PLATFORM	METHOD OF ENGAGEMENT	RESULTS
Instagram	European Instagram users uploaded their own photos of the Ford Fiesta with the hashtag #Fiestagram on Instagram and the global Ford Fiesta Facebook page. Judges chose the best photos as winners and gave out small prizes.	People posted 16,000 photos and Ford earned 120,000 new Facebook fans in Europe.
Pinterest	Elephantine is a jewelry brand on the popular art product site Etsy. Rachel Ball, the owner, increased traffic by pinning her new products to her Pinterest boards when listing them for sale at Etsy.	Since using Pinterest, Rachel's average weekly page views grew 22% and weekly sales increased 20%.
YouTube	Activision, the manufacturer of video games such as Call of Duty, Destiny, and Skylander, uses YouTube to engage and entertain its audience.	Activision became the no. one gaming video franchise on YouTube, with over 2 million subscribers to its channels and half a million video views.
Facebook	One of the first Facebook Timeline campaigns ran in Israel with the anti-drug message "Drugs Set Your Timeline." The campaign developed by McCann Erickson featured a fictional drug addict Adam Barak and his dual lives as a drug addict and non-addict in a split-section design.	In 8 days, the campaign earned 70,000 tweets, but was shut down by Facebook because it violated the terms of service. Adam Barak used his own profile page for the visuals and presented fictitious scenes.

consider this . . .

VIRAL VIDEO ACCIDENT

Video and photographic images are strong potential marketing tools. The vivid nature of both forms of media provides a way for a brand to tell a story in a short period of time that requires little active effort on the part of the viewer. A **viral video** is one that has been widely shared across the Internet and is viewed by many people. A few early adopters of YouTube for communications have benefited from viral campaigns. In most cases, the level of success was purely accidental, and in some cases, the brand was not even responsible for the effort. For example, consider the viral video of Diet Coke fountains in the air fueled by Mentos that was created by professional juggler Fritz Grobe and his friend Steven Voltz at a show in Buckfield, Maine. Mentos was thrilled with the experiment, while Coca-Cola initially indicated that it would prefer people to drink Diet Coke rather than experiment with the beverage. Since that time, Coke has embraced the video and posted it on the company website along with other user-generated content [53].

SUMMARY AND REVIEW

CHAPTER SUMMARY

Brands invest in paid, owned, and social media in order to generate online responses to boost search engine rankings. By creating strong shareable content, brand managers can achieve a number of important goals, such as engagement, brand awareness, and even sales. By understanding the target's use of social media and interaction with content and by tracking the results of customer engagement, marketers can improve their communications efforts.

KEY TERMS

application protocol
   interface (API)
earned media

owned media
paid media
programmatic buying

real-time bidding
   (RTB)
remarketing

social networks
viral video

SUMMARY REVIEW QUESTIONS

1. Define the terms paid, owned, social, and earned media.
2. How do paid, owned, and social media work together to influence earned media?
3. What is an open API? Which social media platforms have open APIs?
4. List three potential goals for brands.
5. Why do marketers use paid media?
6. What is the difference between programmatic buying and real-time bidding?
7. Explain how a firm can use remarketing to enhance a communications strategy.
8. Give two reasons why blogging is important for brands.
9. What is EdgeRank and what is its purpose?
10. The Power of Like study was done in 2012. Given what you have read in this chapter, would the results of the study still hold for brands seeking engagement today? Explain.

APPLICATION QUESTIONS

1. Choose two direct competitors and examine their blogs. Which blog has better content? Evaluate the strength of the two blogs by looking at the quality and quantity of comments.
2. Choose one social network and describe the paid advertising opportunities on the site.
3. Does VKontakte, the Russian social media site, offer paid advertising? What forms of it?
4. Do a Google search for refrigerators by typing into the search bar "buy a new refrigerator." Now, go to three other websites and examine the ads on those sites. What ads appear? Have the ads identified you as a prospect for a new fridge?
5. You are a marketer for a brand of honey roasted pecans. Locate a blogger who writes in this area and compose an email requesting him or her to

post something about your new flavor: Salty Sweet Maple. What aspects of your letter will help convince the blogger to cover your product? What else can you do to encourage him or her to write about your new product?

6. Go to LinkedIn advertising and determine what factors you can use to target people at the site.

7. Go to either Facebook or Twitter and describe one case study on the site that uses paid media to drive a response. What did the brand do and what were the results?

8. Choose a brand and evaluate the brand's social media strategy. What metrics can you use to determine effectiveness? Do all metrics indicate success?

9. What is the difference between programmatic buying, real time bidding and remarketing? Give a clear example of each.

10. What are the steps in the integrated marketing communications process? Give an example of a brand that has an integrated strategy.

11. What is a creative brief and why is it important? Show an example of a brief and the resulting campaign. Does the brief match the campaign and was it a success?

case study aden + anais

aden + anais
made for baby. Designed for you.

Baby products company aden + anais was founded in July 2006 by Raegan Moya-Jones, an Australian business executive, who had moved to the United States. When Raegan had her first child in 2003, she was unable to find muslin swaddles, a product that was popular in Australia for wrapping babies comfortably to promote sound sleep. Moya-Jones decided to design and distribute high-quality, attractively designed muslin swaddles to fill a unique niche market.

By 2014 aden + anais was selling in 7,000 stores in 65 countries and online through various retailers and its own website [54]. The signature product was the muslin swaddle, a large cotton blanket made of thin breathable material designed with bold colors and designs. Other items in the line included: bibs and burp cloths, sleep sacks, blankets, towel and wash cloth sets. In 2012 aden + anais launched a skin-care line called mum + bub, and in 2014 the company started selling clothing made from rayon derived from bamboo [55].

The market was strong for aden + anais as the baby product industry was growing by 3% in the United States and Australia and 1% in the United Kingdom. Experts believed that the market was relatively impervious to economic fluctuations because mothers in developed countries earned their own incomes and did not skimp on baby items. The products were also well suited for gift giving by grandparents, other family members, and friends.

THE TARGET MARKET

The primary target market was first-time and expecting mothers who were 25 to 45 with incomes over $40,000 per year. According to Simmons OneView, there were 4.5 million women in the United States with a child under 2 years old and an income over $40,000, and 6.5 million expectant mothers in this income

Social Media Site Indices for Mothers

INDEX FOR VISITED SITE IN PAST 30 DAYS	EXPECTANT MOTHERS	MOTHERS WITH CHILDREN UNDER 2
Facebook	112	139
Google	82	125
Twitter	125	234
YouTube	83	132

Simmons OneView, 2010

bracket. Mothers were particularly active online and in social media (see Exhibit 9.13). The chart shows indices based on usage of certain websites among expectant mothers and mothers of children under age 2 with incomes over $40k [56].

INTEGRATED MARKETING COMMUNICATIONS STRATEGY

The company used owned, paid, and social media to communicate with mothers; as a result, it earned additional media impressions through social sharing. Aden + anais found that women shared information on pregnancy, birth, and childrearing and also pictures of cute babies and baby products. However, there were many competing outlets for this type of content online.

Aden + anais's social media strategy included a Facebook page, Twitter feed, and some YouTube videos, but the company was not leveraging those media opportunities to build strong engagement among customers or raise its search engine rankings in key categories to drive sales.

In spite of the little time and effort spent on advertising, the company had a loyal following and a number of celebrity customers, some of whom were photographed with their babies and aden + anais products. The website featured a press section that pointed to articles on aden + anais that had appeared in major baby magazines, such as *Baby, American Baby, Parenting, Family, Child, Parent & Child,* and *Pregnancy.* Another section featured celebrities and their babies with aden + anais blankets, including the stars Owen Wilson, Amy Poehler, Kourtney Kardashian, Sandra Bullock, Adam Sandler, Ashley Simpson, Gwen Stefani, Jennifer Garner, Jason Priestley, and Neil Patrick Harris.

The company did some limited traditional advertising in magazines, but relied heavily on word of mouth and retail exposure to drive sales. Originally, the digital strategy was very limited, but the company eventually hired a digital marketing manager and began to build its content offering online, which led to more sharing among members of the target.

Though a Google search for the company name brought the website to the top of the rankings, the other terms associated with the product category, such as "swaddles," "baby blankets," "baby wraps," or "baby fashions," did not lead to high rankings for aden + anais. However, some of the brand's retailers bid for these keywords and paid advertising drove hits to retail sites where aden + anais was sold among other brands of baby items.

According to Alexa, about 30% of traffic to the aden + anais site came from Google, with some traffic (less than 5%) originating from Facebook.

COMPETITORS IN THE SWADDLE MARKET

Competitors in the U.S. market were JJ Cole, Little Giraffe, and SwaddleDesigns. They sold similar lines of products in the United States with comparable price points. JJ Cole was a subsidiary of TOMY, a large public company with strong marketing muscle, while the other brands were small companies with small budgets for promotion [57].

In October 2012 the social media landscape for the competitors in the U.S. market included Facebook, YouTube, and Twitter. Exhibit 9.14 enumerates the competitors and their social media metrics in 2012, and Exhibit 9.15 shows the competition in April 2015.

EXHIBIT 9.14

Social Media Metrics, 2012

	FACEBOOK LIKES	YOUTUBE VIDEOS	YOUTUBE VIDEO VIEWS	TWITTER TWEETS	TWITTER FOLLOWERS
aden + anais	25,950	11	27,153	311	6,287
JJ Cole	23,742	55	384,809	1,297	5,523
Little Giraffe	5,718	6	632	725	2,745
SwaddleDesigns	16,997	5	4,321	11,586	4,843

www.facebook.com; www.Youtube.com; www.twitter.com

EXHIBIT 9.15

Social Media Metrics, 2015

	FACEBOOK LIKES	YOUTUBE VIDEOS	YOUTUBE VIDEO VIEWS	TWITTER TWEETS	TWITTER FOLLOWERS	PINTEREST PINS	PINTEREST FOLLOWERS
aden + anais	112,989	15	122,914	5,245	25.9k	1,924	9,675
JJ Cole	48,298	75	1,326,016	1,675	9,629	1,253	1,928
Little Giraffe	45,562	13	5,724	3,069	7,337	3,098	2,959
SwaddleDesigns	74,238	5	23,313	17k	8,420	889	1,349

www.facebook.com; www.youtube.com; www.twitter.com; www.pinterest.com.

CONSIDERED GOALS FOR ADEN + ANAIS'S DIGITAL STRATEGY

There were a few different goals the company considered:

1. Increase brand awareness within the target market.
2. Drive an increase in unique visitors to the aden + anais website.
3. Increase engagement on social media.
4. Improve the search engine ranking of the brand for keywords.
5. Build online conversations for the aden + anais brand and earned media.
6. Drive online sales.

POTENTIAL STRATEGIES

Aden + anais faced a number of potential opportunities that could be leveraged to help reach its goals. The problem was that the company was unsure as to which goals it should pursue and which strategies would be most effective in generating the desired outcomes. There were a few strategies that could achieve some of the goals:

- Use promotional offerings in social media.
- Reach out to bloggers to encourage them to feature and talk about aden + anais products.
- Build online customer engagement through social media to generate positive emotional connections with new mothers.
- Develop more content, including blogs, videos, articles, and reviews.
- Invest in search engine optimization.
- Buy Google AdWords for key search terms in the category.

Many of the strategies could improve search engine rankings, increase the amount of online buzz surrounding the brand, connect with customers, and ultimately lead to sales. The main hurdle was how to achieve the goals on a limited budget of $25,000.

Aden +anais had a solid business both in its stores and online, but wanted to grow. The brand emphasized its retail strategy and was able to grow the business in stores around the world. However, the digital strategy was also important and the brand had to determine which goals to set and how to achieve them within the limited budget.

QUESTIONS FOR DISCUSSION

1. Evaluate aden + anais's considered goals for its digital strategy using the criteria for effective goals: measurable, time specific and reachable.
2. Rewrite each goal with a performance measure and a specific time frame to strengthen the goal and make it measurable.
3. Using information from the case study, give two examples of paid, owned, and social media for aden + anais. Go online and find two examples of earned media for the brand.
4. Consider the potential strategies that aden + anais developed and the goals outlined here in the "Considered Goals" section. Some of these strategies might work to achieve a number of the goals identified. Match each strategy to a specific goal. How would the strategy achieve the goal to which you matched it?
5. Which combination of paid, owned, and social media would you recommend for the brand? Explain.

6. Evaluate the social media strategy of aden + anais relative to that of its competitors. Which platforms were most effective for driving engagement between 2012 and 2015?

7. Examine aden + anais's content and determine why the company metrics changed between 2012 and 2015. On which social media sites did the brand rely and was this effective? What other factors could have contributed to the changes?

REFERENCES

[1] J. Garside, "Facebook Loses Millions of Users as Biggest Markets Peak," *The Guardian,* 29 April 2013, http://www.theguardian.com/technology/2013/apr/28/facebook-loses-users-biggest-markets.

[2] C. Delo, "By 2017 India to Boast the Most Facebook Users—By Far," *Advertising Age,* 9 May 2013.

[3] The Times of India, "With 243 Million Users by 2014, India to Beat US in Internet Reach: Study," 14 November 2014.

[4] S. Kemp, "Social Media Around the World," We Are Social, June 2014.

[5] Mindshift Interactive, "Kiehl's India Social Media Case Study," 27 December 2011, http://www.slideshare.net/MindShiftInteractive/kiehls-india-case-study.

[6] J. Garside, "Facebook Loses Millions of Users as Biggest Markets Peak," The Guardian, 28 April 2013.

[7] Engauge, "Unwrap the Perfect Reeslationship," 2015.

[8] S. Corcoran, "Defining Earned, Owned and Paid Media," Forrester Blog, December 2009.

[9] V. Beal, "Application Program Interface," webopedia, 13 October 2014.

[10] D. Zarrella, *The Science of Marketing,* Hoboken, NJ: Wiley, 2013.

[11] J. Lee, "No. 1 Position in Google Gets 33% of Results," Search Engine Watch, 20 June 2013.

[12] J. Loechner, "First Position Ads Dominate Click Throughs," MediaPost, 9 October 2014.

[13] S. Hall, "Why the Blog Post Is the New Ad Unit," Hub Spot, 3 April 2013.

[14] D. Boyd and N. B. Ellison, "Social Network Sites: Definition, History and Scholarship," *Journal of Computer-Mediated Communication,* vol. 13, no. 1, pp. 210–230, 2007.

[15] Wikipedia, "Criticism of Coca-Cola," 31 August 2015, https://en.wikipedia.org/wiki/Criticism_of_Coca-Cola.

[16] We Are Social, "Social Media Use," January 2015, http://wearesocial.net/blog/2015/01/digital-social-mobile-worldwide-2015/.

[17] S. Kemp, "Global Social Media Users Pass 2 Billion," 8 August 2014, http://wearesocial.net/blog/2014/08/global-social-media-users-pass-2-billion/.

[18] TS. Kemp, "2016 Digital Yearbook," We Are Social, Jannuary 28, 2016, http://www.slideshare.net/wearesocialsg/2016-digital-yearbook.

[19] A. Lau, "Magna Global: 12 Facts on Digital Advertising in China," 16 February 2014, http://www.clickz.com/clickz/news/2328886/magna-global-12-facts-on-digital-advertising-in-china.

[20] Incitez China, "482M Chinese Visited Social Media Per Month in 2015," China Internet Watch, 9 March, 2016, http://www.chinainternetwatch.com/17191/481-5-million-chinese-social-media-month-2015/#ixzz441o5vhth.

[21] I. Fernandes, "Vkontakte Is Facebook's Formidable Rival in Russia," *Advertising Age,* 12 June 2012.

[22] Experian, "Experian Marketing Services Hitwise," Week of March 19th, 2016. http://www.experian.com/marketing-services/online-trends-social-media.html.

[23] C. Rudder, "We Experiment on Human Beings," OkCupid Blog, 28 July 2014.

[24] C. Rudder, "Race and Attraction, 2009–2014," OkTrends, 10 September 2014.

[25] 360 Degree Content Marketing, "Charles Schwab Case Study," 2013, http://www.slideshare.net/imediaconnection/case-study-360degree-content-marketing-integrating-paid-owned-earned-media-to-earn-consumer-trust-26172447.

[26] Google, "ING Bank Turkey's Mobile-First Strategy and AdWords Campaign Help Quadruple Consumer Loan Sales," September 2014, http://www.thinkwithgoogle.com/case-studies/ing-bank-turkeys-mobile-first-strategy-and-adwords-campaign-help-quadruple-consumer-loan-sales.html.

[27] P. Vaughan, "Demystifying How Facebook's EdgeRank Algorithm Works," Hubspot, 23 April 2013.

[28] DeMers, J. "Why Your Organic Facebook Reach is Still Falling," Forbes, May 13, 2015.http://www.forbes.com/sites/jaysondemers/2015/05/13/why-your-organic-facebook-reach-is-still-falling-and-what-to-do-about-it/#a48e62a2c84b.

[29] V. Goel, "With New Ad Platform, Facebook Opens Gates to Its Vault of User Data," *The New York Times,* 28 September 2014.

[30] Facebook, "Facebook Help," 2012.

[31] TripAdvisor, "Fact Sheet TripAdvisor," 2015.

[32] Yelp, "Overview Press," 2015.

[33] Millward Brown, "Compete," 2015.

[34] New York Times Blog, "Yelp Fights Fake Reviews with Shaming," *The New York Times,* 18 October 2012.

[35] D.-H. Park, J. Lee, and H. Ingoo, "The Effect of Online Consumer Reviews on Consumer Purchasing Intention: The Moderating Role of Involvement," *International Journal of Electronic Commerce,* vol. 11, no. 4, Summer 2007.

[36] Survey Monkey, "Which Review Sites Do People Trust the Most?," 2 February 2015.

[37] Reddit, "International Anti-Poaching Federation," September 2014.

[38] T. Peterson and A. Kantrowitz, "The CMO's Guide to Programmatic Buying," Advertising Age, 19 May 2014. http://adage.com/article/digital/cmo-s-guide-programmatic-buying/293257/.

[39] C. Kalapesi, "Programmatic and Automation—The Publisher's Perspective," Internet Advertising Bureau, 2013.

[40] eMarketer, "Programmatic Direct Takes Majority of Programmatic Dollars," September 28, 2015. http://www.emarketer.com/Article/Programmatic-Direct-Takes-Majority-of-Programmatic-Ad-Dollars/1013035.

[41] Search Metrics, "Search Metrics 2015 SEO Rank Correlations and Ranking Factors," 2015. http://www.searchmetrics.com/knowledge-base/ranking-factors-2014/.

[42] comScore, "comScore and Facebook Release Research Paper: The Power of Like 2: How Social Marketing Works," 11 June 2012.

[43] Blog Rank, "A List of Top Parenting Blogs by Monthly Visitors," 2015.

[44] Nielsen, "Nielsen @plan Q1 2014," 2014.

[45] R. V. Kozinets, K. de Valck, A. C. Wojnicki, and S. J. Wilner, "Networked Narratives: Understanding Word of Mouth Marketing in Online Communities," *Journal of Marketing,* vol. 74, pp. 71–89, March 2010.

[46] L. Dormehl, "Plus-Size Bloggers Invited by Target to Help Critique New Clothing Line," Fast Company, 21 January 2015.

[47] M. Creamer, "Facebook to Brands: You're Posting Stuff Wrong," *Advertising Age,* 7 May 2012.

[48] M. Miller, "Twitter Posting for Best Practices," Search Engine Watch, 8 June 2012.

[49] D. Klamm, "How Ford Used Instagram to Promote the Fiesta's High Tech Features," Mashable, 2 February 2012.

[50] Pinterest, "Etsy Success Story," *Pinterest Case Study,* 2015.

[51] Google, "How Activision Reached over 2M Subscribers on YouTube," *Think with Google,* Octobe 2014.

[52] D. Shamah, "Anti-Drug Message Received Despite Facebook Profile Shutdown," *Times of Israel,* 13 March 2012.

[53] R. King, "The Diet Coke and Mentos Explosion," *Business Week,* 16 January 2007.

[54] M. Overfelt, "No. 30 Aden and Anais," *Crain's New York Business,* 12 October 2014.

[55] aden + anais, 13 April 2015, https://www.adenandanais.com/.

[56] Simmons OneView, 2010,

[57] JJ Cole, 2015, http://jjcolecollections.com/.

CHAPTER TEN

INTEGRATING MEDIA

The number of media vehicles has grown exponentially over the past few years with paid digital joining traditional advertising media options. Marketing managers use integrated marketing communications strategies consisting of a mix of media to communicate effectively with target markets. Sometimes using multiple channels helps marketers reach the fragmented consumer audience or results in more efficient media purchases. Marketers must allocate budgets to various elements of the communications plans to successfully achieve goals. This chapter outlines the research in multimedia synergy, compares digital and traditional media formats, and discusses how social media and mobile technology can enhance a traditional brand communication strategy.

LEARNING OBJECTIVES

After reading this chapter, you will be able to:

- EXAMINE BUDGETING FOR AN ADVERTISING COMMUNICATIONS STRATEGY.

- DETERMINE APPROPRIATE MEDIA VEHICLES FOR CAMPAIGN MESSAGES.

- COMPARE AND CONTRAST DIGITAL AND TRADITIONAL MEDIA FORMATS.

- LEARN DIGITAL AND TRADITIONAL MEDIA PLANNING AND BUYING TERMS.

- EVALUATE MEDIA VEHICLES BASED ON REACH, FREQUENCY, AND COST.

- INTEGRATE DIGITAL AND TRADITIONAL MEDIA STRATEGIES TO MAXIMIZE MESSAGE EFFECTIVENESS.

- IDENTIFY METHODS FOR ENHANCING COMMUNICATIONS WITH SOCIAL MEDIA AND MOBILE TECHNOLOGY.

Do you know where Red Bull, the energy drink, originated? If you don't know, it may be because you think the drink was created for you by marketers who really understand you and your friends. Red Bull does a great job of connecting with the young, hip target of urban risk-taking guys who stay out late and love extreme sports. Red Bull has created television programming (*No Limits* on ESPN), movies (*That's It, That's All*), a documentary on snowboarding shown in theaters (*The Art of Flight*), magazines and inserts (*Red Bull Bulletin*), and tons of online video content featuring snowboarders, sports cars, surfing, cliff diving, and concerts. The brand sponsors Formula 1 drivers, a NASCAR team, four sports teams, and a set of vintage performing airplanes, the Flying Bulls [1]. The entire plan is integrated around the theme "Red Bull gives you wings," the brand's tag line. Using a content-driven strategy, the brand is all over the Internet, has a strong social media presence, and utilizes mobile marketing to build the brand image. At one point, Red Bull was sued over its famous tag line because the complainant claimed that the energy drink did not provide benefits beyond an average cup of coffee, while the advertising promised more. The brand chose to settle and continues to build on its "wings" theme [2].

Red Bull's CEO Dietrich Mateschitz says, "As a major content provider, it is our goal to communicate and distribute the 'World of Red Bull' in all major media segments, from TV to print to new media to our music record label" [1]. Though the statement is very media-driven and less about connecting with customers, it highlights the brand's desire to be front and center in the target's daily activities.

Red Bull engages customers through an integrated marketing communications plan that includes a variety of media formats to reach consumers at times of the day when they might consider drinking a Red Bull. The brand uses mobile to increase the time frame for engaging with customers since the drink is often consumed outside the home. One such campaign, "Red Bull Crashed Ice" launched in Toronto, Quebec, and Montreal, encouraged registrations for an event and loyalty program using multiple media vehicles. Fans could register through a QR code, social networking sites, email, clicks on banner ads, or via text message. By using multiple media formats, Red Bull provided customers with more opportunities to connect at times that were appropriate for them, sometimes on the go. Red Bull's Canadian partner Tagga reported that 10% of registrations occurred via mobile devices and 27% of total registrants engaged with mobile at some point during the "Crashed Ice" campaign [3].

If you are still wondering about the origins of Red Bull, it was first created and sold in Thailand as a

Red Bull's strategy includes daredevil flying and "gives you wings."

© *Shutterstock/Sergey Kohl*

non-carbonated drink called Krating Daeng, which means "water buffalo" in Thai. When Dietrich Mateschitz tasted it on a trip to Thailand in 1982, he approached Thai businessman Cheleo Yoovidhya, the distributor, and the two men began a partnership. The brand was introduced to the Austrian market in 1987 and then to the Hungarian market. Red Bull entered the U.S. market in the 1990s, and the United States represents about a quarter of worldwide sales.

Mateschitz, who is now over 70, still runs the privately held business in spite of efforts by Coca-Cola and others to buy the company. The product is sold in over 150 countries around the world with the same basic integrated message and is now the best-selling energy drink globally, with revenues of over $5 billion [4].

Red Bull's presence in multiple forms of media represents a trend by companies to engage consumers in a variety of ways as the market has become more fragmented. Before the Internet, marketers could reach large percentages of the population by advertising during network prime-time television. But over the years, the network audiences shrunk as people began consuming programming elsewhere, first on cable television and later online. Now in many countries, television viewing is down, while Internet search, social media, and mobile content consumption are up. Advertisers seeking to reach these audiences have naturally gravitated toward the new formats. The challenge for marketers is to determine when, where, and how to communicate best with target markets in the most efficient, cost-effective way.

BUILDING AN INTEGRATED BRAND COMMUNICATIONS STRATEGY

This chapter discusses how marketers can integrate traditional and digital media to achieve their communications objectives. The advertising environment has always been crowded and marketers have long struggled to get people to pay attention to their ads. Now that people have smartphones with them at all times, there are new opportunities and challenges in reaching consumers. On the plus side, marketers can communicate with many new platforms, often using one-to-one communications to interact with targets at moments when they may be considering purchases. The challenge is to integrate the message across many different forms of media that consumers watch, read, hear, and search, sometimes at the same time.

Unfortunately, our knowledge of people's multitasking, multimedia interactions, and consumer behavior in the relatively new social media and mobile environment is limited. We don't know how consumers behave in multichannel environments, how organizations will change based on new media relationships,

EXHIBIT 10.1

Questions on Multichannel Consumer Behavior

LIMITATION	QUESTION
Knowledge of multichannel consumer behavior	Do consumers attend more to television advertisements or tablet ads when multitasking? How do consumers use interactive magazines differently from print magazines?
Internal organizational structure and politics	Who should manage the online, social media, and mobile strategy development and execution for the brand? What are our human resource needs to execute a communications strategy in the digital space?
Communications timing to optimize the customer experience	Are consumers more likely to use a mobile coupon when it is delivered at the point of sale or a Web coupon delivered prior to purchase? When are consumers receptive to text messaging, email, or other media formats?

or how to optimize the timing of communications. Exhibit 10.1 lists some questions marketers may ask in order to improve their integrated marketing communications plans.

Over the past few years, marketers have increased their spending in digital media, while reducing their budgets for traditional media. The annual CMO Survey of 351 top marketers in the Fortune 1,000, Forbes top 200 companies, and the American Marketing Association database found that companies planned to increase digital spending by 10.8%, while reducing traditional media spending by 3.6% [5].

The CMO Survey suggests that many top marketers have significantly increased digital media expenditures. Exhibit 10.2 shows the percentage of unmeasured media spending for certain brands in the United States during a one-year period. The Ad Age Data Center reports media spending in 10 media categories for the top 200 leading national advertisers [6]. Increasingly, Ad Age estimates that firms are spending more on unmeasured media, which include direct marketing, promotion, Internet paid search, and social media.

At this point, you may be thinking that brands should spend their entire budgets in digital and not use traditional media such as television, newspapers, outdoor, radio, or magazines at all. However, there are many reasons to still consider traditional media for executing communications strategy.

EXHIBIT 10.2

Estimated Unmeasured Media Spending

COMPANY	PERCENTAGE OF U.S. UNMEASURED MEDIA SPENDING RELATIVE TO TOTAL MEDIA SPENDING
McDonald's	34%
Amazon	77%
P&G	31%
JP Morgan	79%
IBM	70%

Source: Advertising Age, *"100 Leading National Advertisers," Ad Age Data Center, 2014.*

1. Reach. Reach is the number of people exposed to a message; sometimes, reach is higher in traditional media than digital for certain goals. For example, a study by The Futures Company and the Television Bureau of Advertising (TVB) found that TV commercials drove the highest levels of brand awareness in the automotive category, relative to other forms of media. The study also found that the Internet, especially blogs and review sites, was important to consumers' brand consideration process, but less so than television [7]. A study by the Interactive Advertising Bureau (IAB) found that when brands combined television advertising and digital video advertising, their reach went up by 3.6% for consumer packaged goods and over 6% for other categories such as technology, automotive, and finance. At the same time, the cost per thousand, the amount advertisers spend to reach 1,000 people, declined from $13.82 to $12.31 [8].

2. Target. Certain target markets may interact with traditional media more frequently than digital and may be better persuaded by the familiar formats. Some targets, such as your grandparents, use social media at much lower than average rates. Some people simply don't have access to mobile devices or tablets. A study of consumers in the United States, European Union, and Asia Pacific region asked people which sources they believed were best for marketing and advertising. Forty-seven percent of global customers said traditional media [9]. Even when targets are heavy users of social media, there may be backlash against advertising. Young men have been shown to resent advertising shown during online streaming television more than advertising shown on traditional television media [10].

3. Efficiency. In some cases, traditional media can be more efficient in terms of the amount spent versus the number of people who are reached by a communication. Exhibit 10.3 shows the cost per thousand (CPM) to reach people with video communications. As you can see, some forms of traditional broadcast media, such as day-time, outperform Internet media on a CPM basis for delivering video content [11].

4. Wear-Out. Over time, the effectiveness of an advertisement may diminish. Some research suggests that ads lose their impact the more viewers see them

Cost per Thousand for Video Commercials

VIDEO COMMERCIALS BY PLATFORM	COST PER THOUSAND
Broadcast Daytime	$6.50
Early news	$9.00
Primetime	$19.00
Late evening	$17.50
Syndication Daytime	$5.50
Early fringe	$9.25
Prime access	$17.00
Late fringe	$11.60
Cable Channels Daytime	$3.30
Fringe	$7.55
Primetime	$9.85
Internet Untargeted video	$9.25
Targeted video	$32.75

Source: The Media Book, *Copyright © 2014 Media Dynamics, Inc.*

because people stop attending to familiar messages. Using a variety of media formats, such as radio, print, and digital, may help provide a novel context for a message and increase people's attention levels. In the past, television advertisers limited the number of times viewers saw a commercial to between five and eight exposures over a four-week period. However, advertising repetition is important to build consumer memory for messages [12], and some research does suggest that marketers can intervene to prevent wear-out by varying the execution even when sticking with the same effective messages [13]. For example, a study of Internet advertising found that varying the creative content of Internet ads led to higher conversions for e-commerce sites [14].

5. Clutter. The number of ads aimed at consumers in digital continues to grow, and consumers may start to become overloaded with competitive ads in the same media space. On television, advertising pods of commercials shown during commercial breaks are cluttered with competing messages, leading certain viewers to misidentify brands. Since advertisers in a particular category target similar demographic groups, the brands cluster their ads in the same media spaces. The more individual messages that reach people affect their perceptions of how much advertising exists. For example, if people watch ten minutes of advertising, viewing ten 60-second spots, they will perceive less overall advertising clutter than if they see twenty 30-second spots. As such, the more ads to which people are exposed, the more they will feel bombarded by messages. Also, when there are many directly competitive ads, people have trouble separating the individual brand messages and confuse brands in recall tasks [15]. Smart marketers can use social and mobile media to reach targets without the presence of competitive messages.

6. Synergy. People may respond differently to various media formats, and a mix of media may lead to better results for brands. Researchers refer to the added benefits accrued through additional media formats as **multimedia synergy**: when you use more than one form of media to communicate with a target, the benefits may be greater than when you use only one medium. The idea is that people may respond differently to executions in different formats, so using more than one might achieve more brand goals, thereby enhancing their overall response For example, people may engage with the brand on social media by consuming content, but respond to a coupon via email and purchase. Multiple strategies working together to achieve brand goals have long been part of marketing communications. In fact, even the theory of marketing mix suggests that the four P's operate in tandem to create an image for a brand. In one study, Naik and Rahman found that adding a second media format, such as print, to a television campaign enhanced message effectiveness for Levi's Dockers brand [16].

7. International Targets. In some markets, traditional media may be a better strategy for reaching the local population. In the developing world, people have access to television media even if they share televisions or watch screens in public spaces. Most developing countries do not have high-speed Internet lines and rely on mobile Internet connections, which can be slow or hard to access on older devices. As such, reaching consumers in traditional media may be a more efficient strategy than attempting to connect online or through social networks.

IS ADVERTISING SPENDING JUSTIFIED?

Is there evidence beyond anecdotal that firms which spend more on communications reap financial returns? Advertising and promotional spending has been found to positively affect the market value of a firm [21], [22]. One study found that companies which drop from the top 20% of media expenditures in the industry to the bottom 20% of industry spending decrease their return by almost 5% in the first year and more than 80% over twenty years [23]. The benefits of advertising accrue even during a recession, with a positive impact on future earnings [24].

Some studies of **advertising elasticity**, the percentage change in sales relative to an increase in advertising spending, have shown that advertising effectiveness has decreased over the years. In an examination of fifty-six studies of advertising, the estimate of the overall advertising elasticity for print, television, and aggregate media was .12, meaning that a 1% increase in advertising spending resulted in a .12% average increase in sales. Prior research had shown that advertising elasticity was .22, but these figures have fallen since the 1980s. The conventional explanation for this is that the media environment is more cluttered and fewer messages break through [26]. In general, advertising elasticities are higher for durable goods than nondurable, hedonic (pleasurable) versus utilitarian (functional) goods, and in earlier rather than mature lifecycle stages [27].

Though the research above does not specify social media or mobile advertising as direct influencers of market value, general advertising spending can lead to positive firm results. Since building brand value is one goal of social and mobile advertising, the influence is likely to be positive as well.

BUDGETING FOR MARKETING COMMUNICATIONS

One of the early decisions marketers must make in planning a communications strategy is to determine how much money to spend. Advertisers use different methods for determining advertising spending.

METHODS FOR DETERMINING AD BUDGETS

The most common method for budgeting for advertising is called the **percentage of sales method**; advertisers multiply past or anticipated sales by a certain percentage to determine appropriations. The percentage of sales method is popular because it is easy to execute and prevents overspending. To give you an idea of overall spending levels, according to the annual CMO Survey, firms spend about 8% of their revenues on marketing expenses; B2C firms spend more on marketing as a percentage of revenues than B2B firms [5].

The percentage of sales method, while simple, may not position a brand for the future because it relies on past results. In another advertising budgeting method called **objective and task**, marketers set goals and spend the amount of money required to achieve those goals [17]. In this method, advertisers determine the number of people they would like to reach with their communications and estimate how much that will cost. The budget reflects the costs associated with buying media and creating messaging. For example, the Bulgarian bank UniCredit wanted to reach 30% of the country's total population. The brand determined that 83% of Bulgarians over 18 used Facebook and budgeted to reach them. To do so, UniCredit purchased nine bursts of advertising on Facebook newsfeeds and used a Facebook advertising buy, that guaranteed reaching the entire population. Those expenditures represented the budget for its campaign [18].

Another very commonly used method of budgeting for advertising is **competitive parity**, or spending at levels similar to those of competitors [19]. Sometimes, competitors copy spending levels, target markets, and communications strategies. However, a brand will probably generate better revenues by evaluating strategies instead of guessing competitive actions. How much to spend on strategy is an important decision for firms to make that is often ignored as marketers jump into the next hot social media or mobile tool. For example, as you will see in Chapter Twelve, General Motors continues to rely on traditional media and YouTube commercials to sell cars, while Ford has a strong Facebook presence. GM's decision may be beneficial since automobile brands typically go after a similar demographic group; using different media vehicles may reduce competitive clutter in the automobile market.

MAKING THE MEDIA BUDGET DECISION

The decision of how much to spend on traditional media versus digital depends on the business and how consumers interact with the various forms of media when considering purchases or engaging with brands. Clearly, marketers have been voting with their ad spending dollars, increasing spending in digital media and decreasing spending in traditional format such as magazines and newspapers. While, as we learned in Chapter One, television remains the medium with the highest level of global spending, Internet ad spending, which includes social and mobile media, continues to grow as marketers shift dollars to online ad spending.

Marketers have noticed that people are increasing the amount of time spent with social and mobile technologies and seek to reach them at key moments in the day when they can influence them to purchase. Adults in the United States spend more time with digital media than television, allocating 47% of their day (almost six hours) with digital media such as nonvoice mobile (23%), Internet (18%), and other online activities (6%). But Americans are still watching television over four hours a day, and since television is the dominant method for consuming video, reaching people via commercials is still desirable [20].

consider this...

WHICH MEDIA INFLUENCE SALES MOST?

A comprehensive study of consumer responses to ten forms of media was conducted by researchers on a large Australian retailer. The study examined the customers of the store who participated in the loyalty program, so the researchers could access sales data. The study examined advertisements and sales over a twenty-six-week period and asked customers the forms of media to which they were exposed. The researchers determined that 7 out of 10 formats were effective in driving sales response. The media formats were television, newspapers, radio, magazines, online display, online search, social media, catalog, personal mail, and email. The medium with the strongest impact on sales was television, though the store spent the most on television advertising. The other successful media formats were catalog, newspaper, search, mail, and email. Those with the lowest impact were social media with a close to zero effect, and magazines and online display with negative effects on dollar sales levels for the store [25].

MULTIMEDIA MESSAGE PROCESSING IN ADVERTISING

Marketers face a complicated media environment. People multitask and consume media in many diverse ways so that it is difficult to determine how and when to deliver a message. For example, L'Oréal, Sony, and Walmart were lambasted in the media for publishing fake blogs. The problem was that people expect blogs to be authentic views from individuals, not carefully crafted company messages. L'Oréal's blog Journal de ma Peau ("diary of my skin") detailed the skin-care routine of Claire, who was not a real person, but a persona created by the advertising agency. After complaints from customers, L'Oréal replaced Claire with six real women blogging about their skin-care routines [28]. When attempting to reach customers on social media, marketers have to consider the message, the medium, and how the two interact to influence consumer behavior.

consider this . . .

When consumers multitask, their attention is divided and messages may not be noticed or processed enough to lead to the desired response. In general, multitasking detracts from a person's ability to learn a concept. In order for a person to process information and learn, he or she must be motivated, attentive, and have the ability to understand the communication. Therefore, for multimedia synergy to be successful in driving brand message points, people must process the information in each form of media in tandem, but not simultaneously (as the two formats would cancel each other out). How can a marketer manage the task of delivering optimal messages that people will attend to and process? Advertisers can create multiple messages, so some may match the consumer's preferred method of processing. For example, comparative ads, ads that directly compare competitors, work better on people who tend to process information analytically, while straightforward, image-based ads are better for people who process information visually [29]. Online executions with strong copy or content would be more effective with targets that process verbally [30]. The match results in more persuasive messages, positive brand evaluation, and greater likelihood of purchase.

Can a brand determine in advance the target's preferred method of processing? Consider a hedonic product versus a utilitarian item. A hedonic item appeals to emotion and the senses, whereas a utilitarian product is more practical and useful. Marketers of vacations tend to use strong visual imagery to highlight the beauty of the experience, while vacuum cleaner companies would focus on the attributes of the vacuum, such as speed, power, and strength. Marketers could also consider asking consumers how they prefer to process, using the scale in Exhibit 10.4.

SEARCH ENGINE MARKETING AND TELEVISION

In an advertising tracking study in the Netherlands, researchers examined a multimedia campaign consisting of a search engine, banner and television ads to determine the effectiveness of each media format. The campaign was for a beer company that wanted to build awareness for its new customizable package. Consumers could go online and design a six-pack carton, and have it sent to their homes. The product cost about 4 times the price of a regular six-pack. The brand ran television and banner ads during a ten-week period and tracked consumer search engine data. The researchers also asked a sample of customers to perform controlled Internet tasks related to the purchase of the product and measured their responses to a variety of brand metrics. The study found that search engine ads were effective in building awareness, even when people didn't click on them. Television ads had a positive effect on ad awareness, brand image, and consumption, but banner ads alone did not significantly influence response, unless television ads were also present. One concern was the interaction between search and television ads, which together had a negative effect on advertising and brand awareness. The lesson is that marketers should consider the interaction effects of various forms of media and test such combinations beforehand [31].

EXHIBIT 10.4

Scale Items to Measure Preference of Processing in Words versus Pictures

1. I enjoy doing work that requires the use of words. (W)

2. There are some special times in my life that I like to relive by mentally "picturing" just how everything looked. (P)

3. I can never seem to find the right word when I need it. (P)

4. I do a lot of reading. (W)

5. When I'm trying to learn something new, I'd rather watch a demonstration than read how to do it. (P)

6. I think I often use words in the wrong way. (P)

7. I enjoy learning new words. (W)

8. I like to picture how I could fix up my apartment or a room if I could buy anything I wanted. (P)

9. I often make written notes to myself. (W)

P = pictures W = words

Digital media help amplify television, radio, and print.

© Shutterstock/Subidubi

Research suggests that people process information in varying ways and that reaching individuals through multiple forms of media may have interactive effects—influencing one another. It is no wonder that marketers are excited about new forms of media for their messages. When consumers view messages on television, in magazines, on Instagram during a search for information or within their newsfeed, they process the information differently and may be more likely to attend to one versus another. The findings present opportunities for clever marketers who can also reduce their media spending with smart buys that reach the targets at the time when they are most likely to be receptive to their messages.

You probably watch television, use your smartphone, and go online multiple times a day. Sometimes, you do all three at the same time. But, how can your brain manage all the simultaneous messages and how can advertisers maximize the likelihood that you will get their messages?

ORDER OF EXPOSURE

One factor that affects how you process messages is the order of exposure. **Forward encoding** is when an advertisement in one form of media primes interest in an ad in a second form of media. For example, Heather notices that her friend Amanda watched an old episode of *Sex in the City* on Hulu once Amanda signed in with her Facebook ID. Later, Heather sees an ad on television indicating that past episodes of *Sex in the City* are available on Netflix. In this case, Heather may have been prompted to attend to the Netflix advertisement because of her preexposure to Amanda's viewing. Now, Heather can watch the same episode and discuss its plot with Amanda. Another type of consumer ad processing in cross-media campaigns is image transfer. **Image transfer** occurs when consumers remember previously viewed ads during exposure to a second ad. The second advertisement may prompt memory for the first advertisement and the messages may reinforce one another. For example, when watching Monday night football, Kevin sees an ad for a new tablet that he researched on CNET. The television ad could reinforce positive brand attitudes already established by CNET reviews. Finally, multiple source perception is the belief that a brand must be good if the consumer sees a lot of advertising for the product. In this case, advertising serves as a cue to the brand's market position based on the perceived level of brand spending.

DIFFERENT PROCESSING FOR DIFFERENT MEDIA

An integrated cross-channel strategy is strong because consumers process information differently depending on the medium. For instance, when searching online for product information, individuals scan the screen, reading selective material. Television viewing is more passive, but if the person is watching, he or she tends to view the entire message rather than just scan it. The benefit of advertising in both forms of media is that the response of the consumer differs, but each may contribute to positive brand attitudes or desirable outcomes for the firm. Exhibit 10.5 lists various forms of media and indicates the type of processing associated with each.

ADVANTAGES AND DISADVANTAGES OF MAJOR MEDIA FORMATS

Though marketers continue to purchase ads on television, traditional media's share of total advertising spending is declining. In the United States, marketers are now spending more in digital than in magazines, radio, newspapers, outdoor and direct mail. Globally, digital ad spending is expected to reach 30% of total ad

EXHIBIT 10.5

User Processing of Media Formats

FORM OF MEDIA	PROCESSING
Television	Passive viewing and listening
Search engines	Active search for specific information, possibly brand-related
Websites	Active searching and reading of information, possibly brand-related
Social networks	Active engagement with others, passive and some active engagement with brands
Radio	Passive listening
Outdoor	Active when reading transit posters or passive when viewing billboards
Mobile	Active engagement with mobile activities, including search, or passive when viewing content

consider this . . .

expenditures by 2018. However, marketers should still consider media formats other than social media or mobile because some strategies may benefit from more traditional formats. Additionally, in some cases, traditional media may deliver more efficient results. For example, prime-time television commercials are sometimes inefficient because they cast a wide net for reaching a target. Consider the annual Super Bowl media frenzy and the advertisers who purchase thirty-second spots that cost upward of $4 million, not including the production costs of the commercials [33]. For a Super Bowl ad to be effective, the target market must be well represented in the viewership. So, if a marketer is trying to reach large portions of the U.S. population at one time with a strategy, the Super Bowl could deliver strong reach at a relatively reasonable cost. A Super Bowl ad can reach over 100 million viewers at an average cost of $4 million. The cost to reach a thousand audience members (not including production expenses) would be $40.00, for the media time. That may be a more efficient way to spend money than buying expensive keywords if it leads to sales.

There are times when traditional may be the way to go. When can traditional media help a communications strategy? Either when the target market is more tuned into traditional media than digital or when the product category requires or benefits from traditional executions. As mentioned earlier, some target markets do not own smartphones, while others do not engage on social media. In the developing world, television may still be the best way to reach a large target market, or newspapers may provide more credibility for a strategy. Even in the developed world, young people, the early adopters of Facebook, have begun moving away from the service to more fragmented specialty apps. As such, a well-located billboard in a hip neighborhood might be more effective in attracting attention for a fashion brand. *Advertising Age* recently listed the top 100 campaigns of the twenty-first century. Most of the campaigns listed in Exhibit 10.6 use a combination of traditional and digital media to reach customers and prompt action. If you are not familiar with these campaigns, look them up for inspiration.

When it comes to product categories, certain executions may be more effective in traditional media. For example, direct-to-consumer drug advertising requires a brand to outline side effects. As a result, a mobile banner ad may not provide enough information and a print ad may be more effective. For highly personal products, such as condoms, birth control, or sanitary napkins, social media may not be appropriate. Exhibit 10.7 lists the advantages and disadvantages of major media to help marketers decide appropriate outlets for their advertising strategy.

EXHIBIT 10.6

Advertising Age's Top 10 Campaigns of the Twenty-First Century

BRAND	CAMPAIGN
Dove	Campaign for Real Beauty
Nike	Nike + Fuelband
BMW	BMW Films
Procter & Gamble's Old Spice	The Man Your Man Could Smell Like
Red Bull	Stratos
Burger King	Subservient Chicken
American Express	Small Business Saturday
Apple Mac	Get a Mac
Procter & Gamble's Global Branding	Thank you Mom
American Legacy Anti-Smoking	Truth

http://adage.com/lp/top15/#intro

EXHIBIT 10.7

Advantages and Disadvantages of Major Media

MEDIUM	ADVANTAGES	DISADVANTAGES
Network television	Reaches potentially large markets. Low cost per thousand. Opportunity to develop engaging commercials of varying lengths.	Long lead times and expensive production, declining audiences.
Cable television	Reaches targeted audiences with lower cost per thousand than network TV.	Expensive production and declining audiences.
Newspapers	Highly credible medium with short lead times and targeted (older and affluent) audiences.	High cost per thousand and declining readerships.
Magazines	Strong visual content in a credible medium for targeting audiences by consumer interests.	Long lead times and declining readerships.
Radio	Low cost per thousand with potentially high-frequency opportunities and fast production capability.	Small fragmented audiences limited by audio-only medium.
Outdoor	Delivers local advertising at a relatively low cost per thousand with potentially high frequency over multiple viewings.	Limited by location, short exposure time, and unknown exact audience measurement (based on traffic count).
Direct mail	Highly targeted prospects Can provide detailed information in a vivid piece.	Very high cost per thousand Viewed by some as junk mail.
Online search	Reaches consumers seeking purchase information and delivers strong measurement capabilities.	Requires the consumer to exert effort and search rankings are not controlled by the marketer
Online and mobile display	Low cost per thousand and targeted by content.	May not be noticed and has low click-through rates.
Mobile applications	Owned by the company and can be used to build loyalty.	High start-up costs with low levels of customer commitment.

consider this . . .

SOCIAL MEDIA AND THE SUPER BOWL

Social media have made Super Bowl advertising more efficient by providing additional outlets for viewing Super Bowl spots. After the game, you can view the commercials on the *USA Today* Ad Meter, at company websites, or on YouTube. These additional impressions build the reach for the expensive spots, and Super Bowl water-cooler talk may provide some earned media. Advertisers continue to seek out forms of media that deliver high levels of reach, and the Super Bowl is typically the highest-rated show of the year.

COMCAST GOES DIGITAL

Comcast is another brand that communicates through a variety of channels. Based in Philadelphia, Comcast is the largest U.S. cable operator with over 20 million subscribers in 39 states. Its brands include the NBC television network, XFINITY, Universal Studios, and Universal theme parks [34]. To build these brands and reach multiple targets of customers, Comcast uses many channels.

Comcast still spends a significant amount of its paid advertising budget in television, which makes sense for a traditional cable television brand. However, these days, Comcast has moved more into digital and spends 19% of its budget on paid Internet ads and even more in unmeasured media [6].

Comcast had a rude awakening to social media when a customer videotaped a cable repairman asleep on the job. The video went viral and Comcast was forced to manage an embarrassing situation. The end result was that Comcast increased its digital presence by conducting customer service activities online, saving the firm a lot of money [35].

COMCAST		DOLLARS SPENT IN THE U.S. (IN MILLIONS)	SHARE
Magazines		96.6	<1%
Newspapers		84.4	<1%
TV		901.4	54%
Radio		191.6	12%
Outdoor		78.5	<1%
Internet		310.1	19%
	Measured	1,662.6	54%
	Unmeasured	1,418.7	46%
Total Comcast Spending		3,081.3	

Source: Advertising Age, *"100 Leading National Advertisers," Ad Age Data Center, 2014.*

MEASURING ADVERTISING EFFECTIVENESS

Marketers purchase advertising space in various forms of media based on the number of impressions a communication delivers. An **impression** is when an individual is exposed to a message by seeing or hearing it, such as when a person watches television, listens to the radio, or sees a banner ad on a website or mobile application. The term impressions (see Exhibit 10.8) is a cumulative measure of the total number of audience exposures and is calculated as the size of the audience (reach) multiplied by the number of times each person is exposed to the advertisement (**frequency**). Each form of media has its own methods for determining audience size. In some cases, research firms provide audience data, such as Nielsen for television and radio or the Audit Bureau of Circulations for newspaper and magazine audience sizes.

As a student of social media and mobile marketing, you must know the basic traditional media terms so that you can compare communications strategies and make judgments as to the most effective options. Marketers use the terms in Exhibit 10.8 in both traditional and digital media planning to describe the size of the audience, which makes it easier to compare strategies. However, it is also important to compare the costs associated with each strategy to make informed decisions about which media to buy. A useful metric for evaluating paid media costs is **cost per thousand (CPM)**. CPM (*mille* means "thousand" in Latin) is expressed in dollars (or other currencies) and can be calculated by the formula, below:

$$CPM = \frac{\text{Cost of the Advertisement} \times 1,000}{\text{Size of the Audience}}$$

How much is an eyeball worth? Digital marketers refer to viewers as eyeballs. The answer depends on the cost to reach an individual in one medium compared

EXHIBIT 10.8

Common Media Terms Defined

MEDIA TERMS	DEFINITION
Reach	The percentage of unique individuals out of all potential targets exposed to a message or campaign over a specified time period.
Frequency	The number of times a unique individual is exposed to a message or campaign over a specified time period.
Impressions	A measure of the total number of targets exposed to a communication multiplied by the number of times each person was exposed. Impressions are calculated as Reach × Frequency.

to other forms of media. Using the CPM, we can determine the cost to reach 1,000 people in each medium and compare them. Though this metric suggests that each form of media is equivalent in delivering an impression, it does not take into account the unique attributes of each vehicle. For example, mobile may be very effective in delivering coupons instore, while social media may encourage engagement. Exhibit 10.9 provides some common costs per thousand statistics in media [36], [37].

TELEVISION AND RADIO MEASUREMENT

Social media and mobile marketing take place within the context of brands that use many forms of media to communicate with target markets. In addition, TV is still the medium with the highest level of ad spending both in the United States and globally. Therefore, students interested in integrating media must know television metrics, which also apply to radio media buying.

In television and radio media, planners buy **gross ratings points** (**GRPs**), which reflect the total impressions of a particular campaign. These impressions are calculated as the rating of a program (reach) multiplied by the number of times the ad runs (frequency). GRPs are a measure of the number of unique individuals who view a communication strategy multiplied by the number of times the person sees the communication. Other forms of media such as radio and even outdoor use the concept of GRPs to measure audience size. Exhibit 10.10 presents some of the media terms that are used in television and radio media buying [38].

EXHIBIT 10.9

Cost per Thousand for Media Formats

MEDIA FORMAT	CPM
Digital display	$.27–$1.03
Paid search	
Computer	$.83
Tablet	$.76
Smartphone	$.58
Organic search	Free or SEO
Google paid search	$.25–$3.09
Facebook	$.10–$1.10
Twitter	$.26–$.43
Mobile display	$.51–$1.15
Network prime television 30-second spot	$24.76

TVB, "TV Cost & CPM Trends—Network TV Primetime (M-Su)," 2014, http://TVB.org.
A. Fou, "Digital Advertising Benchmarks," Marketing Science Consulting, 10 March 2014.

consider this . . .

RADIO FINDS SOCIAL MEDIA

Sirius XM, the satellite radio company, has two weekly shows called *The YouTube 15* and *The YouTube EDM 15*. These shows that normally play top forty or electronic dance music are discovering new artists that have YouTube followings, but may not be airing on traditional radio. Google, owner of YouTube, is working with Sirius to provide the playlists, highlight trending songs, and showcase new stars. It's a case of traditional media working with social media content [39].

EXHIBIT 10.10

Television and Radio Media Terms

Rating	A rating is the percentage of the total population that is engaged with a particular program out of all the homes with access to that form of media. In television, the rating is the total percentage of the audience watching a particular show divided by the total number of television households, whether the TV is on or off. Thus, a television program with a rating of 2 would reach 2% of the television household population.
Share	Share refers to the percentage of people who view a medium out of all those who are engaged with the medium at a particular time. In television, share is the percentage of viewers watching a particular show out of all those watching television at that point in time.
Gross ratings points	The sum of all rating points delivered by the media vehicles carrying an advertisement or campaign and a measure of the aggregate reach of the campaign. Gross ratings points can be calculated as Reach × Frequency or Rating × Number of Runs.

Measuring the success of an ad campaign is important and digital media are relatively easy to track. As a result, marketers now demand more accountability from traditional media trackers like Nielsen, the firm that publishes the television ratings. Nielsen samples homes in the United States and local markets to represent the size of the television audience and monitors the homes with TV set meters (also called People Meters) that record viewing. For many years, about 5,000 homes represented the viewing patterns of the U.S. market, but Nielsen has increased the sample by about 30% to improve accuracy at the local level [40]. Nielsen maintains that the company measures television viewing representing 40% of the world's viewing behavior [41] and also measures audiences for Netflix and Amazon Prime with the same methods [42].

Nielsen has been criticized for the procedures underlying the television ratings because over time Nielsen homes are less inclined to press the buttons to indicate who within the family is viewing a particular show, resulting in lower ratings and incorrect data. To respond to advertiser complaints that the ratings did not reflect the true audience when the DVR was introduced, Nielsen started to offer C3 ratings that included viewing up to three days after a show aired and +7 ratings up to seven days after a show aired. According to Nielsen, more than 50% of those 18–34 watch shows in the seven days following a live broadcast [43]. Exhibit 10.11 lists some of Nielsen's television viewing reports [44].

EXHIBIT 10.11

Nielsen Television Viewing Reports

NIELSEN TERMS	DEFINITION
Live	Household viewing at the time the program airs on a specific station or cable channel.
Live + SD	Household viewing at the time the program airs on a specific station or cable channel, and other same-day viewing via DVR or playback.
Live + 7	Household viewing at the time the program airs on a specific station or cable channel, and viewing via DVR or playback up to 7 days after airing.
C3	Household viewing at the time the program airs on a specific station or cable channel, and viewing via DVR or playback up to 75 hours (3 days) after airing. Metric available for shows with national commercial time only.

consider this . . .

YOUTUBE STARS COMPETE WITH TV

Marketers have found aspiring brand ambassadors among the stars on YouTube. These personalities can help brands build audiences or sell products and services. Here some of the more popular personalities and their numbers of subscribers [45] are provided.

These numbers compare favorably to the television viewing audience. The number 10 highest-rated television show has a rating of 6.0 and reaches about 10,000,000. These YouTube stars are not far behind, but there is no guarantee that a message sent by one of the stars will reach each of their followers. Then again, no guarantee exists that people who watch a television show also watch the advertisements.

YouTube Stars' Subscribers

YOUTUBE STAR	FOLLOWERS
Miranda Sings	3,782,689
Michelle Phan	7,631,518
Bethany Mota	8,554,546
Tyler Oakley	6,784,198

www.youtube.com

PRINT AND OUTDOOR MEASUREMENT

Though total ad spending is growing, marketers are spending less of their total budgets on print media such as newspapers and magazines. One reason is because audiences are spending more time with online and mobile communications than with print. Another reason is the cost associated with print advertising, particularly newspapers, which command a high CPM to reach the audience. The decline in print media spending and the associated revenues generated by newspapers and magazines continues. In 2012 newspaper advertising in the United States represented 11.5% of total media spending, but now commands only 7%. Similarly, magazines held 9.2% of total ad spending and will decline to 7% by 2018. Outdoor advertising remains fairly steady at about 4% of total U.S. advertising spending due to its unique attributes and low relative cost [46].

Print media are measured by the size of the audience, which includes subscribers plus those who buy the publication on the newsstand or digitally. Outdoor advertising audiences are difficult to measure, but billboard marketers do provide reach and frequency data for each billboard with total GRPs.

Though newspaper ads are expensive on a CPM basis and newspaper readership is declining as more and more people around the world get their news from online sources, print can still be useful in certain campaigns. Globally, print media circulation has been on the rise. Newspapers are still popular, with 2.5 billion people reading print papers weekly compared to 600 million news readers online [47].

Magazine readership is declining also, but with the tablet's ability to show vivid imagery, the magazine format may continue to appeal to specific targets of affluent individuals with tablets and more of a mass market when more people buy tablet devices.

DIGITAL AND TRADITIONAL METRICS FOR SOCIAL MEDIA

Marketers use both digital and traditional media terms to evaluate social media and mobile paid advertising strategies. The digital strategies provide clear tracking capabilities based on actions that people take online or on a mobile device and are response-based. For instance, the **click-through rate** is the percentage of people who click on a particular ad out of all those exposed to the ad. Click-through rates are extremely low, often less than 1%, so marketers also measure the number of impressions on paid display advertising. Marketers pay for each click on a cost per click basis and each impression on a **cost per impression** basis.

The ultimate metric for a digital campaign is the **conversion rate**, when the target responds by completing a desired action, such as a purchase. Exhibit 10.12 defines some of the digital metrics marketers use to evaluate campaigns.

SEMrush provides some useful data for analyzing cost per click. The screenshot here shows the cost per click for a variety of keywords that deliver people to the Kikkerland website.

EXHIBIT 10.12

Digital Strategy Measures

Click-through rate	A measure of those who click on an advertisement or link out of the total number of exposures.
Cost per click	The price paid by the advertiser when an individual clicks on an ad.
Cost per impression	The price paid by the advertiser when an individual is exposed to an ad.
Conversion rate	The percentage of customers who complete an action out of the total audience. A common use for the term is the percentage of sales resulting from a certain number of visits to a website.

SHARE OF VOICE FOR SOCIAL MEDIA

One analysis that marketers can employ to examine media spending is **Share of Voice (SOV)**. SOV is the percentage of total advertising dollars in a particular category spent by a brand. The calculation is similar to computing market share, but instead of adding up sales, the marketer determines each brand's media

SEMrush estimates the cost per click for keywords on its platform.

SEMrush, www.semrush.com

EXHIBIT 10.13

Share Measures

Share of voice	The share of a brand's media spending relative to competitors' media spending.
Share of conversation	Number of posts discussing a topic and a brand compared to number of posts discussing just the topic.

EXHIBIT 10.14

Social Media Strength for Three Cola Brands in One 24-Hour Period

	COCA-COLA	PEPSI	RC COLA
Strength	22%	30%	24%

www.socialmention.com

spending and divides that number into total spending in the category. The concept is useful for examining share of social media conversations, a brand's share of the online discussions on a particular topic compared to competitors (see Exhibit 10.13). A number of social media listening firms provide clients with information on **share of conversation**, the degree to which people talk about the brand online and in social media, as do some free sites, such as Social Mention.

Exhibit 10.14 shows an example of cola brands and their associated scores on Social Mention's strength metric. Strength is the likelihood the brand was discussed on social media in a 24-hour period divided by the total universe of mentions. Though not limited to a particular product category, the measure represents share of conversation on social media for a particular brand. As you can see from Exhibit 10.14, the top brands are not always dominant in social media conversations.

SOCIAL MEDIA AND MOBILE TECHNOLOGY IN THE MEDIA PLAN

Marketers can enhance communications strategies with social media or mobile marketing by broadening reach, increasing frequency, encouraging interaction, or building relationships. A brand's strategy can include multiple media vehicles, each contributing a distinct element of the message or building on one another to enhance communication in some way. There are some advantages to using multiple forms of media. In a highly cluttered environment, it is difficult for a brand's message to be noticed, so additional formats can lead to more views and increased attention for the brand. Changing the execution of a message can refresh the advertisement and limit potential wear-out. A variety of media also provide different means of delivering the message under varying consumer mind-sets and moods.

Brands also use multiple forms of media to generate broader reach, so more people see the communication. These days, target markets are engaging with many devices, programs, websites, mobile sites, and reading material. It is difficult for marketers to get a strong audience in any one place, so they try to reach people using many forms of media. When the marketer does reach the same person again, the wear-out effect might be reduced because the medium is different and the person may be less inclined to feel annoyance as the message appears in a new format and doesn't seem like exactly the same message . . . again.

One online brand that integrated strategy using traditional media was Zoosk, the dating site. Zoosk's media strategy helped it grow the business by reaching singles in a variety of ways. The online dating service was introduced in 2007 to a very crowded market of strong competitors. Match.com and eHarmony each had 90% awareness among singles. Zoosk was relatively unknown, with only 15% brand awareness. The brand set two goals:

- Increase brand awareness to 50% among adults 18–55.
- Increase subscription rates by 20%.

The brand and agency decided to differentiate from other online dating services. Their insight was that people felt pressure in online dating to find "the one"—in other words, most services emphasized dating for marriage. Zoosk decided dating should be fun and can be casual with many different plans and outcomes. The tag line "Online dating your way" reflected the variety of dating options. The media strategy was integrated across media vehicles and included a social media component to enhance content sharing. The creative strategy centered on humor to highlight the more causal nature of the service. Exhibit 10.15

Online dating is popular with services like Zoosk.

© Shutterstock/Halfpoint

EXHIBIT 10.15

Zoosk's Integrated Strategy

MEDIUM	MESSAGE GOAL	MESSAGE EXECUTION
30-second television spots and national cable	Focus on the casual nature of dating and lightening up the dating scene.	Commercials featuring humorous dates "gone wrong." Zoosk showed a couple on a dinner date inside a movie theater having a great time introducing foods to one another.
Men's and women's magazines	Emphasize the fun of dating when one has control.	Bold headlines in print, with the tag line "Fall in like."
Out-of-door bus station billboards	Increase the reach to singles in major metro areas, such as Chicago, Philadelphia, and San Francisco.	Reinforce the "Fall in like" tagline and the brand name.
Social media	Online website with "mad lib"—style statements to fill in and share with friends on social media sites.	"The best _____ is _____." "You were suddenly feeling frisky, so you asked _____ (name) to _____ (activity) in the _____ (room)." "I _____ while _____ during a date."
Web and mobile banner ads	Drive singles to the website or mobile site for sign-in. Able to connect at any time of day or night.	Zoosk's banner ads feature attractive singles with the tag lines: "Who would you date?" "Who would you prefer?" "Date smarter" "Wanna chat?" "Still single? So are we?"

consider this . . .

MOBILE ADVERTISING ON YOUTUBE

YouTube's TrueView offers mobile users the opportunity to choose when and whether they want to see an ad at a particular time. This allows for engagement with the viewer when he or she is most likely to attend to a message. Over 65% of YouTube online ads offer the option to avoid the ad and YouTube reports that 15%–45% of viewers choose to watch ads [48].

details Zoosk's method for reaching singles. The results of the campaign were that subscriptions increased 98% in the five months from the start of the campaign and awareness reached 50% in eight months, peaking at 60% in the first year.

MOBILE'S CONTRIBUTION TO THE MEDIA MIX

Mobile enhances traditional media strategies in two important ways. First, mobile can connect the message to the retail environment because of mobile's local capabilities. Brands can communicate with customers and reinforce themselves with news, deals, information, and offers in real time or when people are shopping. Most purchases still take place in stores as e-commerce represents less than 7% of retail sales in the United States [49]. Customers may be using their mobile phones in-store to read reviews, locate best prices, and find coupons, which increases their interaction with the brands that can reach them on their devices. Second, people spend a significant amount of time on their phones, checking the device numerous times a day. According to a study by Kleiner Perkins, the average person checks his or her phone starting at 7:31 a.m., looking at email and social media, and completes 140 tasks per day on it, such as food shopping, mapping, or just determining the time. Overall, smartphone users check their phones a total of 1,500 times per week [50].

Mobile engagement differs from social media, and its effectiveness depends on what the individual is doing with his or her mobile device at a particular time. For example, a lot of mobile time is spent gaming. Chances are that people who are playing games are not seeking out products to buy. Those surfing the mobile Web may be looking to engage with marketer information and might be prime targets for communications [51].

The introduction of the tablet provides advertisers with some of the benefits of print with the potential to engage the customer further through a mobile experience. A tablet can link directly to a mobile site, mobile app, Facebook page, or Twitter account. Using a tablet, a consumer can "check in" to receive offers from the brand and engage. Many people use multiple devices at one time, so advertisers can reach people with television and Twitter to ensure their messages get through. Exhibit 10.16 features examples of opportunities for brands to increase reach and engagement via mobile.

EXHIBIT 10.16

Methods for Enhancing Traditional Strategies with Social and Mobile

	SOCIAL MEDIA	MOBILE
Television	Run commercials on YouTube. Announce social media contests on television.	Produce interesting content in ads that people want to share. Run ads on the social media sites of programs or television stars' Twitter feeds.
Radio	Remind listeners about social media promotions. Prompt a visit to a social media site with a radio ad.	Run radio spots on music streaming sites. Encourage app downloads with radio spots.
Print	Publish content on social media sites. Encourage sharing of brand news with links to articles.	Use QR codes in magazine ads. Use print to encourage opt-in for SMS campaigns.
Outdoor	Use signage to encourage "check ins" on social media. Create a social brand destination for customers to meet in real life.	Offer games via billboards that drive store visits. Use beacons to reach customers on their phones.

consider this . . .

INTEGRATING SOCIAL MEDIA AND OUTDOOR

The agency Saatchi & Saatchi set up a life-sized Facebook page in a popular Budapest square, allowing passers-by to use magic markers to post live on T-Mobile's Facebook page. The company hired artists to re-create people's Facebook pages on the giant screen to promote T-Mobile's phone packages and generated a significant amount of buzz for the brand. The campaign used technology to combine social media with real experiences to build engagement, with people interacting with the brand in a fun and exciting way [52].

consider this . . .

MOBILE BOOSTS SOCIAL MEDIA IN CHINA

Cornetto is the leading brand of ice cream in China. To remain top of mind among young consumers and build preferences, the brand created several online videos featuring Chinese celebrities in a love triangle. The eight-second films starred Kai Ko, Bolin Chen, and Ariel Lin in a story inspired by the question "If you had only eight seconds left before the end of the world, how would you express your love?" The films integrated leading networking site Tencent Weishi to allow sharing with friends. The campaign was a good fit for this audience's shorter attention spans and high rate of smartphone ownership. Eighty-five percent of Chinese 15- to 25-year-olds have smartphones. After some success on social media, the brand integrated the campaign to build reach by using display advertising and in-store signage. On May 20, China's day of love, Cornetto encouraged customers to publicly proclaim their love and 70,000 people did so on social media. The results: a 5% year-over-year increase in sales, unaided awareness grew 10%, and scores on key attributes, such as "delicious," were up 5%–20% [53].

SUMMARY AND REVIEW

CHAPTER SUMMARY

Integrated marketing communications is a concerted effort by a brand to be consistent in interacting and communicating with customers. People differ in their media preferences, how they respond to communications, and the actions they take as a result of a promotion. By understanding media synergies, marketers can buy media time more efficiently and take advantage of economies available in new media formats, such as in social networking and mobile communications.

KEY TERMS

advertising elasticity
astroturfing
click-through rate
competitive parity
conversion rate
cost per impression

cost per thousand
(CPM)
forward encoding
frequency
gross ratings points
(GRPs)

image transfer
impressions
multimedia
synergy
objective and task
method

percentage of sales
method
reach
share of conversation
share of voice (SOV)
sock puppetry

SUMMARY REVIEW QUESTIONS

1. What are some of the questions marketers should ask in order to improve their integrated marketing communications plans?

2. Explain the concept of an integrated cross-channel strategy, giving an example.

3. Name some media metrics. What does each metric represent?

4. What are the challenges of measuring different forms of media? Which form of media is the most difficult to measure? Why?

5. Give an example of digital media affecting other forms of media.

6. Compare various media formats. What are some of the advantages and disadvantages of each format?

7. What advertising opportunities did the introduction of tablet devices create? How can advertisers take advantage of such opportunities?

APPLICATION QUESTIONS

1. Visit the major newspaper websites and compare their digital subscription offers (i.e., the number of free articles, the monthly price, etc.). Do you prefer reading a print or digital version of the newspaper? Why?

2. Log in to your Facebook account and "like" three pages of large newspapers (e.g., *The Wall Street Journal, The New York Times, Financial Times*, etc.). Do the latest news headlines that appear on your Facebook newsfeed prompt you to click on the article link and visit the newspaper's website? On which headlines were you the most and least likely to click? Evaluate this strategy and comment on the potential of increasing readership.

3. Visit the Twitter and Facebook pages of your favorite retail stores. Do they offer consumer contests and encourage user-generated content? How can a company use such content in the future? Name some of the benefits from such a campaign.

4. Give an example of the newspaper/magazine ad containing the QR code link to a company's mobile website. Have you scanned it with your mobile device? Comment on the advantages and disadvantages of this type of enhancement to a print campaign.

5. Log on to Twitter.com. Name some of the people who have the largest number of followers. How can advertisers take advantage of these people and their large base of followers in the context of multimedia synergy? Give an example.

6. Over a twenty-four-hour period, track the times that you watch television (include network, cable, and Internet streaming). Write down the time in fifteen-minute increments that you are watching and any other activities in which you are engaged during that same period. For instance, if you watched television from 8 to 8:15 p.m. and ate dinner at the same time, include the dinner activity. Consider which activities led you to be more or less engaged in the show's commercials. Is there a difference?

Axe and Old Spice Battle in Traditional and Digital Media

The men's bath and body-care market was dominated by two major brands that competed head-to-head to attract a young target. Though the competition was fierce, the market was expected to grow 5% per year through 2018, providing an incentive for the brands to advertise heavily to influence consumers [54].

Both Procter & Gamble's Old Spice and Unilever's Axe brands were backed by large global companies with deep pockets for advertising spending. Originally, each focused on young men 18–24 who loved sports and juvenile humor [55]. These consumers were technologically savvy, heavy Internet and mobile users, and watched more online video than the average person. However, after successfully attracting their target, both brands noticed a backlash against the advertisements that showed brainless women who existed to please men [56].

EARLY SUCCESSES

P&G was the first brand to find success using social media to attract the target. Old Spice's YouTube videos focused on the "manly" NFL star Isaiah Mustapha and ran on television, cable, and YouTube. In addition, P&G bought ads on seventeen cable networks that emphasized sports. The strategy also appeared to be targeting women with the tag line "The man your man could smell like." At the same time, Axe's strategy continued to focus on young men with sexualized humor, such as the "Clean Your Balls" campaign. The video spot that ran on YouTube showed women washing soccer balls to an appreciative male audience. For this campaign, Axe purchased ads on thirty-six cable stations, including youth-oriented properties such as MTV and Comedy Central. At that time, Axe spent more money on traditional media than Old Spice [57].

Axe continued its strategy of targeting the "insecure novice" who could rely on Axe to help him meet women. The brand ran the "Axe Effect" campaign in major media and showed images of young men "getting the girl" as a result of using Axe. In "Angels Will Fall," the brand showed angels falling from the sky to smell a young man who used the product. In the Susan Glenn campaign, Kiefer Sutherland regretted not using Axe to help him get the girl.

SUPER BOWL ADVERTISING

The Super Bowl became an important outlet for advertising in this category. A Super Bowl ad cost $4.5 million for a thirty-second spot and reached approximately 114.4 million viewers in 2015 for a CPM of about $40.

Both Axe and Old Spice ran Super Bowl ads. In 2015 Axe significantly altered its message by running an ad with the slogan "Make love, not war," with couples happily expressing their love for one another. The sixty-second spot had over 7 million views and the thirty-second one over 5 million views on YouTube in the three months following the game. Old Spice ran a humorous Super Bowl ad for its electric shaver, with Terry Crews shaving himself. The Crews ad generated over 4 million YouTube views. Elsewhere, the brand continued its videos in which mothers lamented their sons' new-found romantic attraction, singing, "Old Spice, what have you done? You made a sexy man out of my son."

The question was whether buying Super Bowl ads was an efficient use of each brand's media budget. The budget of $4.5 million could buy online video ads to be shown 500 million times over an eighteen-day period. The estimated reach for the video campaign would be 145 million people, with a frequency of 3. Of course, Super Bowl ads were shown once, but viewed more times postgame. The exact same budget could also buy a full-page color ad in every issue of *Men's Fitness, Details, Men's Journal, Rolling Stone, GQ, Golf Digest,* and *Golf Magazine* for a year. Buying banner ads with this budget, an advertiser would garner 1.3 billion impressions on a variety of websites. Finally, $4.5 million could also buy a twenty-four-hour premium Facebook video ad ($750,000), a Snapchat Recent Updates stream ($700,000), a trending topic ad on Twitter ($150,000), and an Instagram video ad ($200,000) and still have budget left for content and posting [58].

GOING FORWARD

In 2015 Axe signed a new global agency, 72andSunny, with a $30 million global budget [59]. Clearly, the intent was to continue to support the brand with interesting creative content from an agency known for its original ideas.

Exhibit 10.17 shows Mediamark Research & Intelligence data for people who purchased Old Spice Red Zone or Axe during a six-month period. The "Total U.S. Population" column gives the medium's audience, and the next two columns offer an index number representing the target market's usage of the medium relative to the average adult in the population. An index of 100 means that the target of interest has the same usage as the overall population. A higher number indicates that the target uses the medium more than the general adult population. Exhibit 10.18 lists the average CPM for a variety of options [4], [60].

Old Spice and Axe have competed head-to-head for years and both brands have seen successes. There may be room in the market for two brands aimed at similar targets, but the brands will likely continue to try to build share by attempting to attract the other's customers, as is often the case in a maturing market. The question remains as to how the brands will use digital and traditional media to reach the target market of young men and to what extent the two brands will continue to raise the bar on irreverent and edgy humor.

EXHIBIT 10.17

Mediamark Research for Old Spice Red Zone and Axe

MEDIAMARK RESEARCH DATA (PURCHASED ITEM IN THE PREVIOUS 6-MONTH PERIOD)	TOTAL U.S. POPULATION AUDIENCE SIZE (000)	OLD SPICE RED ZONE	AXE
TV: Adult Swim	18,106	233	211
TV: ESPN Classic	9,465	257	195
TV: NFL Network	14,879	200	177
Magazine: *Autoweek*	2,076	263	255
Magazine: *Boating*	2,061	286	153
Magazine: *Field & Stream*	7,754	235	169
Magazine: *Inc.*	1,221	329	136
Magazine: *Maxim*	8,309	117	250
Magazine: *Men's Health*	12,877	153	205
Website: MTV.com	3,936	210	115
Website: NASCAR.com	5,891	208	203
Website: ESPN.com	34,962	201	183
Website: NFL.com	17,096	225	179
Website: Yahoo Mail	66,313	109	107
Website: Gmail	74,004	128	123
Website: iTunes	33,037	110	113
Website: Pandora	42,493	129	120
Website: Spotify	3,987	242	133
Radio: Midnight to 6 a.m.	12,347	196	176

GfK Mediamark Research & Intelligence. (2013, Fall Product Report). Personal and Healthcare Products: bought at last 6 months total. Base: Adults. Retrieved from MRI Mediamark University Internet Reporter database.

Average Cost per Thousand for Media

MEDIA	AVERAGE COST PER THOUSAND (CPM)
Network cable television, prime time	$9.85
Network cable television, fringe (before and after prime time)	$7.55
Super Bowl CPM	$37
Internet video (targeted)	$32.75
Online digital display	$.27–$1.03
Radio (spot)	$2.10
Radio (national)	$7.80
Magazines, men's interests	$10.90

C. Smith, "Have We Found the Ceiling for Superbowl Ad Costs?," Forbes, 29 January 2014. http://www.oaaa.org/OutofHomeAdvertising/MediaComparison.aspx.

QUESTIONS FOR DISCUSSION

1. What were the original social media strategies for the two brands? Were they successful?
2. Would it be possible for the brands to replicate their initial social media success today? Why or why not?
3. Is either advertising clutter or wear-out an issue for Axe and Old Spice? Explain.
4. Review the communications strategies for Axe and Old Spice. Which brand has the better strategy?
5. Should Axe and Old Spice continue to advertise during the Super Bowl? Compare the CPM for the Super Bowl to other media options enumerated in the case study and make a clear argument for each brand.
6. Calculate the actual cost to run an advertisement in Maxim magazine.
7. Assuming a $30 million budget, what is the right mix of media for Axe in 2015? Why?
8. If Old Spice has a similar budget, should it pursue the same strategy?
9. Did the backlash against Axe advertising affect the industry? How?

REFERENCES

[1] Bloomberg, "Red Bull's Adrenaline Marketing Mastermind Pushes into Media," 19 May 2011.

[2] A. Jamieson, "Red Bull Drinkers Can Claim $10 over 'Gives you Wings' Lawsuit," *NBC News,* 9 October 2014.

[3] Tagga Media, Inc., "Red Bull Crashed Ice Campaign Summary Results," April 2012, http://www.tagga.com.

[4] C. Smith, "Have We Found the Ceiling for Superbowl Ad Costs?," *Forbes,* 29 January 2014.

[5] C. Moorman, "The CMO Survey," 2014.

[6] Advertising Age, "100 Leading National Advertisers," Ad Age Data Center, 2014.

[7] TVB, "Purchase Funnel 3.0," http://TVB.org.

[8] Internet Advertising Bureau, "Shifting Up to 15% of TV Ad Spend to Online Builds More Effective Reach at a Lower Cost, According to New Research from IAB," 25 February 2013, http://www.iab.net/about_the_iab/recent_press_releases/press_release_archive/press_release/pr-022513_dvresearch.

[9] Adobe, "Click Here: The State of Online Advertising," 12 June 2013.

[10] K. Logan, "And Now a Word from Our Sponsor: Do Consumers Perceive Advertising on Traditional Television and Online Streaming Video Differently?," *Journal of Marketing Communications,* vol. 19, no. 4, pp. 258–276, 2013.

[11] Media Dynamics Inc., "Targeted Online Video CPMs Much Higher than TV," 21 April 2014. Press release.

[12] H. P. Nguyen, J. M. Munch, and M. P. Gardner, "Does Repeated Ad Exposure Impair or Facilitate Recall of Ads with Similar Affective Valence? An Exploratory Study," *Journal of Marketing Theory and Practice,* vol. 22, no. 1, pp. 25–39, Winter 2014.

[13] Millward Brown, "Do TV Ads Wear out?," 2012.

[14] M. Braun and W. W. Moe, "Online Display Advertising: Modeling the Effects of Multiple Creatives and Individual Impression Histories," *Marketing Science,* pp. 753–767, 9 October 2013.

[15] L. Ha and K. McCann, "Advertising Clutter in Online and Offline Media," *International Journal of Advertising,* vol. 27, no. 4, pp. 569–592, 2008.

[16] P. A. Naik and K. Raman, "Understanding the Impact of Synergy in Multimedia Communications," *Journal of Market Research,* vol. 40, pp. 375–388, November 2003.

[17] N. Miller and A. Pazgal, "Advertising Budgets in Competitive Environments," *Quantitative Marketing and Economics,* vol. 5, pp. 131–161, 2007.

[18] Think Digital, "An Investment That Paid Off," 2014.

[19] D. West and G. P. Prendergast, "Advertising and Promotions Budgeting and the Role of Risk," *European Journal of Marketing,* pp. 1457–1476, 2009.

[20] eMarketer, "Mobile Continues to Steal Share of US Adults Daily Time Spent with Media," 22 April 2014, http://www.emarketer.com/Article/Mobile-Continues-Steal-Share-of-US-Adults-Daily-Time-Spent-with-Media/1010782.

[21] A. Joshi and D. M. Hanssens, "The Direct and Indirect Effects of Advertising Spending on Firm Value," *Journal of Marketing,* vol. 74, no. 1, pp. 20–33, January 2010.

[22] M. P. Conchar, M. R. Crask, and G. M. Zinkhan, "Advertising and Promotional Spending: A Review and Meta-Analysis," *Journal of the Academy of Marketing Science,* vol. 33, no. 4, pp. 445–460, 2005.

[23] X. Luo and P. J. de Jong, "Does Advertising Spending Really Work? The Intermediate Role of Analysts in the Impact of Advertising on Firm Value," *Journal of the Academy of Marketing Science,* vol. 40, no. 4, pp. 605–624, 2012.

[24] R. C. Graham and K. D. Frankenberger, "The Earning Effects of Marketing Communication Expenditures during Recessions," *Journal of Advertising,* vol. 40, no. 2, pp. 5–24, 2011.

[25] P. J. Danaher and T. S. Dagger, "Comparing the Relative Effectiveness of Advertising Channels: A Case Study of a Multimedia Blitz Campaign," *Journal of Marketing Research,* vol. 50, no. 2, pp. 517–534, 2013.

[26] R. Sethuraman, G. J. Tellis, and R. A. Briesch, "How Well Does Advertising Work? Generalizations from Meta-Analysis of Brand Advertising Elasticities," *Journal of Marketing Research,* vol. 48, no. 3, pp. 457–471, June 2011.

[27] S. Henningsen, R. Heuke, and M. Clement, "Determinants of Advertising Effectiveness: The Development of an International Advertising Elasticity Database and a Meta-Analysis," *Business Research,* vol. 4, no. 2, pp. 193–239, December 2011.

[28] R. Plummer, "Will Fake Business Blogs Crash and Burn?," *BBC News,* 22 May 2008.

[29] D. Thompson and R. Hamilton, "When Mental Stimulation Hinders Behavior: The Effects of Process-Oriented Thinking on Decision Difficulty and Performance," *Journal of Consumer Research,* vol. 36, no. 4, 532, December 2009.

[30] T. L. Childers, M. J. Houston, and S. E. Heckler, "Measurement of Individual Processing," *Journal of Consumer Research,* vol. 12, pp. 125–133, 1985.

[31] G. Zenetti, T. H. Bijmolt, P. S. Leeflang, and D. Klapper, "Search Engine Advertising Effectiveness in a Multimedia Campaign," *International Journal of Electronic Commerce,* vol. 18, no. 3, pp. 7–38, Spring 2014.

[32] V. Goel, "Twitter and Facebook Wield Little Influence on TV Watching," *The New York Times,* 10 April 2014.

[33] G. Davis, "The Rising Costs of Superbowl Ads in One Chart," *USA Today,* 1 February 2014.

[34] Hoovers, "Comcast Corp Company Information," *Hoovers Company Profile,* 2015.

[35] S. Suri, "Sleepy Comcast Technician Gets Filmed, Then Fired," CNET, 26 June 2006.

[36] TVB, "TV Cost & CPM Trends- Network TV Primetime (M-Su)," 2014, http://TVB.org.

[37] A. Fou, "Digital Advertising Benchmarks," Marketing Science Consulting, 10 March 2014.

[38] P. Farris, N. T. Bendle, D. J. Pfeifer, and D. J. Reibstein, *Marketing Metrics: The Definitive Guide to Measuring Marketing Performance,* Upper Saddle River, NJ: Pearson Education, 2010.

[39] B. Sisario, "Sirius XM Adds Show Based on Popular Dance Songs on YouTube," *The New York Times,* 11 November 2014.

[40] A.C. Nielsen 2, "Nielsen Announces Significant Expansion of Sample Sizes in Local Television Markets," 28 May 2014, http://www.nielsen.com/us/en/press-room/2014/nielsen-announces-significant-expansion-to-sample-sizes-in-local-tv-markets.html.

[41] Nielsen, "Television," http://www.nielsen.com/content/corporate/us/en/solutions/measurement/television.html.

[42] H. Keach and S. Vranica, "Nielsen to Measure Netflix Viewing," *The Wall Street Journal,* 18 November 2014.

[43] A.C. Nielsen 2, "Building Time Shifted Audiences: Does Social TV Play a Role?," 4 November 2014, http://www.nielsen.com/us/en/insights/news/2014/building-time-shifted-audiences-does-social-tv-play-a-role.html.

[44] Nielsen, "Nielsen Monitor Plus—Methodology by Medium," 15 February 2015.

[45] YouTube, "YouTube Subscribers," 18 April 2015.

[46] eMarketer, "Total US Advertising Spending to See Largest Increase Since 2004," 2 July 2014, http://www.emarketer.com/Article/Total-US-Ad-Spending-See-Largest-Increase-Since-2004/1010982.

[47] World Association of Newspapers and News Publishers, "World Press Trends: Print and Digital Together Increasing Newspaper Audiences," 9 June 2014, http://www.wan-ifra.org/press-releases/2014/06/09/world-press-trends-print-and-digital-together-increasing-newspaper-audienc.

[48] C. C. Miller, "Ads Mobile Users Can View or Not," *The New York Times,* 27 August 2012.

[49] U.S. Census Bureau, "Quarterly Retail Ecommerce Sales," *Census News,* 18 November 2014.

[50] V. Woolaston, "How Often Do YOU Look at Your Phone? The Average User Now Picks Up Their Device More Than 1,500 Times a Week," *Daily Mail,* 7 October 2014.

[51] S. S. Sundar, S. Narayan, R. Obregon, and C. Uppal, "Does Web Advertising Work? Memory for Print vs.

Online Media," *Journalism and Mass Communications Quarterly,* vol. 75, no. 4, pp. 822–835, 1998.

[52] I. Slutsky, "At the Bees Awards: Three Great Social-Media Campaigns From Brazil, China and Hungary," *Advertising Age,* 6 May 2011.

[53] Mobile Marketing Association, "Cornetto Express Love in 8 Seconds," *Mobile Marketing Association Case Study,* 2014.

[54] Euromonitor, "Men's Grooming in the US," July 2014.

[55] B. Silverstein, "Axe, Tag, Swagger Body Spray Brands Find Market With Tweens," Brand Channel, 2 February 2010.

[56] J. Zeilinger, "Axe Commercial Suggests That Women's Hotness Is a Danger to Men," Huffington Post, 1 August 2013.

[57] A. Young, "Axe vs. Old Spice: Whose Media Plan Came Up Smelling Best?," *Advertising Age,* March 2010.

[58] J. Marshall, M. Shields, and S. Vranica, "Super Bowl Ad for $4.5 Million? Here's What Marketers Could Buy Instead," *The Wall Street Journal,* 30 January 2015.

[59] A. McMains, "Accounts in Review," *Ad Week,* 30 January 2015.

[60] Outdoor Advertising Association of America, "Media Comparison," 2011.

© Shutterstock/Rawpixel.com

CHAPTER ELEVEN

MOBILE TOUCHPOINTS

Though social media and mobile technology are converging, some elements of mobile marketing are unique to mobile. As people spend larger proportions of their time using smartphones, mobile strategies offer marketers the opportunity to reach potential customers when and where they purchase. The mobile strategies include text messaging, mobile websites, mobile applications, serving advertisements, and sending emails on mobile devices to achieve marketing objectives. This chapter discusses research and goal setting in mobile along with the tools and techniques to reach and engage consumers in mobile.

LEARNING OBJECTIVES

After reading this chapter, you will be able to:

- EXAMINE PEOPLE'S MOBILE USAGE AND PURCHASE BEHAVIOR

- DEVELOP STRATEGIES FOR REACHING CONSUMERS VIA TEXT MESSAGING

- CREATE EFFECTIVE MOBILE ADVERTISING CAMPAIGNS

- PLAN MOBILE APPLICATION STRATEGIES

- INTEGRATE SOCIAL MEDIA AND MOBILE MARKETING CAMPAIGNS

ab.com was a brand with a mission. The company wanted to "help people better their lives through design." The site, originally a gay social network, morphed into an e-commerce outlet for people who wanted to learn about new designs and connect with designers. Sales really took off when the company introduced a mobile shopping app for Android and iOS. Within a year, mobile sales represented over 30% of the site's daily visits, 40% of which were executed on an iPad. The company believed that mobile shopping was more engrossing to consumers because there were fewer distractions on the tablet, which had no banner ads [1]. Fab was already using social media to encourage users to share their finds because customers who shared were more likely to purchase than those who did not. Mobile provided even more opportunities to join the shopping frenzy at Fab.com [2].

So what happened to Fab when the future for the company looked so bright? The company was valued at $1 billion, but could not raise the necessary $300 million in funding to support the business. The CEO Jason Goldberg indicated that the company was spending $14 million a month and had to lay off staff. Fab.com is now a much leaner site, exclusively operating in the United States, with fewer employees and lower overhead [3].

Though Fab had its difficulties, many major retailers have developed mobile apps that either drive sales to stores or enhance the in-store experience. Mobile commerce is still a small percentage of total e-commerce sales, but smart marketers can use mobile to attract new prospects, solidify relationships with customers, and track people's behavior. Exhibit 11.1 lists the most downloaded retailer apps in the iOS and Android stores [4].

Most Downloaded Retailer Apps for iOS and Android

| Amazon |
| Groupon |
| Walgreens |
| Cartwheel from Target Group |
| Etsy |
| Walmart |
| Target |
| Amazon Local |
| Apple Store |
| Living Social |
| Zappos |
| Zulily |

App Annie, "App Annie and Internet Retailer Index," 2014.

MOBILE IS BOOMING

Think about your average day. How many times do you use your cell phone and what are you doing when you use it? If you are like most people, your cell phone is your lifeline to the world and you would be lost without it. And, you are probably not even talking on your phone much. Instead, people are engaged in a variety of activities with their phones all day long. One study of 2,000 smartphone users in the United Kingdom found that people start checking their phones at 7:31 a.m., looking first at personal email and Facebook even before they get out of bed, and use their phones for over three hours a day. The same study also found that people use their phones for 140 tasks in a typical day [5]. In the United States, researchers determined that people spend, on average, 23% of their day with mobile devices [6]. That's a lot of time.

People use their screens interchangeably, so understanding multidevice usage is important for generating responses to marketing strategies. There are two ways that consumers multitask with mobile. The first is sequentially, when people look at one device and then move to a second device to dive more deeply into a task. Most people begin tasks on their mobile phone and continue on a tablet or PC. The most likely tasks to begin on the phone are searching for information, browsing the Web, shopping online, and planning a trip. These activities often result in movement from the phone to a PC [8]. When people start out on the tablet, they are most likely shopping or planning a trip, but since there are fewer tablets, there are fewer searches that start with this device.

Another type of multitasking is to use two devices simultaneously, but this is less common than sequential usage. When people are using multiple screens at the same time, they are most often watching TV with their smartphones, using the PC with the smartphone, or using their PC and watching television. The smartphone is the most common companion device with other screens, likely due to its portability and availability. So, what are people doing with their phones while viewing other screens? They are checking email, browsing the Web, and using social networks [8].

Marketers are particularly interested in how people use phones for shopping. People who buy on their phones are much more likely to be making impulse purchases, with 81% of cell phone purchases taking place spur of the moment [8].

SMARTPHONES

People spend a lot of time using their phones and most agree that they can't live without them. Have you ever tried to live life without your phone? For the next two hours, think about what you would do if you could not take out your phone. What would you be missing?

Smartphones are very dear to people, often representing the screen that wakes them up and the last one they see before going to sleep. Mobile phones are very personal devices, spending the day and night less than 5 feet away from their owners. Arbitron found that 91% of smartphone owners keep their device within an arm's length always or most of the time [7].

By 2017 almost 70% of the world's population will have mobile phones, 50% of which will be smartphones [6]. As a result, marketers around the world can take advantage of a variety of mobile strategies to communicate with customers and interact with them, including short message service, mobile websites, applications (apps), mobile advertising, and email marketing.

You love your phone, but how do you feel about talking on it? Chances are you do a lot more texting than talking, and you would not want a marketer to call you on your cell phone. Originally, marketers attempted to use voice for communications with customers, but found that contacting people via phone was intrusive. Consumers prefer to connect with companies when they control the contact, as when people use click-to-call from their phones or play games on their mobile applications.

Mobile is moving toward full online access for customers from wherever they are at any time. However, there are still limits in connection speeds, which are lower than what consumers experience on desktops or laptops. The phone is an exciting platform for marketers because consumers bring along their phones when shopping and use them as a purchase tool. Mobile is also measurable, which is attractive to marketers. Finally, mobile has become quite social with social networking apps among the most popular on smartphones. Mobile is becoming the dominant way for people to connect and share with their networks.

TABLETS

What about tablets? Tablets are also mobile devices that access the Internet and allow people to search and shop, but are used more for entertainment and shopping than smartphones [8]. People who own tablets spend 3.1 hours a day on them, mostly watching videos or movies, playing games, or reading.

Tablet ownership is growing globally, particularly in the developed world, but less than 10% of the total global population own tablets [9]. In the United States, almost half of households have tablets. These people tend to live in households earning at least $75,000 per year, are ages 30–49 and have college degrees, representing a wealthier and more educated demographic than that of smartphone owners [10]. As a result, tablet strategies differ based on the target and the brand under consideration.

RESEARCHING AND CREATING MOBILE STRATEGIES

Prior to developing a mobile strategy, marketers should consider their target market's ownership and usage of mobile technology. In the United States and United Kingdom, smartphone penetration is around 70% of the total population, but other countries have lower levels of smartphone ownership. For example, fewer than 60% of Chinese citizens have smartphones, while Mexico's smartphone penetration is below 40% of the total population [11]. As a result, depending on the target and whether they have smartphones, marketers may have to alter strategies. For example, Mercedes may find that using mobile advertising to reach wealthy Chinese businessmen may be effective in generating showroom visits, while McDonald's can drive retail store visits using text messaging in India. Exhibit 11.2 lists a series of questions marketers can ask to determine mobile strategy.

Another important consideration for a mobile strategy is the goal that the brand wants to achieve. The question for marketers to answer is which strategy will reach the goal most effectively and efficiently, delivering the best return on investment. Which goals are appropriate for mobile strategies? Well, mobile tends to be very effective in driving immediate response, but can also be used to encourage a number of desired behaviors.

One study found that marketers expected to use mobile marketing to:

Increase sales conversions/revenue.

Generate leads.

Engage customers.

Build brand awareness.

Increase website traffic.

Improve search engine rankings.

Retain customers.

Grow store traffic.

Lower customer acquisition costs [12].

In fact, marketers are using mobile to achieve many of these goals. For example, Trellie is a wearable device that signals when a person's phone is ringing. The product is aimed at busy moms who may not hear their phone ringing in the bottom of a purse. The brand had a $5,000 budget with a goal to increase brand awareness and sales using mobile advertising on Facebook. After running its campaign, the

EXHIBIT 11.2

Key Questions Mobile Marketers Should Ask before Spending to Reach a Target

Not all targets are appropriate for a social media or mobile strategy if the marketer's goal is to reach customers. Marketers should consider the following questions before committing resources to a particular strategy:

For general mobile strategies, marketers must answer the following questions:

1. Does the individual own a cellular phone?
2. What is the type of phone (smart, feature, or other)?
3. What is the operating system on the phone (iOS, Android, or other)?
4. Which carrier does the individual use?

For SMS strategies, the marketer must *also* determine whether the target:

1. Has access to text messaging services on the phone.
2. Knows how to use the text message feature on the phone.
3. Will be charged for text messages and the amount of the charge.
4. Feels negatively toward receiving texts from companies.
5. Feels negatively about the double-opt in procedure.

For mobile Web strategies, the marketer must *also* determine whether the target:

1. Has access to the mobile Web on a phone or tablet.
2. Knows how to access the Web on the mobile device.
3. Can be encouraged to use the mobile Web to search for the brand.
4. Has use for information that can be provided via the mobile Web.

For mobile apps, the marketer must also determine whether the target:

1. Has access to mobile apps on a phone or tablet.
2. Knows how to use mobile apps.
3. Uses an account to download apps and which one.
4. Is willing to download and store the app on the device.
5. Can be encouraged to interact with the brand via an app.

For location-based strategies, the marketer must also determine whether the target:

1. Has turned on the device's location services option.
2. Has downloaded a location-based app or is willing to do so.
3. Is willing to participate in the location-based strategy such that the company or others know where they can be found.

brand found that Facebook "likes" increased by 149%, unique website visitors grew from 1,800 to 7,408, and the company sold 1,400 units in the first four months of the mobile strategy, generating a 675% return on investment [13].

There are new opportunities marketers can consider when attempting to reach customers via mobile, but regulations are more complex in certain aspects of mobile marketing. For example, a text message campaign requires marketers to obtain double opt-in from customers who must agree twice (by texting two responses) to receive messages before a marketer may send messages to their phones.

As with any strategy, marketers must integrate a mobile plan with other components of the marketing and communications mixes. Marketers should never say "we need a mobile strategy" without careful consideration of the costs and benefits of entering the mobile sphere and a clear analysis of return on investment [14].

consider this . . .

ARE YOU BEING SERVED OR TRACKED?

Retailers are increasingly using your phone's wireless signal to track you in their stores. Nordstrom piloted the Euclid tracking system in its stores to determine how long customers shopped and their traffic patterns. However, the company ended the practice after receiving customer complaints once the practice was reported in the media [15], [16].

consider this . . .

VIRGIN'S MOBILE STRATEGY

Virgin Atlantic UK used a mobile strategy aimed at soccer (football) fans ages 18–35 who had iPhones. The goal was to increase awareness of Virgin Media's HD football packages to encourage fans to learn about Virgin media options, such as the ability to sync televised games with the iPhone calendar. The strategy centered on *The Guardian*'s mobile site. *The Guardian* is a popular British newspaper that is accessed via mobile more than any other device. Virgin Media took over the newspaper's mobile website for three consecutive weekends with a full sponsorship and ran ads on the desktop site to drive people to click through to the mobile site. The ads contributed to an additional 100,000 HD subscribers [17].

STRATEGIES FOR SHORT MESSAGE SERVICE AND MULTIMEDIA MESSAGE SERVICE

The most basic form of communication in mobile is via **short message service (SMS)**, also known as text messaging. SMS can be a highly effective method of engaging customers and developing relationships with them. Because people must opt in twice to participate, the marketer knows that those individuals are very interested in receiving communications from the marketer. Most targets that have cell phones can use text messaging and participate in SMS communications even if they don't have smartphones. Finally, SMS can help marketers achieve specific goals, such as to deliver messages, encourage participation in contests and sweepstakes, provide news and information, or simply reach out and say hello to customers.

There are also some caveats associated with SMS. First, marketers must pay for arranging SMS strategies, follow a specific set of guidelines, obtain double opt-in, and agree to end communications when told to do so by users. These rules are stricter than with social media strategies because mobile communications are more heavily regulated than social networks.

An SMS campaign consists of a keyword that a mobile user sends via text message to a **short code**, a "short" phone number usually only 5–6 digits. The keyword identifies the specific text that will be returned to the person who texts that particular keyword to the short code. For example, a marketer can encourage people via in-store signage to text the keyword "ALPHA" to the short code 55467 to receive a daily special from the company. The message will come back to people who sent the keyword "ALPHA" via a returned text message to their phones.

In the United States, the Common Short Code Administration manages short codes so that the numbers work across mobile provider networks and are not duplicated. Short codes in the United States tend to be five or six digits, but shorter codes are sometimes used in other countries depending on the country's own administration system, often ultimately controlled by government entities.

The Common Short Code Administration allows for the short code to be used across wireless carriers such as AT&T, Verizon, or T-Mobile. Marketers can lease short codes for periods of three, six,

An SMS opt-in marketing campaign.

© Shutterstock/blojfo

or twelve months with a minimum flat fee of $500 and then $1,000 per month. A dedicated short code belongs to one entity, while a shared short code may be used by multiple marketers.

Multimedia messaging service (MMS) is a similar service that allows people to send information that is longer than 160 characters, the maximum allowable by SMS. MMS can also be used to send pictures and video content via short code.

SMS is effective for generating a response to offers. For example, Jim Beam wanted to encourage people to enter its sweepstakes to win a set of Live Music Series VIP concert tickets. People were asked to text keyword LMSVIP to short code 66937. The system returned: "Enter Today's Sweepstakes and get alerts. Reply Y to join the Jim Beam Music mobile list." After the receiver of the message typed "Y," the system returned the message "You've joined the Jim Beam Mobile List Reply STOP to cancel, reply HELP for help. Msg&data rates may apply" [18].

consider this . . .

COWS SEND TEXT MESSAGES

In Switzerland, even cows are getting into SMS. Farmers are using a system of sensors to measure the movement of cows and to monitor the times when the cows are in heat. This allows the farmers to plan insemination strategies, while maximizing milk production. The system costs about $1,400 per cow with a correct identification rate of 90% [19].

Marketers can choose to set up their own SMS campaign, though the steps in doing so can be daunting because the marketer must negotiate with each wireless carrier for access. Larger marketers who intend to use SMS often may decide to invest in their own short codes. However, many marketers choose to share short codes and develop campaigns with the help of service providers who aggregate codes for use by multiple marketers. The Common Short Code Administration recommends a variety of firms that run SMS campaigns for clients and will work with them to obtain short codes. Regardless of whether a marketer opts to set it up or hires someone, the process is similar. Exhibit 11.3 outlines the steps in developing an SMS strategy [20].

When using SMS, marketers should stay relevant and offer consumers something they want, such as news, tips, links to sites, product information, or multimedia. The information should be timely with a strong call to action. Since not everyone has smartphones, SMS can help drive consumers to specific in-store deals, and marketers can use a variety of other forms of media to encourage SMS opt-in. SMS is a good method for encouraging participation in contests and sweepstakes and can populate loyalty programs with very good customers.

EXHIBIT 11.3

Steps in Developing an SMS Strategy

1. The marketer begins by obtaining a short code from the U.S. Common Short Code Administration. The website is http://www.usshortcodes.com/. The process takes a long time, so marketers should plan a minimum of 6–12 weeks for an SMS strategy. Each country operates its own common short code administration to manage the process within that country and the short codes differ in the number of digits.

2. The next step is for the marketer to negotiate terms with each wireless carrier so that the carrier will accept routing of the short code through its network. Carriers will assess the promotion to determine whether it is appropriate for its network and the timing of the communication, and if the promotion would interfere with other applications that may operate at the same time. Connectivity aggregators have preexisting relationships with wireless companies, which could expedite the contract. The terms of the contract may include per message fees in addition to the cost of the short code lease. According to Tatango, a firm that provides SMS services, advertising-supported SMS earns $.005 per message for many carriers, such as Sprint and Virgin Mobile.

3. A marketer must then develop a campaign using software that operates with the short code and wireless networks. The campaign specifies the messages returned to customers when they text the keyword to the short code. Applications service providers help marketers develop campaigns if they do not have the technical know-how.

4. The next step is to market the keyword and short codes to encourage customers to opt in to receive communications.

5. Marketers must include a compliant opt-in message that contains the content provider's name, the description of the program, how often the alerts will come, the rate or cost (such as msg&data rates apply), and instructions on how to quit the program such as Reply STOP to end or HELP for help.

Source: *Common Short Code Administration, 2016, https://www.usshortcodes.com/info/*

THE MOBILE WEB

One strategy in mobile marketing is to develop a mobile website that consumers can access on the go. A mobile device will automatically retrieve a mobile site when one is available; otherwise, the device will display the regular website. As discussed in Chapter Seven, marketers are moving toward a system of responsive design. **Responsive design** means that the marketer creates the website so that it can be viewed by many different types of devices, rather than adapt the strategy for different devices. Marketers have to consider the use cases associated with their websites and mobile sites before committing to a particular design strategy.

These days, it is important for marketers to have a mobile site and it is not expensive for brands to initiate a mobile Web presence. Most of the major Web-hosting sites offer a mobile version of the site to companies. For example, marketers who use Shopify, Wix, or Squarespace all have mobile versions of their sites supported by the platform. Mobile sites are particularly important if:

1. There is a local element to the marketing strategy.
2. The customer base has high mobile usage rates.
3. A mobile website can provide current and useful information when the prospect does not have access to wireless Internet, but could benefit from information.

Marketers who do not have mobile-optimized or responsive sites run into problems if the screen displays the regular website. In this case, the user will have to scroll around to locate important information and may become frustrated. Another potential cause of frustration for customers is the slower connection speeds on mobile devices, which limits the number of screens a customer can access and the features he or she can use.

To create effective mobile sites, marketers should first evaluate consumer response on mobile. A good place to start is to look at the site's analytics to determine the percentage of site visits that are generated by mobile and then consider how people use the site on their mobile devices. Google Analytics provides information on the operating system that accesses the site, the screen sizes, and the service provider. Marketers can also evaluate conversions that take place via phone and tablet and track the click stream that leads to key conversions.

The mobile Web presents an opportunity for marketers who wish to reach consumers when they are out and about instead of facing a computer. As with online marketing, mobile users search for product- and service-related information using various browsers that are available on their smartphone or tablet device. Search is a very popular mobile activity, representing 70% of the mobile advertising market, and the dominant player in mobile search is Google, commanding 90% of the global market for mobile search. When people search using their phones, they are even more likely than on a PC to consider the highest-ranked search engine results. Therefore, mobile search engine optimization (SEO) is important and marketers should seek to achieve high mobile rankings [21].

A mobile shopping website.

© Shutterstock/Georgejmclittle

Mobile differs from desktop in terms of software capabilities and tracking. Specifically, mobile websites can support HTML and Java, but not Flash as desktop sites can. Also, cookies are not as useful for tracking in mobile because most browsers are not set to allow third party cookies [22]. However, marketers have methods for tracking consumers on mobile devices. The major social media sites can match a person's mobile usage to PC because people use the same sign-in for their social media accounts on all their devices. Apple and Google have other systems for user identification. Apple requires that developers use identifiers for their software and Google uses Android IDs, which allows for Wi-Fi receiver tracking [23].

consider this . . .

PLUSNET USES RESPONSIVE DESIGN

Plusnet, a U.K. company that sells broadband and phone services, noticed a strong uptick in the number of mobile hits to its website. As a result, the company wanted to optimize the experience across devices to improve the user experience. To ensure the best user experience, the company had to consider how content would show up on various screens and reduce the amount of information. The customers were able to buy Internet services on their phones, which comes in handy when people are moving into new homes. The results were that as mobile traffic doubled, mobile conversions increased with them and the time to complete a sale declined 40% [24].

OPTIMIZING FOR THE MOBILE WEB

As with desktop sites, marketers must optimize mobile websites for search to be noticed. Because the mobile screen is smaller, people look at fewer results when searching, so marketers must ensure their page ranks high in order to drive customers to it. To optimize a mobile site, marketers should consider the available data from the mobile site to improve the performance of the site based on established goals. In addition, it helps to understand how Google crawls sites to rank them. Specifically, Google is looking for mobile sites that give the user the best possible experience, so sites that load fast, have interesting relevant content, and meet the needs of the users rank higher. Because mobile has become so important, Google now expects sites to be mobile optimized and ranks those with good mobile experiences for users higher [25]. Marketers who wish to develop a mobile Web strategy should consider the steps listed in Exhibit 11.4.

Marketers should treat mobile campaigns as distinctively mobile, meaning that the mobile outlet should take advantage of its functionality and location information, and focus on consumers' immediate needs. Marketers should optimize sites following the basic rules for Web SEO as outlined in Chapter Seven.

EXHIBIT 11.4

Steps in Developing a Mobile Web Strategy

1. Determine your mobile audience by using analytics for organic mobile traffic.

2. Evaluate your current website and determine the potential mobile use case scenarios.

3. Analyze the mobile behavior of your target market by examining mobile keywords.

4. Examine how your site shows up on various mobile platforms.

5. Assess your current content to identify the content that is most mobile friendly.

6. Determine whether you need a dedicated mobile site or can use responsive design.

7. Optimize the site for search engines.

8. Consider costs and measure return on investment for a mobile site.

consider this . . .

TD AMERITRADE LEVERAGES MOBILE SEARCH

In order to attract new customers to TD Ameritrade's trading desk, the brand evaluated people's search behavior to determine how best to reach them. TD Ameritrade noticed that mobile Web traffic rose on new market information and that people used their phones to determine whether to buy specific stocks. The company then purchased keywords for the major stock purchase searches and drove potential customers to a dedicated mobile landing page. For example, two very successful keyword phrases were "Buy Apple Stock" and "APPL Stock Split." The campaign led to a 10% increase in mobile conversions for the company [26].

QUICK RESPONSE CODES

Have you ever used your phone to scan a square-shaped bar code in a magazine ad, or on a store sign or poster? These 2D bar codes, also called **quick response (QR) codes**, are read by special scanners that link to the camera in a smartphone. Originally, QR codes were created in Japan for use in the automobile industry. The codes were useful because they could store large amounts of data. Once the bar codes became available for free online so anyone could create and use them, they grew in popularity [27].

Whereas marketers like QR codes because they can deliver an immediate response at a low cost, people have not widely embraced the technology in spite of

You can generate your own QR code at www.goqr.me.

QR Code Generator, www.goqr.me

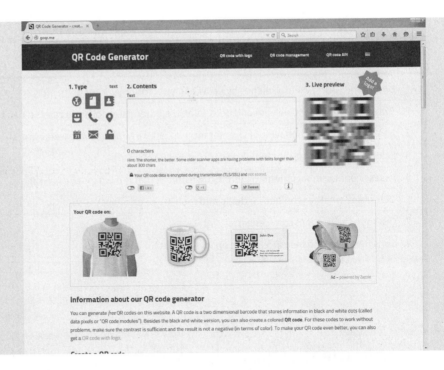

the growth of smartphone usage overall. When was the last time you stopped to scan a QR code? In the United States, younger consumers are more likely to scan QR codes than older consumers, but the incidence is still fairly low at under 40%. The most likely place to scan a code is in a magazine, followed by regular mail, posters, and packages [28]. Whereas QR codes are more popular in Asia than in the United States, they are less commonly used in Europe [29]. One reason is that QR readers are often preloaded on cell phones in Asia, but not in the United States where people have to download readers in order to scan codes.

Anyone can generate QR codes easily by going to www.goqr.me. The site is run by a German company that also offers customizable QR codes. To use the service, you first have to decide the type of content to which you want the QR code to link. You may want the QR code to lead to a website URL, a dedicated landing page, a set piece of text, a call to a number, an email, a location (in latitude and longitude), or an event's date and time. Once you input the information, the system delivers a QR code, such as the one pictured, that you can put anywhere you like. Of course, where you place the QR code and how you promote it influence the likelihood that people will scan it. In order for marketers to use the strategy, they should consider the requirements listed in Exhibit 11.5.

Marketers can place QR codes in a variety of locations, including in magazine advertisements, on billboards, on packaging or shelving, or even on t-shirts. The strategy is important and marketers must make sure that the offer is valuable to the target—it will lead to a working and useful outcome—and that the person can actually scan the QR code easily. There are many examples of QR codes that are hard to scan. For example, one company placed QR codes on cupcakes that were eaten, another put a QR code on a poster in a subway station where people would have had to go on the tracks to scan it, and many QR codes have appeared on people's shirts, which could result in an awkward interaction.

Requirements for Consumers Reading QR Codes

1. Smartphone with optical scan

2. Applications with a QR code reader for Android, iOS, or other smartphone system

3. Consumers with the motivation and opportunity to scan a QR code at a particular time

consider this...

CHOOSING QR CODES VERSUS SMS

Marketers who would like to reach consumers quickly in a particular location may choose between using a QR code or SMS since both share the goal of immediate response. When people opt in on an SMS campaign, the messages appear on their phones, even if they did not scan or download a scanning application. As a result, SMS is good for connecting with highly engaged and interested customers who are willing to text a keyword to a short code and agree to receive messages from a marketer even if they do not have smartphones. SMS is a strong strategy for reaching customers in the developing world. QR codes are for those willing to participate in the action once, but may not want to receive future text messages. The codes are good for purchases that require some consideration and consumers can use them to gain more information. A QR code can also be styled so that it represents the brand's logo and is therefore viewed as more upscale than reaching someone via SMS and may provide a brand identification if the code is created to look like the brand logo.

MOBILE APPLICATIONS

Mobile applications (apps) are software programs that run on mobile devices, such as a smartphone or tablet [30]. They provide a specific type of function, such as a game, search engine, or calculator, and can pull data from the Web into the application or use the functions of the device, such as scanners, cameras, or sounds. The most popular applications are games and social networks.

Most people who have smartphones have downloaded apps, and they spend over thirty hours per month using applications. Though people have many applications on their devices, they use only about twenty-five apps per month [31]. Not only that, but people prefer the apps they have. Sixty-six percent of smartphone owners do not download an app in a typical one-month period [32].

Marketers are interested in consumers' app behavior because of the amount of time people spend using apps and the e-commerce opportunities in mobile shopping. Internet Retailer found that conversion rates were 30% higher when people used apps compared to connecting with a store's mobile site. One advantage of apps over the mobile Web is the fact that an Internet connection is not necessary because the app is stored on the device. People using dedicated store apps are more likely to have a task at hand, rather than just searching the mobile Web [33].

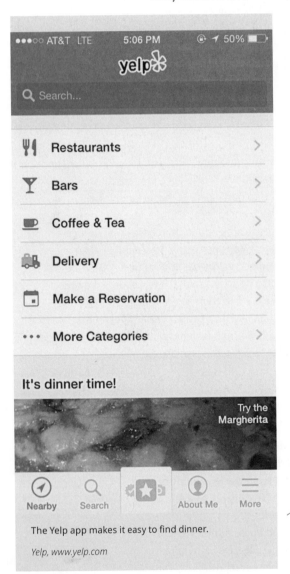

The Yelp app makes it easy to find dinner.

Yelp, www.yelp.com

As with any strategy, marketers must first set goals and determine whether an application is the most effective and efficient means of reaching the goal. For many communications strategies, apps may not provide a strong return on investment if the goal is to reach a large proportion of a target market. However, apps may provide a strong level of engagement among a targeted group of customers. Marketers can use apps to:

- Build a social media presence.
- Improve store ratings.
- Increase user engagement.

Another key to a successful app strategy is to research the target and know their behaviors regarding the brand. An app would have to fit neatly into the customer's brand-related behavior in order for the person to be willing to take the time to download and then use the app. The target would have to perceive a strong benefit to using the app in order to participate and perhaps see others use it or at least be aware that the app exists. In essence, people adopt apps based on the same criteria as they adopt new products. The new product adoption process is discussed in detail in Chapter Four.

Apps provide marketers with the opportunity to run advertising within apps that already exist, run customized experiences in existing apps, or build their own apps to offer added value to customers. The most complicated of these strategies is building an app, but it also affords the marketer the most control over the content and customer experience. Exhibit 11.6 lists the most downloaded categories of apps [34].

EXHIBIT 11.6

Percentage of Mobile Users with Apps and Time Spent by Category

APPS DOWNLOADED	PERCENTAGE OF PEOPLE WITH THIS TYPE OF APP	SHARE OF USER TIME SPENT IN THE CATEGORY
Games	65%	6%
Social networking	57%	14%
Weather	54%	3%
Entertainment/Video	51%	9%
Radio/Music	38%	6%
Utilities	38%	3%
Finance	37%	2%
Sports	27%	3%
Newsstand	20%	3%
Retailer	19%	5%

Sources: *K. Sruoginis, "Who Are the Mobile Gamers and Why Do They Matter?," lab.net, 20 November 2014.*
Perez, S. "Consumers Spend 85% of Time on Smartphones in Apps, but Only 5 Apps See Heavy Use," TechCrunch, 22 June, 2015.
http://techcrunch.com/2015/06/22/consumers-spend-85-of-time-on-smartphones-in-apps-but-only-5-apps-see-heavy-use/

APP DEVELOPMENT

A strong app builds on brand objectives and offers customers an engaging brand experience that often adds value to the brand and its users. App development requires marketers to commit both in terms of time and expense. Apps are meant to be ongoing, but must be updated regularly to continue to deliver value.

Globally, Android systems represent over 80% of the market compared with Apple running on less than 15% of global devices. Windows phones have less than 3% share and Blackberry is under 1%, so they are less important to consider when designing applications [35]. App development involves creating a program that can operate across multiple platforms and for various-size devices.

Most marketers hire outside firms to develop applications and the costs vary substantially depending on the task, variety of platforms, and complexity of the program. At a minimum, a very basic application costs $10,000, but a decent functioning app is at least $20,000 [36].

Google charges a one-time developer registration fee of $25, but an Apple development account costs $99 per year. Both Apple and Google take 30% of the revenues generated by the app [37].

Marketers should seriously consider the need for an application because of the time and cost associated with development. A study of mobile businesses by Kinvey found that 56% indicated that it takes from seven months to over a year to build an app, and 18% indicated they spent from $500,000 to over $1,000,000 per app, with an average of $270,000 per app [38].

Additionally, there are rules. Developers must follow specific guidelines so that Apple or Google will accept the app in their stores. Apple will reject apps that fail to protect children, do not provide a unique or useful function, are not well designed, or are just "plain creepy." Some examples of the iTunes store rules appear in Exhibit 11.7 [39].

The Google Play Store offers apps for Android devices and has its own set of rules for app development and sales. Though Android has fewer rules than Apple,

EXHIBIT 11.7

Summary of Apple's Rules for Developing Apps for iOS

RULES FOR IOS	
Functionality	The app operates as intended, is useful and not overtly advertising-based, limits its data collection and dispersion outside the app itself, doesn't encourage excessive alcohol consumption.
Metadata	The app does not mention other mobile platforms, icons are consistent across similar apps, keywords are appropriate, developers do not attempt to manipulate iTunes ratings or rankings.
Location	Apps get consent from users before using location data, location data can only be used if appropriate to the app, apps may not be used to control vehicles.
Push notification	Push notifications must have user consent and use the Apple format, notifications must be free of charge.
User interface	Apps must be visually appealing with simple clear designs, apps may not alter standard switches or their functions.
Purchasing and currencies	Apps may not lead to purchases of physical goods outside of the app, expensive apps are heavily scrutinized.
Others	Apps may not damage the device or use excessive battery power, they may not be offensive or mean-spirited, they can't be overly violent, users' privacy must be protected, sweepstakes rules must be followed.

Source: Apple, "App Store Review Guidelines," accessed June 3, 2016.

there are more screen sizes to consider because of the variety of devices. Other major differences are that developers can manipulate device buttons, use widgets (mini programs within an app that perform one function), alter the appearance of the screen more, and use near field communication (NFC) technology [40].

RETAIL APPS AND PAYMENTS

Retailers have begun to offer apps that drive traffic to stores and enhance the shopping experience once the customer is in the store. Initially, stores were concerned that people would browse in the store but seek a better-price deal online. While customers can certainly shop around using their mobile devices, many retailers have decided to fight back with their own apps that offer consumers a unique experience and incentives to buy from the store in which they are browsing. For example, Target introduced its Cartwheel application to attract loyal customers and reward them. The mobile coupon clipping app has been very successful. The amount of time Target shoppers spent on mobile apps rose 251% in one month and Target's app was used 76% of the time, with Target's mobile site accounting for the remaining mobile visits. In addition, Cartwheel users spent 30% more per store visit according to Target [41].

Mobile is also growing as a medium for payments. Initially, people were reluctant to use their phones to buy goods and services because they did not trust mobile systems. And, some of the fear remains. A study of 4,200 U.S. households found that two-thirds prefer to use a mobile app from a bank rather than a third party and 65% were concerned with security [42]. Younger people are more likely to use mobile payment systems, which accounts for much of the success of PayPal's Venmo. Venmo is a mobile platform for making and sharing payments, which is popular among those under age 30. The Venmo platform processes more payments as Starbucks's system, and had $1 billion of transactions in one month [43]. Though finance apps do not command the attention of other applications, they are likely to be important in the mobile sphere for executing purchases going forward.

consider this . . .

WHAT IS A BEACON?

A **beacon** is a small radio transmitter that can signal applications on a mobile device and deliver a message to someone in a particular location. Marketers can use beacons to offer coupons when app users approach a particular area. If you have an iPhone with the iTunes App Store application and you approach an Apple store, you might receive offers or notifications from Apple. Beacons only work with certain apps—usually, those placed by a particular marketer. The transmitters do not store data, but the applications on the phone do. American Eagle installed beacons to work with the Shopkick application to deliver incentives to shoppers in its stores. In a store study, half the customers were told they would earn rewards for trying on clothes and the other half were not offered incentives. Twice as many who received the offer tried on clothes. How did American Eagle learn that? The store had placed a beacon in the dressing rooms to determine whether or not the subjects entered [44].

consider this . . .

RITZ CARLTON KNOWS ITS CUSTOMERS

App marketers can benefit from use case scenarios. For example, Ritz Carlton developed a mobile app that offers different services for customers who are at home versus those on site. When in the hotel, people want to check in and get their key. When people are home, they are shopping for hotel services. These two use cases require the app to deliver a different experience—optimized for location [45].

MOBILE GAMING

A very important segment of the mobile applications market is mobile gaming. Traditionally, gamers were young men 18–24 who played on home gaming devices or handheld systems. The advent of mobile led to a shift in the segment of individuals who play games. Now, the most likely gamer is a professional woman in her early thirties who earns an above-average income.

More than half of U.S. adults are mobile gamers and almost 70% of smartphone owners. Mobile gamers are an attractive target market because they are engaged with both mobile marketing and traditional advertising, and are more likely than average adults to be planning purchases.

According to Nielsen, 93% of gamers are willing to pay for games. They are also sticky, with players spending an average of 14.7 hours a month on iOS games and 9.3 hours a month on Android games [46]. As a result, games are the most lucrative segment of the app market. What games do you play when you take out your mobile phone? You probably play one of the top grossing games in the United States, but the game that makes the most money is one that is popular in Japan (see Exhibit 11.8) [47]. Have you ever heard of Puzzles & Dragons?

Highest Grossing Mobile Applications in the United States

COMPANY	TOP GAME	ESTIMATED DAILY REVENUE
Supercell	Clash of Clans	$1,118,457
King Digital Entertainment	Candy Crush Saga	$884,676
Machine Zone	Game of War—Fire Age	$572,498
King Digital Entertainment	Farm Heroes Saga	$271,378

R. Borison, "The 15 Highest Grossing iPhone and iPad Games," Business Insider, 20 May 2014.

consider this . . .

THE SUCCESS OF FREMIUM

People download most apps from either the Apple or Google Play stores depending on whether they have an iOS or Android system. Most apps are free to download initially, but may charge for add-ons. This type of pricing is called the **fremium model** and has been very successful in generating revenue for developers. Over 90% of apps are offered for free, but they represent 69% of iOS app revenues and 75% of Android revenues. Among the most downloaded and used apps are those for gaming. The freemium model works well in the gaming genre because it encourages people to try a game and then, if the app is lucky, the players get hooked on it and buy more lives, virtual items, or currency that advances the game [48].

Mobile game marketing consists of two basic strategies. The first is for a brand to develop a mobile application. Marketers who wish to develop gaming apps must carefully consider the investment. Good apps are expensive to produce and games have a limited shelf life. People will play a game for a period of time, tire of it, and move on to the next exciting option. As such, marketers must be very clear about the goals they set.

The first goal for a gaming app is brand engagement. Marketers may wish to encourage targets to think about their brand and what it stands for. For example, Chipotle developed a mobile app as part of a broad campaign to get people to consider how food is raised. In the game, a Scarecrow works in a factory producing processed foods, but longs to grow and serve healthy burritos. A video trailer produced for the game and running on YouTube earned 11.6 million views,

52,000 Facebook posts, 31,000 tweets, and a total of 126 million impressions in eight months [49].

In addition, Chipotle's game was downloaded 530,000 times in the first four months it was available and people continued to download the game around the world, even in countries that did not have a Chipotle restaurant. The game reinforced the healthy food message and drove business to the stores by offering "buy one get one free" coupons for in-store purchases of burritos, bowls, and tacos. In the first four months of the campaign, 57,000 customers earned coupon cards through the game [50].

A second mobile game marketing strategy is to advertise within successful existing games. Some mobile games accept third party advertising, but much of the inventory is sold through advertising networks.

MOBILE ADVERTISING

Mobile advertising spending in the United States has been growing at a rate of 5% per year and represents more than 50% of total digital ad spending in the United States and 25% worldwide [51]. The push toward mobile will continue in the developing world as marketers seek to reach more people on their devices.

PURCHASING AD SPACE ON MOBILE

Marketers can buy advertising on mobile websites or within applications in a variety of formats including video. The most popular format is the 300×250 banner advertisements because the size works on multiple devices and screen sizes. Mobile advertising networks sell advertising space on a cost-per-impression or cost-per-click basis, depending on the needs of the advertiser. Click-through rates on mobile devices are higher than for desktop or tablet search, in social media and for display ads [52].

Buying mobile advertising is similar to buying Web advertising as more programmatic buying and real-time bidding options emerge. Mobile ad networks sell mobile advertising space programmatically to advertisers by aggregating the mobile ad inventory. Advertisers can purchase ads on premium networks, which provide information on the apps and sites on which ads run. Alternatively, blind networks run advertising, but the buyers do not learn which mobile sites are in the network, so these ads are cheaper, but less targeted.

The mobile ad market is dominated by the big Internet companies. Google's network represents 32% of U.S. mobile ad revenues and Facebook's platform controls about 20% of mobile advertising [51]. Advertisers who wish to run mobile ads on these networks can simply specify mobile ads as part of the display ad purchase process when buying advertising on Google's or Facebook's platforms. Both of these companies offer developers the opportunity to run the network ads in their apps by installing the Google or Facebook **software development kit (SDK)**, a set of instructions for designing apps so they meet specifications for running network ads.

Marketers can also purchase mobile advertising space through real-time bidding systems served by advertising exchanges, which aggregate publishers' ad space and provide the software for bidding on and serving the ads to mobile Web or app viewers.

Mobile advertisers can take advantage of location information and the type of person who uses a particular application in terms of demographics and interests. Increasingly, mobile ads identify consumers based on their unique characteristics and serve ads with interactive elements that drive response.

Burger King is offering breakfast coupons to consumers who have the Pandora app and enter the vicinity of one of its restaurants. The coupons show up within the app, so listeners are not taken away from their music. Hershey's created mobile video ads for the Scharffen Berger brand and made a deal with AT&T to cover the mobile data charges for watching the ad. L'Oréal has used specialized software to determine people's hair colors on a mobile device, so it can recommend a hair color product [53].

NATIVE ADS

Brands, particularly in mobile, try to run **native ads**. Native ads are those that fit seamlessly into the content on a mobile device or on the Web so that viewers don't feel bothered by the advertising. Since people prefer to view content more than advertising, brands want to be able to appear in a natural setting. For example, ads that run in people's newsfeeds on the Facebook mobile app fit in with the format of Facebook and match the type of content that people engage with on the platform. Native ads fit the form and functionality of the page design, are well integrated with the look and feel of the application, and match the user experience. There are six types of native ads according to the Internet Advertising Bureau (IAB) [54]:

In-feed units (unpaid messages in the newsfeed)

Paid search units (paid messages in the newsfeed)

Recommendation widgets (lists of recommendations to viewers)

Promoted listings (product listings with purchase information)

In-ad advertising units (banner ads)

Custom designs

MOBILE CLICK-THROUGH RATES

According to a study by Smart Insights, click-through rates are really low. For display ads the CTR is .06% meaning that per 1000 viewers fewer than 1 person on average clicked on the ad. That doesn't mean that the person didn't see the ad, just that he or she did not click on it. Are other CTRs better? The bright spot appears to be mobile where click through rates for search, social media, and display ads are all higher than for desktop. For example, the CTR for social media on mobile is .86% compared to .54% on a desktop computer. Mobile search has a 2.14% click-through rate. And click-through rates are higher, a whopping 4.4%, for the top search position than items that rank lower when people search on mobile. [55], [56].

MOBILE EMAIL

Email is one of the most cost-effective methods of reaching customers, and **mobile email** reaches people at moments when they may be making purchases in the real world. Mobile email is particularly effective in delivering coupons or encouraging a store visit because people check their email regularly and expect communications from marketers. In fact, checking email is the number one smartphone and tablet activity [57]. Not only that, but mobile open rates have been climbing, and almost 50% of those emails opened are on a mobile device [58]. Because of increased mobile usage, revenues from mobile email are significantly higher than those generated via desktop email, and the low cost of serving an email message leads to a very solid return on investment.

Mobile email is a good way to stay in touch with customers, provide news and updates, and drive people to respond. When developing a mobile email strategy, marketers should:

- Consider the size of the screen and use bold graphics.
- Keep the message short with a strong opening line.
- Use a consistent brand message.
- Optimize for mobile, recognizing that screens are small and load times must be quick.
- Include easy clickable buttons.
- Consider the timing of the message.
- Create mobile friendly landing pages.

LOCATION-BASED MOBILE MARKETING

The expression SoLoMo suggests mobile's importance to location-based strategies. The acronym SoLoMo stands for social, local, and mobile and represents the expectations marketers had for mobile early on. It is true that people are very social on their mobile devices and use them on the go. Of course, mobile devices are also used extensively from home because people find them so convenient to pick up.

Marketers have found that mobile is well suited for location-based strategies because the phone travels with people wherever they go. Any strategy that takes location into account in finding and reaching customers is location-based. Originally, location-based mobile strategies emphasized "check-in" apps that allowed people to indicate their presence in particular places. On Foursquare, a user could become the "mayor" of a bar, restaurant, school, apartment building, or any other place frequently visited. Ultimately, people grew weary of checking in and the company changed its focus to emphasize reviews. The company still does "neighborhood sharing" under the name Swarm.

Some other location-based strategies include mobile search, which can lead customers to a location; mobile advertising that runs in certain locations; beacons or geofences that operate with mobile applications; billboards that interact with mobile devices; check-in offers and deals; mobile email that is opened in a location; and even opting in to SMS as a result of a location.

consider this . . .

A LOCATION-BASED EMAIL STRATEGY

One of the great advantages of mobile is that it can target people based on their locations. Quirky, a company you may remember from Chapter Five, created a mobile-controlled air conditioner. The company used location-based marketing to reach consumers when the temperatures rose beyond 75 degrees in New York and Boston. The weather alert system Poncho sent mobile emails and text messages to users. Quirky inserted a promotional link in these messages to encourage people to go to their landing page for the product. Poncho indicated that the open rate on the email was 60% and close to 100% on text messages. That's a fairly strong response [59].

SUMMARY AND REVIEW

CHAPTER SUMMARY

Marketers are increasingly adding mobile to their communications mixes as consumers spend more time with their mobile devices. Mobile marketing strategies include sending opt-in text messages, offering mobile websites, developing applications, serving mobile advertisements, and sending emails. Each of these strategies can take advantage of the fact that consumers frequently bring their phones everywhere they go; their phones are always within reach. Mobile lends itself particularly well to location-based strategies and many executions rely on knowing where people are.

KEY TERMS

beacon
fremium model
mobile applications (apps)
mobile email
multimedia message service (MMS)
native ads
quick response (QR) code
responsive design
short code
short message service (SMS)
software development kit (SDK)

SUMMARY REVIEW QUESTIONS

1. What does SMS stand for and how is it used?
2. What are three goals a brand could achieve using mobile marketing?
3. What are the advantages and disadvantages of developing a mobile app for a brand?
4. How can a marketer buy mobile advertising if he or she wants to show mobile users advertisements on applications?
5. Which mobile strategy provides the highest return on investment for most companies? Why?
6. What is a beacon and how can a company use one?
7. Describe two location-based strategies that can be executed via mobile.

APPLICATION QUESTIONS

1. For a full 24-hour period, keep a log of your phone usage, indicating what you are doing with your phone and for how long. What are the activities that hold your interest the longest? What else are you doing while using your phone?
2. Imagine a day when you could not use your phone. List three problems you would encounter during the day if you left your phone at home. How would you solve those problems?
3. Go to the Common Short Code Administration website and list three application service providers. What do these companies do?
4. What does the company SiteScout do? Go to its website and explain how it serves mobile ads.
5. Go to Google's www.howtogomo.com and create a mobile version of a website you like. What is different about the mobile site versus the regular website?

6. Examine a mobile email from a marketer that you have received. Does the email meet the criteria for successful email outlined in the section on mobile email in this chapter? What would you recommend to improve the communication?

7. Have you ever "checked in" using an application? Examine closely a time when you used your location-based app to check in. Why did you choose to announce your presence? What benefits did you obtain and what were the risks? If you have never checked in, look at your social media accounts and see if any of your friends have done so. Why do you think your friends chose to check in? What are their motivations?

case study Mobile Payments Take Off with Apple Pay

Have you been one of the bold ones to throw away your wallet and pay for all your purchases using your phone? While you may be able to buy your morning coffee at Starbucks, a hamburger at McDonald's, or healthier options at Whole Foods, you may not be able to buy everything you may want using your phone to pay.

Mobile payments have been a long time coming. What has been the hold-up? You have probably already split a check using Venmo and you likely have a PayPal account, so what's the problem?

OBSTACLES TO ADOPTION

There were a number of obstacles to mobile payment systems, including technological limitations, banking issues, and consumer reluctance to embrace virtual wallets. As a result, no one system dominated the market, though many companies tried. Competitors in the mobile payment space included Google Wallet, Softcard, PayPal, Alipay, and various bank apps. One of the largest players in mobile payments was Starbucks, which completed over 7 million mobile transactions per week [60]. In 2014 mobile payments represented a $50 billion market, but Forrester Research had predicted that mobile payments would grow to $142 billion by 2019. One big reason for the expected growth was the introduction of Apple Pay [61].

Mobile payment systems were slow to gain traction for a number of reasons. First, there were numerous types of payment technologies, but each merchant had its own payment system that often did not work with the mobile wallet applications on people's phones. Point-of-sale payment systems and the employees who ran them were not mobile-ready, and stores were reluctant to invest in new hardware and training. The goal of the store was to obtain payment in the easiest way possible, not spend a lot of time worrying about whether a payment system would work.

Another obstacle was that stores had to choose between offering Apple or Android systems for payments because of the different technologies on the two types of devices. Google Wallet worked only with near field communication (NFC) technology that allowed a phone to interact wirelessly with a payment system. Apple phones were not NFC capable until the iPhone 6, which enabled NFC for the Apple Pay system only. Of course, Android systems dominated the global marketplace and Apple could only offer Apple Pay on its iPhone 6 or higher models. This greatly limited the reach of Apple Pay, but provided Apple with a hook for consumers to upgrade their phones [62].

Believe it or not, the credit card was a problem for mobile payment systems. It was very easy for people to take out a credit card, swipe it, and pay for an item. Why should a customer need a phone system to do that? After all, there were security and privacy issues with using phones for payments. Among people *who already used* mobile payment services, a study found that 41% were concerned with privacy. Additionally, 37% of active mobile payment users compared to only 20% of average consumers indicated that using a smartphone for payments wasn't safe [63].

APPLE PAY BREAKS BARRIERS

Apple Pay was introduced in October 2014 in the United States. Apple's mobile payment system was only available to iPhone 6 owners, representing about 10 million people. Prior to the launch, Apple signed up over 220,000 stores, the major payment networks such as Visa and MasterCard, and more than 500 banks [64].

After a few months, Apple Pay indicated that the system accepted payments from vendors representing 90% of the credit card purchases made in the United States, including Staples,

Winn-Dixie, Albertsons, and Amway Center. McDonald's reported that half of its mobile payments through NFC occurred via Apple Pay in the first two months following its introduction.

The Apple Pay system required that the vendor install an NFC reader device in the store. The company chose to integrate its system with NFC-based tap-to-pay systems previously available on the market, and did not develop its own wireless standard. As a result, Apple Pay could be used in stores with a variety of NFC systems and even worked internationally on systems when customers' payment systems were linked to U.S. credit cards [65].

Customers with an iPhone 6 had to adjust their settings and include a credit card's information within their Apple Passbook application to use the system. In stores, users touched the phone to the in-store device and identified themselves via a fingerprint scanner on their phones. As NFC technology was not new— Google Wallet had been using NFC technology since its introduction in September 2011—what was the hook?

Apple CEO Tim Cook announced the payment system at a media event, but did not heavily promote its introduction. However, banks were eager to promote their connection with Apple and did so via digital and traditional media. Wells Fargo sent out Apple Pay emails to its customers, advertised the service on its site, and ran a TV spot showing the ease and use of Apple Pay. In one ad, a man showed up early to his own surprise party when he was supposed to be out shopping, because that trip went faster than his wife anticipated as a result of Apple Pay. Wells Fargo also offered its customers $20 to sign up with the service. Chase ran promotions offering a free music album and added a Chase Visa card to the Apple Passbook application [66].

In the first few weeks of its introduction, the Apple Pay app gained more market share than Google had when it launched Google Wallet in 2011. Apple Pay accounted for .1%–1.6% of transactions among the top five retailers in the month after the launch. At the same time, Google announced that it had purchased Softcard, the mobile payment system formerly known as ISIS, which was founded by a consortium of mobile carriers like AT&T and T-Mobile [67]. Apple Pay was also expanding beyond the US and UK to China and other parts of Europe [68]. Clearly, the mobile payments market was moving forward, but with customers still showing reluctance to give up their wallets, how far would it go?

QUESTIONS FOR DISCUSSION

1. Why are people reluctant to use a mobile wallet?

2. What technology is Apple Pay using to connect iPhones to store readers?

3. Describe the barriers that Apple faced when introducing Apple Pay. How was it able to overcome those barriers and why?

4. Why do consumers adopt mobile pay systems? What would you recommend as a strategy for Apple Pay to encourage adoption?

5. Have you used a mobile payment system? Describe how it works and your feelings about using it.

6. What types of apps do you typically use on your smartphone? Does a payment app fit in with your lifestyle? How?

7. Consider your parents or other relatives older than yourself. Is their use of smartphones similar to yours? What do they do differently? How would they feel about using a mobile payment application on their phones?

8. Is Apple Pay a B2B or B2C application? Explain.

9. How could Apple Pay expand internationally? Which countries would be good candidates?

REFERENCES

[1] J. Wortham, "Fab Revamps Mobile Shops Ahead of the Holidays," *The New York Times,* 11 October 2012.

[2] N. Singer, "Learning to Chase Online Word of Mouth," *The New York Times,* 26 May 2012.

[3] I. Lundun, "Fab Was Burning Through $14M/Month Before Its Layoffs and Pivot," TechCrunch, 20 October 2014.

[4] App Annie, "App Annie and Internet Retailer Index," 2014.

[5] Tecmark, "Tecmark Survey Finds Average User Picks Up Their Smartphone 221 Times a Day!," 8 October 2014, http://www.tecmark.co.uk/smartphone-usage-data-uk-2014/.

[6] eMarketer, "Smartphone Users Worldwide Will Total 175 Billion in 2014," 16 January 2014, http://www.emarketer.com/Article/Smartphone-Users-Worldwide-Will-Total-175-Billion-2014/1010536.

[7] Google, "Navigating the New Multi Screen World," 29 August 2012, http://googlemobileads.blogspot.com/2012/08/navigating-new-multi-screen-world.html.

[8] Marketing Charts, "Most Smartphone Owners Feel Naked without Their Devices,"11 April 2012.

[9] European Travel Commission, "Tablet Penetration and Demographics," 2014, http://etc-digital.org/digital-trends/mobile-devices/tablets/.

[10] Anderson, Monica "The Demographics of Device Ownership," Pew Internet Research, October 29, 2015, http://www.pewinternet.org/2015/10/29/the-demographics-of-device-ownership/.

[11] Poushter, J. "Smartphone Ownership and Internet Usage Continues to Climb in Emerging Economies", February 22, 2016, http://www.pewglobal.org/2016/02/22/smartphone-ownership-and-internet-usage-continues-to-climb-in-emerging-economies/.

[12] Marketing Sherpa, "Marketing Sherpa Mobile Marketing Benchmark Study," 2012,

[13] Mobile Marketing Association, "Mom Influencer Campaign," 2014, http://www.mmaglobal.com/case-study-hub/case_studies/view/32209.

[14] Baglia, M., "The Golden Rule of SMS Marketing." January 7, 2016, Business to Communityhttp://www.business2community.com/infographics/golden-rule-sms-marketing-infographic-01387772#kqBHGhkLgGDrUQ4c.97.

[15] K. Rabon and A. Kane, "Some Stores Track Users by Wifi on Smart Phones," The Denver Channel, 29 April 2013.

[16] J. Cook, "Nordstrom Ends Smartphone Surveillance Program That Tracked In-Store Behavior of Shoppers," GeekWire, 13 July 2013.

[17] D. Butcher, "Sir Richard Branson's Virgin Media," Mobile Marketer, 23 November 2010.

[18] R. Kats, "Top 10 SMS Campaigns Q2," 11 July 2012, http://www.mobilemarketer.com/cms/news/messaging/13280.html.

[19] J. Tagliabue, "Swiss Cows Send Texts to Announce They're in Heat," The New York Times, 2 October 2012.

[20] D. Johnson, "The History of Carrier Pass Through Fees in SMS Marketing," Tatango, 27 January 2014.

[21] T. Wasserman, "How Google Could Lose Its Grip on Mobile Search," Mashable, 22 October 2012.

[22] E. Zalman, "Mobile Resolutions," 5 January 2012, http://www.adexchanger.com/now-serving-mobile/mobile-resolutions.

[23] J. McDermott, "Can Mobile Tracking Ever Be as Accurate as Cookies on the Desktop?," 21 March 2013, http://adage.com/article/digital/mobile-targeting-accurate-cookies-desktop/240464/.

[24] Google, "Plusnet Uses Responsive Web Design, Sees Traffic Grow 2x and Sales 10x on Smartphones and Tablets," Think With Google Case Study, August 2013.

[25] V. Fox, "The Definitive Guide to Mobile Search," 8 July 2013, http://searchengineland.com/the-definitive-guide-to-mobile-technical-seo-166066.

[26] Mobile Marketing Association, "Leveraging Mobile to Drive Acquisitions," Mobile Marketing Association Case Study, 2014.

[27] Denso Wave Inc., "History of QR Code," http://www.qrcode.com/en/history/.

[28] eMarketer, "US Ahead of Western Europe in QR Code Usage," 28 January 2013, http://www.emarketer.com/Article/US-Ahead-of-Western-Europe-QR-Code-Usage/1009631.

[29] K.-M. Cutler, "People Actually Use QR Codes (In China)," 29 May 2013, http://techcrunch.com/2013/05/29/people-actually-use-qr-codes-in-china/.

[30] C. Jannsen, "What Is a Mobile Application?," 2014, http://www.techopedia.com/definition/2953/mobile-application-mobile-app.

[31] Nielsen, "So Many Apps So Much Time," 1 July 2014,http://www.nielsen.com/us/en/insights/news/2014/smartphones-so-many-apps--so-much-time.html.

[32] S. Tweddie, "Most Americans Download Zero Apps Every Month," 22 August 2014, http://www.businessinsider.com/how-many-apps-people-download-per-month-2014-8.

[33] Internet Retailer, "IR Mobile 500," 15 January 2015, https://www.internetretailer.com/mobile500/print/.

[34] K. Sruoginis, "Who Are the Mobile Gamers and Why Do They Matter?," Iab.net, 20 November 2014.

[35] D. Reisinger, "Android Continues to Lord Over the Smartphone Biz," CNET, 1 December 2014.

[36] S. Porges, "Eight Things You Should Know Before Building a Mobile App," CNN, 3 February 2012.

[37] SensorTower, "Everything Developers Need to Know About App Store Transaction Costs," 5 March 2014.

[38] Kinvey, "State of Enterprise Mobility," 2014.

[39] Apple, "App Store Review Guidelines," 22 March 2012.

[40] Mobile Marketer, 2014.

[41] P. Wahba, "Target Finds Rare Tech Edge: Its Popular Cartwheel Shopping App," *Fortune,* 5 June 2014.

[42] The Week, "Venmo Users Transferred $1 billion in January alone," February 16, 2016, www .theweek.com

[43] The Week, "Venmo Users Transferred $1 billion in January alone," February 16, 2016, www. theweek.com.

[44] M. McFarland, "American Eagle Outfitters Lures Customers into Fitting Rooms with Help of Beacons," *The Washington Post,* 15 October 2014.

[45] Usablenet, "The Ritz Carlton Hotel," 2015.

[46] S. Schroeder, "Mobile Games Dominate Smartphone App Usage [STATS]," Mashable, 7 July 2011.

[47] R. Borison, "The 15 Highest Grossing iPhone and iPad Games," Business Insider, 20 May 2014.

[48] S. Perez, "Paid Apps on the Decline: 90% of iOS Apps Are Free, Up from 80–84% during 2010–2012, Says Flurry," TechCrunch, 18 July 2013.

[49] K. Lukovitz, "Chipotle's 'Scarecrow': 5.5+ Million Views and Counting," *MediaPost Marketing Daily,* 18 September 2013.

[50] C. Blank, "Brands' Mobile Games Build Customer Sales, Loyalty," *QSR Magazine,* December 2013.

[51] eMarketer, "AOL, Millennial Face Uphill Battle to Capture Mobile Ad Dollars," September 8, 2015. http://www.emarketer.com/Article/AOL-Millennial-Face-Uphill-Battle-Capture-Mobile-Ad-Dollars/1012954

[52] Marin Software, March 25th, 2015, "Mobile Ad Spend to Overtake Desktop by End of 2015,"http://www .marinsoftware.com/resources/news/marin-software-mobile-ad-spend-to-overtake-desktop-by-end-of-2015.

[53] C. Tode, "Top Ten Mobile Advertising Campaigns from the First Half of 2014," Mobile Marketer, 1 July 2014.

[54] Internet Advertising Bureau, "Native Advertising Playbook," 4 December 2014.

[55] Chaffey, D. "Display Advertising Click Through Rates," Smart Insights, 1 April, 2015, http://www.smartinsights.com/internet-advertising/internet-advertising-analytics/display-advertising-clickthrough-rates/.

[56] Ackley, M. Quantifying the Mobile Revolution, March 18, 2015, http://searchengineland.com/quantifying-mobile-revolution-2014-benchmark-mobile-advertising-progress-216696.

[57] eMarketer, "Mobile Email Opens Trump Those on Desktop," 14 January 2014.

[58] A. Gesenhues, "Report: Climbing to 48%, Mobile Email Open Rates Nearly Overtake Desktop in 2013," Marketing Land, 12 June 2014.

[59] L. Johnson, "4 Location-Based Marketing Tactics That Are Working Payments, Beacons and Coupons Are Top Priorities," *Adweek,* 4 August 2014.

[60] M. Wohlsen, "Forget Apple Pay: The Master of Mobile Payments Is Starbucks," *Wired,* 3 November 2014.

[61] M. Isaac, "U.S. Mobile Payments Market to Boom by 2019, Research Firm Says," New York Times Bits Blog, 17 November 2014.

[62] N. Hughes, "Mobile Payments Still Facing the Same Big Obstacles," *Street Fight,* 28 October 2014.

[63] C. Martin, "41% of Active Mobile Payments Users See High Risk," MediaPost, 3 October 2014.

[64] J. Graham, "Apple Pay Launches Today, Here's How to Use It," *USA Today,* 20 October 2014.

[65] S. Oliver, "Apple Pay Already Works Internationally, But Only with US Credit Cards," AppleInsider, 21 October 2014.

[66] J. Clover, "Wells Fargo Apple Pay Advertisement," Macrumors.com, 2 December 2014.

[67] M. Geuss, "Google Will Launch Android Pay at the I/O in May," ARS Technica, 25 February 2015.

[68] Reuters, "Apple Pay to Launch in China Despite Stiff Competition in Mobile Payment System,"The Guardian, 16, February 2016, https://www.theguardian.com/technology/2016/feb/16/apple-pay-china-mobile-payment-system

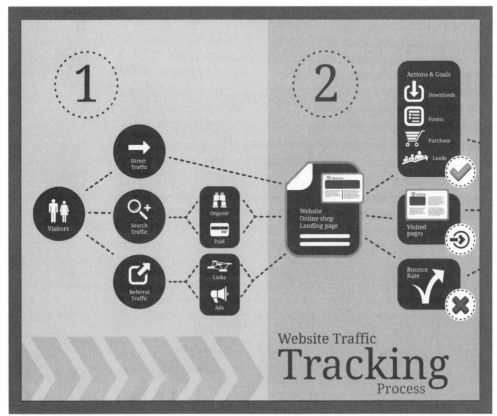

CHAPTER TWELVE

EXAMINING METRICS

One of the major advantages of social media and mobile marketing strategies is that marketers can track the results of marketing efforts. Tracking can occur in real time so that brands can alter the campaign while it is taking place to maximize the return. Marketers can measure the outcomes of strategies by examining both financial and nonfinancial measures of success. However, ultimately strategies must deliver clear returns on investment or marketing dollars may be wasted. This chapter examines how to use metrics to improve a social media and mobile marketing strategy.

LEARNING OBJECTIVES

After reading this chapter, you will be able to:

- LEARN THE IMPORTANCE OF MEASUREMENT

- REVIEW FINANCIAL AND NONFINANCIAL METRICS

- EVALUATE DIGITAL MARKETING STRATEGY USING METRICS

- DETERMINE COSTS IN SOCIAL MEDIA AND MOBILE MARKETING

- JUDGE STRATEGIES USING GOOGLE ANALYTICS

- TRACK ATTRIBUTIONS IN TRADITIONAL AND DIGITAL MEDIA

General Motors (GM) and Ford have long gone head-to-head in the automobile industry. Both use social media and mobile marketing to engage their customer base, but one is more committed to a social media strategy than the other. Do you have any idea which one that is? One way to make a judgment on the success of a strategy is to examine the numbers. Exhibit 12.1 shows how each brand performed in 2015 on social media sites, based on its number of followers. Which brand appears to have a more developed strategy?

A few years ago, GM publicly announced that it would suspend all advertising on Facebook. The announcement suggested that social media advertising may not have been delivering the desired outcomes for GM. While the company eliminated all Facebook advertising, it decided to retain a Facebook page. During the same period, Ford Motor Company indicated that it would maintain its Facebook strategy, including advertising and content posting.

The data in Exhibit 12.1 were gathered three years after GM eliminated Facebook advertising [1], [2]. As you can see, GM has fewer social media followers than Ford, which generates more buzz around its brand [3], [4]. With more customers engaged in social media, Ford saw more value in Facebook [5].

The publicity surrounding GM's decision to stop buying Facebook ads got a lot of attention in the media at the time. However, a year after publicly ending its

EXHIBIT 12.1

Metrics for General Motors and Ford Motors 2015

	GENERAL MOTORS	FORD MOTOR COMPANY
Facebook Likes	633,718	2,945,850
Twitter Tweets Followers Following	11,400 406,000 6,313	17,200 710,000 32,200
Google+ Followers	2,260,022	3,861,240
YouTube Videos	9,347	195,666
Klout Score Topics	58	94
Instagram Followers Post	5,291 153	407,000 698

Twitter, YouTube, Instagram, and Klout, accessed 24 April 2015

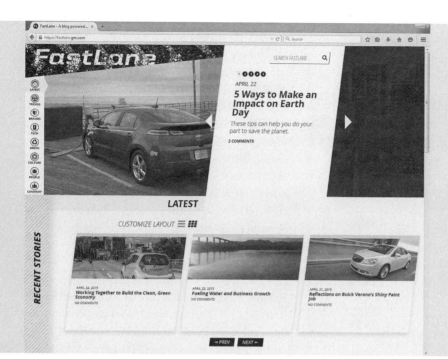

General Motor's blog is called Fastlane.

General Motors,
www.generalmotors.green

Facebook advertising, GM debuted its Chevrolet "Find New Roads" campaign on social media, buying paid Facebook ads on its mobile platform [6]. GM simply could not ignore the vast reach of Facebook.

Before digital media, marketing managers often relied on gut instinct to determine communications strategy. Though some still make snap decisions, we've seen throughout this book that there are many more tools available to help marketers plan, execute, and evaluate strategies. Both GM and Ford evaluate their campaigns using a variety of measures and metrics to ensure that they maximize profitability. This chapter describes many of the available tools marketers use to evaluate strategies.

MEASUREMENT IN DIGITAL MARKETING

A major advantage of digital media over traditional media is that marketers can track the results of digital strategies by examining the consumer response online and on company websites. Specifically, marketers can tag site visitors with cookies, pieces of code stored on users' computers that marketers can track, website analytics, or tracking software from a variety of vendors. These efforts can tell marketers the characteristics of those who have been to their site, the actions people have taken there, and whether visits resulted in a sale or other positive outcome.

EXHIBIT 12.2

Top Ten Measures Used by Companies

MEASURES	PERCENTAGE OF COMPANIES USING THIS METRIC
Hits, visits, page views	68%
Number of followers	45.0%
Repeat visits	38.7%
Conversion rate	31.3%
Buzz indicators (Web mentions)	24.2%
Sales levels	16.8%
Online product and service ratings	14.0%
Customer acquisition costs	13.7%
Net promoter score	12.8%
Revenue per customer	12.5%

C. Moorman, "The CMO Survey," 2014.

Marketers rely heavily on website performance to examine response. Exhibit 12.2 lists the top ten ways that marketers examine their performance according to the CMO Survey. The most important metrics measure the number of people who visit the site, how many pages on the site they view, and whether they make repeat visits. The fourth measure on the list is conversion, referring to the number of site visitors who completed a desired action, such as made a purchase, downloaded content, or entered their email address. Though conversions are very important for e-commerce sites, they may be less important to content sites, where success relies on site visits and page views to sell advertising.

Marketers also use some of the measures listed in Exhibit 12.2 to evaluate social media and mobile strategies [7]. For example, social media strategies may lead to more website visits, increased buzz, better ratings, or sales and revenues. The net promoter score measures the likelihood that a person would recommend a company, asking the question "How likely is it that you would recommend this company to a friend or colleague?" The net promoter score does not directly measure outcomes from social media strategies, but can help a firm determine how people feel about its company.

The term **metrics** refers to the set of measures that assist marketers in evaluating the success of marketing strategies; **key performance indicators (KPIs)** are those metrics most important in determining success or failure for a strategy. Measuring outcomes has become an important priority for marketing management for a number of reasons. First, managers often must defend their marketing budgets to firm management by showing that investments in marketing spending lead to sales. Second, measuring outcomes helps brand managers determine which strategies are the most effective and should be repeated, and which are not effective and should be eliminated. Some metrics can help managers determine whether a strategy that is ongoing is working and may indicate how to change the strategy to make it stronger. Third, metrics help companies set clear quantifiable goals to evaluate strategies. Finally, metrics can be used to set goals for performance and reward employees, marketing service firms, and advertising agencies when the brand meets the goals.

Marketers have vast sources of digital data to analyze. The companies that specialize in data management, data analysis, data storage, and data consulting are all part of an industry known as **Big Data**. These companies help other firms collect and analyze information on consumers, products, competitors, and industries. The term **analytics** refers to the evaluation of patterns within available data to make business decisions. Smart marketers take advantage of the data analysis tools to examine Web, social media, and mobile metrics to assess strategies and alter them to improve results.

How can you determine if your social media or mobile strategy is working? As always, you have to go back and look at the goals you set for your strategy and determine the appropriate way to measure the relevant outcomes. A social media or mobile strategy can help build engagement, encourage opt-in or conversions, increase website response, or improve search engine rankings.

Exhibit 12.3 provides some examples of the ways in which brands are using metrics to evaluate their goals [8] [9] [10]. As one example, LEGO is seeking to build engagement with fans through its Rebrickable website and can measure response using certain metrics.

EVALUATING MARKETING STRATEGIES

The most effective way for marketing managers to show the impact of marketing strategies and defend their budgets is to use financial metrics. **Financial metrics** are measures that evaluate revenues and expenses associated with strategies. Some

Evaluating Goals with Metrics

GOAL	EXAMPLE	METRICS TO CONSIDER
Build engagement	LEGO introduced Rebrickable.com, a social media site that showcases LEGO customer creations. The site has no advertising, but hopes to generate future positive word of mouth.	Postings, tweets, and retweets about the site; customer demographics; search results
Encourage opt-in	Starbucks uses an SMS strategy to encourage opt-in on its My Starbucks Rewards program by texting the keyword GOLD to a short code.	Opt-in rate and conversion rate
Encourage conversions	Rovio, the developer of the Angry Birds app, increased revenue to $100 million with over 600 million downloads.	Price, cost per download, return on investment
Increase website responses and improve search engine rankings	Bombfell, the monthly clothing subscription service for men, used Twitter to interact with their young-male target. Along with some video advertising, the brand increased conversions by 25% during the campaign.	Views, popularity, how the video was discovered, search terms employed, demographics, bounce rate, rewind rate, and reviews

financial metrics focus on building revenues, while others reduce expenditures. In either case, a financial metric is expressed as a dollar (or other currency) value. One important financial metric that we've referred to throughout this text is **return on investment (ROI)**, the amount of revenue (in a currency) a strategy delivers after accounting for expenses.

Financial metrics are the ultimate measure of success or failure because firms must make money on marketing investments or the firm would fail employees, shareholders, and investors. However, financial measures are not the only way to evaluate strategy, and since such an analysis would likely happen after a strategy is completed, another set of metrics can be helpful in guiding the strategy. Specifically, **nonfinancial metrics** focus on consumer actions and results that are not measured in dollars or other currencies. Though nonfinancial metrics should never determine the ultimate success or failure of a strategy, these metrics can help guide strategy. Social media platforms provide a vast array of nonfinancial metrics that indicate whether the brand's strategy is getting attention online.

Some popular social media metrics are Facebook likes, Twitter followers, blog posts, comments, and Yelp reviews. These nonfinancial metrics are also called intermediary or navigational metrics because marketers can measure these metrics before the strategy is complete and they can be useful to steer strategy in the right direction [11]. Such measures should be considered guideposts on the way to reaching and evaluating financial impact, but not the final determinant of success. Exhibit 12.4 provides examples of both financial and nonfinancial metrics.

Marketers must ensure a positive ROI for marketing strategies. Often, marketers must justify spending to financial gatekeepers who require a convincing quantitative argument to support marketing budgets. A strong potential ROI may provide the documentation required for the finance department and may lead

EXHIBIT 12.4

Financial and Nonfinancial Metrics

FINANCIAL METRICS	NONFINANCIAL METRICS
Reduced costs in customer service	Positive and negative mentions
Increase in sales during a campaign	Net new Twitter followers
Reduced advertising costs	Facebook "likes"
Net new customers acquired and average purchase	Increased website impressions
Increase in sales from a specific vehicle	Pinterest repins
Reduced market research costs	Number of times an item was shared

decision-makers to increase marketing spending if the investment pays off. However, marketers are not always certain how to calculate their return on social media spending. Only one-third of businesses surveyed by Social Media Examiner agreed that they were able to measure their ROI on social media activities [12]. In order to calculate ROI, marketers should follow the steps outlined in Exhibit 12.5.

consider this . . .

THE ECONOMIC VALUE OF ENGAGEMENT

Some marketing strategies deliver clear economic value to firms, resulting in either revenue generation or cost savings. Avinash Kaushik, a social media evangelist and former Google founder, suggests that social media engagement can often deliver economic value more efficiently than traditional media. For instance, if a marketer reaches the target through social media and compares the costs to running a television commercial, the social media strategy may be more efficient. Social media can reach the target directly without casting a wide net and the traditional strategy requires more people, including copywriters, art directors, producers, production companies, illustrators, editors, casting directors, actors, account management teams, and agencies.

According to Kaushik, economic value is easy to determine for commerce and lead generation. In e-commerce, marketers can track the stream of clicks that delivered the customer to check out. In lead generation, marketers can determine the new customers who have never visited the site and where they came from digitally. Kaushik determined the economic value of a visit that originated from a particular site for the sale of his books. When a customer originated from Twitter, Kaushik found that he earned 87 cents in book sales.

Those who arrived via StumbleUpon were even more likely to buy, as shown here

PROPERTY ORIGINATING THE CUSTOMER	VALUE OF A VISIT
Twitter	$.87
Facebook	$.27
Stumble Upon	$4.30

http://www.kaushik.net/avinash/best-social-media-metrics-conversation-amplification-applause-economic-value/

Kaushik computed the conversion rate on Amazon with an affiliate code and tracked customers back to social media origination points. He followed those who visited his blog, signed up for email, and posted comments using Google Analytics. He recommends that to maximize the response, the valuable content to selling rate should be 90 to 10. Most of the time, the site should be generating useful and engaging content, and only 10% of the time should a marketer be talking about the company, its services, products, and benefits. The notion is that delivering value to people engages them with the brand and they become more open to communications, purchases, loyalty, and other favorable outcomes for brands.

EXHIBIT 12.5

Key Steps to Determine Financial Impact

1. **Determine the Cost of the Investment.**
   The costs include personnel, content development, media expenses, agency fees, and technology.

2. **Set Guidelines for the Expected Outcome.**
   For each strategy, determine the expected response. For example, if the marketer makes significant improvements to scheduling the Twitter feed, what result would be expected in terms of customer response to Twitter?

3. **Measure the Nonfinancial Impact of the Strategy.**
   Examine the nonfinancial metrics. These are the intermediary metrics that show the marketer the direction the results are taking prior to examining the financial return. These metrics include social media followers and comments.

4. **Calculate the Financial Impact.**
   The financial impact is always measured in currency such as $U.S. There are a number of formulas for calculating the ROI, but the results are similar. The following equation is easy to use and provides a clear result for ROI in dollars:

$$ROI = \frac{\text{Gain from the Investment} - \text{Cost of the Investment}}{\text{Cost of the Investment}}$$

   Marketers can also express the ROI as a percentage by multiplying the result from the equation above by 100.

5. **Evaluate the ROI Opportunity Cost.**
   The next step is to evaluate the return relative to the other marketing investments that you have undertaken to determine whether this ROI is strong. A positive ROI is only one element of the decision to invest in a strategy and in some cases another investment might yield a lower ROI, but higher overall income.

USING FINANCIAL AND NONFINANCIAL METRICS

People often think that social media are free. After all, anyone can set up a Facebook page or Twitter account without paying. However, as we've seen throughout this book, it's clear that there are many costs associated with social media strategies for businesses. According to the Social Media Examiner, a majority of companies (64%) spent over 6 hours per week on social media strategy, 37% spend more than 11 hours, and 19% spend over 20 hours a week on social media marketing [12]. Much of the cost associated with social media requires hiring staff to develop and post content, manage customer service, develop strategies, and evalute performance. More important, the costs associated with social and mobile strategies rise with more commitment by a firm [13]. Exhibit 12.6 lists the categories of spending associated with social media strategies.

EXHIBIT 12.6

Costs of Social Media

The Costs

<u>Internal Soft Costs</u>
Staff, training and research

<u>Customer–Facing Initiatives</u>
Media spending
Agency costs
Influencers or blogger costs

<u>Technology Investments</u>
Customer relationship management
Platform development
Monitoring and management systems

ACTIONS That Cost

Brand monitoring
Social media content
Social media promotion
Social media engagement
Social media conversion
Post purchase support
Social media analytics
Customer service
Agency fees

SOCIAL MEDIA STRATEGY COSTS

So, how much do firms actually spend on social media? The answer depends on the company and the structure the company uses for executing its social media strategy. In general, the costs have been on the rise. According to the CMO Survey, social media spending represents over 20% of a firm's marketing budget [7].

One way to quantify the costs associated with social media is to determine how much a strategy would cost if the business hired an outside firm to manage the process. Exhibit 12.7 shows some of the functions associated with a social strategy and how much it would cost a small- to medium-sized company (under 500 employees) to hire a firm to complete the action [14]. Some of the costs are ongoing, and the costs vary significantly depending on the type of business and the firms the company hires.

Marketers who calculate ROI must include the costs associated with developing, managing, and monitoring the social media strategy. As you can see, the costs can be very high, particularly for a small- to medium-sized business.

MOBILE MARKETING STRATEGY COSTS

The costs in mobile marketing can vary widely depending on the strategy. Mobile banner advertising is relatively inexpensive (with a low cost per thousand impressions or CPM) because there is a significant amount of unused stock available on mobile platforms. The low CPM is an opportunity for marketers given that people spend a lot of time with mobile devices—not actually talking.

Strategies such as short message service (SMS) or a mobile app can be expensive to execute depending on the vendors, scope of the project, and the expectations for functionality. The costs to develop a mobile strategy are outlined in Exhibit 12.8 [15] [16] [17] [18].

EXHIBIT 12.7

Costs of Outsourced Social Strategies

ACTION	MONTHLY COST
Total Industry Average Cost of Outsourcing Social Media Services	$4,000–$7,000
Social Media Strategy Developing the roadmap for how to execute the social media strategy	$5,000–$10,000
Social Media Build Setting up the social media channels for a business	$2,000–$5,000
Social Media Content Development Designing, writing, and producing the shareable materials for the social strategy	$3,000–$5,000 (ongoing)
Social Media Channel Management Posting, responding, and managing the social media strategy e.g. Twitter New Account Set Up and Management PR firm rates for Facebook Management	$3,000–$5,000 (ongoing) $2,000-$4,000 $2,500-$5,000
Social Media Campaigning Planning and executing the paid social media strategy	$1,500–$3,000 (ongoing)
Social Media Monitoring and Management Tools Using a system for posting content and analyzing results	$10–$5,000 (ongoing)

J. Sandler, "How to Effectively Budget Your Social Media Program in 2013," ClickZ, January 9 2013; Content Marketing Factory, Accessed April 5, 2016, http://www.contentfac.com/how-much-does-social-media-marketing-cost/

consider this...

CALCULATING ROI FOR AN SMS STRATEGY

You are a marketer of fashion sunglasses sold in specialty stores, but have found that people don't notice your display in the back of many retail locations. The goal of the strategy is to increase sales from the display by attracting people from the front of the stores. As part of a prior SMS, text-messaging strategy, you already have a short code and decide to leverage the asset to build engagement with your displays. You may remember that a short code is the number that your customers use to send a keyword text via cell phone.

Your SMS strategy over a three-month period costs $6,000, and 90% of your retailers have agreed to support your strategy with in-store signs. The signs to attract customers to text the keyword to your short code cost an additional $10,000. The target market consists of the traffic exposed to your signage at the various locations. The estimate of the number of targets who are exposed to your signs and opt-in is 100,000. The incremental sales you will generate by converting those who opt into the SMS campaign is $15.00 per person, and you have a 2% conversion rate.

The gain is   100,000 targets × .02 conversion × $15.00 sale = $30,000

The costs are $6,000 + 10,000 = $16,000

The ROI is $\dfrac{\$30,000 - \$16,000}{\$16,000}$ = .875 or an 87.5% return on investment

EXHIBIT 12.8

Costs for Mobile Strategies

STRATEGY	EXPENSES	COSTS
Mobile SMS	Short code Messages	$1,000/month plus set-up fee $.01 to send and $.005 to receive
Mobile app	Development costs Design costs	$5,000–150,000 average of $6,453 according to developers surveyed
Mobile website	Design and hosting Custom development	Free services available $150+/hour
Mobile banner advertising	Cost per thousand (CPM)	iOS banner ads $.20-$2.00; Android banner ads $.15-$1.50; (cost to reach 1,000 targets)

www.twilio.com/pricing, Accessed April 7, 2016
Formotus Blog, March 12, 2016, http://www.formotus.com/14018/blog-mobility/figuring-the-costs-of-custom-mobile-business-app-development.
Monetize Pro, May 17, 2016, http://monetizepros.com/cpm-rate-guide/mobile/.

NONFINANCIAL METRICS FOR STEERING STRATEGY

If ROI is such a good measure of the success of a campaign or strategy, why not use it all the time? Well, sometimes sales are not realized quickly, and the consumer slowly brews before he or she makes a decision to buy. During this time, the consumer may still be engaging with the brand at some level, and since it is helpful to know how the strategy is developing, marketers use nonfinancial intermediary metrics.

Intermediary metrics help firms monitor the day-to-day responses to strategies to determine whether to continue on a particular path or alter their efforts.

For example, if a brand runs a paid Facebook ad and sees no click-through activity on the ad, the marketer may decide to improve the message, increase the offer, change the target, or use different images. In addition, intermediary metrics can help focus a social media strategy by showing people's engagement with the content that brands produce.

According to the *Social Media Examiner Industry Report,* [19] most marketers (68%) indicate that they do examine their social media strategies. However, the same survey found that most (88%) want more information on how to measure social media results. The major social media sites provide metrics for examining brand performance on their sites, but these measures frequently do not show ROI, which is much more difficult to assess.

Marketers can use the metrics social media properties provide to evaluate engagement. For example, Facebook, Twitter, and Pinterest give marketers information on the number of followers for pages and responses (likes, retweets, and repins). These data show impressions for a brand strategy, and since they are positively valenced, they are a measure of positive feelings. Exhibit 12.9 lists and describes the metrics marketers can find on the most popular social media platforms [1] [2] [4] [20] [21] [22] [23] [24] [25].

consider this . . .

SOCIAL MEDIA METRICS TO FIND A DUCK

When Aflac had to find a new voice for its duck, the Kaplan Thayler Group, the brand's long-time agency and the creative force behind the Aflac duck, turned to social media. The agency did not use traditional methods for communicating; instead Aflac posted a job opening on Monster.com, continued the duck's tweets, and conducted live auditions that were uploaded to social media. How did Aflac measure the results of the campaign without looking at actual revenue? It used intermediate metrics and reported the following results:

99,000 people viewed the job on Monster.com.

143,000 people visited the quackaflac website.

There were 70,000 media stories generating 900 million media impressions.

Twitter followers of the duck increased 14.5% and Facebook fans increased 5%.

Traffic to the Aflac site increased 20%.

These interim measures suggest that the campaign successfully generated impressions. There were also significant sales increases during the campaign. Sales leads increased 80% over the year before, and Aflac increased the number of agents recruited by 13.5% [26]. It also found a new duck.

EXHIBIT 12.9

Social Media Site Metrics

SOCIAL PLATFORM	MEASURES AVAILABLE FROM THE SITE
Facebook Insights	*Page Reach:* Total number of people who were shown your page and posts. *Page Likes:* Number of people who indicate they like the page. *Engagement:* The number of unique people who have clicked, liked, commented on, or shared posts during the last 7 days.
WeChat	*Views:* Total number of those who see the post. *Likes:* Those who indicate appreciation for the post.
Google+ Social Reports	*Page Views:* Number of unique viewers. *Shares:* Number of reshares through partner URLs. *Ripples:* An interactive graph of sharing.
Twitter Ad Measurement	*Impressions:* The number of times users are served the promoted account. *Follows:* Followers gained from a promoted account impression. *Follow Rate:* Followers divided by impressions. *Profile Visits:* Number of viewers in a 28 day period.
LinkedIn Reports	*Page Reach:* Allows comparison of performance by days, weeks, 3 months, or 6 months. *Engagement Rate:* Engagement is the number of times members clicked, liked, commented on, or shared content in both organic and paid campaigns and the number of followers acquired through paid campaigns. *Content Marketing Score:* Unique engagement divided by the total target.
Tumblr	*Volume:* The number of people interacting with posts. *Size of Community:* This metric tells you the size of the community; top contributors, curators, and content producers within it. *Reblogs:* The extent to which people share content. *Likes:* Shows a general interest in content.
Pinterest	*Pins:* The pin metric is the daily average number of pins from a verified website. *Repins:* The daily average number of pins from a website that were repinned by others. *Reach:* The daily average number of people who saw pins on Pinterest.
Instagram	*Followers:* Number of those subscribing to a feed. *Following Trends:* Tracks followers over time. *Likes:* Number of likes. *Comments:* Number of comments.
Snapchat	*Snap Score:* A metric examining the number of Snaps sent and received. *Audience Size:* Number of friends.

(continued)

EXHIBIT 12.9 (Continued)

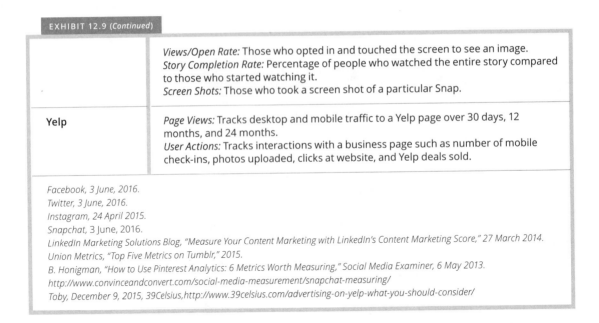

	Views/Open Rate: Those who opted in and touched the screen to see an image. *Story Completion Rate:* Percentage of people who watched the entire story compared to those who started watching it. *Screen Shots:* Those who took a screen shot of a particular Snap.
Yelp	*Page Views:* Tracks desktop and mobile traffic to a Yelp page over 30 days, 12 months, and 24 months. *User Actions:* Tracks interactions with a business page such as number of mobile check-ins, photos uploaded, clicks at website, and Yelp deals sold.

Facebook, 3 June, 2016.
Twitter, 3 June, 2016.
Instagram, 24 April 2015.
Snapchat, 3 June, 2016.
LinkedIn Marketing Solutions Blog, "Measure Your Content Marketing with LinkedIn's Content Marketing Score," 27 March 2014.
Union Metrics, "Top Five Metrics on Tumblr," 2015.
B. Honigman, "How to Use Pinterest Analytics: 6 Metrics Worth Measuring," Social Media Examiner, 6 May 2013.
http://www.convinceandconvert.com/social-media-measurement/snapchat-measuring/
Toby, December 9, 2015, 39Celsius,http://www.39celsius.com/advertising-on-yelp-what-you-should-consider/

Twitter shows summary data for a 28-day period and compares traffic to the prior period.

Twitter, www.twitter.com

GOOGLE ANALYTICS FOR STRATEGY EVALUATION

One important tool for analyzing Web results is Google Analytics. As we first noted in Chapter Three, this free program provides key metrics for evaluating a social media or mobile strategy. Google Analytics is set up on a webpage using a snippet of code that allows Google to track a variety of data on a company website.

The Google Analytics dashboard lets the user choose the period of time to analyze. Companies can look at a single day, particular weeks, several months, or years of data to watch for trends. The first section of the dashboard shows the number of sessions, unique users, page views, pages per session, average session duration, and the percentage of new sessions. These data tell marketers how many new and returning people have visited the site, how long they have stayed on the site, and the number of pages they searched. The dashboard also indicates the bounce rate for the site, which is the percentage of people who come to the site, but leave after viewing the first page. These basic statistics can help a business determine whether its site interface is strong and leads people to become engaged in terms of time commitment to the site. The more time people stay on the site, the more opportunities for them to convert by downloading content, buying something, or sharing information.

The next section of the dashboard presents information on the languages people use to access the site and the countries from which the site draws its audience. For global businesses and Internet businesses with customers in more than one country, these data can help determine strategies to best reach people. Google Analytics also shows the browsers people are using to access the site, such as Chrome, Safari, or Firefox; the operating systems (Windows, Mac, or iOS); and the Internet service providers (Verizon, Comcast, Time Warner). Marketers can tailor the look and feel of their sites to match the requirements of the various systems. A growing area of interest for marketers is the devices people use to access the site. Google Analytics shows whether traffic is coming from mobile devices and the mobile operating system (iOS, Android, or Windows).

Marketers have the option of monitoring their site in real time to see how many people are on the site, what they are looking at, or which other sites referred them. This view changes moment-by-moment, so marketers can observe what is happening in a quick snapshot of time. Another option is to set up daily, weekly, or monthly intelligence alerts to indicate when traffic is high or low or when users complete certain actions, such as a purchase. As a result, marketers don't have to sit and watch a site, but still can know when important events take place.

The major additional categories of information that Google Analytics tracks are audience, acquisition, behavior, and conversions. In the audience section, marketers can set up tracking that will provide age and gender information on those visiting the site. Google Analytics can also show the interests of visitors (for a fee) from Google's Display Advertising Network that tracks people's website visits through cookies and thereby knows a person's browsing habits.

The acquisitions section tells marketers where inbound traffic originates, showing the site from which a user came immediately prior to arriving at the website. The options for traffic are:

- *Organic Search:* The user searches using keywords.
- *Referral:* A user arrives from another website.
- *Direct:* A user types the URL directly.
- *Paid Search:* The traffic comes from paid advertising click-throughs.
- *Social:* The source is a social media site.
- *Email:* A user clicked on a link in an email.

Google Analytics then divides all the overview information by these sources, so marketers can see which sources delivered people who interacted more or less with the site or who performed certain actions like a purchase. Marketers can delve deeply to determine which exact keyword searches (paid and organic), blog sites, social media sites, ads, and strategies delivered people to the website and which were most effective in leading to desired outcomes. In the Google Analytics page for a business school, the organic searches that delivered people to the site were words such as "tuition," "business school," "MBA," and even the names of particular faculty members. The business school also earned hits from Facebook, Twitter, LinkedIn, Quora, and Google+.

In the behavior section of Google Analytics, marketers can see graphically where users tended to go on the site, which exact pages they viewed and where they exited. There are data on site speed and loading time for each landing page.

As stated earlier in this chapter, one of the most important metrics for marketers to track is conversions, the number of customers who perform a desired action on a website. In this case, marketers have to set up goals that show a visitor has completed the desired task. For example, many e-commerce sites set a goal on the website's "thank-you" page. This is the page that appears after a customer purchases a product from the site and goes through the full process of shopping cart and payment. Tracking these sales and from where they originated can be a valuable tool for determining marketing efforts.

consider this . . .

REFINING MOBILE STRATEGY WITH GOOGLE ANALYTICS

Certain Affinity, a Texas-based game development company, used Google Analytics to determine that people play games for longer periods of time on game consoles than on mobile devices. The company examined mobile game time data for its game Age of Booty, an asynchronous turn-based tactics game. By looking at mobile response data, the firm created optimum-length games to entertain and retain customers on mobile devices. The results were that the company reduced time spent on turns, games, and screen loads, while increasing gamers' overall usage of a game relative to other activities [27].

consider this . . .

COMPANIES PROVIDING DATA ANALYTICS

Marketers must determine which measures will be appropriate under varying circumstances to both maximize the information provided and justify the research expense. One of the reasons why nonfinancial metrics are so popular is because marketers can access such measures for free. Firms hire analytics companies because some of the measures are complicated and the measurements may require specific technological expertise to execute. For instance, some analytics firms use Web crawlers to collect information to evaluate strategies. Radian6 uses a combination of RSS feeds and crawlers to index publicly available data on the social Web. Clients determine the important keywords connected to conversations about the brand, and Radian6 collects information on consumer demographics, influence, geolocation, sentiment, and topics of interest to a company and its competitors.

A number of firms offer services to marketers to help evaluate social media and mobile executions. Radian6 is known for its ability to listen, track conversations, and also provides a dashboard for social media monitoring. Omniture, now owned by Adobe, consults in the area of search, search engine optimization (SEO), and key performance indicators (KPIs). HubSpot and Constant Contact target smaller businesses with a full range of marketing and evaluation services to enhance sales and ROI.

ATTRIBUTION TECHNIQUES IN SOCIAL MEDIA AND MOBILE

Attribution refers to the task of assigning values to the various elements that may have influenced a consumer to take a particular action, such as purchase a product. In the digital realm, marketers can evaluate click-stream data within a website to see where customers visited, how long they stayed, and what they examined when browsing. Brand managers can also examine the click streams of consumers before they arrived at the website to determine the best referral sites for a marketing communications strategy. The process of determining which elements of the marketing strategy delivered the desired response is called **attribution analysis**. The concept behind attribution is that many elements of a strategy may have contributed to the final decision to purchase. For example, a customer may go online and read reviews to decide which brand of air conditioner to buy, but wait four weeks before typing "air conditioners" into the Google search engine to find retailers who sell the product. The decision to purchase the brand was made four weeks before the actual search for the retailers. Which communication was more important for the brand manager of the air conditioner?

Though it is easier to determine attributions in digital media, there are techniques that evaluate traditional media attributions so that marketers can compare strategies across media formats. These methods are explained in Exhibit 12.10 and detailed within the chapter with specific instructions on using the techniques to determine media impact.

EXHIBIT 12.10

Methods of Attribution Analysis	
Response modeling	A regression model to determine the weights of various elements contributing to an outcome
Media timing analysis	Determining the timing of media executions and the effect on outcomes
Media equivalent analysis	A method for equalizing the value of an advertisement in different forms of media using impressions and costs

CUSTOMER TRACKING

To determine digital attributions, a good place to start is with Google Analytics Multi-Channel Funnels. This free tool on a brand's Google Analytics site examines the click streams of consumers who visited the site or completed a transaction. This function in Google Analytics allows marketers to give weights to various positions in the click stream, such as first, last, or middle clicks, to better distribute the influence of any one strategy. The **last click attribution model** is the default in Google Analytics and the method most businesses use to evaluate referrals, but marketers can change the weights.

The last click model of attribution gives 100% of the weight of the conversion to the website that delivered the visitor. The assumption is that the prior website was successful in encouraging the sales, but does not account for the possibility that the customer moved between sites to evaluate brands, read reviews, or engage with the brand's Facebook page, particularly if the last action undertaken by a customer was typing in the direct URL to get to the site. Exhibit 12.11 describes some of the options for attributions in Google Analytics.

Researchers who analyze click-through behavior suggest that analyzing the "last click" undervalues the role of social media. The assertion is that social media influences the purchase decision process early, perhaps sparking problem recognition or driving consumers to particular purchase-related information, but may be less likely to function as the final factor in the sale. In the "last click" model, credit for the sale is more likely to go to a "search" strategy because search results may serve as reminders to consumers to execute a purchase after the decision is already made. As a result, marketers should consider how they use attrributions and which elements of the strategy might contribute to a conversion.

EXHIBIT 12.11

Attribution Models in Google Analytics

MODEL	DESCRIPTION
Last click	Attributes a conversion to the site clicked immediately prior to the website visit.
First click	Counts the touchpoint that initiated the path to conversion.
Last nondirect interaction	Eliminates direct attributions (typing in the URL) and attributes conversions to the last channel before the website visit.
Linear	Each element of the conversion path receives equal weights for the conversion.
Time decay	The closest interaction to the conversion earns the most credit followed by earlier touchpoints in backwards time order.
Position based	Gives more weight to first and the most credit to last clicks.

About the Default Attribution Models
https://support.google.com/analytics/answer/1665189?hl=en

Which Attribution Model?

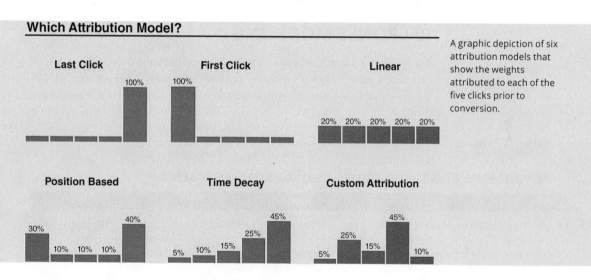

A graphic depiction of six attribution models that show the weights attributed to each of the five clicks prior to conversion.

Last Click 100%

First Click 100%

Linear 20% 20% 20% 20% 20%

Position Based 30% 10% 10% 10% 40%

Time Decay 5% 10% 15% 25% 45%

Custom Attribution 5% 25% 15% 45% 10%

TRACKING WITH COOKIES

Marketers use cookies to track consumer responses. The process works when a marketer embeds a cookie on a user's PC to track the number of unique visits to the site. **Transient cookies** are used to aggregate data from a particular visit and are erased after the user logs off. A **persistent cookie** remains on the computer, delivering data for as long as the cookies is set and is used to recognize a unique visitor. Both transient and persistent cookies may be set by first parties, companies with whom a customer has agreed to do business (by visiting the site) and hence agrees to allow cookies. A third party's cookies are set by another entity that the first party has agreed to allow on a customer's computer.

Cookies are very useful for tracking customer responses, though other methods are possible, such as a unique sign-in by customers. Companies like Google Analytics, Facebook Insights, Omniture, and comScore use cookies to track customer behavior.

There are numerous opportunities for marketers to collect vast amounts of consumer online click behavior. The data sets are so large that average applications and computers can't handle them. These days, data scientists use open-sourced software called Hadoop to store data sets and MapReduce software to process the data into usable information.

Customer tracking data have some advantages and disadvantages (see Exhibit 12.12). First, the data are reliable because they measure actual behavior rather than the perceptions of consumers. The disadvantage is that impression and click-through behavior for an individual is not available when the person was exposed to a traditional ad or marketing strategy or purchased from a retail location, rather than from a digital one.

RESPONSE MODELING

Marketers can use a number of techniques to evaluate the impact of various elements of a media strategy involving multiple consumer touchpoints, including social media, search, retail, traditional advertising, promotions, public relations,

EXHIBIT 12.12

Advantages and Disadvantages of Customer Tracking

ADVANTAGES	DISADVANTAGES
Uses reliable digital measures.	Does not consider traditional media or outlets for purchase.
Does not provide for consumers' perceptions of media influence.	Recognizes that consumers may be limited in their abilities to remember media exposures.
Can be used over a variety of digital touchpoints.	Does not control for extraneous influences such as traditional media interactions.
Can be automated to collect data over time and track huge numbers of consumers.	Retains concerns over cookie deletions, robots, and other fraudulent clicks.

mobile, and other strategies. The methods can yield a series of weights or attributions for the various touchpoints.

One technique is a large-scale perception study to examine the media elements that consumers believe influence their own purchase behavior. The advantage of analyzing customer perceptions is that customers can provide information on traditional and nontraditional media. However, people do not always clearly remember the media with which they interacted prior to making a purchase, particularly a low involvement purchase. Therefore, this technique works better when the product or service requires some thought as part of the purchase decision. To conduct a customer perception study, marketers generally follow the steps enumerated below. It often helps to engage the services of a market research firm to manage the task, create the stimuli, and evaluate the data. The steps are:

1. Define and contact a representative sample of members of the target market of interest. Include subjects who purchased the product and those who did not for group comparisons.

2. List each possible form of media or touchpoint with which a consumer may have engaged over a particular time period. These should include all the strategies the firm executed in a particular time period. In addition, the marketing team should identify a few phantom forms of media, strategies that were not executed. The phantoms will help identify customers who do not remember or who may not be taking the study seriously.

3. Create brief descriptions of each form of media and a representation of the medium, such as a picture. For example, a picture of a television with notable images from the commercials shown could serve as a stimulus. The images can be created in electronic form and displayed to the sample.

4. Develop a questionnaire asking each sample subject whether he or she remembers seeing the image and how much the image, on a scale of 1 to 100, influenced his or her attitude toward the item of interest. Include subjects who did not buy the product, asking them about the influence of forms of media on their attitudes toward the product or service. Include additional variables such as demographics, purchase outlet, and other brand-specific questions.

5. Aggregate the data for all customers to create a response model that identifies the variables associated with a positive attitude toward purchase.

6. Enter all the data into a statistical data analysis program and run logistic regression to determine the appropriate weights for the variables.

Let's see how this works with a specific example. Say that over a three-month period a marketer executed four strategies: a television commercial, a magazine ad, a search engine keyword campaign, and a mobile application. A questionnaire asks subjects whether or not they were exposed to the execution and the degree to which the execution influenced their attitude, on a scale of 1 to 100. The researcher enters the data into an SPSS program to run a logistic regression. Whereas a **multiple regression model** predicts the value of a numeric variable, a **logit model** predicts the value of a categorical variable (0–1) based on a set of inputs. In this case, the model will predict whether a person purchased the product or did not purchase the product based on their perceptions of the influence of each media execution. A basic logit model equation is provided in Equation 12.1.

$$\text{Logit}(p) = \alpha + b_1 x_1 + b_2 x_2 + b_3 x_3 \ldots$$

Equation 12.1 Logit Model

Let's say the researcher runs a logistic regression and finds the results in Exhibit 12.13 [27]. To understand the output, look at the B, the estimated coefficient for the values of the predictors and at the Wald statistic. If the Wald statistic is significant (<.05), then the variable is useful to the model. The corresponding regression equation is shown in Equation 12.2.

Product Purchase Prediction =
$-10.183 + .063^*\text{commercial} + .063^*\text{magazine} + .041^*\text{search} + .024^*\text{mobile app}$

Equation 12.2 Regression Equation

The marketer can then plug in values for the variables to predict the likelihood of purchase. General advantages and disadvantages of response modeling are summarized in Exhibit 12.14

EXHIBIT 12.13

Logistic Regression for Response Modeling

		VARIABLES IN THE EQUATION					
		B	S.E.	WALD	DF	SIG.	EXP(B)
Step 1*	Commercial	.063	.031	4.205	1	.040	1.065
	Magazine	.063	.026	5.659	1	.017	1.065
	Search	.041	.028	2.195	1	.138	1.042
	Mobile app	.024	.022	1.245	1	.265	1.025
	Constant	–10.183	3.543	8.261	1	.004	.000

*Variable(s) entered on Step 1: Commercial, Magazine, Search, Mobile app.

EXHIBIT 12.14

Advantages and Disadvantages of Response Modeling

ADVANTAGES	DISADVANTAGES
Equates traditional and nontraditional media quantitatively.	Does not take advantage of digital measurement.
Provides for consumers' perceptions of media influence.	Consumers may be limited in their abilities to remember media exposures.
Can be used over a variety of touchpoints.	Does not control for extraneous influences.
Eliminates concerns over cookie deletions, robots, and other fraudulent clicks.	Limited sample predicts behavior of the population and perceptions may vary widely.

MEDIA TIMING ANALYSIS

Marketers know when certain marketing actions have been executed and should have an idea of when to expect a consumer response from a medium in their market space. For example, a marketer may have experience running an email campaign with a direct response indicator that establishes where the customer originated. After running a few email campaigns, the marketer may conclude that a majority of the customer response is driven within two days of opening the email. To use this technique, the marketer must track each communication implementation over a period of time to determine the level of sales or other desired outcome generated by a particular strategy. To execute a **media timing analysis**, the marketer should:

1. Set a time period during which to track outcomes. Use a minimum of three months and a maximum based on the longest response time of your communications methods plus 50%. For example, if a magazine advertisement generates response for one to six months following a run and magazines are the longest time-to-outcome medium, set the maximum at nine months.

2. On a calendar timeline, mark each communications event during the time period. Use days if the strategy can be broken down into specific days; otherwise, use the shortest time denominations possible. Some strategies are

executed on a weekly or monthly basis and can't be tied to a day. Mark the calendar timeline for the length of the execution as consumers see it.

3. Track sales levels and other desired outcomes on each day.

4. Determine, based on past data, which media execution led to the sales level on a particular day. If more than one communication influenced the sales level, estimate a percentage of each medium's impact.

5. Evaluate the degree to which each execution led to a particular sales level attributing a percentage of the total sales to each medium.

The chart in Exhibit 12.15 represents the media strategy for a brand that executed communications in television, outdoor, and search and held two events during the nine-month period January through September. As you can see, the marketer ran a television campaign during February and sales spiked. On the other hand, the event in August had virtually no impact on sales levels. The revised Facebook strategy launched in May also seems to show an increase in sales in May. However, this analysis has to be carefully considered. It does not account for extraneous variables that could influence sales. For instance, let's say this is a brand of snowboards. An event in August might generate sales in December. The marketer's experience in each medium will help predict the appropriate time periods and outcome slots to examine. Exhibit 12.16 summarizes the advantages and disadvantages of media timing analysis.

consider this . . .

MEGARED ANALYZES A FACEBOOK CAMPAIGN

MegaRed is a brand of fish oil supplement that decided to run Facebook ads to build customer engagement. The company wanted to target those who already used fish oils or who were concerned with heart health, using emotional stories in multiple ads that stretched over days and weeks. The campaign started in November and reached 18.1 million women aged 45 and older on Facebook, 56% of the total target audience. The intermediary results for the campaign were strong, with 1 out of every 84 Facebook users who saw the campaign liking, commenting, or sharing it—a rate 3 times as high as MegaRed's prior campaigns. MegaRed tracked sales through the following February, using Datalogix's loyalty card program, and found that the brand gained a full share point in the heart–health market [29].

EXHIBIT 12.15

Media Timing Analysis Chart

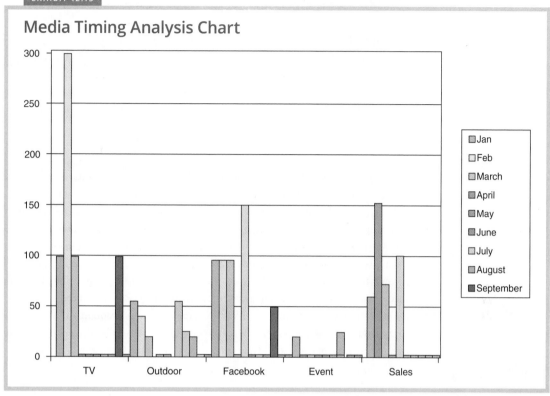

EXHIBIT 12.16

Advantages and Disadvantages of Media Timing Analysis

ADVANTAGES	DISADVANTAGES
Examines traditional and digital media.	Does not consider consumer engagement outside of strategic campaigns.
Does not rely on consumers' perceptions of media influence.	Recognizes that consumers may be limited in their abilities to remember media exposures.
Can be used over a variety of digital touchpoints.	Requires significant tracking of strategies over time.
Allows the marketer to consider sales results from strategies.	Marketer must know the timing of outcomes for various strategies and does not account for new untested actions.

MEDIA EQUIVALENT ANALYSIS

Media equivalent analysis, also called advertising equivalence, is a method of comparing forms of media in terms of reach and costs using the CPM measure described in Chapter Ten. Cost per thousand refers to the cost to reach 1,000 members of the target and can be expressed with Equation 12.3.

$$\text{CPM} = \frac{\text{Cost of an Advertisement} \times 1,000}{\text{Size of Audience}}$$

Equation 12.3 Cost per Thousand

The size of the audience depends on the medium. In print media, the audience is circulation. In television, the size of the audience may be the number of households that see an advertisement or the number of people in a particular target tracked by Nielsen. In digital media, the audience consists of those who see the communication online, in an app or mobile advertisement, or on a social media site. The assumption behind media equivalent analysis is that a consumer viewing a message in each form of media is equal in terms of the value to the firm. Though certain media may deliver stronger prospects, media equivalents operate on the notion that an impression in one form of media is the same as an impression in another. Therefore, viewing a 30-second spot on television is the same as seeing a Facebook ad or an organic ranking of the brand when the customer searches Google.

EXHIBIT 12.17

Example Using Media Equivalence

MEDIUM	ADVERTISEMENT	AUDIENCE	COST	VALUE ($) CPM
Keywords "laptop computers"	Bid on key word during the campaign	246,000 global monthly searches; avg. click through 2.36%	Avg. cost per click $1.50	$354
People magazine national edition	2/3rds -page 4-color ad	3,450,000	$305,900	$88.66
NBC Sunday Night Football	30 seconds	20,860,000	$637,330	$30.55
A prime-time television commercial on a network	30 seconds	14,074,000	$502,500	$35.70

SpyFu, "Competitive Data," 2014.
People Magazine 2016 Rate Card, accessed April 7, 2016. http://www.people.com/people/static/mediakit/media/pdf/ratecard.pdf
Steinberg, Brian, TV Ad Prices: Football, Empire, Walking Dead Grab Highest Rates, Variety, 29 September 2015. http://variety.com/2015/tv/news/tv-advertising-prices-football-empire-walking-dead-big-bang-theory-1201603800/

The example in Exhibit 12.17 compares the cost per thousand for buying a keyword on a search engine with a magazine ad, sports programming ad, and a prime-time television ad [30]. If you assume that an impression holds the same value in any form of media, which is the most efficient purchase on a CPM basis?

The analysis comes from the public relations world. For years, PR firms have tried to equate the value of an impression in a news article or story to an advertisement. Using ad equivalence was one way to evaluate the contribution of PR. One mistake the industry made was to assume that a PR mention was worth more than an ad and attempt to multiply the effect of the media communication. The multiplier effect reduced the credibility of the process. However, using conservative estimates of value, media equivalents can be very useful for comparing traditional and digital strategies, but there are still advantages and disadvantages to using this method (see Exhibit 12.18).

consider this . . .

BIG DATA'S PREDICTIVE ABILITY

Marketers collect so much data on customers that their ability to predict behavior is growing. However, consumers still like to believe that they control their information. Through data mining, Target has been able to determine whether a female customer is pregnant or not, often before she has told friends and family members. Pregnant women tend to purchase certain products, such as unscented lotions and larger purses, so Target can determine with a scary level of accuracy the likelihood that a woman is having a baby. Having a baby is a life-changing event that comes with many purchases. Target's information would seem like a great opportunity to connect with customers and convince them to buy at Target. But, when Target sent exclusively baby-related coupons to pregnant women, the response was anxiety. Women did not appreciate the fact that Target had obtained this knowledge. Now, Target sends a variety of coupons with baby items embedded within them so that women will not feel spied upon [33].

EXHIBIT 12.18

Advantages and Disadvantages of Media Equivalency

ADVANTAGES	DISADVANTAGES
Equates all forms of media using CPM.	Does not consider strategies without a CPM measure, such as the retail touchpoint.
Does not depend on consumers' perceptions of media influence.	Has been criticized for using a multiplier.
Can be used over a variety of digital and traditional media.	Assumes that all impressions are equal regardless of medium.

MARKET RESEARCH

Marketers can also take advantage of tried and true market research techniques to evaluate social media or mobile strategies: surveys, observation, and experimentation.

A **survey** is a questionnaire that marketers use to ask people questions regarding their attitudes and behaviors. **Observation** is simply watching or monitoring people's behavior, and **experimentation** involves comparing the responses of two or more groups to different strategies.

SURVEYS AND OBSERVATION

Through surveys, research brands can measure levels of awareness, attitudes, or brand equity both before and after executing social media or mobile strategies and examine the differences. Social media engagement should positively affect all three measures, which are defined in Exhibit 12.19. Surveys can be useful, but always have the potential problem of nonresponse. It is difficult to encourage people to answer surveys, but with some incentive, it is possible. One reason to use a survey over social media monitoring is that many people do not express themselves on social media, and marketers would then lose the opportunity to include members of the target in the data.

We have already looked at a common form of digital observation. Do you know how marketers "observe" digital consumers? Marketers examine consumer click-stream behavior and people's real-time responses. For example, Google Analytics shows a snapshot of activity on a site, while other dashboards display data gleaned from observing customers, such as heat maps or bubbles representing visitor clicks on elements of a website.

EXHIBIT 12.19

Measures of Awareness, Attitudes, and Brand Equity

BRAND VALUE MEASURES	
Awareness	The degree to which people are aware of the brand in both aided (with response choices) and unaided response.
Attitudes	A positive or negative valence toward a stimulus expressed as cognitive, affective, and intentional responses to a brand.
Brand Equity	The value inherent in a brand's name or symbol.

MEASURING THE SOCIAL MEDIA BRAND EQUITY EFFECT

Do social media and mobile strategies build brand equity? If so, can a marketing manager measure the effect? **Brand equity** has been defined as "a set of brand assets and liabilities linked to a brand, its name and symbol that add to or subtract from the value provided by a product or service to a firm and/or that firm's customers" [34]. The concept can be measured by examining four brand elements: awareness, perceived quality, brand associations, and loyalty.

Brand Equity Strategies

BRAND EQUITY ELEMENT	EXPLANATION	STRATEGIES TO ENHANCE BRAND EQUITY
Awareness	Recognition of the brand name.	Customers searching for local businesses may use their smartphones to locate previously unknown retailers or use social media sites such as Yelp to find a business in a new area.
Perceived quality	Belief that the brand performs strongly on key attributes.	Social media sites offer reviews of products, and potential buyers can judge quality based on the firm's response to complaints in social media.
Brand associations	Elements of the brand are accessible by consumers who can describe key brand attributes.	The brand can create a Pinterest page with strong visuals that express the brand's identity. Tweets of important news for the brand can build associations.
Loyalty	A favorable attitude toward a brand coupled with repeat purchase behavior.	Brands can offer discounts, premiums, and value via social media and mobile to loyal customers.

EXPERIMENTATION

Experiments provide a powerful way to evaluate the influence of a strategy on brand value. In a controlled experiment, the researcher randomly divides a group of subjects into treatment and control groups. The researcher exposes the treatment group, but not the control group to a particular strategy and measures the differences in outcomes among the groups. This technique is just as useful for social media and mobile marketing as it is in more traditional marketing strategies.

Marketers sometimes call experimentation A/B testing because they will compare two strategies (A vs. B) to determine which is more effective. However, marketers can evaluate more than two strategies at the same time as long as they have enough people to study. A common use of experimentation is to test email offers, but marketers can also test social media strategies.

To test email offers, marketers develop the various offers, send them to different targets of randomly selected consumers, and determine which customers responded to each offer using a tagging code. Marketers must plan this effort in advance, a method known as forward tracking so that they can embed the code within the appropriate communications platform and tie the code to the specific promotion. A marketer could do the same with Twitter by sending out tweets to different groups with varying offers and measuring the response. One option is to use a special Bit.ly URL to track the campaign. **Bit.ly** is an online tool for shortening URLs and tracking the response to them.

consider this . . .

USING EXPERIMENTATION TO DETERMINE BRAND EQUITY EFFECTS ON PINTEREST

Let's say you would like to run an experiment to determine if your new Pinterest site generates brand equity value for your firm. Here are the steps to take to study the brand equity effects of Pinterest:

1. Locate an email list of customers who are in your target market or use your company email list.
2. Randomly assign the members of the list to two groups. You can do this by starting at a random point on the list and assigning every other person to either the treatment or control group.
3. Develop a Pinterest site that represents your brand, and its values, products, and identity.
4. Send an email inviting the treatment group to view your Pinterest site with a link to the site. Send an email to the control group inviting them to view a Pinterest site that is not specific to your brand, such as a brand-neutral general-interest Pinterest site. Offer everyone the same incentive to participate in the study.
5. After a significant proportion of study subjects have viewed the Pinterest site, send an email link to the survey that includes a customer-based brand equity scale for your brand.
6. Analyze the results of the study to determine brand impact.

A variation on the study is to measure equity or attitudes prior to viewing the Pinterest sites for a before and after direct view of the response to the site.

THE CUSTOMER-BASED BRAND EQUITY SCALE

The Customer-Based Brand Equity Scale measures consumers' preferences, awareness, and perceptions of a brand's level of quality on a seven-item Likert scale, ranging from strongly agree to strongly disagree. Some of the items are marked reverse to indicate that the scale goes from strongly disagree to strongly agree [35].

1. Even if another brand has the same features as Brand X, I would prefer to buy Brand X.
2. Brand X must be of very good quality.
3. I consider myself to be loyal to Brand X.
4. I know what Brand X looks like.
5. It makes sense to buy Brand X instead of any other brand, even if they are the same.
6. I can recognize Brand X among other competing brands.
7. I will not buy other brands if Brand X is available in the store. I am aware of Brand X.
8. If there is another brand as good as Brand X, I prefer to buy Brand X.
9. Brand X is of high quality
10. I would like to buy Brand X.
11. The likelihood that Brand X would be functional is very high.
12. Brand X is desirable.
13. Brand X is nice.
14. Brand X is attractive.
15. Brand X is undesirable. (reverse)
16. Brand X is bad. (reverse)

SUMMARY AND REVIEW

CHAPTER SUMMARY

Digital marketing provides vast amounts of data for brands to process and manage. However, marketers who evaluate strategies with sound metrics can determine effectiveness both during and after a campaign. Some of the techniques include digital tracking, media analysis, and traditional market research methods. Whereas marketers can and should evaluate both financial and nonfinancial metrics, ultimately marketers should show a ROI for any marketing strategy.

KEY TERMS

analytics
attribution
attribution analysis
Big data
Bit.ly
brand equity
experimentation

financial metrics
key performance
    indicators (KPIs)
last click attribution
    model
logit model

media equivalent analysis
    (or advertising
    equivalence)
media timing analysis
metrics
multiple regression
    model

nonfinancial metrics
observation
persistent cookies
return on investment
survey
transient cookies

SUMMARY REVIEW QUESTIONS

1. How do firms determine spending for promotional strategies?
2. Why are both financial and nonfinancial metrics important to examine for performance?
3. What criteria are important in evaluating metrics?
4. What information is needed to determine ROI, and how can a marketer obtain it?
5. Can traditional media measures be used for measuring social media and mobile strategies?
6. Explain the concepts of attribution analysis and media equivalence.
7. Using media equivalence, explain why marketers may prefer to buy traditional media.

APPLICATION QUESTIONS

1. You have developed a mobile gaming application that allows children to connect with one another to create drawings together. The app costs 99 cents and has additional incentives within the game, for a total average cost of $1.49 per buyer over a three-month period. Typically, games are downloaded and played and then dropped after a relatively short time period. Your firm spent $100,000 to develop the game and an additional $40,000 in marketing costs and registration costs. The game is available for iPhone and Android, but not yet for tablet use. You earn income from selling the game and sponsorships and in-app advertising totaling $10,000. The target market for the game is U.S. moms who buy the game for their children ages 5–9 to play. The conversion rate is 2%. Eighty-four percent of moms have smartphones, [36] and there are approximately 20 million children ages 5–9 in the United States. What is the ROI for the game developers? Show your work.

2. An advertiser buys Facebook ads aimed at adults 18–24 to sell a new brand of beer. The ad runs on the right side of the target's newsfeed. Go to Facebook and begin creating this advertisement. Put in any URL and then add the following criteria: men and women 18–24 who have an interest in food and dining or beer/wine/spirits. What is the cost per click and how much does it cost per impression? What do these numbers mean?

3. Calculate the total impressions and cost per thousand of the luxury automobile campaign in Exhibit 12.20 featuring multiple advertisements and promotions over a one-week period.

4. Evaluate the social media strategies of Coke and Pepsi using nonfinancial metrics. What stands out with regard to their competitive strategies? Do the two brands continue to go head-to-head in social media?

5. Go to your browser's cookie section and look at the last ten cookies set on your computer. Which cookies do you want to have on your computer and which would you prefer to delete? If you are not sure what a particular cookie does, type its name into your search bar and check out the result.

    (If you do not know how to find the cookies, type "find cookies" and the name of your browser into a search engine and find out how to look at them. In Firefox, go to settings and click on privacy. In Google Chrome, you have to click on the wrench on the right side of the page, click on settings, advanced settings, privacy, cookies, and all cookies and site data.)

6. Using Google or a library database (like ABI Inform), find a study that shows a content analysis (try typing in "content analysis," "market research," and "journal" into the toolbar). What did the researchers examine and how was the content analysis conducted?

EXHIBIT 12.20

Luxury Automobile Campaign

MEDIUM	VEHICLE	CIRCULATION/REACH	COST FOR SINGLE ADVERTISEMENT
1 Television commercial run in prime time for 5 nights	*60 Minutes* prime time with rating of 5.3	8,096,000 viewers	$108,956 Production costs of $200,000
1 Full-page ad in each newspaper, run ad in 2 papers daily for 5 days	*Wall Street Journal* *New York Times*	2,061,142 daily 876,638 daily	$277,776 (weekday Global Edition) $194,166 (business section weekday)
2 Tweets per day	Number of Twitter followers	500,879	$1,000 (allotment of staff time for posting)
YouTube commercials over a 5-day period	YouTube ad run on *60 Minutes* in network prime time	1.234,789 views/day for 5 days	$1,000 (allotment of staff time for posting) and responding to comments

7. Find a case study on Think with Google, Facebook, or Twitter that discusses the financial impact of a social media strategy. How much did the brand spend and what was the return?

8. Choose a brand and evaluate the brand's social media strategy. What metrics can you use to determine effectiveness? Do all metrics indicate success?

9. You would like to reach 18- to 24-year-olds with a message about your new social network for college students to help them prepare for their coursework and meet students at other schools. Which form of media would you recommend as having the highest reach for this target at the lowest possible cost? Show the alternatives you considered.

case study Pretty Pushers Evaluates Its Strategy

Pretty Pushers is a brand of birthing gowns sold online and through select stores in the United States. The company, founded by Mary Apple, was the first to offer a beautiful 100% cotton garment that could be worn during labor and delivery. Early on, the company earned approvals from doctors and hospitals for its design as the gowns had openings for fetal monitors, IVs, and epidural access, with enough coverage to maintain the mother's privacy [37].

Pretty Pushers, Inc., www.prettypushers.com

In 2013 the brand reached $255,000 in sales and expected to hit $340,000 in 2014. However, the owner was concerned because her product was sold on Amazon.com and some discounted websites at lower prices than available on her website. This was a big problem because a sale on the Pretty Pushers website earned the company a much higher margin than a sale through a third party site. As such, Mary Apple set the goal for the brand to build website sales 100% in 2015. The website revenues were approximately $86,000 for the year

ended November 2014. These revenues represented a little less than 30% of total sales [37]. The brand set the 2015 total revenue goal at $680,000.

INDUSTRY

Sales of Pretty Pushers birthing gowns was directly tied to the U.S. birthrate as close to 90% of Pretty Pushers online sales, as indicated by Google Analytics, originated in the American market. The U.S. birthrate was approximately 4 million in 2013, a decrease of 7% compared to the historical high of 4.3 million in 2007 [38]. The U.S. states with the highest birthrates were: California, Texas, and New York [38], important markets for Pretty Pushers.

Pregnant women were heavy consumers of both baby products and maternity wear. The baby products market was expected to grow 2% between 2013 and 2018, compared to less than 1% between 2008 and 2013. The maternity clothing industry generated revenues of $2.2 billion in 2012 and was also expected to grow as the birthrate increased following the U.S. recession of 2008–2010. The market for birthing gowns appeared to be poised for growth.

Pretty Pushers' competitors included standard hospital gowns as well as more fashionable options from BG&Co, Dressed to Deliver, Gownies, and My Bella Mama. Although the products were comparable, some competitors offered additional features such as convenient pockets, matching pillow cases, and personalization. Only Pretty Pushers and Gownies offered their most basic (and most popular) gown online for $29.99, the lowest price point among the major competitors before shipping.

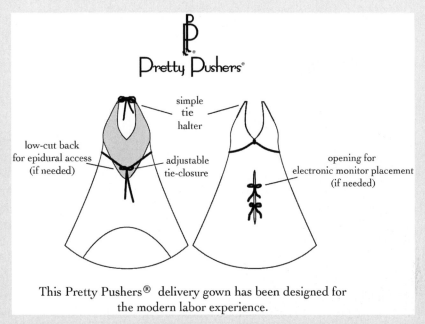

This Pretty Pushers® delivery gown has been designed for the modern labor experience.

Pretty Pushers, Inc., www.prettypushers.com

THE BUSINESS

The Pretty Pushers' website was hosted by Shopify, a platform for online stores. Shopify provided some analytics data on the site to help retailers evaluate site performance. The dashboard included sales, traffic, and order information as well as data for individual products. Retailers could also see the referral sources through Shopify's last click method of attribution.

Pretty Pushers inserted a snippet of code in the Shopify platform to allow for Google Analytics tracking. Google Analytics reported that in a one-month period from October 24 to November 24, 2014, about 45% of the site visits were from iOS devices and an additional 21% from Android, suggesting a large mobile audience. Over this time period, the bounce rate for the site was 36%, and the average time spent on the site was 1 minute, 36 seconds. There were 100 total orders with most coming from direct sources. Exhibit 12.21 shows that the

EXHIBIT 12.21

Conversion Rates by Traffic Sources

Direct	51
Search engine	41
Referrals (blogs)	7
Social (Facebook)	1
Total orders	100

Shopify, "Pretty Pushers Data," 2014.

conversion rate was weakest for social media sites.

According to the Shopify site metrics over a longer ninety-day period, the average per customer order was $54.00 and the conversion rate on the site overall was 4%. Annual website hits were 159,699 for an estimated monthly sales rate of 532. The 2013 annual expenses for the business were $153,000.

The following information from the company founder indicated the costs to deliver a gown and the problem associated with diverted sales:

Our most popular gown, the solid black, is $29 on the website. They pay on top a flat $6.25 for shipping, so a total of $35.25. Our Cost of Goods Sold on that gown is about $6.50, and then we pay $5.05 to ship to that customer, so our total cost to get it to the customer is $11.55. This is obviously before all of our operating costs–rent, monthly credit card processing fees, etc.

That same black gown is $16 wholesale, and still costs us $6.50 to make. But most wholesale orders were through a rep, so their commission is 15%, so that's coming out of that $16 right away. The customer pays UPS shipping, and we pay UPS to ship the boxes of product, but it's not nearly as much per item.

TARGET MARKET

Pretty Pushers' target was women 25–44 who were expecting a baby. Most of the people (88%) who purchased maternity clothes were women, and it was likely that most women made the birthing gown decision on their own.

The maternity wear market matched closely the target for Pretty Pushers. Women who had purchased maternity clothing generally lived in the southern part of the United States with household (HH) incomes of over $40,000. In terms of media, these women watched child-oriented programming on channels that included ABC Family and the Disney Channel as well as E! Entertainment Network.

Women who bought maternity clothes were heavy Internet users, and 67% accessed the Internet at least once a day, compared to only 57% of the overall adult population. Some of the websites that indexed high for these women were IMDb (178), Pandora (144), WebMD (208), and Groupon (192), which suggests that they were interested in celebrities, music, and deals [39]. In addition, pregnant women were more likely than the average adult to access the Internet from mobile devices, which explains the relatively high sales rate from mobile for Pretty Pushers [40].

Women in the target market were fashion- and brand-conscious. Approximately 80% of the target indicated that "it is important to look attractive to others" and almost 90% reported that they "dress to please themselves." In addition, 80% had a few favorite brands that they always followed and 60% normally looked for their favorite brands first [41].

DIGITAL STRATEGY

Pretty Pushers had a limited digital strategy that emphasized bloggers and social sites such as Facebook, Twitter, and Pinterest. One blogger, in particular, drove significant sales to the site, Birth Without Fear, a blog on which Pretty Pushers bought paid display ads and as a result was often mentioned in the editorial. Pretty Pushers relied heavily on organic search, and almost 50% of organic search hits to the site came from the keywords "Pretty Pushers." Pretty Pushers did not buy any Google Ad-Words, because the recommended word phrases such as "maternity clothes" were too expensive relative to the click-through rate they delivered.

POTENTIAL STRATEGIES

Pretty Pushers had many options for increasing sales to its website. The question was which would deliver the strongest level of conversions relative to the costs. Exhibit 12.22 lists a set of strategies the brand might consider, and Exhibit 12.23 shows the cost per thousand and click-through rate data for various options.

EXHIBIT 12.22

Options for Strategy

a. Paid search/keywords

b. Search engine optimization

c. Blogger outreach

d. Email

e. Paid display advertising

f. Building social media presence on Facebook, Twitter, Pinterest, or other sites

g. Video and YouTube channel

h. Mobile website and mobile advertising

i. Mobile SMS

j. Daily deals promotions such as Groupon

k. Traditional advertising (magazine ads, commercials, radio spots, outdoor, direct mail, newspapers, others)

EXHIBIT 12.23

Cost per Thousand and Click-Through Rates for Strategies

MEDIA	CPM	CTR
Digital display	$.27–$1.03	.20%
Paid search		
Computer	$.83	2.29%
Tablet	$.76	2.70%
Smartphone	$.58	3.75%
Organic search	Free or SEO	13%–69%
Google paid search	$.25–$3.09	
Facebook	$.10–$1.10	.03%–.92%
Twitter	$.26–$.43	
Mobile display	$.51–$1.15	
Network prime-time television, 30-second spot	$24.76	

Media Dynamics Inc., "Targeted Online Video CPMs Much Higher than TV," 21 April 2014. Press release.

The brand could estimate ROI from strategies to determine how to reach its goals.

Pretty Pushers was headed into the busy Christmas season and hoped to increase sales with a Black Friday deal. However, the purchase was not seasonal in nature and sales were steady throughout the year. In addition, women tended to purchase only one gown and repeat business was not a huge revenue generator. As such, to expand her business in 2015, Mary Apple had to develop a sustainable strategy that would deliver sales directly to her site.

QUESTIONS FOR DISCUSSION

1. Consider a blogger outreach strategy. How would you determine which bloggers to approach and what would be your strategy for doing so?
2. Choose five bloggers and calculate the ROI for advertising with those bloggers, assuming a 2% response from each of their sites. You will have to find traffic data for each one.
3. Using sites such as SpyFu and SEMrush, determine five keyword phrases you would recommend to Mary Apple. For each one,

determine the average monthly searches, the click-through rate, and the cost per click. Calculate the ROI for this strategy.
4. Both Facebook and Pinterest deliver hits to the Pretty Pushers website, but Twitter does not. Does this mean Twitter is not an effective strategy? Defend your response considering the attribution method used by Shopify.
5. Consider a mobile SMS strategy. Would you recommend this strategy to Mary Apple? Why or why not?
6. Would mobile advertising be effective? Calculate the ROI using data from Exhibit 12.23.
7. Compare Pretty Pushers' conversion rates for Facebook and the blog Birth Without Fear. If the blog ad costs $500 per month, which is a better strategy?

REFERENCES

[1] Facebook, 24 April 2015.

[2] Twitter, 24 April 2015.

[3] YouTube, 24 April 2015.

[4] Instagram, 24 April 2015.

[5] Klout, 24 April 2015.

[6] C. Delo and M. McCarthy, "GM Returns to Facebook Advertising after Public Split a Year Ago," Advertising Age, 9 April 2013.

[7] C. Moorman, "The CMO Survey," 2014.

[8] T. Bradshaw, "'Angry Birds' Lays $100m Egg for Rovio," Financial Times, 16 December 2011.

[9] A. Young, "Axe vs. Old Spice: Whose Media Plan Came Up Smelling Best?," Advertising Age, March 2010.

[10] Twitter, "BombFell: How Does a Unique Styling Service Drive Potential Customer to Their Website?," February 2015.

[11] O. Blanchard, *Social Media ROI,* Indianapolis: Que, 2012.

[12] M. Stelzner, "2014 Social Media Marketing Industry Report," May 2014, http://www.socialmediaexaminer.com/Social MediaMarketing IndustryReport2014.pdf.

[13] J. Sandler, "How to Effectively Budget Your Social Media Program in 2013," ClickZ, January 9 2013.

[14] Content Marketing Factory, accessed April 5th, 2016, http://www.contentfac.com/how-much-does-social-media-marketing-cost/.

[15] www.twilio.com/pricing, accessed April 7th, 2016.

[16] J. Harper, "The True Cost of Developing Your App," Apps Marketing.Mobi, 26 September 2011.

[17] Mopub, "Mobile Advertising Insights," 2013.

[18] Astegic, "How Much Does It Cost to Develop a Mobile App?" 10 July 2013.

[19] Stelzner, Michael 2015, "Social Media Marketing Industry Report, Social Media Examiner.

[20] R. Fu, "Why Wechat Marketing Metrics Could Be All Lies," China Internet Watch, 5 August 2014.

[21] LinkedIn Marketing Solutions Blog, "Measure Your Content Marketing with LinkedIn's Content Marketing Score," 27 March 2014.

[22] Union Metrics, "Top Five Metrics on Tumblr," 2015.

[23] B. Honigman, "How to Use Pinterest Analytics: 6 Metrics Worth Measuring," Social Media Examiner, 6 May 2013.

[24] Cicero, Nick, Four Important Snapchat Metrics Your Brand Should Be Measuring, Convince and Convert, accessed April 7, 2016, http://www .convinceandconvert.com/social-media-measurement/snapchat-measuring/.

[25] J. Beese, "Yelp Introduces New Metrics for Local Businesses," Sprout Social, 27 March 2012.

[26] Effie Awards, 2012, "The Search for the New Duck Voice, Effie Bronze Award, Aflac. https://effie.org/ case_studies/by_category/51/by_year.

[27] Google, "Certain Affinity," Google Analytics Case Study, 2013.

[28] BGSU, "Annotated Output," Bowling Green State University, 2006.

[29] V. Goel, "How Facebook Sold You Krill Oil," The New York Times, 3 August 2014.

[30] SpyFu, "Competitive Data," 2014.

[31] People Magazine 2016 Rate Card, accessed April 7, 2016, http://www.people.com/people/static/ mediakit/media/pdf/ratecard.pdf .

[32] Steinberg, Brian, "TV Ad Prices: Football, Empire, Walking Dead Grab Highest Rates", Variety, 29 September 2015, http://variety.com/2015/tv/ news/tv-advertising-prices-football-empire-walking-dead-big-bang-theory-1201603800/.

[33] C. Duhigg, "How Companies Learn Your Secrets," The New York Times, 16 February 2012.

[34] D. A. Aaker, Managing Brand Equity, New York: Free Press, 1991, p. 2

[35] J. H. Washburn and R. E. Plank, "Measuring Brand Equity and Evaluation of a Consumer-Based Brand Equity Scale," Journal of Marketing Theory and Practice, Winter 2002, 46–62.

[36] Edison, 2015, Moms and Media Report, http://www. edisonearch.com/wp-Edison Research content/ uploads/2015/05/Moms-and-Media-2015-Final.pdf.

[37] M. Apple, "Pretty Pushers," Pretty Pushers.com, 2014.

[38] Babycenter, "Surprising Facts about Births in the US," 2014.

[39] MediaMark Research & Intelligence, Fall 2013 Product Report, Maternity Clothing.

[40] Shopify, "Pretty Pushers Data," 2014.

[41] Nielsen, "@Plan," 2014.

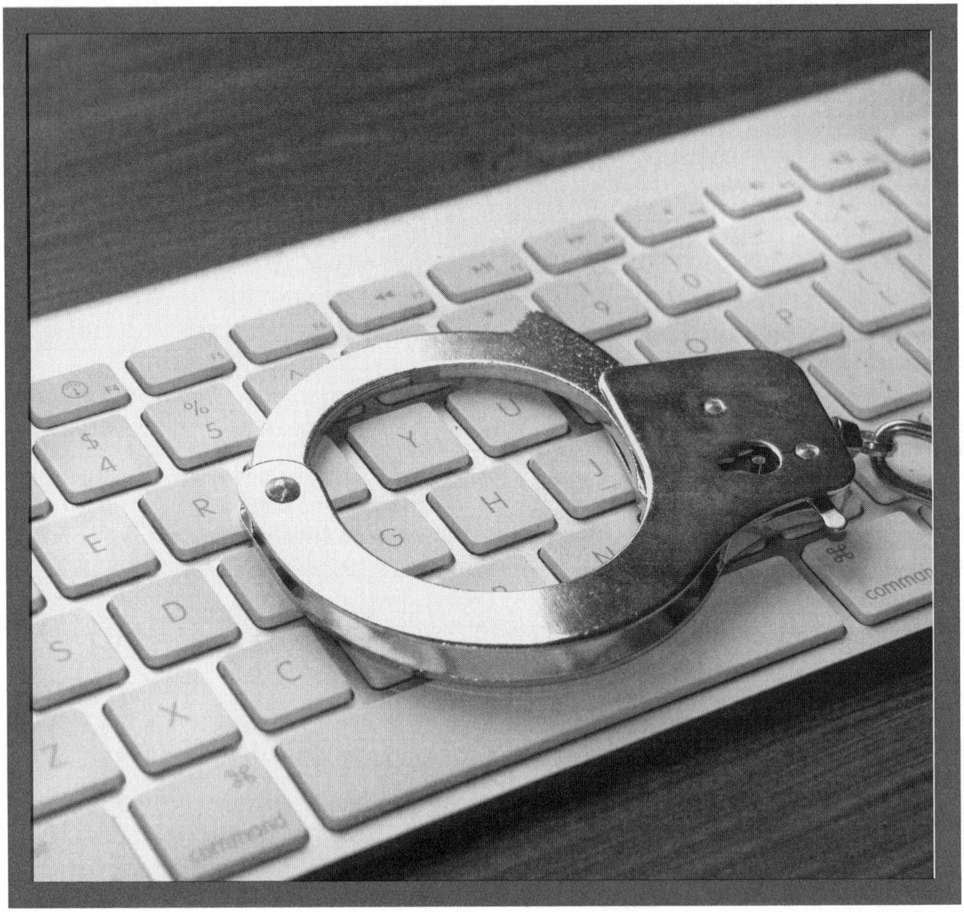

© Shutterstock/PTstock

CHAPTER THIRTEEN

LEGAL MATTERS

The deluge of information collected on private citizens by online marketers is unprecedented, and laws regulating the flow of data have just begun to emerge. Marketers use consumer data to offer products and services for purchase, but may also abuse the responsibility, sometimes failing to properly safeguard personal data. A number of current regulations aimed at protecting consumers from unsolicited emails, deceptive advertising, and aggressive data collectors do apply to social media and mobile marketing activities. Other laws protect copyrights, cellular phone numbers, and children's data. This chapter reviews issues of privacy, the various regulations, and both the Federal Trade Commission (FTC) and advertising industry enforcement procedures.

LEARNING OBJECTIVES

After reading this chapter, you will be able to:

- EVALUATE THE LEGAL IMPLICATIONS OF SOCIAL MEDIA AND MOBILE STRATEGIES

- DETERMINE THE APPROPRIATE RULES AND REGULATIONS FOR CAMPAIGNS

- IDENTIFY GOVERNMENT AND ADVERTISING INDUSTRY REGULATORY AGENCIES

- CREATE LEGAL SOCIAL MEDIA AND MOBILE MARKETING CAMPAIGNS

- CONSIDER CONSUMER PRIVACY IN EXECUTING SOCIAL MEDIA AND MOBILE STRATEGIES

Have you ever downloaded a book to read on your Kindle device, iPad, or smartphone? Do you think anyone is tracking your reading habits? Would anyone care? There are over 40 million e-readers and more than 65 million tablets in the United States generating $282 million in sales quarterly. By examining reading behavior, publishers can determine which books you like to read, how long it takes you to read them, what you highlight, what you skip, when you put the book down for a break, and when you keep reading and can't stop. And, the major brands—Barnes & Noble, Apple, Google, and Amazon—are tracking your reading habits. Barnes & Noble shares the information with publishers so that they can locate the points of boredom with books and potentially alter the works to make them more interesting. The company has also found that sci-fi, romance, and crime genres tend to be read more quickly than novels and that nonfiction is read slowly, with breaks in between reading sessions.

Publishers have responded by adding video and content on pages in digital versions where readers get bored. But publishers also can deliver content in books that matches what people like. For instance, digital analysis shows that women prefer romance novels featuring men in their thirties who have dark hair and European accents [1]. Will all romance novels now have such men as their heroes?

So, is it legal for the e-book sellers to track your reading habits? More importantly, do you want booksellers tracking your reading? What if you are reading a book on a disease you may have? Do you want your insurance company to be able to buy data that documents your book purchase? Do you want the government to know if you purchased a book on creating Internet viruses? Are there books whose content might embarrass you or get you into trouble? Well then, you had better be careful. It's perfectly legal for e-book sellers to track you because when you signed on to download books, you agreed to the terms of service, which includes permission for Kindle to store information from the device [1].

Given the chance, all sorts of companies will follow you online and would track you off-line if they could do so. Marketers really try to understand what leads you to make a purchase, so they can figure out how to sell more to you and your friends. Have you ever noticed how the terms and conditions of using all sorts of websites change regularly with updates? How many times have you read an agreement from the same site? Even if you were to read it once, which most likely you have not, the website owner could change it at any time, forcing you to read the agreement again and again not knowing what marketers are doing with your data. In essence, when you use a website, you are giving your implicit trust to a company to do what it wants with your information. However, most online terms and conditions not only give the company with whom you are dealing access to your information, but also extend that right to numerous third parties such as advertising networks, research companies, and others who also want to track your click stream. In many cases, the original company to which you granted the right to see your information doesn't even know who else might be using it.

SHOULD YOU TRUST MARKETERS?

We implicitly give our consent for marketers to track us, but what about when we post personal information on social media sites. Most marketers have privacy policies that they suggest serve to protect consumer data, but, in fact, protect the marketer from lawsuits. The regulations allow marketers to collect any information they like and only one state, California, in the United States requires firms to indicate that are doing so in their company privacy policies. Other states, such as Connecticut and Delaware require a policy if certain data are collected.

TYPES OF CONSUMER DATA COLLECTED

There are two types of data marketers can collect on consumers: personally identifiable information (PII) and non-personally identifiable information (non-PII). **Personally identifiable information (PII)** includes data such as a person's name, email address, Social Security number, and other information that identifies an individual. **Non-personally identifiable information (non-PII)** is also about individuals, but does not reveal the actual person associated with the data. Marketers defend their practices by indicating that they only collect non-PII data. However, the tracking does affect what a person sees on the Internet and alters the experience. For example, if a marketer can identify a consumer as a high-income individual who may be willing to pay more for a service, the high-income customer could then be quoted a higher price than an economy or deal shopper. If you search for prices for an airline flight and the vendor is tracking you, the company can see that you really want a particular flight and charge you more to get it.

Luckily, a smart consumer can avoid tracking by browsing in private mode, eliminating cookies, or setting browser preferences to avoid advertising. Each

consider this . . .

MOBILE APPS TRACK YOU

Are you familiar with the Whisper app? It is a social media site that prompts users to post their secrets with the promise of anonymity. To use all the features in Whisper, users have to permit tracking. What the company did not tell users was that Whisper was tracking them even if they opted out of the geolocation services.

Not only that, but the app shared data with news outlets and law enforcement. At one point, *The Guardian* newspaper reported that Whisper was tracking a "randy D.C. lobbyist." The company then boasted that "he's a guy we'll track for the rest of his life, and he'll have no idea we'll be watching him" [2].

browser has its own settings for tracking, but consumers can find most in their tools, settings, or at the bottom of the browser's page.

LOSS OR MISUSE OF DATA

There are many recent examples of marketers losing consumer data or accidentally making data public. Hackers stole credit card information from 119 Staples stores, affecting 1.16 million customer credit and debit cards [3]. Anthem, the health-care company that runs Blue Cross and Blue Shield in 14 states, found that hackers accessed data for 78 million people [4]. Even banks can be violated, as when Citigroup lost the account numbers of 200,000 customers to hackers [5], and JP Morgan Chase had to file a report with the SEC disclosing that user contact information was stolen for 76 million households and 7 million small businesses in the United States [6].

So many breaches of security occur that the Identity Theft Resource Center tracks them for the U.S. Department of Justice annually. In 2015 there were 781 data breaches in the United States—the second highest since tracking began in 2005 [7]. A breach occurs when someone steals or a company divulges a person's name and Social Security number, driver's license number, medical records, or financial credit card information.

HOW MARKETERS TRACK YOUR BEHAVIOR

Marketers use cookies on computers to track your behavior. A **cookie** is a small text file that is stored on your computer which records the sites you visit online, how long you stay there, and what you do at those sites. A **persistent cookie** is one that stays on your computer feeding information back to the source until you erase it or the marketer does. These cookies have tags that identify the specific computer. Another type of file that a marketer can load onto a computer is a flash cookie. This type of cookie is an image file that also tags the user to track information. Originally developed to improve loading speed, the file is stored in the cache of the browser. The cache now serves to slow down the browser when the flash cookie is used to serve ads to consumers. Adobe, the company that owns Flash software, can store trackers in Flash when marketers use the program on their sites [8].

Sometimes, the consumer chooses to be tracked by providing a unique sign-in to the marketer to facilitate purchase or other Web-related actions. When consumers log on, the marketer can track them via their log-in name and history. This individualizes the information to the person, so the marketer can identify an individual rather than a computer, providing even better information about purchase behavior. Facebook can track you from your PC, to your phone, to your tablet because you log on to the social network with your unique ID on all those devices.

The World Wide Web Consortium developed a set of policies for those who wish to track individuals using cookies. The consortium established three-letter P3P compact codes that marketers can use when they embed cookies to indicate the privacy policy in effect when collecting information. For example, the P3P protocol indicates that no personally identifiable information is collected by the cookie and the data will be used for a certain amount of time. The code NOI means that no identified information will be collected, while OTC means other data, not described by the marketer, may be collected [8].

MARKETERS TRACK MOBILE DEVICES, TOO

Marketers can collect a significant amount of data on individuals to target the proper consumers and deliver messaging that drives a desired response. It is no secret that marketers track people's click streams to determine which sites consumers visited prior to making an online purchase. Marketers can also track click streams on mobile devices as well as mobile device codes embedded in phones or tablets. The challenge for marketers is to tie the click-stream behavior to off-line purchases. One answer to this problem is encouraging mobile payment or other means of payment that marketers can track, such as credit cards.

Mobile applications are the Wild West of data collection. When you download an app onto your mobile device, you are often giving the app permission to look at data collected from other apps. Did you know that your Facebook app can access your contacts and calendars? Facebook allows third party advertisers to track people's usage and tie the data back to desktop usage so that marketers can observe mobile shopping behavior and remarket online. You can opt out, but you have to go through a procedure to do so as the default is opt-in [9].

Researchers at Carnegie Mellon examined the top 100 apps in the Google Play store and found the following 10 requested the most access to users' hardware: Backgrounds HD, Wallpaper, Brightest Flashlight, Dictionary.com, Google Maps, Horoscope, Mouse Trap, Pandora, Shazam, and My Talking Tom. Does a wallpaper app need access to your camera, locations, and contacts [10]?

consider this . . .

WHAT IS HISTORY SNIFFING?

History sniffing is secretly gathering online information from consumers by accessing their browser queries to see which websites they have visited. The FTC prohibited the company Epic Marketplace from using its technology for history sniffing. Epic is an advertising network that collected information about consumer browsing around the Internet, but only told customers in its privacy policy that it would collect information about their visits to sites within the network. The FTC consent order required Epic to destroy all data it had collected through history sniffing [11].

BIG DATA AND THE DATA COLLECTORS

The term "Big Data" refers to the aggregate data that marketers and other entities collect on the population and that they then analyze to make predictions about behavior. We learned in Chapter Twelve how marketers can use statistical techniques to determine what types of consumers are more likely to buy their product or respond to a particular communication. Research firms work with marketers to help them cull through the large amounts of data and organize the information for their purposes. The information is very valuable to firms because companies can determine which customers are the best prospects, which marketing efforts lead to the highest levels of conversions, and what steps the consumer takes in the purchase of the product or service. As a result, numerous firms collect data on Internet users (see Exhibit 13.1) [12].

A number of different types of firms collect data about your online behavior. The data collectors include advertising networks, advertising servers, publishers, widgets, supply-side platforms, demand-side agency trading desks, exchanges, and others. Most of these collectors are tracking customers' behavior in an attempt to figure out their likely next purchase and then use that information to deliver highly targeted advertisements.

EXHIBIT 13.1

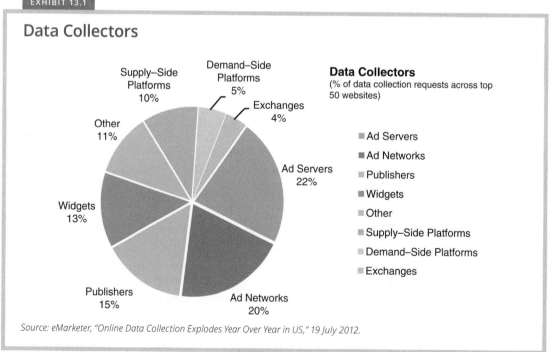

Data Collectors

Data Collectors
(% of data collection requests across top 50 websites)

- Ad Servers
- Ad Networks
- Publishers
- Widgets
- Other
- Supply–Side Platforms
- Demand–Side Platforms
- Exchanges

Supply–Side Platforms 10%
Demand–Side Platforms 5%
Exchanges 4%
Other 11%
Ad Servers 22%
Widgets 13%
Publishers 15%
Ad Networks 20%

Source: eMarketer, "Online Data Collection Explodes Year Over Year in US," 19 July 2012.

ADVERTISING SERVERS

The largest group of data collectors are **advertising servers.** Ad servers are companies that help marketers track advertisements; they represent nearly one-third of all online data collected by marketers. These servers provide tools for managing and tracking the online advertising of campaigns when advertisers buy on a cost per thousand (CPM) or cost-per-click (CPC) basis. Some marketers find these services useful because it is often difficult to track the actual delivery of an ad once it has been purchased. The server can also provide more detailed information about consumer behavior through tracking.

ADVERTISING NETWORKS

Advertising networks are groups of websites that are packaged together so that advertisers can easily buy advertising space, such as banner ads, on the network's website and mobile apps. Networks typically sell their inventory based on impressions, the number of "eyeballs" a campaign will reach. Advertisers will buy a certain number of impressions or page views to satisfy the campaign requirements. For example, a network might sell 50,000 impressions to the mobile gaming app Jetpack Joyride, placing its ads on gaming websites to encourage downloads of the game. Approximately 20% of the data collected by marketers online is gathered by advertising networks.

PUBLISHERS

Publishers are websites that deliver content to consumers, such as news outlets, blogs, special-interest websites, and others that have information or entertainment people want to see. Some examples of publishers are magazine websites, video-sharing sites, or content sites such as Yelp, which publishes reviews. Sometimes, publishers sell their inventory of advertisements directly to advertisers, and because of that, they track consumer data to make the sale more attractive. Publishers represent about 15% of online data collection.

WIDGETS

Facebook, Twitter, and Pinterest use widgets, small software applications, on websites to encourage people to connect with them. The widgets also serve the purpose of feeding data back to the company when individuals click on them. So, as in the real world, be careful who you "like" as you may enter into a longer relationship with a site than you realize and breaking up will require some effort [13].

REAL-TIME BIDDING: DEMAND AND SUPPLY SIDE PLATFORMS

Real-time bidding is a method marketers use to buy advertising space on websites and is a growing avenue for serving ads. **Demand-side platforms** are companies that use proprietary technology to allow advertisers to buy ads aimed at customers who have particular desirable characteristics, including favorable demographics and specific purchase behavior. This method of purchasing audiences occurs through a real-time bidding system that advertisers use to find appropriate online prospects. Advertisers determine their budgets and target market requirements and place bids to earn the right to show ads to the target. For example, a data collector can determine which people are looking at rugs on various websites. Target stores might then bid to place an ad on pages viewed by the rug seekers. The transaction occurs through a bidding system, with the highest bidder winning the advertising space.

Another aspect of the real-time bidding system occurs on the supply side. Supply-side platforms sell online advertising inventory to advertisers. Publishers use supply-side platforms to fill their advertising spaces with ads. Together, demand- and supply-side platforms represent about 20% of online data collection.

EXCHANGES

Exchanges sell website advertising inventory through a specific method of buying and selling advertising space similar to what occurs on a stock exchange. Exchanges sell available advertising inventory to bidders who purchase immediately, but represent only about 4% of total data collection in the industry [14].

CONSUMER ATTITUDES TOWARD DATA COLLECTION

Consumers are worried about the personal data that firms collect, but many believe they are protected by "strong" laws governing their data. A study by the Berkeley Center for Law and Technology found that 60% of Internet users in the United States prefer regulation to stop websites from collecting information about them [15]. Exhibit 13.2 shows just how concerned Americans are about their data, yet few do anything to protect their online privacy. When asked, only 64% of Internet users have cleared cookies, 41% have erased something they personally posted, 41% have set their browser to disable cookies, and 36% have not used a website that asked for a real name. Only 14% have encrypted communications online [16].

Consumers are obviously concerned when their personal identifiable information is available to firms and third parties, but often do not understand the risks associated with non-personally identifiable information. People may think that if the company does not know who is doing the surfing in terms of a name, address, phone number, or Social Security number, they can't be harmed. In fact, because marketers track data to a unique computer IP address (the address that identifies a person's computer), they can alter an individual's online experience.

EXHIBIT 13.2

Americans' Concern about Online Privacy

PERCENTAGE OF ADULTS WHO:	
Agree or strongly agree that consumers have lost control of how personal information is collected and used by companies.	91%
Say they are not confident that records of their activity maintained by the **social media sites** they use will remain private and secure.	87%
Believe that being in control of who can get information about them is "very important."	74%
Feel that controlling what information is collected about them is "very important."	64%

Source: Pew Research, "The state of privacy in America: What we learned," 20 January, 2016.
http://www.pewresearch.org/fact-tank/2016/01/20/the-state-of-privacy-in-america/

GENERAL REGULATIONS THAT APPLY TO DATA COLLECTION

The **Federal Trade Commission (FTC)** is the U.S. government body that regulates interstate commerce and is responsible for protecting consumers, establishing guidelines for fair competition, and setting policy regarding false and misleading advertising.

There are relatively few laws governing data collection on individuals in the United States, though the FTC has published a draft report titled "Protecting Consumer Privacy in an Era of Rapid Change." The report suggests that marketers should promote consumer privacy within their organizations, provide consumers with choices about how the data will be used, and establish higher levels of transparency in data-collection activities. The report is a warning to marketers to follow these principles or face potential regulation. However, there are no consequences for marketers if they do not abide by these guidelines, yet.

consider this . . . .

FTC WARNS NORDSTROM RACK

The FTC issued a warning to a Nordstrom Rack store in Boise, Idaho, with regard to its "VIP Tweet-Up" campaign. The store invited active Twitter users to a private party with drinks, food, and gift cards. The store encouraged those influencers to tweet about the event, which violated FTC guidelines requiring anyone endorsing a product to disclose payments—or free gifts or gift cards [17].

ESTABLISHING CLEAR AND VISIBLE PRIVACY POLICIES

Consumers may agree to share data with a marketer with whom they do business, but they may not be aware of third party cookies that the marketer places on their computer to allow other entities to freely track activities. Though no federal law requiring privacy policies exists, marketers can protect themselves from lawsuits or unhappy customers by setting clear consumer data privacy policies—and then following those guidelines when developing marketing and data-collection strategies. Also, since the State of California does require websites doing business in the state to have a privacy policy, it makes sense for most companies operating in the United States to post one. The California Online Privacy Protection Act (CalOPPA) also specifies how companies must respond to "do not track" signals and whether third parties can access data. Every marketer should publish a privacy policy that is explicit regarding the data the firm is collecting and with whom the data are shared. One option for companies is to use TRUSTe's visual icons to indicate to consumers the data that companies collect during online interactions [18]. Another is to publish a strong policy following the best practices in Exhibit 13.3.

consider this . . .

EXHIBIT 13.3

Best Practices for Privacy Policies

Privacy policies should:

1. Clearly communicate in easy-to-understand language.
2. Explain the information that will be collected.
3. Indicate how the data are collected.
4. Allow individuals to alter their personal information.
5. Provide a method for opting out.
6. State that the policy will be updated regularly.
7. Be easy to find.

With regard to social media, consumers who post online should not assume privacy protections unless they make efforts to secure their information. So, if you post your activities on Facebook, assume everyone has access to that information. Email and text messaging are different in that those vehicles come with a greater expectation of privacy and are therefore more strongly protected from public view. Also, children have more protection under the law than adults, as mandated by the Children's Online Privacy Protection Rule enacted in 2000.

consider this . . .

FOLLOW YOUR PRIVACY POLICY

Consumers filed a class action lawsuit naming Google Buzz for violating the Electronic Communications Privacy Act, the Stored Communications Act, the Computer Fraud and Abuse Act, and other laws inconsistent with the company privacy policy. Google shared people's private posts when they signed up for Gmail.

The FTC ruled that Google had acted deceptively and is now subject to independent audit through 2031 to ensure compliance with the privacy program. By the way, the FTC also found Facebook in violation when they changed users' privacy settings without their consent [20].

consider this . . .

A SAMPLE PRIVACY POLICY

Kayak is an online travel booking service that searches numerous sites for low prices. The company indicates that its goal is to be the most trusted company in online travel, so it offers a one-page privacy policy written in plain English. It also explains why the company collects information. For example:

WE'LL KEEP YOU IN THE LOOP

If you book a travel product via the Platform, we may need additional information from you. This information can include your name (and traveler's name if different),

passport number, email address, telephone number, credit card information, billing address, itinerary, and frequent flyer details. You can also choose to store personal information in your user account for future bookings.

IN THIS CASE, SHARING IS NOT CARING

We collect your personal information directly from you. For example, when you provide us your personal information when you register or book travel.

We also collect your personal information passively. For example, we collect information about you over time and across different Web sites when you visit this Platform. We also use tracking tools like cookies and beacons.

We collect your personal information from third parties. This can include when you log in using a third party platform, such as Facebook. Kayak has authored a very folksy privacy policy that sounds friendly and unobstrusive to consumers. However, the company can still collect a lot of data on you and share that information with others [21].

The two sample paragraphs above represent the tone of the company's privacy policy, but the substance is still there. Kayak makes clear in the rest of its policy statement that it uses cookies and allows third party networks to fill ad space with advertisements that may use non-personally identifiable information to serve ads which might include information from other sites you have visited.

STANDARDIZED AD PRIVACY PROGRAMS

A few organizations offer marketers the opportunity to post their privacy icon on a webpage so that consumers can click on the icon to receive privacy information. Though marketers are not required by law to inform consumers each time a website collects data, the FTC highly encourages that companies provide to consumers both transparency and control over their data. Icons help consumers by drawing attention to clicks that may lead to tracking and allow people to opt out.

One industry program that helps companies monitor privacy issues is the Ad-Choices program. Developed by the Digital Advertising Alliance, the plan requires members to monitor the advertising they serve online and report on their use of icons to the Alliance. Marketers can then use another system such as TRUSTe to monitor their privacy compliance, while still collecting data on consumers. Both companies place icons on company websites that sign up for their service and then provide each business with reports on digital ads that third parties may place on consumers' computers through the company's cookies. Marketers must monitor their privacy systems because they will not otherwise know when other firms have placed cookies on consumers' computers using their access.

The AdChoices icon opens a window on the user's computer that indicates how the ad targeted the user and how to click through to opt-out of behavioral targeting [22]. Right now, some big companies such as Google, Yahoo, AOL, Facebook, and Microsoft participate in the AdChoices program.

One issue with the AdChoices icon is that consumers do not understand its purpose. Carnegie Mellon conducted research that showed consumers did not recognize the AdChoices icon and did not understand its meaning or how to use it. The subjects were shown the icon on websites, and only 15 out of 48 people indicated that they had seen it before. Some people also believed that if they clicked on

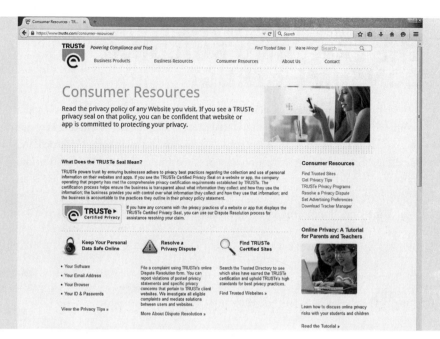

The TRUSTe symbol indicates that a company abides by TRUSTe's privacy policies.

TRUSTe, www.truste.com

the icon, something bad would happen, like launching a pop-up advertisement [22]. Whereas companies may prefer that consumers remain unaware of their efforts to provide transparency, the government regulatory bodies around the world might not believe that AdChoices meets their standards for informed consent.

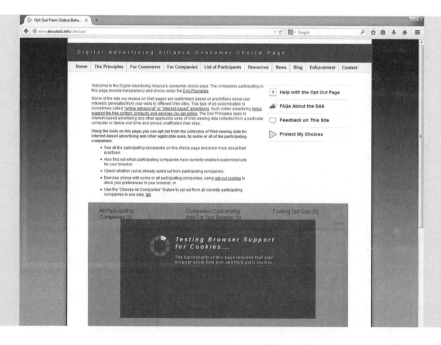

Consumers can identify the companies serving ads on their computers using the Consumer Choice Page accessible at http://www.youradchoices.com/control.aspx.

About Ads, http://www.youradchoices.com/control.aspx

CONSUMER PRIVACY, THE LAW, AND BUILDING CONSUMER TRUST

As with most laws, permissible actions are subject to definition by the courts when a complaint or violation is lodged, so until there is a legal case, marketers may not know where to draw the line on acceptable behavior. As such, following the FTC guidelines in its draft report can protect in the instance of lawsuits. In addition, marketers should recognize the value of their customers' trust. Since trust is an inherent aspect of business, marketers should protect consumers' privacy if they hope to maintain long-term relationships with them.

consider this . . .

A VIOLATION OF COPPA

Mobbles is a kid's mobile gaming app that took its product off the market when a privacy group threatened to file a complaint with the FTC. The game encouraged kids to find, capture, and trade virtual pets. The app did not have a privacy policy and was capable of geotracking children. In addition, the app collected personal information from kids, such as email addresses without parental consent [23].

PRIVACY PROTECTIONS IN THE UNITED STATES

The laws related to consumer privacy in the United States include:

1. **The Computer Fraud and Abuse Act (CFAA).** This law suggests that marketers may be committing fraud when accessing a computer without authorization or intentionally obtaining financial records of consumers with the intent to defraud. Violations of the act can lead to imprisonment or a fine.
2. **The Electronic Communications Privacy Act (ECPA).** This law makes it illegal to access stored communications without authorization. Companies that hold consumer data, such as in the cloud, must protect those data and may not divulge the information without a court order. This act protects consumers' personally identifiable information from disclosure.
3. **The Children's Online Privacy Protection Rule (COPPA).** This is the strongest privacy legislation enacted by Congress. The rule applies to children under the age of 13 and prohibits marketers from requesting personal information from children, allowing kids to post publicly, and passively tracking

children without parental consent. This law is the reason why Facebook requires users to be at least 13 years old.

4. **The Controlling the Assault of Non-Solicited Pornography and Marketing Act**. Also known as the CAN-SPAM Act, this regulation relates to commercial email messages and prohibits marketers from sending messages without obtaining consent or sending misleading information when the return email address is unknown.

5. **The Telephone Consumer Protection Act**. Also known as TCPA, this law restricts use of telephone equipment and prohibits calls using automatic dialing systems to cellular telephone numbers without prior consent or an established business relationship [24].

Each of the above laws may apply when marketers execute strategies in social media or mobile. As mobile becomes an increasingly social medium, the laws related to fraud and abuse of personal data, user-generated content, and children's privacy protection may also apply.

consider this . . .

CAN A COMPANY TEXT ME ANYTIME?

Consumers filed a class action lawsuit against Papa John's Pizza, claiming that its SMS campaign violated the TCPA. Franchises sent text messages to consumers without their approval. The US District Court for the Western District of Washington allowed consumers to recover $500–$1,500 per unlawful message [25].

PRIVACY PROTECTIONS IN THE EUROPEAN UNION

Other countries, including China and member-states of the European Union (EU), have stricter laws governing data collection than the United States. The EU Cookie Law that took effect in May 2012 applies to computers and mobile devices. The rule states:

Personal data shall be adequate, relevant and not excessive in relation to the purpose or purposes for which they are processed. This is the third data protection principle. In practice, it means you should ensure that: you hold personal data about an individual that is sufficient for the purpose you are holding it for in relation to that individual; and you do not hold more information than you need for that purpose.

The EU Court also handed down its "Right to Be Forgotten" ruling in 2014. As a result, Google, which controls 80% of the European search engine market, removes links when formally requested by individuals in certain geographic areas [26].

The EU regulators have their eyes on Google since the company alters its privacy policy whenever it changes strategy. For example, Google changed its policy to allow Google sites to share information across platforms to show ads on YouTube to Gmail users using consumer data. Google has the power to scan emails to determine what topics a person discusses and can feed ads based on that knowledge. In the United States, the Electronic Privacy Information Center (EPIC) complained to the FTC about Google's privacy policy, but the FTC took no action.

consider this . . .

THE FTC VERSUS GOOGLE

The FTC ordered Google to pay fines and refunds to consumers whose children made in-app purchases from apps downloaded from the Google Play store. Google is now required to get informed consent from parents before charging fees for in-app purchases. However, the FTC chose not to pursue an antitrust case against Google for the way in which it orders its search results when users search.

DEVELOPING SOCIAL AND MOBILE STRATEGIES IN A LEGAL CONTEXT

With social media and mobile marketing activities converging, marketers need to make sure they consider rules for both types of marketing activities when developing a strategy. Marketers execute many social media strategies via mobile on mobile apps such as Facebook or Twitter. These might include contests, sweepstakes, or user-generated content campaigns using social media or mobile SMS or mobile apps. Therefore, the laws apply to these executions regardless of the medium. In addition, advertising must be truthful and claims substantiated in all social media and mobile strategies.

The law is playing catch-up with social media technology, but a few legal issues affect how a business operates in the social media and mobile marketplace. Marketers should familiarize themselves with the following areas of existing law:

1. Developing a social media policy
2. Disclosing third party endorsements

3. Managing user-generated content
4. Running contests and sweepstakes
5. Avoiding deceptive advertising
6. Monitoring e-commerce and payment systems

DEVELOPING A SOCIAL MEDIA POLICY

A **social media policy** differs from a privacy policy as it focuses on behavior related to employees and their social media behavior, while privacy policies are for customers. Some firms encourage employees to be the voice of the company, encouraging them to tweet, pin, and post about the firm, its products, and brands. Other firms hold stricter views about who is allowed to speak on behalf of the company, with only certain individuals authorized to post. In the United States, companies can't limit employees' private speech and are prohibited from telling employees that they may not discuss the firm at all on social media because employees have the right to free speech. Companies may not prohibit social media usage during nonwork time, prevent the use of the company name or logo, limit posting on inflammatory topics, or stop criticism of the employer [27]. Because of the oversight of the National Labor Relations Board, companies should limit restrictions on speech, but encourage employees to behave properly on social media, respect the privacy of others, and abide by the law.

Every marketer should publish a social media policy for employees. A social media policy should reflect company expectations regarding social media behavior and include the following elements:

1. A clearly stated purpose for the policy
2. An indication that the policy matches company policy
3. Clear language
4. Brevity
5. Approval of legal counsel

For example, Coca-Cola's social media policy begins with an introduction indicating that the company wants to participate in social media the right way. The policy then outlines the company vision and suggests that employees consider the company's values when engaged on social media. In addition, Coca-Cola asks employees to be careful about what they post, accept personal responsibility, disclose that they work for the company when interacting online, let the experts respond in their areas of expertise, keep business separate from personal postings, and get training to become an official company spokesperson before posting on behalf of Coca-Cola [28].

Official Coca-Cola spokespeople have additional sets of guidelines, which include remembering that they represent the company, disclosing their company affiliation, not posting when in doubt, keeping records, giving credit without violating the rights of others, and considering the global and permanent nature of posts.

DISCLOSING THIRD PARTY ENDORSEMENTS

Companies are responsible for the veracity of online endorsements and testimonials and must disclose the relationship the endorser has with the company. An **endorsement** is any advertising message that consumers are likely to think represents the thoughts, feelings, or beliefs of someone other than the company. Marketers must disclose any connections that have economic value which could affect a customer's belief in the unbiased nature of the comment. Even when the consumers themselves comment on a product or service, the advertisers may have to disclose the relationship, as when customers received something for free or have been somehow compensated. Even if the marketer does not have ultimate control over the content, the law still requires disclosure. The discloser must be noticeable on the site, easy to understand, and near the endorsement. Marketers can also be held liable for false statements by bloggers or customers and must monitor them when they give endorsers free products [20].

consider this . . .

IS IT LEGAL?

1. A company providing cosmetic surgery services posted fake consumer reviews online and hired people to post testimonials. (The company was fined $300,000 for doing this.)
2. A mommy blogger posted positive reviews of a new wearable baby carrier on her site after receiving a free one. (She must disclose the fact that the merchandise was free.)
3. A company wrote a positive blog post about a new tech gadget and sent it to a blogger who posted it as his own. (The blogger must disclose that the company wrote the review.) [20]

MANAGING USER-GENERATED CONTENT

A few laws also come into play when marketers allow customers to create and post content. The first question is who owns the content. Often, users of websites post materials that do not belong to them and are copyrighted. At other times, users post material that may be offensive. Luckily for the website operators, they are protected by two laws:

1. The **Digital Millennium Copyright Act** protects a website from individuals who upload copyrighted material from claims of copyright infringement from the users, provided the operators do not know the material is owned by others and do not materially benefit. However, marketers must follow a set of procedures, including managing the content and setting website policies.
2. The **Communications Decency Act** allows website operators to monitor and restrict material that is lewd, lascivious, or excessively violent.

Sometimes, marketers encourage consumers to post their own creative material on a website, either as a submission to a contest or just for fun. When marketers want to post ads, artwork, music, written works, or videos created by customers, they are subject to the Copyright Act. The materials belong to the customers who hold exclusive rights to the works unless they assign the rights to the company. Marketers must obtain written permission from customers when posting their creative work.

The **doctrine of "fair use"** allows people to reproduce written materials, to comment on them, report news, parody content, or use it for teaching and research. The four factors that determine fair use are:

- Purpose and character of the use and whether it is for commercial purposes
- Nature of the work and degree of creative expression
- Amount used relative to the whole of the work
- Effect of the use on the potential market for the copyrighted work [29]

However, most social media users do not fall into these categories and may be violating copyright laws by posting or sharing content owned by others.

consider this...

DOES PINTEREST VIOLATE COPYRIGHT LAWS?

Pinterest encourages users to "pin" interesting pictures that may be owned by others. The site indicates that the copyright is the responsibility of the person who pins it and not Pinterest. For users, the doctrine of "fair use" could protect people from a violation, but only if the result is a highly transformed version of the original or contributes a significant aesthetic beyond that of the original.

Adbusters can parody advertising under the doctrine of "fair use."

Courtesy of Adbusters Media Foundation

RUNNING CONTESTS AND SWEEPSTAKES

Contests and sweepstakes are popular methods of building an audience, generating engagement with customers, increasing traffic, and sharing user-generated content. A contest requires a level of skill on the part of participants, while people win by chance in a sweepstakes. Marketers must be aware of the legal aspects of contests and sweepstakes to avoid accidentally creating an illegal lottery. Marketers who consider a contest to achieve a particular audience-building goal must abide by the legal requirements. Among the existing legal requirements are the following:

1. Sweepstakes must have official rules in effect for the duration of the sweepstake, can have no eligibility limits, must have a free method of entry (e.g., no purchase required), and provide prize and chance details.
2. Contests must identify the sponsor, the method for judgment, who will evaluate the entries, and start and end dates of the promotion.

Each state has its own laws and requirements, so marketers should review the process for their particular state (or states) with an attorney before proceeding [20].

Some companies use third parties, such as TRUSTe, to verify their security measures.

© *Shutterstock/Christos Georghiou*

ADVERTISING REGULATION IN SOCIAL AND MOBILE STRATEGIES

As indicated earlier in this chapter, the Federal Trade Commission (FTC) is the U.S. government body that regulates advertising and marketing communications. Section 5 of the FTC Act prohibits unfair or deceptive actions that are likely to harm consumers which are not avoidable or outweighed by benefits. An ad is only deemed deceptive when the damage is substantial to the individual. A communication can be true and still legally labeled "deceptive" if it deceives the consumer and leads to substantial damages. An ad is not considered deceptive if the consumer was confused about something not related to the purchase decision.

FALSE ADVERTISING

The FTC enforcement procedure involving deceptive advertising usually begins with a complaint from a consumer or competitor alleging false advertising. The FTC will then investigate the complaint by asking the advertiser to substantiate the claims it made in the advertisement. If the advertiser is unable to validate the claims in an advertisement, the FTC may ask the advertiser to revise the message; if the advertiser refuses to change its message, the FTC may issue a cease and desist order. If the advertiser continues to run the deceptive ads, it is subject to fines and the named employees to possible imprisonment. Sometimes, the FTC deems the ads are so deceptive that the messages cause long-term damage, in which case the Commission may order the advertiser to run corrective advertising.

consider this . . .

L'ORÉAL SETTLES CHARGES OF DECEPTIVE ADVERTISING

L'Oréal, the cosmetics giant, agreed to an FTC administrative settlement that prohibited the marketer from claiming any of its products could boost people's genes to make their skin look younger. Two of the company's products, Génifique by Lancôme and L'Oréal's Youth Code, made unsubstantiated claims about the products' anti-aging properties. For example, Génifique said its product was "clinically proven" to "boost gene" activity and lead to "visibly younger skin in just 7 days." The statements ran in print and on radio, television, the Internet, and social media. After receiving a notice from the FTC, L'Oréal agreed to no longer make anti-aging claims about these two products [30].

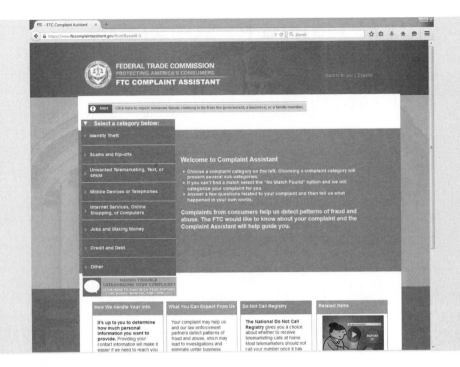

You can file a complaint with the FTC by using the FTC.gov Complaint Assistant.

Federal Trade Commission, www.ftc.gov

Both marketers and their agencies can be liable for deceptive advertising. However, the punishment for deceptive advertising is usually mild, particularly when the advertiser agrees to abide by FTC decisions.

FTC enforcement can be expensive for firms that make false claims. The marketers of the Your Baby Can Read learning program suggested that babies as young as 9 months could be taught to read and hired bogus experts to support the false claim. The settlement prohibited Infant Learning, the creator, from using the phrase "Your Baby Can Read" to name its product and fined the company $185 million, the company's total gross sales. The program had been marketed on You-Tube, Twitter, and Facebook, as well as in traditional media [31].

TRADEMARK INFRINGEMENT

Another law that affects how firms advertise is the **Lanham Act**. The act protects competition by prohibiting trademark infringement or dilution of that trademark with regard to advertising or promotion. In such cases, a competitor might sue for damages. For example, the SUBWAY sandwich chain sued Quiznos over a contest that asked consumers to create disparaging videos comparing a SUBWAY sandwich to a Quiznos Prime Rib Cheesesteak. SUBWAY sued, asserting that the contest produced ads that were false even though they had been created by third parties. The case was settled when the U.S. district court in Connecticut ruled that Quiznos participated in the development of the videos by creating the forum and theme [20].

SELF-REGULATION IN THE ADVERTISING INDUSTRY

The advertising industry, in an effort to avoid regulation by external agencies, set up self-regulatory agencies to address the FTC and EU concerns over data collection and misleading advertising. The industry, consisting of advertisers and agencies, believes that by monitoring its advertising governments around the world may be less inclined to impose restrictions on it.

The advertising industry maintains monitoring organizations within the EU and in the United States, Canada, Australia, India, and other countries to investigate complaints that advertisers or consumers submit over advertising claims that may or may not be deemed false. This process helps limit the caseload at the government regulatory agencies and allows industry insiders to participate in the process.

U.S. Self-Regulation

In the United States, the Advertising Self-Regulatory Council (ASRC) sets policies for the National Advertising Division (NAD), the National Advertising Review Board (NARB), the Children's Advertising Review Unit (CARU), the Electronic Retailing Self-Regulation Program (ERSRP), and the Online Internet-Based Advertising Accountability Program (OIBAAP).

The NAD focuses on misleading advertising, CARU reviews ads aimed at children, and the ERSRP regulates direct and interactive advertising. The OIBAAP reviews cases involving behavioral targeting and also examines infractions committed by advertisers who fail to inform consumers of online ad data collection and serving. Advertisers involved in disputes can appeal the decisions of any of these bodies to the NARB when they disagree with the ruling. The NARB is the appellate division that then hears the case and acts like a court, rendering a decision.

The NAD, CARU, ERSRP, and OIBAAP settle disputes when competitors make complaints against other advertisers, that may not have obtained proper consent for data collection, or ran messages unacceptable for children. Both ASRC members and nonmembers can participate for a fee and agree to voluntarily abide by the rulings. The process is a faster alternative for advertisers than the typical FTC procedure, as the self-regulation process provides written decisions within sixty days. In addition, rulings are confidential except for final decisions.

Though the NAD, CARU, ERSRP, or OIBAAP do not have the enforcement power of the FTC, the ASRC can publicize its rulings in the media to encourage compliance. Another way to encourage compliance is through the FTC, which will likely be interested in cases brought by the ASRC regulatory bodies [32].

The ASRC focuses on national advertising and can mediate between advertisers regarding questions over misleading messaging on television and radio, in magazines, and online. Since social media tools such as Facebook, Twitter, Pinterest, and others reach national audiences, the industry self-regulation body can hear disputes in these areas. More often though, claims are made that cover multiple forms of media. For example, Procter & Gamble, maker of Crest 3D White whitestrips, challenged Colgate-Palmolive's claims that its Optic White toothpaste had the "same whitening ingredient as strips." Colgate's claim ran in print; on television, packaging and store signage; and online. The NAD ruled that although Colgate's product contained the same 1% hydrogen peroxide ingredient and the company's advertising was truthful in this claim, the product did not deliver the same result. Though Colgate disagreed with elements of the NAD decision, it agreed to consider the NAD's decision in future advertising for the product Optic White. The end result was that for Colgate to be in compliance with the NAD decision, it could not run the prior claims for Optic White in any form of media, including social media or mobile advertising [33].

Global Advertising Regulation

The European Advertising Standards Alliance (EASA) regulates advertisers to ensure that ads are legal, decent, honest, truthful, and prepared with a sense of social responsibility [34]. The Internet Advertising Bureau (IAB) in the United Kingdom asks its members to abide by a set of behavioral advertising guidelines providing more transparency to consumers. Throughout the EU, an icon (similar to the AdChoices one) appears on people's computers near display advertising. Clicking on the icon leads individuals to information on behavioral advertising and provides a method for managing preferences or stopping such advertising [35].

The Advertising Standards Council of India (ASCI) is the industry body for advertising self-regulation in India. However, the national government there has recommended that an investigative agency monitor advertising, suggesting that the self-regulation board is not strong enough since not all advertisers (including some large multinationals) in India are members [36].

Brazil has a comprehensive and successful advertising industry self-regulatory system with a strong code that provides a guide for advertisers. Conselho Nacional de Autorregulamentação Publicitária (CONAR, National Council for Advertising Self-Regulation) is the organization that enforces the Brazilian advertising code. Advertising regulation in Brazil is more stringent than in the United States and requires that ads should not create fear or incite violence, may not stimulate pollution, or even use improper grammar [37].

The Australian Association of National Advertisers (AANA) set up a self-regulation system based on a set of codes and member compliance. The codes are similar to those enacted by the European self-regulatory body, EASA [38].

COORDINATING STRATEGIES ACROSS COUNTRIES

Marketers of global brands may develop advertising strategies that are standardized across multiple countries or adapted to reflect individual country or regional differences. For example, McDonald's agency in Germany developed the "I'm Lovin' It" campaign and the company chose to leverage that message around the world. The advantages of standardization include a single message to consumers and reduced costs of creative development and execution. To take advantage of the benefits, marketers could aim global ad strategies at the lowest common denominator or the country that has the strictest rules (e.g., China), but then they would lose the opportunity to reach consumers in other countries with a more nuanced message. An alternative is to develop a strategy that is standardized to some extent, but executed recognizing local forces [39].

In spite of these advantages, brands often develop campaigns for specific countries, in part due to differing regulations, but also because consumers themselves may differ by country. In the social media sphere, marketers find standardizing particularly challenging given that they do not have control over the message when consumers become involved.

consider this . . .

EXAMPLES OF ILLEGAL ACTS IN EUROPE AND CHINA

The European Commission's Unfair Commercial Practices Directive enacted in 2005 mandates that a commercial practice is unfair if it distorts economic behavior for the average consumer. Other illegal acts are aggressive commercial practices, misleading ads, ads with unsubstantiated claims, and untruthful comparative ads. European law even protects a customer from a merchant who explicitly tells the buyer that his or her livelihood will be at risk if the person doesn't buy the product [40].

China banned ads on television dramas in 2012, one more addition to a long history of restrictions on advertising. The Chinese State Administration of Radio, Film and Television (SARFT) regulates advertising with the objectives of cleaning up the advertising environment, protecting consumer rights, suppressing unfair competition, and protecting domestic products. Chinese laws prohibit the use of the national flag in advertising, require that people be able to close an online pop-up ad with a single click, and regulate tobacco ads. Chinese regulators fined Procter & Gamble $963,000 for using a computer to whiten the teeth of a celebrity endorser in a commercial, ruling that the act was false advertising [41].

REGULATING MOBILE PAYMENTS

In the United States, there are seven different government bodies that have jurisdiction over mobile payments: the Federal Reserve System, the Federal Deposit Insurance Corporation (FDIC), the Office of the Comptroller of the Currency (OCC), the National Credit Union Administration (NCUA), the Consumer Financial Protection Bureau (CFPB), the Federal Trade Commission (FTC), and the Federal Communications Commission (FCC). The FCC oversees mobile standards and the FTC covers consumer protection and privacy. The Federal Reserve defines mobile payments as "purchases, bill payments, charitable donations, payments to another person, or any other payments using a mobile device."

The law itself does not cover mobile transactions, but focuses instead on the payment methods such as credit or debit cards or prepaid access. The Mobile Payments Industry Workgroup has suggested that the current laws adequately cover mobile payments, but regulators continue to monitor the situation as adoption by consumers grows. The concern for agencies other than the FTC is risk to the financial system as a whole, rather than consumer protection [42].

SUMMARY AND REVIEW

CHAPTER SUMMARY

As consumers adopt new means of communications, laws are springing up to regulate these communications—but the laws lag behind. It takes Congress and other government bodies time to react to changes in the marketplace and enact laws to protect consumers or regulate trade. Though people are concerned with privacy, few individuals take steps to protect themselves. As a result, for the most part, social media marketers are able to track people, collect their information, and serve them ads based on their own data. This chapter outlined some of the current restrictions on marketers, but marketers generally have free reign as long as they disclose their practices to consumers.

KEY TERMS

advertising networks
advertising servers
Communications
    Decency Act
cookie
demand-side platform

Digital Millennium
    Copyright Act
doctrine of "fair use"
endorsement
exchanges

Federal Trade
    Commission
Lanham Act
non-personally
    identifiable
    information (non-PII)

persistent cookie
personally identifiable
    information (PII)
publishers
real-time bidding
social media policy

SUMMARY REVIEW QUESTIONS

1. Explain why Facebook's policy is to only allow those who are 13 years of age and over to register for accounts.
2. What is the difference between an advertising server and an advertising exchange?
3. What should be included in a good privacy policy? How do privacy policies protect companies?
4. How do European laws differ from U.S. laws on advertising regulation?
5. What is the doctrine of "fair use?" What are the limitations of this doctrine?
6. What are three rules specific to contests in the United States?

APPLICATION QUESTIONS

1. Go to the Industry Theft Resource Center. Determine the number of breaches over a particular time period and the number of records exposed. List three of the top breaches and the industry in which each cited company operates. What percent of total breaches occurred in the industries you listed?
2. Using a search engine, determine how to browse privately using your browser. Your browser is the software you use to access the Internet, such as Internet Explorer or Firefox. Before setting your browser to private mode, do a search for a popular news event that took place over the past month. After setting your browser to private, do the same search and note the differences in the results and pages that you see.
3. Go to www.ftc.gov and locate one case that involves deceptive advertising. What did the advertiser do and what was the response of the FTC? Did the case involve any social media or mobile marketing activities? Do you now feel differently toward the marketer involved in the case?
4. Do a search to find out how to determine who is tracking you on your computer. In Google Chrome, look at the "Ads Preferences Manager." When this author looked at her advertising preferences, eighty-six companies were delivering ads through her Google Chrome browser. How many are tracking you and what types of companies are they?
5. Go to Truste.com and determine the types of monitoring that the company can do for websites.
6. Find one contest on social media that a company ran or is currently running. Describe the contest and evaluate whether the contest meets the legal requirements.
7. What is the "right to be forgotten"? Who is responsible for complying with the corresponding rules and in which countries is this important?
8. What is disconnect.me and what does it do?
9. Using a search engine, find the FTC complaint assistant. What categories of complaints can you file as a consumer?

case study Snapchat and the FTC

Snapchat is a mobile communication and social networking platform that was built on a unique premise—that items shared would disappear in ten seconds or after a designated time set by the sharer. The founders of Snapchat, Evan Spiegel, Bobby Murphy, and Reggie Brown, launched the app on iTunes in September 2011 and downloads grew quickly. By August 2014 the app had more than 100 million monthly users [43].

BACKGROUND

Snapchat operated somewhat differently from other social networks. There was no Internet presence and users communicated by providing their cell phone numbers. Users typically snapped photographs or videos and set the amount of time, up to ten seconds, that they would allow their item to be viewed by others. The photos/videos could include various filters and words in a variety of sizes and colors to accompany the visuals. Users then selected the groups or individuals to whom they wanted to send the photo or video. Alternatively, users could elect to send the photo to "stories," which aggregated pictures to be sent together.

The allure for many on Snapchat was the fleeting nature of the photos. This offered many opportunities to show illicit, unacceptable, sexual, or other secret content with the assurance that the material would not appear on the sender's permanent record. This was particularly attractive to teenagers who might want to remain anonymous when posting certain content.

Snapchat was also very popular with millennials (those 18–34); it became the third most downloaded app after Facebook and Instagram among this demographic. Thirty-three percent of 18- to 34-year-olds had downloaded the app

by June 2014. Almost 20% of the adult population of smartphone users had downloaded the app as well. Of course, more established apps had more users, with Twitter at 271 million monthly log-ons and WhatsApp with over 600 million monthly users [44], [45].

The website Niche asked 7,000 users of its service who were graduating from high school in 2014 to indicate which sites they used daily. Niche.com provided reviews on neighborhoods, schools, and colleges. The site was founded in 2002 by students at Carnegie Mellon, originally as CollegeProwler.com. The students in the Niche survey indicated that they logged onto the sites in Exhibit 13.4 on a daily basis [46], [47].

Snapchat attracted a desirable young audience, but because the platform could not offer demographic data on its users, the app decided to only court big advertisers. Brands that wanted to advertise had to pay to $750,000 a day for ads that would also disappear in less than ten seconds, but that required users to press the screen to view them, indicating at least some level of engagement. Only the largest brands could afford the fee, so Snapchat's advertisers included McDonald's, Samsung, big budget movies, and large retailers.

SECURITY BREACHES

In 2013 an anonymous group of developers created a Web tool called Snapsaved that saved Snapchat photos and videos in an online location. The photos began surfacing on message boards, and it is believed that between 40,000 and 200,000 files were stolen. Snapchat was made aware of the security breaches and the ability of third parties to hack its system, but dismissed the claims. That was when the Electronic Privacy Information Center asked the FTC to look into Snapchat's security practices [48].

In December 2014 the FTC issued a five-count complaint against Snapchat, indicating that the company:

1. Marketed its services as sending disappearing photos when tools could be easily accessed to save pictures—including via screen save.
2. Issued statements claiming senders of photos that had been saved in a screenshot would be notified—but were not.
3. Tracked location information when promising it would not do so.
4. Represented that in using its "Find Friends" feature, the app would only collect phone numbers, although it also collected information from users' address books.
5. Failed to secure user accounts such that third parties could create accounts using the names of others [49].

The FTC found Snapchat in violation of the Federal Trade Commission Act and issued an order requiring that Snapchat no longer misrepresent its services and protect consumer privacy and security. In addition, the FTC required Snapchat to maintain a comprehensive privacy policy and submit to third party monitoring of this policy every two years for twenty years following a 180-day period of initial assessment. The order terminates on December 23, 2034. By January 2015 Snapchat had altered its privacy statement and its terms of use [50].

Sites Teens Use Daily

SERVICE	PERCENTAGE WHO USE EACH APP OR WEBSITE DAILY
Facebook	65%
YouTube	55%
Instagram	51%
Snapchat	46%
Pandora	37%
Twitter	35%
Phone call	34%
iTunes	32%
NetFlix	29%
Google	23%
Pinterest	16%
Vine	16%

D. Thompson, "The Most Popular Social Network for Young People? Texting," The Atlantic, 19 June 2014; Niche, "Best and Worst Media Habits of the Class of 2014," 2014.

QUESTIONS FOR DISCUSSION

1. Which law or laws did Snapchat violate according to the FTC? Examine the various laws cited in the chapter to answer this question.
2. What is your perception of the promises that Snapchat made to you or other users of

its service? Would you have expected others to see your photos?

3. What makes the Snapchat service so popular? Will teenagers or young adults continue to use Snapchat or switch to another service?

4. Evaluate the study done by Niche to determine the usage of various applications

by teens. Is this a good representative sample?

5. Evaluate the decision by some advertisers to spend $750,000 a day for Snapchat advertising. What are the advantages and disadvantages? How much does it cost to advertise on other platforms?

REFERENCES

[1] A. Alter, "Your eBook Is Reading You," *The Wall Street Journal,* 19 July 2012. http://www.wsj.com/articles/SB100014240527023048703045774909500 51438304.

[2] D. Goodyear, "Open Secrets," *The New Yorker,* 8 December 2014.

[3] B. Hardekopf, "The Big Data Breaches of 2014," *Forbes,* 13 January 2015.

[4] C. Humer, "Anthem Says at Least 8.8 Million Non-Customers Could Be Victims in Data Hack," Reuters, 24 February 2015.

[5] M. C. White, "Citi Data Breach: Are Hackers Getting Smarter?," *TIME Magazine,* 9 June 2011.

[6] JP Morgan Chase & Co., "United States Security and Exchange Commission 8K," 2 October 2014.

[7] Identity Theft Resource Center, "2015 Data Breaches," 25 January, 2016, http://www.idtheftcenter.org/ITRC-Surveys-Studies/2015databreaches.html.

[8] C. A. Dwyer, "Behavioral Targeting: A Case Study of Consumer Tracking on Levi's.com," *Behavioral Science,* 30 April 2010.

[9] A. Bereznak, "Everything You Need to Know (and Fear) About Facebook's New Ad Platform, Atlas," Yahoo Tech, 1 October 2014.

[10] K. Komando, "Facebook is watching and tracking you more than you probably realize," USAToday, 29 March, 2016, http://www.usatoday.com/story/tech/columnist/komando/2016/03/18/facebook-watching-and-tracking-you-more-than-you-realize/81803796/

[11] Federal Trade Commission, "FTC Settlement Puts an End to 'History Sniffing' by Online Advertising Network Charged With Deceptively Gathering Data on Consumers," 5 December 2012. Press release.

[12] eMarketer, "Online Data Collection Explodes Year Over Year in US," 19 July 2012.

[13] Ad Traders, "Why Third-Party Ad Servers Are Necessary in the Emerging DSP Market," AdExchanger.com, 8 June 2010.

[14] R. Karpinski, "Ad Networks and Exchanges 101," Advertising Age, 19 April 2010.

[15] C. J. Hoofnagle, J. Urban, and S. Li , "Berkeley Consumer Privacy Survey," Berkeley Center for Law and Technology, 3 December 2012.

[16] Pew Research, "Public Perceptions of Privacy and Security in the Post Snowdon Era," *Internet Project,* 12 November 2014.

[17] A. Lu, "Nordstrom Tweet Racks Up FTC Warning," FindLaw, 28 March 2013.

[18] TRUSTe Blog, "TRUSTe and Disconnect Introduce Visual Icons to Help Consumers Understand Privacy Policies," 23 June 2014.

[19] S. Hawkins, "How to Craft a Privacy Policy for Your Website," Social Media Examiner, 2 February 2012.

[20] R. McHale, *Navigating Social Media Legal Risks,* Indianapolis, IN: Que, 2012.

[21] Kayak, "Privacy Policy," April 2011, http://www.kayak.com/privacy.

[22] K. Kaye, "Obama's Approach to Big Data: Do As I Say, Not As I Do," Advertising Age, 16 November 2012.

[23] Center for Digital Democracy, "CDD Charges Mobile Game Company with Violation of COPPA," 11 December 2012.

[24] Federal Trade Commission, "TCPA Rules," 2003.

[25] A. Moscaratolo, "Papa John's Facing $250 Million Text Message Spam Lawsuit," *PC Magazine,* 14 November 2012.

[26] Information Commissioner's Office, "Guide to Data Protection," https://ico.org.uk/.

[27] Heidelberger, B., "Eight Ways Your Employee Social-media Policy may Violate Federal Law" 12 June 2012, Advertising Age.

[28] Coca-Cola Company, "Social Media Principles," 2015.

[29] U.S. Copyright Office, March 2016, http://www.copyright.gov/fair-use/more-info.html.

[30] Federal Trade Commission, "L'Oreal Settles FTC Charges Charges Alleging Deceptive Advertising for Anti-Aging Cosmetics," 30 June 2014. Press release.

[31] Federal Trade Commission, "Ads Touting 'Your Baby Can Read' Were Deceptive, FTC Complaint Alleges," 28 August 2012. Press release.

[32] Advertising Self-Regulatory Council, "A Service of the Advertising Industry and the Council of Better Business Bureaus," 2014, http://www.asrcreviews.org/.

[33] Advertising Self-Regulatory Council, "NAD Recommends Colgate Discontinue Certain Claims for 'Optic White Toothpaste' Following P&G Challenge," 14 August 2012, http://www.asrcreviews.org/2012/08/nad-recommends-colgate-discontinue-certain-claims-for-optic-white-toothpaste-following-pg-challenge/.

[34] European Advertising Standards Alliance, "Click More to Learn About Your Ad Choices," 2014, http://www.easa-alliance.org/.

[35] Internet Advertising Bureau UK, "IAB UK's Guide to the EU Self-Regulatory Initiative for Behavioural Advertising," 2014.

[36] D. Jain, "Industry Body Bids for Self Regulation in Advertising," *Times of India,* 8 October 2012.

[37] V. Rocha, C. Hungria, and D. Umekita, "Advertising in Brazil—The Success of Self-Regulation," Global Advertising Lawyers Alliance, 2003.

[38] Advertising Standards Bureau, "Self Regulation System," 2014.

[39] S. Zou and Y. Z. Voltz, "An Integrated Theory of Global Advertising: An Application of the GMS Theory," *International Journal of Advertising,* vol. 29, no. 1, pp. 57–84, 2010.

[40] European Commission, "Unfair Commercial Practices," *Consumer Rights,* 23 March 2015.

[41] A. Doland, "China Just Overhauled Its Advertising Law: Here's What You Need to Know," Advertising Age, 29 April 2015.

[42] Federal Reserve Board, "The U.S. Regulatory Landscape for Mobile Payments," Atlanta, GA, 2012.

[43] G. Sloan, "Snapchat Is Asking Brands for $750,000 to Advertise and Won't Budge," *Adweek,* 14 January 2015.

[44] S. Perez, "Snapchat Is Now the #3 Social App Among Millenials," TechCrunch, 11 August 2014.

[45] D. MacMillan and E. M. Rusli, "Snapchat Is Said to Have More than 100 Million Monthly Users," *The Wall Street Journal,* 26 August 2014.

[46] D. Thompson, "The Most Popular Social Network for Young People? Texting," *The Atlantic,* 19 June 2014.

[47] Niche, "Best and Worst Media Habits of the Class of 2014," 2014.

[48] M. Isaac, "A Look Behind the Snapchat Photo Leak Claims," *The New York Times,* 17 October 2014.

[49] Federal Trade Commission, "Snapchat Inc., In the Matter of:," FTC Matter/File Number, 31 December 2014.

[50] Federal Trade Commission, "In the Matter Of: Snapchat, Inc.," Decision and Order Docket Number C-4501, 23 December 2014.

GLOSSARY

Active control Desired participation in a network and the ability to control behavior to obtain benefits.

Active deal-prone customers Consumers who switch brands to get the deal whenever available.

Adaptive design A method for developing websites that optimizes the user experience by altering the site to match particular devices.

Advertising A nonpersonal paid form of persuasive communication aimed at target markets through various forms of media by identified sponsors.

Advertising networks Groups of websites that are packaged for sale together so that advertisers can easily buy advertising space, such as banner ads, on the network's websites.

Advertising servers Platforms that provide tools for managing and tracking online advertising campaigns when advertisers buy on a CPM (cost per thousand) or CPC (cost per click) basis.

Affinity targeting When marketers reach consumers who are fans of particular entertainment properties on websites that feature entertainment.

Algorithm A mathematical equation that determines the links that will be listed for a particular keyword search by a particular individual.

Alternative evaluation When consumers review the attributes of various products and brands to determine the optimum choice for potential purchase.

Analytics When marketers use patterns within available data to make business decisions.

Android The operating system for Google devices.

Application protocol interface A term that specifies a set of routines for how a type of software interacts with the user.

Astroturfing Creating seemingly grassroots efforts around an issue, often online, but actually in an attempt to sell products.

Attitudes Positive or negative valences toward a stimulus made up of cognitive, affective, and intentional responses.

Attribution analysis The process of determining which elements of a marketing strategy delivered the desired response.

Awareness The degree to which people are familiar with a brand using both aided (with response choices) and unaided response measures.

Basic communications model A representation of human communications in which a source encodes a message and sends it through a medium to receivers who decode the message.

Beacon A small radio transmitter that can signal applications on a mobile device and deliver a message to someone in a particular location.

Behavioral segmentation A process by which marketers divide the market into smaller groups based on how people use or respond to a product category.

Big data A term for the collection and analysis of large amounts of marketing and consumer data available to firms due to the Internet and mobile devices.

Bit.ly An online tool for tracking posts consisting of a URL shortener and data site.

Black hat tactics Taking advantage of questionable means of improving search engine rankings by linking to a variety of unrelated sites, having people pay to share content, or creating useless content for links.

Blog A discussion or informational site published on the World Wide Web and consisting of discrete entries ("posts") typically displayed in reverse chronological order (meaning the most recent post appears first).

Bloggers Writers publishing online that may have followers who read their blogs and whom the blogger may influence.

Brand associations Elements of a brand that are cognitively accessible by consumers who can describe key brand attributes.

Brand equity The value inherent in a brand's name or symbol.

Brand sentiment Attitudes and perceptions people hold about a brand that range from positive to negative.

Business feasibility The degree to which a firm can execute product or service development strategies given available resources and capabilities.

Business-to-business market (B2B) The market of transactions between businesses, such as between a manufacturer and a wholesaler, or between a wholesaler and a retailer.

Business-to-consumer market (B2C) The market consisting of goods and services sold by individuals or businesses to the end-user.

Children's Online Privacy Protection Rule (COPPA) A U.S. government rule that applies to children under the age of 13 and prohibits marketers from requesting personal information from children, allowing kids to post publicly, and passively tracking children without parental consent.

Click-through rate A measure of those who click on an advertisement or link out of the total number of exposures.

Communications Decency Act (CDA) The congressional act that requires website operators to monitor and restrict material that is lewd, lascivious, or excessively violent.

Competition-based methods Strategies that establish the price for a product or service based on the prices of competitors.

Competitive advantage When one company is more skilled in a business area than another and ideally can use that advantage to lead in the marketplace.

Competitive clutter When the environment for viewing advertising is crowded with many other brands' advertisements in the same product category.

Competitive parity method A method for determining advertising spending in which advertisers match the spending levels of competitors.

Complementary product A product that is often purchased in tandem with another product or service.

Computer Fraud and Abuse Act (CFAA) The law that forbids marketers from accessing a computer without authorization or intentionally obtaining financial records of consumers with intent to defraud.

Concept testing A research technique that involves writing clear descriptions of ideas and asking potential customers to evaluate them.

Content Information and materials posted online that provide value to an end-user/audience.

Content analysis A qualitative research method that is used to judge information.

Content development Determining the appropriate materials that brands can produce and distribute online to attract targets, engage customers, or build relationships with the goal of encouraging sharing on social media.

Contest A promotion in which people compete to win prizes based on skill or merit and are then evaluated based on objective criteria.

Contextual targeting When marketers reach consumers with digital ads on websites, mobile sites, or social media because the site is directly related to a product or service category.

Controlling the Assault of Non-Solicited Pornography and Marketing Act (CAN-SPAM Act) A congressional act related to commercial email messages that prohibits marketers from sending messages without obtaining consent or sending misleading information when the return email address is unknown.

Conversion The metric indicating that site visitors completed an action desired by the company, such as making a purchase, downloading content, or entering their email address.

Conversion rate Out of a total audience, the percentage of customers who complete an action.

Cookie A small text file that is stored on a computer that records information about the websites someone visited online and the tasks associated with those visits.

Cost per click The price paid by the advertiser when an individual clicks on an ad.

Cost per impression Amount the advertiser pays for each person who views an ad when it is shown even if the viewer does not click on the ad.

Cost per thousand The cost to reach 1,000 people with a particular communication in any of a number of different media formats such as television, print, or online.

Cost-based methods A pricing method in which the marketer determines the cost to produce or offer a particular product or service, and then tacks on an additional amount for the profit to arrive at the final price.

Creative brief A short document written in outline form for use by the advertising industry to highlight the key requirements for a brand's communications strategy.

Creative collaboration Opportunities for groups to develop creative ideas together.

Credence attribute A characteristic of a product or service that the consumer is unable to evaluate prior to or even after consumption because such information is not available.

Cross platform strategy Using two or more forms of media to run brand messaging.

Crowdsourcing The process of obtaining needed services, ideas, information, or content by soliciting contributions from a large group of people, often online.

Customer value A measure of the set of benefits provided by a purchase relative to the costs borne by customers.

Customer value proposition The set of benefits and costs that a marketer offers to consumers that represents the total offering to the buyer.

Day part targeting When marketers reach consumers with communications at particular times of the day.

Demand-based methods Determining how much customers may be willing to pay for a product or service and pricing accordingly.

Demand-side platforms Companies with technology that pairs advertisers who wish to reach consumers online through automated bidding systems with the correct ad space to reach the desired target.

Demographics The statistical data associated with a particular population, which includes variables such as age, income, marital status, and ancestry.

Digital marketing strategy Planning marketing efforts involving a brand's website and blog, social media executions, mobile advertising and applications, email marketing, and search engine strategies.

Digital Millennium Copyright Act (DMCA) The congressional act that protects a website from individuals who upload copyrighted material from claims of copyright infringement, provided the operators do not know the material is owned by others and do not materially benefit.

Digital strategy Marketing strategies involving technology-related executions, such as search engine marketing (SEM), search engine optimization (SEO), website development and management, email marketing campaigns, and social media and mobile strategies.

Digital tracking Monitoring a brand's performance on a variety of digital platforms.

Direct marketing Selling to the final consumer with no other businesses assisting within the channel of distribution.

Disruptive technology An innovation that helps create a new market and value network, and eventually disrupts an existing market and value network (over a few years or decades), by displacing an earlier technology.

Distribution The process of making a product or service available to the business or consumer for use through direct means or via intermediaries.

Doctrine of "fair use" A rule that allows people to reproduce written materials, under a certain set of guidelines, to comment on them, report news, parody their content, or use for teaching and research.

Earned media Content created by people online and shared through various platforms that potentially provides benefits to companies that are mentioned in that content by increasing the reach of communications or improving search engine rankings.

Electronic Communications Privacy Act (ECPA) A congressional act that makes it illegal to access stored communications without authorization.

Employee-based crowdsourcing Leveraging a company's own employees, who may have specialized knowledge about products or processes, to improve business operations.

Encoding The act of composing a particular communication for broadcast to others in the communication process.

Endorsement Any advertising message that consumers are likely to think represents the thoughts, feelings, or beliefs of someone other than the company. Marketers must disclose any connections that have economic value that could affect a customer's belief in the unbiased nature of the comments.

Endorsers Professionals who share product category information online and include experts and celebrities.

Enduring involvement When consumers regularly monitor product category information because they have a strong interest in the product or service.

Ethnography When researchers deeply analyze consumers by observing them in their personal spaces.

Exchanges Selling website advertising inventory through a specific digital method of buying and selling advertising space, similar to what happens on a stock exchange.

Experience attributes A characteristic of a product or service that the consumer can only evaluate after consumption or usage.

Experiential marketing A set of product- or service-related activities designed for consumers to directly interact with a brand in real life.

Experimentation Comparing the responses of two or more randomly selected groups to strategies by manipulating a single key variable for one or more selected groups (treatment), but not a control group.

Experts Individuals with professional knowledge regarding products or services, such as doctors or bloggers.

External pricing factors Those elements that contribute to defining the price of a product that the company does *not* control, such as consumer demand for the product or service and the competition.

External reference prices Prices supplied by marketers to consumers to encourage people to frame the context in an advantageous way for a company's profitability.

Fad A product or service that gains strong momentum early in the product lifecycle by growing very quickly, but then droping off in sales almost as fast.

F-commerce A term that mimics the concept of e-commerce and refers to selling on Facebook.

Federal Trade Commission (FTC) The U.S. government body that regulates interstate commerce and is responsible for protecting consumers, establishing guidelines for fair competition and setting policy regarding false and misleading advertising.

Financial metrics Measures that evaluate revenues and expenses associated with strategies.

First click attribution model Attributing a conversion to the touchpoint that initiated the path to conversion.

Forward encoding When an advertisement in one form of media primes interest in an ad in a second form of media.

Forward tracking: Determining the means through which a strategy will be evaluated prior to executing it. Often includes inserting codes into digital posts so that they can be tracked.

Four P's of the marketing mix The set of marketing strategies that brands undertake in their efforts to attract target markets. The four factors, price, product, place (distribution), and promotion work together to create an image for a brand.

Fragmented The extent to which viewers expose themselves to different communications such that marketers find it difficult to reach people using a limited set of media options.

Framing The consumer's perception of price relative to his or her expectations or knowledge regarding prices within a product category.

Fremium model A type of pricing model that initially provides a free app download, but may charge for add-ons or specialized content.

Frequency The number of times a unique individual is exposed to a message or campaign over a specified time period.

Geofencing A technological method of identifying the presence of individuals in a particular place using mobile-connected devices and potentially communicating with them.

Geographic segmentation When marketers divide consumers based on the location of individuals by countries, cities, metropolitan areas, census tracts, or neighborhoods.

Geo-social marketing Reaching consumers through social networks with a marketing strategy based on their geographic location.

Gross ratings points (GRPs) A measure of the number of unique individuals who view a communication multiplied by the number of times each person sees the communication.

Hedonic shoppers Buyers who seek the sensory experience offered by products and services.

Idea generation A set of processes for generating insights on new products, services, ideas, or solutions.

Image transfer When consumers remember previously viewed ads during exposure to a second ad. The second advertisement may prompt memory of the first advertisement and the messages may reinforce one another.

Impressions A cumulative measure of the total number of audience exposures that is calculated as the size of the audience (reach) multiplied by the number of times each person is exposed to the advertisement (frequency).

Inbound marketing Attempts by marketers to encourage people to visit their website or otherwise connect with the company by using content and messaging.

Industry analysis A section of a situation analysis that describes the state of an entire industry and reports competitive information.

Influencers Consumers who are highly engaged with certain brands and who persuade their connections through social media or mobile properties.

Information search When consumers conduct either an internal memory search or use external sources to find information to help them complete a purchase.

Informational group influence When members of social groups share ideas, thoughts, attitudes, and beliefs and affect one another's purchase behavior.

Innovators The earliest adopters of new technologies.

Insight A marketer's ability to understand consumer behavior by examining data and relying on industry experience and knowledge.

Integrated marketing communications A set of strategies for communicating with target markets using a variety of media that work in tandem to provide a positioning.

Integrated marketing communications planning Using various forms of media in tandem to communicate with and engage customers.

Intention analysis A method for determining how a particular person may act or behave based on the information her or she types into search engine toolbars.

Intermediary metrics Those measures used by firms to analyze tactics, rather than more advanced measures, known as key performance indicators, used to analyze broader business strategies.

Internal pricing factors Those elements that contribute to defining the price of a product that the company controls, such as production costs and firm objectives.

Internet marketing All the elements of the marketing mix used to attract and sell to people online.

Inter-rater reliability A measure of the degree to which two judges agree on an evaluation.

iOS The operating system for Apple devices.

Key Performance Indicators (KPIs) Metrics that evaluate the success of a business strategy.

Lanham Act Protects competition by prohibiting trademark infringement or dilution with regard to advertising or promotion.

Last click attribution model When marketers attribute a conversion to the site clicked immediately prior to the website visit.

Last nondirect interaction attribution model Using the last click attribution method and also eliminating direct attributions (typing in the URL) to determine the factor that led to a website visit.

Lifestyle compatibility A characteristic of a product or service that suggests it fits well with a person's daily activities.

Lifetime customer value The dollar value of all the revenue an individual customer generates for a firm over his or her lifetime.

Linear attribution model A method for determining media influence in which each element of the click-stream path receives equal weight for leading to a website visit or conversion.

Link When a website's URL or address is posted on another webpage.

Location-based marketing Reaching consumers with a marketing strategy based on their geographic location.

Logit model Predicting the value of a categorical variable (0-1) based on a set of inputs using regression analysis.

Loyalty A favorable attitude toward a brand coupled with repeat purchase behavior.

Many-to-many communications When consumers interact with one another with messages that are passed between individuals and among groups.

Market segmentation The process of dividing a market into homogenous groups that share common needs.

Marketer-generated content Any content produced and distributed by a marketer.

Media equivalent analysis (advertising equivalence) A method for equalizing the value of an advertisements in different forms of media using impressions and costs.

Media timing analysis Determining the timing of media executions and the effect on target market response.

Metrics A set of measures that assists marketers in evaluating the success of marketing tactics.

Microblogging A broadcast medium that allows users to exchange small elements of content such as short sentences, individual images, or video links with others.

Mobile applications (apps) Software programs that run on mobile devices, such as smartphones or tablets.

Mobile email A strategy for communicating with customers by sending email messages that people read on mobile devices.

Mobile marketing strategy A set of strategies involving mobile devices, such as sending opt-in text messages, offering mobile websites, developing applications, serving mobile advertisements, and sending emails.

Model development Building a representation of the product or service for testing.

Multimedia message service (MMS) Text messaging services with image and video capability.

Multimedia synergy The benefits accrued when brands use more than one form of media to communicate with a target.

Multiple regression model Predicting the value of a dependent variable using a series of independent variables.

Multitasking When individuals engage in two or more tasks at the same time.

Native ads Advertising that fits seamlessly into the content of a publisher on a mobile device or on the Web so that viewers don't feel bothered by it.

Netnography A technique that researchers use to examine the behavior of consumer tribes by becoming part of the community and interacting with them. The term "netnography" is a combination of the term eth*nography* and Inter*net*.

Niche market A small subset of the overall market that represents the target for a particular product or service.

Nonfinancial metrics Measures of business performance that focus on consumer actions and results that are not represented in dollars or other currencies.

Non-personally identifiable information (non-PII) Information about individuals that does not reveal a person's name or Social Security number.

Objective and task method A method for determining advertising spending in which marketers set goals and spend the amount of money required to achieve them.

Observability A characteristic of a new product or service suggesting that the consumer can see the item in use prior to purchase.

Observation A research technique that involves watching or monitoring people's behavior and recording the results.

Opinion leaders People who are highly involved with a product or service and enjoy sharing information on the product category with their close friends, family, and others online or in person.

Organic rankings The unpaid result that appears in the center of the search engine page when people search for keywords or phrases.

Organizational objectives A set of business goals focusing on maximizing profits, dominating markets, or reducing costs.

Owned media All content and data that a company owns and controls with its desired messages, imagery, and distribution, such as websites and blogs.

P3P compact codes Embeded information on webpages that indicates the privacy policy in effect when collecting the information, usually represented by a short series of letters. For example, a NOI code means that no identified information will be collected.

Paid media Space or media time, either online or in traditional media, which advertisers buy to feature their brand messages.

Paid search results The sponsored keyword advertising that appears above and to the side of organic results listings on search engine results pages.

Passive deal-prone customers Individuals who stockpile products and only buy when the marketer offers a deal.

Pay per click A method of buying impressions in which the advertiser pays each time a searcher clicks through to the site from an online advertisement or search result.

Perceived quality The belief on the part of the consumer that a brand performs strongly on key attributes.

Percentage of sales method A method for determining advertising spending in which advertisers multiply past or anticipated sales by a predetermined percentage.

Persistent cookie A small text file that stays on a computer feeding information back to the source until the user or marketer erases it.

Personal selling Interactions between salespeople and potential customers on a one-to-one basis with the goal of selling products and services.

Personally identifiable information (PII) Includes information such as a person's name, email address, Social Security number, and other data that identify him or her.

Podcast A digital medium consisting of an episodic series of audio, video, radio, PDF, or ePub files subscribed to and downloaded through Web syndication or streamed online to a computer or mobile device.

Position-based attribution A method for determining media influence that gives more weight to the first interaction prior to a conversion and the most weight to the last interaction prior to a conversion.

Postpurchase behavior A set of thoughts and actions taken by consumers after a purchase, such as evaluation of satisfaction based on previously determined expectations of performance.

Premiums Additional products or offers that add to the value of a product or service.

Price compression When prices for particular goods and/or services in the marketplace converge, eliminating premiums.

Price penetration Offering a product or service at a low initial price in the hopes that people will become loyal to the product and continue to buy more as its price goes up over time.

Price sensitivity The responsiveness of the quantity demanded of a good or service relative to a change in its price.

Primary research A type of data collection when marketers define a problem, develop a research plan, execute a study, and report their findings, rather than rely on existing data.

Problem recognition (need recognition) The first stage of the purchase decision process, which takes place in the mind of the consumer when he or she recognizes an unmet need.

Product lifecycle A graphic representation of the sales of a product, service, or category over time from its introduction through growth, maturity, and eventual decline.

Product testing A stage in the product development process that involves researching the viability of a product or service model.

Production and commercialization The stages in the product development process spent developing the product and introducing it to market.

Programmatic buying Any process that includes buying advertising space through automated networks.

Promotional mix The integration of advertising, public relations, sales promotion, and personal selling for the purposes of communicating with target markets.

Prospecting The act of seeking out potential customers as the first part of the sales process.

Psychographic segmentation A process where marketers divide the market into groups based on people's activities, interests, and opinions.

Public relations An indirectly paid form of communication in which marketers seek to gain media attention in order to persuade people, without paying for media time.

Publishers Websites that deliver content to consumers, such as news outlets, blogs, special-interest websites, and others that have information or entertainment people want to see.

Purchase decision process (the consumer journey) The process by which consumers recognize their needs and engage in a set of behaviors aimed at satisfying them. The stages include problem recognition, information search, alternative evaluation, purchase and postpurchase behavior.

Purchase funnel Represents the path consumers take through the purchase decision process and the goals the marketer wants to achieve in moving the consumer down the path toward purchase.

Q scores A metric that shows the likability of celebrities, icons, and known individuals and people's emotional connections to them.

QR code A two-dimensional graphic that when scanned by a mobile scanning app leads to a result such as a website landing page, click to call, or video view.

Qualifying Determining whether a prospect has the ability and willingness to purchase so that the salesperson doesn't waste time.

Rating The percentage of the total population that is engaged with a particular media entity (such as a television program) out of all the homes with access to that form of media.

Reach The percentage of unique individuals out of all potential targets exposed to a message or campaign over a specified time period.

Real-time bidding A method marketers use to buy advertising space on web and mobile sites and apps in which advertisers bid for particular target markets that may consist of those who have completed a certain online action, such as examining a website.

Reference prices Prices of similar products or competitors that consumers consider when evaluating products and services.

Relative advantage A characteristic of a new product or service that suggests there are no available alternatives that provide the benefit at a set level of cost.

Remarketing A technique for finding customers who have interacted with a brand's website and serving them messages on other sites to encourage purchase.

Response modeling A regression model to determine the weights of various elements contributing to an outcome.

Responsive design Developing websites so they can be readily viewed on a wide range of mobile devices.

Retailer A member of the marketing channel that distributes products to the final consumer mostly through physical or online stores.

Return on investment (ROI) The amount of revenue (in a currency) a strategy delivers after accounting for expenses.

Sales promotion A short-term incentive offered to consumers or the trade to induce purchase.

Search attribute A characteristic of a product or service that is easy for the consumer to determine prior to consumption or usage.

Search engine marketing (SEM) Paid advertising on search engines and search engine optimization that marketers use to reach targets when people search online.

Search engine optimization (SEO) The process of affecting the visibility of a website or webpage in a search engine's "natural" or unpaid ("organic") search result.

Sentiment analysis A method for determining how people who engage in online conversations feel about particular topics.

Share The percentage of people who view a particular media entity (such as a television program) out of all those who are engaged with the medium at a particular time.

Share of conversation The number of posts discussing a topic and a particular brand compared to the number of posts discussing the topic only.

Share of voice (SOV) The share of a brand's media spending relative to competitors' media spending.

Shopping app A mobile application that guides consumers in retail establishments by providing information during a store visit.

Short message service (SMS) A strategy for communicating via text messaging.

Showrooming Using a retail store to obtain information related to a product and then purchasing it online or through a mobile device.

Simplicity of use A characteristic of a product that allows the consumer to learn the usage basics quickly without significant time and attention.

Situation analysis A comprehensive research document that guides a company's strategic planning, implementation, and evaluation process.

Social media Platforms owned by companies that provide online spaces for people and companies to build profiles and share information.

Social media channel management Posting, responding, and managing a firm's engagement on social media platforms.

Social media listening The act of evaluating online data using keywords and phrases to determine social media conversations about a brand, product category, issue, or other area of interest.

Social media monitoring and management tools A set of Web platforms for posting social media content and analyzing results.

Social media policy A document that provides behavior and etiquette guidelines for employees using company social media platforms.

Social media strategy Planning and executing marketing efforts focused on developing content for the various social media platforms or engaging constituencies through social networks.

Social networks A set of online services that individuals use to create profiles, define a set of others with whom they connect, and interact with those connections in a variety of ways.

Sock puppetry When companies post comments using many different names, so it appears that they have received many comments and positive customer feedback.

Software development kit (SDK) A set of tools and instructions that developers use to create applications for software packages, systems, games, consoles, operating systems, or other platforms.

SoLoMo An acronym representing marketing strategies that combine social media and location-based efforts delivered via mobile device.

Sponsorships A form of nonpersonal communication in which marketers seek brand attention by purchasing naming rights to an event, entity, or activity that they do not own.

Stickiness The degree to which a website leads users to remain on the site for a long period of time.

Supply-side platforms Companies with proprietary technology to facilitate the sale of online advertising inventory to advertisers through a set of Web properties.

Survey A questionnaire that marketers use to ask people questions regarding their attitudes and behavior.

Synchronicity Compatible timing of information transmitted and received based on the responsiveness of the system.

Telephone Consumer Protection Act (TCPA) The congressional act that restricts use of telephone equipment and prohibits calls using automatic dialing systems to cellular telephone numbers without prior consent or an established business relationship.

Time decay attribution model A method for determining media influence in which the closest interaction to the conversion earns the most credit, followed by earlier touchpoints in backwards time order.

Touchpoints All the potential places where marketers interact with customers, such as through products, advertising, retail establishments, or events.

Trade promotions Special sales and discounts to wholesalers or retailers sometimes requiring them to purchase certain amounts, merchandise the product in particular ways, or participate in joint marketing efforts.

Transient cookies Small text files stored on a user's computer that aggregate data from a particular website visit and are erased after the user logs off.

Trial-ability A characteristic of a new product such that consumers have the opportunity to try the product or service prior to purchase.

Two-way communication A form of interaction in which both parties can share information with one another.

Usage rate segmentation Dividing the market of consumers into groups based on how much of a product or service they buy or consume.

User-generated content (UGC) Pictures, videos, and other materials created by average people, customers, or other individuals, sometimes related to a company's branded contest.

Utilitarian shoppers People who seek products with a purpose, carefully consider prices, and do not tend to buy impulsively.

Viral marketing A strategy that attempts to build online word-of-mouth communications for a product or brand often through social networks.

Viral video Video content that has been widely shared across the Internet and is viewed by many people.

Virtual workforce Using social media and mobile technology to locate workers to perform services for pay.

White hat tactics A set of strategies for improving search engine rankings by creating strong content and sharing the information in appropriate ways or tweaking a website to perform better.

White paper An authoritative report or guide helping readers understand an issue, solve a problem, or make a decision. White papers are used in two main spheres: government and business-to-business marketing.

Wholesaler A distributor who may move a product from the producer through the channel to retailers, or who may arrange for the product to move through the channel.

Word-of-mouth communications (buzz, guerilla marketing, or viral marketing) When consumers share information among themselves, sometimes about products and services.

INDEX

A

prospecting, 189
protesting, 16
psychographics, 252, 254*e*
psychographic segmentation, 39*e*,
    46–47
Publicis, 268*e*
public relations (PR), 176*e*,
    186–87, 411
publishers, 431, 432
publishing, 261
purchase
    attitudes, 255*e*
    behavior, 47–48, 166, 255*e*, 432
    decision-making process, 105–6,
        107*e*, 108, 109, 111–12
    funnel, 105–6, 107*e*, 108
    postpurchase processes, 106,
        107*e*, 111
    process, 202

Q

QR codes. *See* quick response codes
Q scores, 41–42
Qloo app, 109
qualifying, 189
quick response (QR) codes, 317, 365,
    366, 367
Quirky.com, 13*e*, 55*e*, 136, 138, 377
Qwikster, 80

R

radio, 44, 327*e*, 330*e*, 331*e*, 333, 334*e*,
    342*e*, 371–72
ratings, 334*e*
reach, 178, 319, 332*e*
real-time bidding (RTB), 52, *299*, 300,
    431–32
Recession, 273
recommendation widgets, 375
Red Bull, *316*, 317
Reddit, 6, 299
Reddi-wip, 38
reference prices, 174
regulations
    of advertising, 445–48
    data collection, 433–37
    of Internet, 432

relationships
    bloggers, 303
    with customers, 170
    with marketers, consumers, 114–15
    among media, 282*e*
relative advantage, 124
remarketing, 299–300
requests for proposals (RFPs), 269
research
    dangers of failing to, 80
    market, 412–15
    mobile, 92–93
    process, 72*e*, 73
    strategy development, 71–74, 138*e*
    texting and, 92–93
response modeling, 402*e*, 404–5,
    406*e*, 407*e*
responsive design, 215, 362–63, 364
retail environments, 152
retailer apps, 354*e*, 371–72
retailers, 150–51
return on investment (ROI), 8, 22,
    390–91, 392*e*, 393, 396
    calculating, 223
    email marketing, 219, 223–24
    for SMS strategy, 394–95
retweets, 121
reviews, 48, 49–50, 110, 297–98
review sites, 45–46, 297–98, 298*e*
RFPs. *See* requests for proposals
Rhapsody, 60
The Richards Group, *260*
Ridiculousness, 54
risk, 212, 213*e*, 304
Ritz Carlton, 372
ROI. *See* return on investment
Rotten Tomatoes, 104, *105*
RTB. *See* real-time bidding
Rubio, Gatsy, 81
"Run For," 241–42
Russia, 291

S

Saatchi & Saatchi, 342
sales, 292*e*. *See also* promotion
    automobile, 272*e*
    of beverage, global, 192*e*, 193*e*
    media and, 323

mobile devices, 21
    percentage of sales method, 321–22
    personal selling, 176*e*, 188–90
    Porsche, 272*e*
    process, 188–89
    promotion, 176*e*, 180–81
    tablets and online, 155–56
Salesforce.com, 18
samples, 179*e*
Samsung, 252
Saudi Arabia, 181–82
scan-able codes, 109
Schafer, Tim, 141
Schreier, Martin, 136
Scoutmob, 183
Screwfix, 227–28, 229*e*, 230, 231*e*,
    232*e*, 233*e*, 234*e*, 235*e*
scribecontent.com, 288
SDK. *See* software development kit
search. *See also* Google search
    attributes, 109, 110, 111*e*
    behavior, 58
    mobile devices, 218
    organic, 7, 204, 207, 209,
        228–29, 287
    paid, 205, 207
SearchDex, 202
search engine marketing (SEM),
    203–4, 325
search engine optimization (SEO),
    202–4
    black hat tactics, 208
    for blogs, 288
    firms, 208
    HTML, 210*e*
    links, 210*e*
    meta tags, 210*e*
    mobile devices and, 363, 364
    recommendations from
        Google, 210*e*
    rules of, 208–9
    Screwfix, 228–30
    site maps, 210*e*
    title tags, 210*e*
    URLs, 210*e*
    white hat tactics, 208
search engines, 7, 28, 203–4, 327*e*
    algorithm, 204
    brands and, 20
    Chobani's strategy for, 96–97

Lady Gaga, *251*
language use on, 116
monitoring, 5
name ownership on, 80
of Pepsi, 193, 195
promotions, 181–82
psychographics, 254*e*
retweets, 121
television and, 328
tools, 81
traffic, *398*
trends, 84
value of visit, 391
two-step flow of communications, 116
two-way communication, 212*e*
Tyco, 159–60

U

Uber, 172, 219
UGC. *See* user-generated content
Ulukaya, Hamdi, 95
Unilever, 72, 144, 245, 246, 249–50,
   345–48
unmeasured media, 259
URLs, 210*e*, 288, 414
usage, 47
usage rate segmentation, 48
use case scenarios, 215, 216*e*
usefulness, 125
user-generated content (UGC), 55,
   178, 422–43
user identification, 364
user types, 14*e*
UTest, 143
utilitarian shoppers, 174

V

value, customers, 145–46
Venmo, 17, 371, 379
videos, 153, 266*e*, 292*e*
   cost per thousand for commercials,
      319*e*
   viral, 121, 305, 331
Vikander, Alicia, 56

Vine, 10*e*, 14, 122
viral marketing, 118, 120–21
viral mavens, 121
viral videos, 121, 305, 331
Virgin, 359
virtual workforce, 141–42
Vkontakte, 291

W

Wald statistic, 406
Walking Dead, 7
Walmart, 8, 155
wear-out, 319–20, 339
Weather Channel, 301
web browsers, 399
   history sniffing, 429
   private mode, 427
   tracking and, 427
Web crawlers, 76
Web Marketing Association, 214
website design, 210
   active control, 212*e*
   adaptive, 215
   country-specific, 217
   cultural factors in, 216–17
   good, 213–14
   interactivity in, 211, 212*e*
   maximizing effectiveness
      in, 214*e*
   mobile, 117*e*, 215, 216*e*, 218, 219*e*,
      230, 362–63
   perceived risk and, 212, 213*e*
   responsive, 215, 362–63, 364
   synchronicity, 212*e*
   two-way communication, 212*e*
   use case scenarios, 215, 216*e*
website marketing, 211*e*
websites, 6*e*, 327*e*
WeChat, 397*e*
Weibo Wallet, 182
weRead, 113*e*
Westpac Impulse Saver, 11*e*
WhatsApp, 8, 10*e*
Whisper app, 427
white hat tactics, 208
white papers, 19–20, 266*e*

wholesalers, 150–51
Wickes, 235*e*
widgets, 431
Wikipedia, 6, 18, 289
wireless carriers, 362*e*
wireless networks, 14
The Wisdom of Crowds (Surowiecki),
   139–40
Wish, 22*e*
Wix.com, 267
WOM. *See* word-of-mouth
   communications
women, social networking
   and, 43
word-of-mouth communications
   (WOM), 78, 104, 118–20
WordPress, 264*e*, 286
words, advertising and, 325*e*. *See also*
   keywords
WordStream, 85*e*
Wordtracker, 85*e*
World Wide Web Consortium, 428
WPP Group, 268*e*
WriteAPrisoner, 113*e*

Y

Yahoo, 204
Yammer, 145, 159–61, 175
Yelp, 19, 45–46, 297, 298*e*,
   368, 398*e*
Yik Yak, 4, 55*e*
Yoovidhya, Cheleo, 317
Your Baby Can Read, 446
YouTube, 14, 153, 206
   advertising, 340, 440
   API of, 284–85
   engagement methods of, 305*e*
   mobile advertising on, 340
   stars, 335*e*
   television and, 335

Z

Zappos.com, 215
Zoosk, *339*, 340*e*, 341
Zynga, 155